AMERICAN HEROINE

Jane Addams, *ca.* 1915

AMERICAN
HEROINE

*The Life and Legend
of
Jane Addams*

ALLEN F. DAVIS

New York   Oxford University Press   1973

For
Marjorie L. Davis
1934–1965

The greatest gift she gave to her time was not what she wrote or what she said or even what she did in the development of Hull House. The greatest gift she gave to her time was herself.

GLEN FRANK

The long impressive chronicle of her deeds is comparatively unimportant because she was greater than what she did.

LILLIAN WALD

She, more than any other contemporary American, represented through her leadership what might be called the altruistic element in a civilization that is on the whole too acquisitive.

WILLIAM ALLEN WHITE

Most truly and fully was she a representative American. She could have come to maturity in no other land than her own.

S. F. RATCLIFFE

Preface

EGENDS and myths surround almost all the famous women in the American past, and capsule summaries of their careers contained in textbooks and general accounts often distort their importance or hide their significance behind a veil of half-truths. More has been written about Jane Addams than about most women in American history, both by scholarly and popular authors, but still she remains an enigma. The image that comes through in the popular accounts of her life is that of a precocious child who became a saintly woman. She founded Hull House in a spirit of self-sacrifice and went on to lead movements for humanitarian reform and peace.

The scholarly studies define and interpret Jane Addams in different ways and for different purposes, but they are also affected by the legend, and often use her to represent a movement or a point of view. Richard Hofstadter, in the *Age of Reform*, published in 1955, cites her as a prime example for his "sense of guilt" thesis in explaining the reform impulse during the progressive era.[1] Staughton Lynd, writing a few years later, attacks Hofstadter and the other consensus historians who "have made Jane Addams a principal exhibit in their collection of curious cases." Confronting the evidence presented by Hofstadter, Lynd asks: "Does he mean to say that it was wrong or abnormal for a member of the urban middle class in 1900 (or for that matter, today) to feel guilt about living in comfort when millions of immigrant families battled tubercu-

1. Richard Hofstadter, *The Age of Reform* (New York, 1955), 208.

losis and the sweatshop in filthy and over-crowded tenements?"[2] Writing in 1965, Christopher Lasch answers Lynd's argument. "The question," he argues, "is not whether it was wrong to pity the victims of industrialism, or even to feel guilty about them: the question is whether that was what Jane Addams felt guilty about." He decides that she was most frustrated by "the life her mother was trying to get her to lead," and that it was a rebellion "against the family claim" that was the most important reason behind the decision to found Hull House.[3] Lasch's interpretation is a refinement of the Hofstadter thesis with the emphasis still on the internal need for reform. Yet at the same time he uses the date of the establishment of Hull House as the symbolic beginning of what he calls "the new radicalism." Other scholars have interpreted Jane Addams' life for their own purposes, in fact almost every book on reform, peace, and the woman's movement in recent years has a section on Jane Addams, until she has come to represent and symbolize the movements she participated in.[4]

All of this is very confusing for anyone wishing to understand the importance of Jane Addams in the story of the American past, or to study the role of women in American history. One good reason for another book on Jane Addams at this time is to try to clarify some of the confusion about her significance. There are other reasons as well. The recent discovery of a large number of letters and other material makes possible a clearer explanation of the steps which led to the founding of Hull House. But more important than that is the need to deal with her symbolic importance and with the myths and half-truths that have circulated about her from the moment she moved to the West Side of Chicago in 1889. Most accounts of her life, including her own autobiograph-

2. Staughton Lynd, "Jane Addams and the Radical Impulse," *Commentary* XXXII (July 1961), 54-59.
3. Christopher Lasch, *The New Radicalism in America, 1889-1963* (New York, 1965), 3-37.
4. See for example: Sondra R. Herman, *Eleven against War: Studies in American Internationalist Thought, 1898-1921* (Stanford, 1969); William L. O'Neill, *Everyone Was Brave: The Rise and Fall of Feminism in America* (Chicago, 1969); Gail Parker, ed., *The Oven Birds: American Women on Womanhood, 1820-1920* (New York, 1972); Jean B. Quandt, *From Small Town to the Great Community: The Social Thought of Progressive Intellectuals* (New Brunswick, 1970); Morton and Lucia White, *The Intellectual Versus the City* (Cambridge, 1962).

ical writing, make the story too easy. By depicting her as precocious, or by crediting a conversion experience at a bull fight with the idea for founding Hull House, they reduce the complexity and the significance of that decision. By turning her into a benevolent saint, her contemporaries and her later chroniclers have blunted the edge of her criticism of American society. But she cooperated in creating a comforting public image of herself. She helped to convince her generation of the need to improve living conditions in the nation's cities, yet she explained the problems and outlined the solutions in such a way that many people underestimated the danger, and in fact credited her with providing the only solution necessary. She revolted against the stereotype of woman as submissive, gentle, and intuitive, yet she did not publicly challenge the stereotype. In her own writing she stressed feminine intuition as a special womanly technique for changing society, and she helped to create, or at least acquiesced in, the public image of herself as a self-sacrificing saint, and friend of the down-trodden, rather than emphasizing the administrative talent and the ability to compete in a man's world that actually made her a success. Still, the way people viewed her and the legends that swirled about her name can tell us a great deal about American society in the years from 1889 to 1935. It is the major task of this book to explore the legend of Jane Addams, but also to relate the legend to the facts of her life and to show how the two became intertwined.

This is something more and something less than a biography. It does record and interpret the basic story of her life in roughly chronological order, but it is in no sense a definitive account of her life and times. Nor is it primarily an intellectual biography; the development of her thought is part of the story, but she was always more important as a publicist and popularizer than as an original thinker. I have not attempted a psychoanalytic study, such as John Cody's sensitive analysis of Emily Dickinson, or Erik Erikson's unique and remarkable interpretations of Luther and Gandhi. I have, however, profited from the work of these men and from that of other psychobiographers, psychologists, and anthropologists. I am interested in motivation, in the development of the Jane Addams' personality, and in her relationship with other people, for these things are connected very directly to what she achieved and to the way she responded to that achievement. At every point I have tried to suggest the complexity of her personality and to deal with her human strengths and weaknesses. I have tried not to explain away her commitments by using a simple psychological thesis. Human actions cannot be neatly explained by citing concepts such as "status anxiety," or "identity crisis," and anyone who has tried to understand his own complex motives, or has attempted to write biography, must remain humble about the possibilities of ever discovering the truth about human motivation. At the same time it is important to try to understand.

I write from a perspective that is basically sympathetic to the movements for social reform, woman's rights, and world peace that Jane Addams participated in during her lifetime. But nothing is to be gained from another laudatory account of her life. I am often critical of her tendency to compromise and equivocate, of her failure to act more vigorously in pursuit of her goals. It is easy to be critical of the limited accomplishments and of the naïve optimism of Jane Addams' generation, but I have also tried to appreciate the problems and difficulties from the perspective of her generation. I write not so much to judge as to understand.

An explanation is perhaps necessary as to why a man came to write this book about the life and legend of a woman. I do not accept the dictum that only women can write about women, or blacks about blacks (though I am willing to concede that there is a special empathy that can be gained from being female or black). This book is a natural outgrowth of my work on the settlement movement, though its purpose and point of view are quite different. Over a period of several years I have developed my own scholarly and personal understanding and empathy that enables me to write critically, but sympathetically, about Jane Addams and her generation. I do not claim to write without prejudice however, and I have certainly been influenced by growing up male in America. Yet in this study I have tried to avoid a sexist interpretation of Jane Addams.

The first four chapters of this book trace in some detail the influences and the circumstances which led Jane Addams to found Hull House in 1889. It is necessary to tell the story carefully and to relate her experiences to her generation in order to dispel the idea that she decided to found the settlement when she was a precocious child of seven, or that the plan emerged because of one dramatic incident. It is also important to suggest that Jane Addams' experiences were not unique, that many of her problems and many of her solutions were similar to those of other women of her generation, especially those who went to college and came from the upper-middle class.

The rest of the book is concerned with her reputation and her public image—with the legend of Jane Addams. She was one of those rare individuals who became a sounding board for her time, a symbol of her age, a representative American woman. I pay special attention to her autobiography, *Twenty Years at Hull House*, because it was through this book that most people learned about Jane Addams, and about the stories that surrounded her life. I have been influenced by the American Studies, symbol-and-myth school of historiography, especially by the work of Henry Nash Smith, Leo Marx and John William Ward. But I have tried to avoid some of the pitfalls of this school by carefully relating the facts of Jane Addams' life to her image as projected in the press, periodicals, and the letters she received. By using both unpublished correspondence and published writing I have attempted to avoid the limitations of literary sources. I have been careful not to claim that a particular point of view was accepted by all Americans, and yet this is not a scientific study using content analysis or some other device to measure public opinion. My methods are impressionistic, but the evidence that Jane Addams played a symbolic role for many Americans is overwhelming. I have tried to explore and explain that evidence. By studying Jane Addams and her changing reputation perhaps we can learn something about shifting American attitudes toward poverty and reform, toward women, and toward the social order in the years from 1889 to 1935 and beyond.

A.F.D.

Swarthmore, Pennsylvania
April 1973

Acknowledgments

N the process of doing the research and the writing for this book I have accumulated debts that can never be repaid, and some that cannot even be recalled. Research and travel grants from the University of Missouri, Temple University, and the American Philosophical Society provided funds that were indispensable. A grant from the American Council of Learned Societies allowed me the free time to finish the writing.

I would never have completed this project without the aid and cooperation of many librarians and archivists. These include the staffs of the Chicago Historical Society, Special Collections, Columbia University Libraries, the Hoover Institute for War, Revolution, and Peace, Stanford University, the Library of Congress, the Rockford College Archives, the Arthur and Elizabeth Schlesinger Library, Radcliffe College, Social Welfare History Archives, University of Minnesota, the Sophia Smith Collection, Smith College Library, the Stephenson County Historical Museum, the Libraries of the University of Chicago, the University of Kansas, the University of Missouri, and the Wisconsin State Historical Society. A special word of appreciation must be reserved for the two major repositories for Jane Addams' material—the Swarthmore College Peace Collection and the Jane Addams Memorial Collection at the University of Illinois-Chicago. My home for the past few years has been within walking distance of the Swarthmore Peace Collection, where Bernice Nichols and her staff have created a friendly atmosphere, answered my annoying questions, and tolerated my uncharted explorations through boxes, folders, and film. I have always received a warm welcome and helpful assistance at the Jane Addams Memorial Collection where Mary Lynn McCree became friend, adviser, and co-author. Permission to quote from material in all these collections and libraries is gratefully acknowledged.

Alice Kessler Harris and Mary Lynn McCree read the entire manuscript. They prevented many errors and asked difficult questions, forcing me to re-think and rephrase large sections. They will be able to detect the places where I was unable to answer their questions, but I am solely responsible for the final product. I have also profited from Blanche Wiesen Cook's reading of the sections on the peace movement, and from the criticism of my colleagues in the American History Seminar at Temple University, and in the American Civilization Seminar at Columbia where I tried out some of my ideas. Several students at the University of Missouri and at Temple University helped with the research, shared their own work with me, and listened patiently as I talked about Jane Addams. Especially helpful were: Sally Benson, Susan Ellmaker, Daryll Hartley, Barbara Haug, Toni Joseph, J. Stanley Lemons, Elizabeth Lightbourne, and David Wigdor. A number of scholars shared their ideas (and occasionally their notes) with me, told me about sources, and often, without realizing it, contributed to this book. Among these were: Clarke Chambers, Jill Conway, the late John Farrell, Barbara Kraft, John Lankford, Christopher Lasch, Anne Firor Scott, Louise Wade, and Edith Wynner. A number of friends and associates of Jane Addams shared their memories with me. Most helpful were the late Jessie Binford, the late William Bryon, the late Alice Hamilton, Katherine Ewing Hocking, the late Albert Kennedy, Wallace Kirkland (who also granted me permission to use some of his photographs), Mercedes M. Randall, and Lea Taylor. Sheldon Meyer of Oxford University Press was always patient and encouraging when he might have become exasperated. Sally Dufek improved the manuscript with her blue pencil and with her searching questions about both form and substance.

For permission to quote from the published and unpublished writings of Jane Addams I would like to thank her literary heirs: Mrs. Alice DeLoach, Mrs. Eri Hulbert, Mrs. Mary Hulbert, Mrs. Stanley Linn, and Mrs. Elizabeth Murray. A portion of Chapter 8 has been published previously as an introduction to a new edition of Jane Addams' *Spirit of*

Youth and the City Streets. It is republished here with the permission of the University of Illinois Press.

Finally a word of appreciation for my wife, Roberta, and my sons, Gregory and Paul, who tolerated this project and the interruptions it caused far beyond the call of family loyalty.

List of Illustrations

Contents

AMERICAN HEROINE

I

Formative Years

ANE Addams was born in 1860 in a little village in Illinois. Her generation missed the pioneer stage but witnessed the technological and industrial revolutions that not only transformed the country but also changed the roles of women. Her generation of women was the first to go to college, the first to develop professional careers in government, research and social work, the first to be relieved of some of the drudgery of housework by factory-produced clothing and prepared foods, the first to win the vote. But the new situations and opportunities, the shifting status and role caused Jane Addams and her generation much remorse and pain.

Jane Addams was a generation younger than Susan B. Anthony and Elizabeth Cady Stanton and the other pioneer feminist leaders, and like most of the women of her age she was not especially militant in pushing the struggle for woman's rights. She had little in common with these older women, and she did not look to them as heroines; in fact, like most of her generation, she seems to have had no heroines while growing up, except her mother, who died when she was two and a half, her older sister and the virginal, adolescent characters in Louisa May Alcott's *Little Women*. She had only heroes—Emerson, Carlyle, Mazzini, and her father. In her own writing Jane Addams made creative and imaginative use of her childhood memories. The person who always dominated those recollections was her father.

John Huy Addams, was the epitome of the nineteenth century American self-made man although he never aspired to become a millionaire.

He chose northern Illinois as a place to begin his adult, married life, in part because relatives from both sides of the family had settled there, but also because he saw an opportunity to build and prosper in the rolling prairies just south of the Wisconsin border, where the land was barely settled and the pioneer era just passed. He studied various sites along the Rock River, but finally purchased a sawmill and grist mill on the banks of Cedar Creek six miles north of Freeport. It was hardly an auspicious place to make a fortune. The stream was too small to support a very large mill, and the village of Cedarville, which had been settled only nine years before, was still unincorporated, unsurveyed, unnamed, and contained only a few scattered families. But Addams was not only interested in amassing a fortune; he also wanted to help build a community. He planted the hill across from his mills with the seeds of Norway pines, which he had brought all the way from Pennsylvania, and set to work.

He was one of the second wave of pioneers, one of those who came to organize and develop what others had discovered and settled. In 1844 he and his bride moved into a simple two-room house with a loft and a lean-to addition; ten years later they built a large gray-brick, two-story house on a hill overlooking the mills and on the main road between Freeport and Wisconsin. They also constructed a large new mill at a cost of more than $10,000. Addams invested in railroads and banks, and in land near Cedarville and as far away as Iowa and the Dakota Territory. In 1864 he helped to organize the Second National Bank of Freeport and became its president. He was also president of a life insurance company in Freeport. When he died in 1881 at the age of fifty-nine he left an estate of about a quarter of a million dollars.[1]

Success was the product of careful planning and hard work for John Addams. He was a serious, self-contained man with a reputation for inscrutable honesty, but success did not change his habits; he still found time to join the hired help to get in the hay on the home farm and to work side by side with his employees at the mills. He believed in hard work, and he had faith in God. He called himself a Hicksite Quaker, but that was an inadequate discription of his simple religious faith, which might better be described as non-denominational Protestant.

Addams' interests and concerns spread beyond the little village of Cedarville. In 1846 he drove all over the county in a successful campaign to gather subscriptions to bring a railroad through the area, and for a time the whole village prospered. Addams himself helped organize the first church, the first school and the first subscription library as well as the cemetery.

In 1854 he was elected to the State Senate and was re-elected every two years until 1870, when he refused to run again. He attended the meeting in 1854 at Ripon, Wisconsin, where the Republican Party was born, and he remained a Republican for the rest of his life. During the Civil War he raised and helped to equip a company in an Illinois Regiment, called after him "The Addams Guard." Politically he was a conservative, small-town Republican, though he did take a special interest in improving the prisons, the insane asylums, and the state industrial and normal schools.[2]

John Addams was the dominant force in the family. He made most of the major decisions, set the rules, and demanded obedience, but the management of the household and growing family fell largely to his wife, a gentle and serene woman with soft brown hair which she parted in the middle and gathered into a knot in the back. Sarah Addams had no delusions about a career; she was untouched by the movement for woman's rights. There was never any doubt in her mind that a woman's place was in the home, and in fact, bringing up a large family and managing a home in the mid-nineteenth century was no small task. Behind the gentle façade she had a quiet determination, an ability to command, and a strength of purpose just as strong as her husband's though she always deferred to him. There were always two or three hired girls, and Sarah supervised the operation of what was virtually a domestic factory; she also did a great portion of the actual work herself. The household produced its own soap, lard, candles, rugs, quilts, and stockings; it preserved fruits and vegetables, salted meats, baked bread, and prepared meals for as many as twenty farm and mill hands in addition to the family.

Like most mothers in the nineteenth century Sarah Addams had to steel herself to tragedy. She watched one child die at two months, another at ten months, and still another at two years. In January 1863, when she was pregnant with her ninth child, she went in the best tradition of the rural village to the aid of another woman in labor. The doctor was out on another call, and Sarah took complete charge. She managed to save the life of both mother and child, but on the way home she stumbled and fell. Her own baby was born prematurely and died within a few minutes. A week later Sarah Addams, at the age of 49, also died, and was buried beside her infant.[3]

Jane Addams was only a few months over two years old when her mother died, and she had only a vague, childish memory of the tragedy. When Mrs. Addams died Jane's sister Mary was seventeen, Martha thirteen, James Weber ten and Alice nine. Mary took over the management of the household, with the aid of the hired girls and especially of Polly Bear, a nurse who had long been employed by the family. The routine of family and village life continued, but the loss of their mother left a void for the Addams children.

Jane, or Jennie as she was usually called, had a succession of illnesses in childhood, the most serious being tuberculosis of the spine, which left her with a slight curvature of the back and caused her to be pigeon-toed and to carry her head cocked a bit to one side. It was quite natural that she should be pampered and protected by her sisters, and even by her austere father. As a young child she was quiet and introspective. She adored her father, who was often away from home on business or in Springfield as a member of the legislature, but she depended on her older sisters, Mary and Martha. When Jane was six, Martha died suddenly of typhoid fever. Years later Jane recalled the horror she felt at staying home alone during the funeral, and once admitted to her sister Alice that "my horrible dream every night would be Mary's death and no one to love me." After Martha's death Jane attached herself even more strongly to Mary and to her father.[4]

Two years after Martha's death Jane's life was again altered. Her father remarried, and at about the same time Mary moved away; first to Rockford Seminary where she took a few courses, then, after marrying John Linn, a Presbyterian minister, she left Cedarville permanently.

Jane's stepmother, Anna Haldeman Addams, the widow of William Haldeman of Freeport, was a high-strung, attractive woman who considered herself an aristocrat and intellectual. She had little formal education, but she had grown up in a family of intellectuals and was herself a talented musician and an avid reader, though she also never questioned the traditional belief that a woman's place was in the home. She made fun of the woman's rights advocates who "would do away with *baby* and *cradle* and ape instead a statesmanship or professorship."[5] But the new Mrs. Addams believed it was her responsibility to make the home a center of culture and art. She rarely lifted a finger in a household chore; rather she directed, organized, and played the role of mistress and cultural leader in the home. She read widely and she talked to the children about what she read. She moved her piano into the living room where a new bay window let in more light. She had wardrobe closets installed in the bedrooms to replace the hooks, and insisted that linen table cloths and the best china and silver be used daily. She added elegant furniture to the well-designed pieces that were already in the house and she entertained her friends, and the business and political associates of her husband, in a style unusual for a tiny hamlet in northern Illinois. Growing up in this relatively sophisticated environment, Jane Addams acquired a social assurance, a sense of position, an easy identity with those who represented wealth and culture, that would stay with her all her life.[6]

Anna Addams brought more than culture to the Addams household however; she also brought discipline, order, and a certain amount of tension. At first Jane, who had been spoiled by doting sisters and servants, found the adjustment to a more rigid system difficult to take. She also was somewhat aghast at her stepmother's outbursts of temper. Yet, it was not long before Jane became accustomed to the new regime, and despite a difference in temperament a real bond of affection developed between her and her stepmother. Jane referred to her very naturally as "Ma," and Anna treated the quiet, retiring child as one of her own

The new Mrs. Addams had two living children of her own and had lost two others. Harry Haldeman was eighteen when his mother remarried. He was brilliant, gregarious, and independent. He studied in Germany, became an able doctor and then a shrewd businessman. When he was twenty-six he married Jane Addams' sister, Alice, though neither his mother nor her father approved. George Haldeman was seven, six months younger than Jane, when the two families combined. The two youngsters quickly became inseparable playmates and rivals. George was an imaginative boy with a quick mind always ready for a new adventure. He had an important influence on Jane Addams as she grew and matured—he helped her realize that she had ability too. If he could dream of becoming a scientist or physician, why couldn't she?

Despite her complex family and her frequent sicknesses, Jane had a happy, rural childhood not significantly different from others of her generation, except that she early developed a sense of purpose and commitment. She was sickly, but she never became a hypochondriac; she suffered in silent determination. Jane and the other children in the village went to a one-room school. Her grades were good, though she did not seem in any sense precocious. She did not excel at spelling, a humbling deficiency because the spelling bee was one of the social events of the school year. But she early became an eager reader and one of the leaders in the literary society at school.[7]

Jane Addams grew up believing in the American dream of democracy, equality, and equal opportunity for all. She was aware, of course, that her father was the wealthiest and most prominent person in the village, that her house was bigger than all the other houses, that she had advantages that many other children did not have, such as drawing and music lessons in Freeport and fine clothes. But still there was a basic equality in Cedarville. She played with the sons and daughters of the mill hands and went to the village school as did everyone else in town. Of course, there were no recent immigrants and nearly everyone was a Protestant. The hired girls at the Addams' house were just that, girls from the community who agreed to work for a year or two, in part to learn how to cook and sew and manage a house. They were not treated as servants but included in the family circle along with Polly, the family nurse. They sat with the family in the evening and knitted while Mrs. Addams read and Jane and George played checkers on the big table or wrote letters to brothers and sisters who were away at school or lived in nearby towns.

The natural equality of the small town counteracted the aristocratic tendencies of her stepmother. The two conflicting influences led to some ambivalence and contradiction which Jane Addams never completely overcame.

At sixteen Jane Addams was slender and attractive, five feet three inches tall and ninety-five pounds. She wore her soft, brown hair pulled back and gathered in a bun in the back. Her dark eyes gave her face a look that strangers mistook for sadness. She could even on rare occasions laugh at herself. She wrote to a distant cousin whom she had never met that she could cover pages trying to vindicate her nose "which is simply a piece of flesh, expressing no character whatever, and contains eight freckles horrible to relate (I counted them this morning.)" Yet in many ways her upbringing was sheltered. "I cannot number dancing among my accomplishments," she admitted, "and my knowledge of 'cards' is very limited indeed."[8]

She had the usual feminine interests in lace, pretty dresses and "fancy work," but she also liked to roam through the hills and fields around Cedarville with George and assorted neighborhood children, to play chess, and to skate on the millpond in winter. She also liked to read. John Addams was a serious reader himself, and the subscription library which he had helped organize was located in the Addams' house. He inspired his daughter to read; he also bribed her by offering her five cents for every one of *Plutarch's Lives* she finished, and twenty-five cents for every volume of Irving's *Life of Washington*. She tried Pope's translation of the *Iliad* and Dryden's *Virgil*, but as a young girl she preferred somewhat lighter fare, especially Louisa May Alcott. She re-read *Little Women* several times and decided that "it never seems to grow old." She liked Dickens ("he never wrote anything stupid"), but was not impressed with Scott ("instructive novels are to me a bore"). She early developed the habit of keeping a notebook, in which she copied the passages which appealed to her, together with her random thoughts and observations. She also had the Victorian notion that reading too much fiction was somehow a sign of weakness. "As I am a little inclined to 'overdo' things when I get started," she reported, "I now have an arrangement with Pa, that I am to read a certain amount of history first."[9]

John Addams not only helped his youngest daughter appreciate literature and history, he also passed on to her some of his own driving sense of ambition and purpose. He taught her that achievement and integrity were important, that one should work hard, and do every task as well as possible. This sense of destiny and commitment was part of the Christian tradition, part of the Protestant ethic which was deeply rooted in American life. This sense of purpose and achievement was reinforced in the Addams family by her stepmother, who encouraged Jane to think of herself as an intelligent woman, and by George Haldeman who was passionately interested in science and philosophy. John Addams believed that women should be educated and for years he supported the Female Seminary at near-by Rockford, and he had sent his two older daughters there. But he also believed that women should be taught to become better wives and mothers, not scientists or professors. While George was encouraged to become a doctor or a scientist Jane was quietly discouraged from any such ambition. The contradiction and the conflict between the sense of destiny and the belief that she could do something important, on the one hand, and the traditional role of submissive, domestic woman on the other, troubled and confounded her for years.

Jane Addams' rural childhood was important in molding her personality, and affecting her career. Her family, though complex and filled with tensions and conflicts, was a close-knit unit whose members wrote constantly to each other. Some of the tragedies and disagreements which beset them left scars on her personality. But once she was finally able to break away from the burdens and guilt placed on her by her particular family situation she was able to use her own experience to interpret the conflicts which troubled all families in a changing America.

Like a great many others of her generation she left the small town to move to the city, but she had a warm affection for her hometown, a real sense of place, and she returned frequently even after she became famous. Cedarville and the memories of her rural childhood became a reference point for evaluating and understanding the massive changes that took place during her lifetime.

Jane Addams was one of the first generation of college women. A few girls had attended Mount Holyoke, Oberlin, or one of a small handful of other colleges before the Civil War, but they usually received the equivalent of a high school rather than a college education. It was not until the founding of Vassar in 1861, Smith in 1872, Wellesley in 1875, Bryn Mawr in 1886, and the gradual movement toward limited co-education at Cornell, Harvard, and a number of state universities that college education for women became a reality. The proper course of study and the effect of higher education on women remained topics of controversy for years, but those women who entered college in the 1870's and 1880's did so with a sense of mission and a feeling that they were participants in a new venture.

Jane Addams' college years were crucial in her development. For the first time she became a part of a group more important than family and village, and she developed a sense of solidarity with other women. She discovered that she could write and speak in public and that other women looked to her for leadership. Her college experience reinforced her childhood desire to do something important with her life. It took her eight years after college to settle on a career and to determine her role in the world, but in a real sense that career began in college.

Before entering she had read of the new Eastern colleges and was determined to go to Smith, perhaps because, more than the others, Smith tried to maintain the same standards as the best men's colleges. Her father, however, insisted that she stay closer to home. Reluctantly she agreed to go for a year to the Female Seminary in nearby Rockford as her older sisters had done. Rockford Seminary, which she entered in the fall of 1877, had been chartered thirty years before by the Presbyterian and Congregational Conventions to provide education and religious instruction for the daughters of the farmers and small businessmen of the upper Mississippi Valley. It was not, however, until Anna Peck Sill arrived in 1849 that anything was done about actually establishing a female seminary. In 1849 she raised $5000 from the citizens in the Rockford area and in the fall of 1851 admitted the first class of fifteen girls.

Anna Sill patterned her institution after Mary Lyon's Mount Holyoke. Almost from the beginning the seminary became known as the "Mount Holyoke of the West," though it was also similar in purpose and design to a number of other women's seminaries scattered across the East and Midwest. The object of the school was to combine domestic and industrial training with religious and cultural instruction; to promote piety, purity, submissiveness, and domesticity. "The chief end of Woman's education is not simply to shine in society, but to elevate and purify and adorne the home," Miss Sill announced, and "to teach the great Christian lesson, that the true end of life is not to acquire the most good, whether of happiness or knowledge, but to give oneself fully and worthily for the good of others; recognizing, of course, that "the Bible is the only true textbook of practical morality." By the time Jane enrolled at Rockford Miss Sill was an old lady (she retired in 1884), and Rockford was in a state of transition between a seminary and a full-fledged woman's college. Yet her philosophy and personality still dominated the school.[10]

Each girl had to tend the stove in her room, furnish her own linen and table service, and she was expected to devote an hour each day to domestic tasks. The bell rang at 6:30 each morning, and breakfast was served at 7. Each student had to keep an account book and turn it in for inspection once a month. Demerits were issued to those who misbehaved, and occasionally a girl was expelled. A faculty member presided at the head of each table in the dining room; no one sat down until Miss Sill gave the signal. No one could leave the campus without special permission, and parents were urged not to send jewelry or expensive clothes or even food to their daughters. Daily chapel was, of course, required, as were weekly prayer meetings and church on Sunday, as well as Sunday School in the afternoon. There were also regular monthly fast days, an annual prayer week in January and informal devotions between the two study periods in the evening. Miss Sill was proud of the fact that a large proportion of the Seminary's graduates became missionaries, and she did her best to win more converts from each new class.[11]

There were seventeen girls in Jane Addams' graduating class, and a half-dozen more who dropped out before graduation. Most of them came from small towns in Illinois and Wisconsin. Their fathers were farmers, ministers, or small businessmen, although there were a few who had wealth and position. Several Rockford students corresponded with girls at Eastern colleges, and a few talked of transferring to a college that awarded a bachelor's degree. Even though Rockford did not have collegiate rank many of the women in Jane Addams' class were self-consciously aware that they were college women.

To be a college woman, whether at Vassar or Rockford, took some courage and dedication in 1877. Just four years earlier Dr. Edward H. Clarke, a professor at Harvard Medical School, had written a little book, *Sex in Education*, in which he argued that higher education for women would interfere with the reproductive system and lead to nervous prostration and a general decline in health. "Must we crowd education on our daughters, and for the sake of having them 'intellectual' make them puny, nervous, and their whole earthly existence a struggle between life and death?" another critic asked. Both of the older Addams girls had gone to Rockford, and they had not been unfitted for marriage and motherhood by the experience, and that may have been part of the reason John Addams preferred Rockford to Smith for his youngest child. But Jane Addams went to Rockford not just to be a seminary student; she was determined to be a college woman.[12]

The Rockford women talked, argued, and discussed. They debated Darwin's theories, talked about the role of women, a novel by Dickens, a Shakespearean play or one of Carlyle's books. They even argued about religion, though Miss Sill assumed that religion was not debatable. They had little interest in politics or social issues and were oblivious to the great rail strikes and the labor unrest around the country in 1877. Apparently this was not unusual for college students in the 70's. Florence Kelley, who had entered Cornell the year before, remembered: "My freshman year was one continual joy. . . . Little did we care that there was no music, no theater, almost no library; that the stairs to the lecture halls were wooden, and the classrooms heated with coal stoves. No one, so far as I know, read a daily paper, or subscribed for a monthly or a quarterly. Our current gossip was Froude's *Life of Carlyle*. We read only bound volumes."[13]

Jane had many friends, but the best and most important was Ellen Gates Starr, a slight and intense girl with a quick wit and a passionate interest in art who came from the small Illinois town of Durand. More spiritually and aesthetically concerned than Jane, she forced her friend to define her own religious beliefs. Ellen stayed at Rockford only one year and then turned to school teaching, at first near her home town and then in Chicago. The two friends saw each other infrequently after that first year, but they wrote long and intimate letters to each other. Another close friend made during her first year was Sarah Anderson, a young woman in her early thirties who was the college accountant and an instructor in gymnastics as well as English. Miss Anderson, unlike most of the teachers, did not hold herself aloof from the students, but became intellectual companion to several of the girls.[14]

She also had many casual friends in college, indeed even at this stage in her life there seems to have been something about her that attracted all kinds of people. Her room, in the words of one friend, became "an available refuge from all perplexities." Many girls tried to become her confidante, asked her for her picture, begged her to write to them and generally fawned over her. But she held herself from the sentimental flirting that seems to have been commonplace at many women's colleges at the time.[15] She was also more formal than most of her classmates.

All the girls were addressed as "Miss" in class, and the custom was even continued outside the classroom. "Apparently the formality was part of the solemn business of higher education for women," she wrote years later, but she was obviously more impressed by it than were most of her friends. She preferred "Miss Addams" to "Jane" and on one occasion aroused Ellen Starr's mild reproach when she told some of her classmates that her friend preferred "Miss Starr" to "Ellen." Miss Anderson tentatively mentioned after she had known Jane for four years: "Do you never think of me as 'Sarah'? If natural and pleasant for you to do so I would like it." College changed Jane Addams in many ways, among other things it transformed Jennie Addams into "Miss Addams," and "Miss Addams" she remained for the rest of her life.[16] Her formality and aloofness also seem to have affected her relationship with the men who occasionally visited the campus. Beloit College was only a few miles away, and there were a number of romances between students at the two colleges. Jane had several friends and at least two admirers at Beloit. One of these was her stepbrother, George Haldeman, who came to think of her as something more than a sister, though she did not return the affection and was somewhat troubled by it.

A number of her classmates dropped out of school to get married but apparently Jane never contemplated marriage for herself. She visited her sister Mary, who was married to a minister and lived in a nearby town. She loved to take care of the children, although the rest of the housework did not interest her. It is probably true that for the first generation of college women, a decision for a career effectively ruled out marriage. Not all her classmates were career-oriented, however; one of them wrote: "My highest aspirations now are not any more probable than in my younger days—only a little lower—to marry a rich man and live comfortably." Even Jane on occasion was restless and envious of the girls who had dropped out of school and were doing something real and useful. In writing to Ellen, who was in Chicago, she remarked: "There is something in being in a big city, in giving somewhat as well as taking all the time, in gaining the ability not to move in ruts, that will give you a self-reliance and an education a good deal better than a boarding school will. . . ." And again: "Sometimes when I think of being hemmed in by these four walls I grow perfectly restless, but when I think what a good quiet place it is for study I become quite contented again."[17]

The notebooks from her years at Rockford reveal the inward drive, the ambition to succeed, to become someone, that was an important part of Jane Addams' personality. "Solitude is essential to the life of man," she wrote, "all men come into this world alone and all leave it alone. . . ." "Deeds make habits, habits make character, character makes destiny." "Nothing is more certain than that improvement in human affairs is wholly the work of uncontented characters." "We are haunted by an ideal life and it is because we have within the beginnings and possibilities of it." "Better far pursue a frivolous trade by serious means than a sublime art frivolously." "Our doubts are traitors and make us lose the good we often might win, by fearing to attempt." "We (women) strain our natures at doing something great far less because it is something great to do, than happy we so commend ourselves as being not small."

There is also an indication in her notebooks of religious questioning and doubt. There is a paragraph on death, a speculation that "Nature is the ambassador of God," but mostly the notebooks are filled with unformed scepticism. "If we pray at all we pray no longer for our daily bread, but next century's harvest." At one point, perhaps referring to Miss Sill or to one of her other teachers, she wrote: "She does everything for people merely from love of God, and that I do not like." Her scepticism, her questionings and doubts were not unlike those of other intelligent young men and women of her day, but her situation was complicated by the conservative religious atmosphere at Rockford. Like others of her generation she was attracted to the new critical spirit which applied the test of science, or at least reason, to all areas of life even religion. Yet she hesitated to push the rational analysis of religion too far, because emotionally she wanted to believe.[18]

It is easy to misunderstand Jane Addams' religious questioning during her college years, to make her seem a rebel and free thinker, or see her as terribly confused and despondent over her doubts. The best way to understand her religious questioning is to see it as a part of her larger drive for self-improvement, as part of her attempt to find herself. Her religious quest was also complicated by her friendship with Ellen Starr, who forced her to worry about religion. The letters written between the two young women are the best surviving evidence of what Jane was thinking during college, but they are distorted by Ellen's great fascination and concern for solving her own religious dilemma.

During the summer after her sophomore year Jane tried to reassure Ellen and in the process revealed some of her own religious thinking and confusion. "Don't you see that you are all right—what do you understand by being saved? I don't know, of course, whether I have the correct idea or not, but what I call it is this—that a people or a nation are saved just as soon as they comprehend god . . . Comprehending your deity and being in harmony with his plans is to be saved. If you realize God through Christ, it don't make any difference whether you realize Christ or not, that isn't the point. If God has become nearer to you, more of reality through him, then you are a Christian. Christ's mission to you has been fulfilled . . . I am afraid I haven't expressed my idea very clearly, if you read Tennyson's 'In Memoriam' and look out for it, may be you can see something that will be exactly what you need; I did once but I am far enough away now, and I beg of you not to think that I am trying to preach. . . ."[19] "I can work myself into a great admiration for his [Christ's] life, and occasionally I can catch something of his philosophy, but he don't bring me any nearer the deity—I think of him simply as a Jew living hundreds of years ago, surrounding whom there is a mystery and a beauty incomprehensible to me, I feel a little as I do when I hear very fine music—that I am incapable of understanding. This is the nearest that I get to it and it is very rare—as a general thing I regard with indifference. . . ." But she had no more written that than she tried again to explain her thinking. "Lately it seems to me that I am getting back of all of it—superior to it, I almost feel—back to a great primal cause, not nature exactly but a fostering mother, a necessity, brooding and watching over all things. . . ." But then she gave up in despair. "Everytime I talk about religion, I vow a great vow never to do it again, I find myself growing indignant and sensitive when people speak of it lightly, as if they had no right to, you see, I am not so unsettled, as I *resettle* so often, but my creed is ever *be sincere* and don't fuss."[20]

It was difficult, however, in the religious atmosphere of Rockford Seminary not to worry and fuss about religion. The "unconverted" girls were the objects of rather intense pressure not only to become practising Christians but missionaries as well. Jane resisted the pressure, but she was affected by it. After an especially impressive chapel service during her junior year she even admitted that for the first time she was glad she belonged to a "Christian School." Belonging to a "Christian School" or joining a church or knowing that you were a Christian didn't help much, however, for to Jane her religious beliefs and her life work seemed closely intertwined.[21]

Her friend and instructor Miss Anderson provided a practical answer when she said: "I do not think we are put into the world to be religious, we have a certain work to do, and to do that is the main thing." But as much as Jane wanted to accept this simple solution she could not. "I for my part am convinced that . . . I can never go ahead and use my best powers until I do settle it, it seems to me sometimes—I suppose when I am wrought up—could I but determine *that* and have it for a sure basis, that with time and space to work in I could train my powers to do anything, it would only remain to choose what—of course this must be a false stress laid on religion, but I don't fuss anymore, since I have discovered its importance, but go ahead building up my religion where ever I can find it, from the Bible and observation, from books and people and in no small degree from Carlyle."[22]

Jane Addams was doing what a great many intellectuals in both England and America did in the nineteenth century when they became disillusioned and perplexed by the church; they "looked to literature for authority and to the writer as prophet." And to this end Carlyle became especially important. "If I could claim one promise in the Bible," Jane Addams wrote to Ellen, "I would care for no other—'He restoreth my soul.' Carlyle says everyone must sooner or later find out it is not with work alone he must contend but with folly and sin in himself and others, I have laid too many plans simply for work."[23]

What exactly that work was she was not sure, but a few months later she again emphasized the importance of religion as a way of helping her organize her life and get on with her real task. In explaining to Ellen how she thought their religious conceptions and needs differed she remarked: "You long for a beautiful faith, an experience . . . I only feel that I need religion in a practical sense, that if I could fix myself with my relations to God and the universe, and so be in perfect harmony with nature and deity, I could use my faculties and energy so much better and could do almost anything."[24]

Her introspective nature, her strong sense of purpose and her ability to organize and to work hard enabled her to excel in her classes. She studied Greek, Latin and German, Geology, Astronomy and Botany, Medieval History, Civil Government, Geography and American Literature, as well as the inevitable courses in Bible, Evidence of Christianity, and Moral Philosophy. During her freshman year she had an occasional 8 on examinations, but most of her grades were 9.5, 9.8, 9.9 with a few perfect 10's.[25]

For all the high grades, however, there were not many moments of intellectual excitement in the classes at Rockford. Most were routine, some were just boring, but she did even the most pedestrian assignments with care, and she complained little. The general tedium was occasionally broken by the excitement of studying Homer in the original Greek, or by dissecting and stuffing a hawk sent by an anonymous donor.[26]

Her interest in dissecting animals and other scientific endeavors came in part from her two stepbrothers and from the vague feeling that she someday wanted to be a doctor. Harry Haldeman had studied medicine in Germany, while George, her childhood playmate, was fascinated with scientific experiments. Together they studied comparative anatomy during the summer after her sophomore year. During her freshman year she had helped to found a scientific society at Rockford which sponsored lectures and tried to collect equipment for use by the Science Departments at the Seminary. Her interest in science continued during her senior year; she suggested to George that during the summer they could go thoroughly into mineralogical chemistry, "it is clean and accurate and lots of fun."[27]

She had other abiding concerns, however, and often during college she seemed torn between the science she felt she ought to learn and the literature and writing that fascinated her. She took part in debates, was elected president of the Literary Society and worked hard for the *Rockford Seminary Magazine*. During her junior year she became editor of the column called "Home Items" and was also in charge of magazine exchanges with other colleges. The magazine had always been a propaganda vehicle for the college. "We publish the quarterly in the interest of the Seminary and the cause of Christian education in general," Miss Sill announced. During her junior year, however, a small group of women set out to change the magazine and make it reflect student concerns rather than official dogma. They were influenced by the other college magazines they read. Their goals for reform were very meager, yet inevitably they clashed with Miss Sill, who wanted to maintain control over the magazine. Jane was by no means the most radical of the group. She often played the role of compromiser. Yet she was clearly a part of the reform movement. "You are *progressive* Jane, or you would not have joined the revolutionaries," a friend remarked.[28]

She wrote essays for the magazine, the first appearing in the spring of her freshman year. They had such titles as "Plated Ware," "The Element of Hopefulness in Human Nature," "The Macbeth of Shakespeare." Her essays were not any different from those of her classmates. They reveal an intense, idealistic young woman, steeped in literature and trying desperately to apply literature to life. Even in college she thought of herself as a writer. She worked hard on her college themes, and she wrote other essays and sketches. She carefully preserved her essays, even the most humble college themes, reworking them, adding material and eventually using some of the ideas in her later writing. She never had any desire to become a novelist, in part because fiction to her seemed frivolous and in part because most women writers composed sentimental novels or feminine books steeped with religion. She wanted to write about something important, and she began to develop the habits of a writer while she was in college.

Jane's social and political ideas as revealed by her college themes are what one might expect from a small-town girl from a good Republican family. In a theme entitled "The Present Policy of Congress," written during the fall of her freshman year, she wrote: "Our late war was inevitable, it might have come a little sooner or a little later but come it must. The disease of the nation was organic not functional, it needed the knife not soothing herbs, war was its only remedy and we are better and stronger for it. Thousands died on both sides, to have stopped before the end was attained, or if Congress now yields one inch of the principle then advanced, will make all that terrible loss of life mere butchery. But the negroes are free, that is a settled fact, and something must be done with them, the plight of the nation reminds us of the Vicar of Wakefield, who paid an enormous price for his family portraits and then didn't know what in the world to do with them." She went on to state that the South should be treated "with justice not mercy," and that "Hays should remember 'to the victor belongs the spoils' and not put a democrat, his political enemy, into office when there is an honest republican to be found in the neighborhood." She predicted that "if he deserts the big republican north, for the sake of soothing the big democratic south, he will find 'midst a whole country full of friends he has none.' "

The next spring she wrote an essay on "Tramps" that revealed little sympathy for their lot, and no suggestion that environment or circumstance had anything to do with their predicament. "The country is flooded with tramps," she wrote, "but where they come from and whither they go is a conjecture, we only know they are trying to evade the principle set down from the foundations of the earth, that a man must give a full equivalent for everything he receives; by disregarding this principle they render themselves abject and mean and merit their universal contempt . . . for a man to go around the country expecting help and to be pleased is an absurdity . . . an utter impossibility, for it is contrary to the laws of nature."[29]

The Class of '81 at Rockford, inspired by their correspondence with girls at other colleges, especially those at Vassar and Smith, introduced several new activities. They started a ceremony similar to Vassar's "trig day," organized a junior exhibition, composed a class song and designed their own class stationery with a picture of hops and wheat and their motto "breadgivers." Jane explained to her sister that their motto "is the primitive meaning of the word 'lady' and there are sixteen girls at R.F.S. who mean to do all they can to restore the word to its original sense, probably because they are so far now from its accepted meaning."[30]

Jane Addams, like many of the first generation of college women, was self-consciously a feminist, not so much concerned with woman suffrage as woman's role in the world. "The impervious will of man," she announced in a college debate, "is at last forced to admit that woman like himself possesses an intellect [and] that she exerts a potent influence in the age in which she lives. . . ."[31] At the junior exhibition she spoke in more muted tones and suggested that the changes over the last fifty years had been most marked in women's education which had "passed from accomplishments and the arts of pleasing, to the development of her intellectual force and her capabilities for direct labor. She wishes not to be a man, nor like a man, but she claims the same right to independent thought and action. . . . We . . . are not restless and anxious for things beyond us," she assured her audience, "we simply claim the highest privileges of our times, and avail ourselves of its best opportunities. But while on the one hand, as young women of the 19th century, we gladly claim these privileges, and proudly assert our independence, on the other hand we still retain the old ideal of womanhood—the saxon lady whose mission it was to give bread unto her household. So we have planned to be 'Breadgivers' throughout our lives, believing that in labor alone is happiness, and that the only true and honorable life is one filled with good works and honest toil, we will strive to idealize our labor and thus happily fulfill woman's noblest mission."[32]

Jane Addams' address was a shrewd, yet guarded declaration of independence and it marked her first open break with the traditional role of women. It was also a veiled attack on Miss Sill's educational philosophy. In place of the time-honored goal of womanly submissiveness, she offered the right to independent thought and action, with the comforting proviso that of course they did not want to be like men. Never once did she mention the importance of womanly piety, of religious training or Christian morality. Yet by stressing work and the Protestant ethic, she could hardly be faulted. She spoke of "good works and honest toil," and suggested that the ideal of womanhood, was not to be submissive, pious and pure, but rather to reassert the ancient role of woman as provider, as "breadgiver." One could, of course, be a "breadgiver," as a wife, mother and homemaker, but she implied that women could also fulfill their ancient role in other ways.[33]

Despite her other activities, she found time to go to a few lectures and to read several books not assigned in her classes. She mourned the death of Carlyle and worried that Emerson might also die before she had a chance to meet him. Her world sometimes seemed bound by the mundane details of Miss Sill's rules, the short trips to Cedarville, or Winnebago or Freeport, the trials of negotiating with the dressmaker, the domestic chores she willingly performed when she visited her sister, but then she would remind herself that what she was doing was significant, that Carlyle and Emerson did matter and that she was going to do something important.

She got a glimpse of a slightly wider world in the spring of her senior year when she and another magazine editor, Hattie Wells, received an invitation to attend the Interstate Oratorical Contest in Jacksonville, Illinois, and a meeting of college magazine editors. The girls were entertained by the committee, met all the participants and were taken to a literary contest between Knox and Illinois College by two young editors from the Illinois College Student Magazine. "We could not possibly have been better provided for," she wrote home. "It was an experience entertaining and decidedly different from anything I ever had before, we got more into the spirit of college life than I had ever dreamed of." The two young women also took time to visit the state institutions for the deaf, dumb and insane in Jacksonville.

In her letters to her sister Alice, describing her adventure, she seems confident and filled with enthusiasm. But in the letter to her father she played the roll of a humble daughter. "Of course I would have felt much better satisfied and comfortable if there had been time to write home and see what you and Ma thought of such an undertaking, but unfortunately there was not time," she explained, "I have sometimes doubted the wisdom of it and I hope it won't seem to you sudden and erratic."[34]

She had no more than returned from her Jacksonville adventure than the whirlwind of getting ready for graduation began. The trustees and the faculty agreed to add a post-graduate year, and those who completed the program would be entitled to the degree. "Now I have had a little more than a full years extra work," she explained to her stepbrother, "And there upon Miss Sill has offered to me this degree." The offer of a B.A. from Rockford put her clearly on the spot. The degree meant a great deal to her; it marked her as a college woman officially and irrevocably, but she had always planned to take the degree from Smith. Yet there was obvious pressure from Miss Sill and also from her classmates (who wanted the Class of '81 to be the first to have a degree) and she knew it would please her father. She asked George for help in solving her dilemma. "I know better than anyone else how little my scholarship is worth," she wrote, "and I do hate a spread, especially if I have the first class honor, and too if I will take a degree at Smiths it will be perfectly absurd to have had this one first." What advice her brother gave her it is now impossible to learn, but she did refuse to take the degree probably for the reasons she gave, the most important of which was her expectation to enroll at Smith the next year.[35]

Graduation day was a day of triumph for Jane Addams. In her senior essay, well written and ringing with confidence and conviction, she spelled out some of her developing ideas, and her thinking about the special role and responsibility of women. Her title was "Cassandra"—the Trojan woman who was given the power of prophecy and who predicted the victory of the Greeks and the destruction of her father's city. "But the brave warriors laughed to scorn the beautiful prophetess and called her mad. The frail girl stood conscious of Truth but she had no logic to convince the impatient defeated warriors, and no facts to gain their confidence, she could assert and proclaim until at last in sooth she becomes mad." This was the tragedy of Cassandra, and implicitly of all women, "to be right and always to be disbelieved and rejected."

It was a feminine trait of mind, she maintained, to have "an accurate perception of Truth and Justice which rests contented in itself and will make no effort to confirm itself, or to organize through existing knowledge." So the goal of women should not be to become more like men, for there was a great need for womanly intuition in a nineteenth-century world that emphasized physical and mechanical knowledge. But women must gain "what the ancients called *auethoritas*, right of speaker to make themselves heard . . . ," and demonstrate that intuition is a way to knowledge and truth. Yet women should not depend on intuition alone, they should use their special talents. "Let her not sit and dreamily watch her child, let her work her way to a sentient idea that shall sway and ennoble those around her. All that subtle force among women which is now dream fancy, might be changed into creative genius."

In more personal terms she went on to describe how women could convert their wasted intuition to use. They should study at least one branch of science. "With eyes accustomed to search for the Truth, she will readily detect all self-deceit and fancy in herself; she will test whether her intuition is genuine and a part of nature, or merely a belief of her own. She will learn silence and self-denial, to express herself not by dogmatism, but by quiet, progressive development." In addition there were discoveries to be made in science by the trained intuitive mind, but women's responsibilities were not to science alone for she must also take an active role in solving the social problems of the world."[36]

This essay was the most original, the least stilted piece of writing she had done in college; it was personal yet grounded in a knowledge of the classics. Her thesis about woman's special intuitive genius, of course, was debatable, but it was one which in modified form she would pursue in much of her later writing. Her essay "Cassandra," and another, "Breadgivers," represented her growing convictions about the special role of women and her own determination to do something important as an educated woman. Breaking away from her stepmother's and Miss Sill's conception of a woman's role based on piety, purity, domesticity, and submissiveness; she was groping toward a conception of the role of woman that would make her a more active participant and a special leader in the world's affairs, while preserving and making special use of her womanliness. Jane Addams' use of the "Cassandra" image and the ancient idea of woman as "breadgiver" were original at least in part, but her defense of an active role for woman was a product of her college years. Around the country at Vassar, Smith, Wellesley, and other colleges women were coming to similar conclusions. Even at Rockford Jane Addams was far from alone. Several other girls in her class and the class behind her, as well as a number of the young instructors were planning to become something more than mothers and homemakers. But not everyone agreed with her. Kate Louise Turner, a member of Jane's class, in her senior essay attacked the woman who ignored the home and strove "for more avenues to power, more opportunities for employment." A woman who neglected her home in order to reform the world was simply "no more a lady."[37]

During the summer after her graduation her friend and former teacher Sarah Anderson wrote: "I think just at this stage of the woman question one does the most good who does good work in one of the professions or higher departments of teaching and yet maintains her true womanly way of helpfulness." Jane certainly must have agreed. Filled with confidence, and with plans to enroll at Smith, earn her BA, then travel in Europe before entering medical school, she said goodby to friends, sold her college furniture for $100, and prepared for a summer of study and relaxation before the new adventures of the fall.[38]

II

Despair and
Disillusionment

FTER graduation Jane Addams returned to Cedarville, and suddenly became ill and despondent. By early July she had given up her plans to enroll at Smith College in the fall.[1] She had never been especially robust or strong. She had frequent back aches, seemed to catch cold easily, and had periodic bouts of "horse fever." Yet she had led a vigorous and active life in college apparently untroubled by health problems, or no more afflicted than her classmates. Her undefined illness and breakdown coming so quickly after graduation has to be seen in the context of her family situation, and in terms of what was expected of a young woman in 1881.

In the 1870's and 1880's young women of the upper and middle classes were often afflicted by nervous prostration and periodic breakdowns from overwork. William Dean Howells remarked in 1872 that American society seemed little better than a hospital for invalid women. Menstruation usually caused this generation of young ladies to take to their beds (something their mothers rarely did). Dr. Walter C. Taylor, in a popular guide published in 1872 called *A Physician's Counsels to Woman in Health and Disease*, advised that "every woman should look on herself as an invalid once a month." Jules Michelet, the popular French writer on women, maintained that much of the month, "Woman is not only an invalid, but a wounded creature." She is held by nature in a bondage of weakness and suffering." While an English authority argued: "Although the duration of the menstrual period differs greatly according to race, temperament, and health, it will be within the mark of state that women are unwell, from this cause, on the average two days in the month, or say one month in the year. At such times, women are unfit for any great mental or physical labour. They suffer under a languor and depression which disqualify them for thought or action and render it extremely doubtful how far they can be considered responsible beings while the crisis lasts. Much of the inconsequent conduct of women, their petulance, caprice and irritability, may be traced directly to this cause." It was also a general assumption that the female nervous system was more frail, more irritable, more prone to overstimulation than the male nervous system.[2] This kind of pseudoscience could obviously be used to document women's basic inferiority, and even many young women who argued for the equality of the sexes fell prey to the popular rhetoric, especially when friends and relatives fully expected them to play the role of semi-invalid. It was an easy way to avoid difficult and anxiety-filled situations. The new college women seemed especially susceptible to illness and nervous prostration; because it was assumed that too much mental exertion led to nervous and physical breakdown. One writer in *Scribner's Monthly* described the new women's colleges as breeders of "diseases of body, diseases of imagination, vices of body and imagination—everything we would save our children from. . . ."[3]

A number of girls dropped out of Rockford Seminary because of physical and mental breakdown. At Cornell, Florence Kelley was taken ill with diphtheria, and it was three years before she was well enough to continue. Almost all of the first generation of college women seemed to have suffered from poor health and nervous prostration. Simultaneously with Jane Addam's illness, Ellen Starr was stricken at her home not far away. "I have been sick in bed for more than a week . . . ," Ellen wrote, "The Dr. says it is serious prostration caused partly by overwork. I suppose I shall be obliged to admit it is a smash up, and thank my good health that it's no worse."[4]

How ill Jane Addams was in the summer of 1881 it is now impossible to determine. She may have had an emotional and physical relapse after her strenuous year at college, but it is significant that she became ill after she returned home to her family and Cedarville. Her father and stepmother did not want her to go to Smith College, and they probably helped to convince her that she was too ill to continue her studies. It was easy to be confident and self-reliant on the college campus, but at home her family almost encouraged her to play the role of invalid daughter.

A tragic event of the summer of 1881 also had its impact on Jane's emotional state. On July 2 Charles Julius Guiteau shot President James Garfield at the railroad station in Washington. Guiteau, a mentally disturbed young man who had dabbled at law, politics, and preaching, was the stepbrother of Flora Guiteau, probably Jane's closest friend in the Freeport-Cedarville area. Flora had been a frequent visitor at the Addams' house, and her father (also the father of the assassin) worked at John Addams' bank in Freeport. President Garfield lingered through the summer before dying on September 19, 1881. But all that summer Freeport became the center of great publicity, and Flora Guiteau the object of much attention and abuse. Jane naturally felt sorry for her friend and worried about the tragedy and notoriety that had befallen her family.

In part to escape the turmoil, as well as to give Jane a change of scenery, John Addams took his wife and daughter on a combined business and pleasure trip to northern Wisconsin early in August. While exploring mining property near Marquette Mr. Addams suddenly became ill. Jane and her stepmother took him to a hospital in Green Bay, but within thirty-six hours he was dead, the victim of "inflammation of the bowels" or a ruptured appendix.[5]

Her father's sudden death was a great blow to Jane. She had always admired him. She lovingly called him "Pa" and shared many of her college experiences with him in long letters. Shortly after his death she wrote, briefly and simply about her memory of him:

> He was respected for his stern honesty and the tricksters either in politics or in the legislative halls were afraid of him. He was the uncompromising enemy of wrong and of wrong doing. He was a leader as well as a safe and fearless advocate in right things in public life. My own vivid recollection of John H. Addams is the fact that he was a man of purest and sternest integrity and that bad men feared him. This fact was proverbial at Springfield where as Senator and in other public positions he distinguished himself both as an able man and an honest man.[6]

"I will not write of myself or how purposeless and without ambition I am," she admitted to her friend Ellen two weeks later. "Only prepare yourself so you won't be too disappointed in me when you come. The greatest sorrow that can ever come to me has past and I hope it is only a question of time until I get my moral purposes straightened." "I shall never be disappointed in you," Ellen replied, "you are too much like your father, I think, for your 'moral purpose' to be permanently shaken by anything, even the greatest sorrow." It was a shrewd analysis of Jane's personality, for she had a sense of determination that was not easily defeated. Indeed in the letter to Ellen in which she described "her greatest sorrow" she spent most of the space advising her friend to take a bottle of malt and desiccated blood in order to recover from her illness. She did not collapse in confusion after her father's death nor did she give in to the temptation to become an invalid. "You have the faculty which I wish I had and yet which I believe you would be better off without," Sarah Anderson wrote, "that of doing good work when tired and sick." Within a few weeks she was traveling to Philadelphia to enroll as a student at the Women's Medical College.[7]

Why she chose to start medical school at this juncture, after she had given up the idea of going to Smith because of her health, is not clear. A large part of the impetus seems to have come from her stepmother, now a widow for the second time, who felt the need to get out of Cedarville for the winter. Philadelphia was a logical place to go, especially because there were a number of relatives in the area and her older son Harry and his wife would be there for part of the time. The Women's Medical School in Philadelphia was one of the few medical schools in the country which accepted women. "To be in Philadelphia studying this winter would be the realization of the brightest dream that I have ever entertained," one of her college friends wrote, but it did not seem so ideal to Jane after the first few weeks. The courses were not espcially interesting. She wrote despairingly in her notebook about her "utter failure" and her inability "to work at the best of myself." "I am growing more sullen and less sympathetic every day."[8]

Before many weeks she was ill again, and by February she had given up her studies and entered S. Weir Mitchell's Hospital of Orthopedic and Nervous Diseases. Mitchell was a brilliant physician, who had experimented with the relationship between mental condition and physical ailments. He treated wealthy women who were troubled by nervous exhaustion and a variety of other complaints. Some of his patients arrived on litters, some had convulsions, some were partly paralyzed, others had uncontrollable fits of tears and laughter. Many, like Jane Addams, had backaches and simply felt run down and depressed. Mitchell's cure consisted mostly of rest, and seclusion—no visitors, no books or papers. He sought to "fatten and redden" his patient until her health and moral courage were restored. He also wanted to change the patient's routine and get her away from the over-protective sympathy of relatives, especially mothers. Occasionally there was a patient who liked the rest cure too well and refused to get out of bed at all. On one occasion Mitchell, who played the role of the "tranquil tyrant," threatened to get into bed with a young woman if she did not get out. He took off his coat and had started to loosen his trousers when the patient leaped out of bed.[9]

Mitchell had many theories to explain why women developed the symptoms of nervous illness. In part, he suggested, it was the very traits which men had come to admire in women; their helplessness, submissiveness and modesty which, if exaggerated, led straight to invalidism. Sometimes it was a shock or trauma, a death or disappointment in love which precipitated the crisis, but often it was the inability to meet the demands placed upon her which led to a "breakdown through overconformity." Part of Jane's difficulty in Philadelphia was her inability to reconcile her career ambitions, her need to study hard and to learn material which was not innately interesting to her, with the sense of responsibility she felt toward her family, especially toward her stepmother. Mrs. Addams, freed from the provincial small town, wanted to go to concerts, visit museums, entertain relatives and friends, and she expected Jane to share these activities with her, little appreciating the time and discipline demanded by her studies. But instead of insisting on her priorities, Jane usually went along with her stepmother's ideas. She felt a responsibility even in medical school to play the traditional womanly role of companion, homemaker, and entertainer. A few years later she would recall that her main trouble in Philadelphia was "trying to fulfill too many objects at once." It was not as easy to maintain the old ideal of womanhood, as she had suggested in her Junior Exhibition speech, and still assert one's intellectual independence.[10]

Dr. Mitchell's rest cure did not seem to help her very much. She was impatient with the inactivity. "I have come to the time when I could not read and then found how much I had depended on that," she wrote. But the rest did seem to improve her back. By April she was well enough to travel, and she returned to Cedarville with her stepmother. But familiar surroundings did little to improve her outlook, and her back continued to bother her. Cedarville and the old homestead were depressing and lonesome when she returned, not the happy place they had seemed when she had come home from college. She had lost her purpose. She tried to imagine that she could be happy managing the household, and busying herself with domestic chores. She wrote in her notebook of feeling "failure in every sense," and lectured herself about the need to pay more attention to the feelings of others. "People expect certain things of me. I have every chance to obtain them and yet fall far short." To complicate matters George apparently pressed his affections on his stepsister during the spring and summer of 1882. Jane had no interest in a romantic relationship with George (or probably with any man), yet she did not want to hurt him. She worried about their relationship and about her own sexual identity. "We can set a watch over our affections . . . as we can over our other treasures—Geo and me both," she cryptically wrote in her notebook.[11] Most college women in the 1880's believed that they could not combine marriage and a career, and in fact almost one half of the first generation of women college graduates never married. If Jane Addams wavered a bit in the summer of 1882 she did not seek a lover to solve her dilemma, least of all a lover she thought of as her brother. Instead, she was determined to go back to college. She decided once again to enroll at Smith, and even stopped in Northampton to inspect the campus in July while she was traveling with her family in New England. But she was advised by a college friend already at Smith that she should not come unless she was completely well. "To begin a life of self sacrifice without strength enough to carry on makes one lead a life of duplicity and falsehood," she wrote bitterly in her notebook.[12]

The self-searching, the mental anguish, the illness and loneliness that Jane Addams went through in the year after graduation was not unique and cannot be explained entirely by her special family situation or by describing it just as a woman's problem. In America, William James and Henry Adams, to name only two, went through similar periods of questioning and inaction and self-doubt. In Victorian England a time of "depression and *ennui*" was almost commonplace among writers and intellectuals and became a major theme in Victorian literature, much of which was familiar to Jane Addams. John A. Symonds recalled his "utter blackness of despair"; Carlyle wrote frequently of the fatal misery of "languor and paralyses"; Huxley wrote, "I can't think; I can't write; I can't run; I can't ride; I have neither wit, nerve nor strength for anything. . . ." Ruskin blamed the "ennui, and jaded intellect and uncomfortableness of soul and body" on the loss of faith. A later generation would see deeper psychological reasons for the languor. It was also related to the fantastic changes in all areas of life being brought about by industrialism and urbanization, and this a few physicians like S. Weir Mitchell recognized.[13]

No group felt more adrift than the first generation of college women. Released from the close-knit fellowship and the purpose of the women's colleges, many women graduates had a difficult time finding a suitable career, or even a feeling that they were needed. "Suddenly they found themselves not merely alone, but alone in a society that had no use for them," William O'Neill has written. "Their liberal education did not prepare them to do anything in particular, except teach, and the stylized, carefully edited view of life it gave them bore little relation to the actual world. In consequence graduation was often a traumatic experience for those young women who had been educated to fill a place that did not yet exist."[14]

With marriage, teaching or possibly charity work the only acceptable or socially approved occupations for young ladies, those who sought an alternative found it a lonely and frustrating search. In 1882, the same year that Jane Addams dropped out of medical school and felt so depressed and helpless, Marion Talbot, a graduate of Boston University, who had drifted aimlessly after college, organized the Association of Collegiate Alumnae. The object of the new organization was to help raise the standards of women's education, but also to restore the lost sense of purpose and fellowship that college women had felt on the campus.[15]

Jane Addams' predicament in 1882 was not unique but that did not make it any more bearable. She finally became convinced by family and friends that a large part of her problem was physical, that if her back problem, resulting from a curvature of the spine, could be corrected she then could solve her problem of lack of purpose and direction. So in the fall of 1882 she once again postponed her enrollment at Smith and traveled instead to Mitchelville, Iowa, where her stepbrother, Harry Haldeman, a skilled surgeon, operated on her back. He injected irritant into the tissue near the spine, then she lay flat on her back for months while the scar tissue which formed supposedly pulled the spine straight. He then fitted her with an elaborate straight-jacket made of leather, steel and whalebone to support her spine.[16] After six months spent mostly in bed being waited on by her older sister, Jane was almost convinced that she was an invalid. She wrote few letters during those months of convalescence because she was "ashamed to show even my good friends against what lassitude, melancholy and general crookedness I was struggling. I have had the kindest care, and am emerging with a straight back and a fresh hold on life and endeavor, I hope," she wrote without too much conviction.[17]

In the spring she returned to Cedarville only to have a new burden thrust upon her. Her older brother, Weber, who was married with a family and lived on a farm on the outskirts of Cedarville, had a complete mental breakdown. Most of the burden of making arrangements, comforting his wife, and handling the financial affairs fell on Jane. Mrs. Addams was in Florida, Mary, who lived not many miles away, had her own problems, George was still at college, and Alice was in Iowa. Family responsibilities seemed to interfere with her own ambitions and career, and she postponed her plans to go back to college and took over the practical management of the family. "I find myself becoming quite absorbed in business affairs and am afraid I shall lose all hold of the softer graces," she admitted to Ellen. Jane had inherited a 247-acre farm, sixty acres of timberland, and eighty acres in Dakota as well as considerable stock, bonds and other property—worth a total of between $50,000 and $60,000. Weber acquired a farm in Cedarville, in addition to the mills.[18] So with her brother ill, Jane for a time took over the management of the whole operation in addition to handling her own investments. She had arguments with a neighbor over a disputed boundary line, and disagreements with her sister Alice over who was going to pay Weber's bills. In addition she made frequent trips to Mary's house to help her care for her children, while she continued to read extensively and to write a few essays.

She also maintained an interest in Rockford affairs. She helped to raise money for a telescope and a new library, and in 1883 was appointed a member of the board of trustees, a real honor for one so recently graduated. She was also the principal speaker at the alumnae meeting held during graduation week. In her new capacity she quickly became embroiled in a controversy arising over the rebellion of some of the younger faculty and many of the students over the repressive actions of Miss Sill. In all, she had many chances to sharpen her skill at organization and compromise.[19]

She sometimes complained of being "smothered with business cares," but she was pleased to be back in the old house in Cedarville and associated again with the college, and her health was much improved. "I can do a great many things without getting tired which last summer would have used me up completely, but now are a pleasure to undertake," she reported to her sister. She had discovered as she would again and again in the next few years, that activity both physical and mental as well as a direct purpose to work for made her stronger and happier.[20] Yet she decided once again not to continue her education in the fall of 1883, but instead to go abroad. "It seems quite essential for the establishment of my health and temper," she wrote to Ellen, "that I have a radical change, and so I have accepted the advice given to every exhausted American, 'go abroad.'" Several writers have perpetuated the story, using this letter as evidence, that she went abroad to seek better health and to solve her problems and frustrations.[21] But her health was already better, and she had long planned to take a European trip as well as to go to Smith and medical school. Now having failed at the first two goals, she set out on the third, but with some fear: "I quite feel as if I were not following the call of my genius when I propose to devote two years' time to travel in search of a good time and this *general* idea of culture which some way never commanded my full respect. People complain of losing spiritual life when abroad, I imagine it will be quite as hard to hold to full earnestness of purpose."[22]

Her European venture was similar to the cultural excursions of other moderately wealthy Americans in the late nineteenth century, and yet there was a difference. She was a careful observer of the European scene. She did not avoid the prejudices and the foibles of most American tourists, but she noticed things that they did not. Most of all it was the intensity of her study of art and history books, of literature and people that marked her apart. She was determined to study Europe, not just to observe, then to do something useful with the knowledge of art and language, literature and history. She was driven to her study by the same compulsion that made her excel in college.

Unlike most of the young American ladies who went to Europe as a finishing touch to their education before they settled down to become proper wives and mothers, she kept a careful record of her trip. She had discovered in college that she had some talent and interest in writing, and somehow writing about her adventures became part of her scheme to make her trip more than just sightseeing. She jotted down her thoughts and reactions in notebooks, and she wrote long "journalistic" letters to her sisters Alice and Mary and to other members of the family.[23]

The party, which consisted of her stepmother, Mary and "Puss" Ellwood, two college friends, their aunt, and Sarah Anderson, her teacher from Rockford, sailed from New York on August 22, 1883, and returned in June 1885. They landed in Ireland and with their six trunks and other baggage, traveled to Scotland, then to England. They crossed the channel to Holland in November, went to Berlin and then to Dresden, where they settled for ten weeks in a pension. Early in the spring they were off again to Bavaria, Austria, Italy and Switzerland, before spending some time in Paris. They made a second trip to England before settling down for the second winter in Berlin. Finally they returned for a few months in Paris, then sailed for America. The party occasionally split into smaller groups. Sarah left after the first year, and George Haldeman came over to spend two months with them during the summer of 1884.

Jane's health and spirit remained good throughout the whole trip. She was seasick every time she got on a ship, but she even convinced herself that it did her good. After a short time she abandoned the special jacket or brace that was supposed to help her back and never wore it again. She found no difficulty climbing mountain trails, clambering up the steep, winding staircases in cathedrals, tramping endlessly through museums and riding in trains and cabs. Indeed, she gained weight, from 98 to 115 pounds during her stay in Europe.

In addition to the usual fare of museums and cathedrals, with operas and concerts in the evenings, the party stopped at most of the universities and all the literary landmarks. They visited the homes of Thomas Carlyle and Horace Walpole and inspected the graves of Matthew Arnold and William Wordsworth. They read and recited Tom Moore in Ireland and *Rob Roy* in Scotland. When they went through the palace of Frederick the Great, Jane recalled Carlyle's description of him, and she compared the moral struggle in Wagner's Tannhauser to Victor Hugo's Jean Valjean. She read John Ruskin's *Mornings in Florence* and William Dean Howells' *Italian Journey* as well as George Eliot's *Romola*. She often made literary references and comparisons in her letters home, but occasionally she revealed a more practical background. Impressed with the Mediterranean Sea, she remarked: "I never saw such blue water, it is just exactly the shade of a tub of blueing to wrinse clothes in."[24]

Scattered throughout her communications on the trip are passages that show her basic concern for the poor and the depressed, but it was a concern more filled with curiosity than with indignation. On the Irish countryside she remarked: "In one little field about an acre square we counted thirteen men at work making hay. It was pretty and thrifty looking and we saw little of the squalor, though the men average but six shillings a week in wages. We were beseiged by troops of children . . . begging for pennies, the more we threw the more the crowd increased. They were all well-fed, very pretty and saucy."[25] Later she described a trip into the slums of the East End of London, where they watched the Saturday night marketing. "The poorest people wait until very late Saturday night as meats and vegetables which cannot be kept over Sunday are sold cheaper. We reached the neighborhood by the underground railway and then rode on top of a streetcar for five miles through rows of booths and stalls and swarming thousands of people." In a characteristic literary reference she referred to the area as a "Dickens' neighborhood." "We took a look into dingy old Grubb St.," she continued. "It was simply an outside superficial survey of the misery and wretchedness, but it was enough to make one thoroughly sad and perplexed." In the very next sentence, however, she described an eloquent minister they heard preach the next morning.[26]

Perhaps because of her recent business experience she seems to have been impressed with the long list of taxes paid by two New England ladies who ran a boarding house in London. "They pay rent of 136 pounds a year, general tax, Queens tax, water rates, poor rates, land rates until it is perfectly amazing to look over their tax list. Besides that the man owning the house pays so much a year to the Duke of Portsmouth who has a life lease on the land. It is the big fish living off the little fish over and over again."[27]

In Bavaria she remarked: "The skies and the forest are beautiful, but we saw a great deal of misery at Coburg . . . right across the market were a dozen or fifteen women going backward and forward with huge casks— almost barrels—fastened on their backs. These were filled with hot beer which they were carrying to a cooling house. The stuff stirred and spilled, of course, as they were walking, often scalding their heads and shoulders. They did this from five in the morning until seven at night for a mark and a half—37½ cents."[28]

These passages, however, are not typical of her reactions to the sights and sounds of Europe, and they seem to have had little or no impact on defining her purpose, though she strongly implies that they did in her autobiography, where the scene in the East End of London and the sight of the Bavarian Brewery become part of the influence which led directly to Hull House. In the letters she wrote home during the trip she seemed much more impressed by the palaces, the glimpses of royalty and the pomp and circumstance which she witnessed in Europe.

The great cathedrals, the religious art and the other monuments to Christianity seem to have done little to settle her religious questioning, and the letters she wrote home barely mention religion. During the summer before sailing, burdened with new difficulties and responsibilities she remarked to Ellen who had just joined the Episcopal Church, "My experiences of late have shown me the absolute necessity of the protection and dependence on Christ, his 'method and secret' as Matthew Arnold put it . . . the good men and books I used to depend on will no longer answer."[29] But she made no move at this point to join a church, Episcopal or otherwise. A sense of fellowship, a sense of community, was more important than theology. "I believe more and more in keeping the events and facts of Christ's life before me and letting the philosophy go," she wrote Ellen on Palm Sunday from Paris.[30]

Politically, she had few doubts, and she had not progressed beyond the high-tariff Republicanism of her father. She asked that the Reverend Mr. Linn, Mary's husband, send her pamphlets on the tariff question. She had met so many Americans in Europe who believed in low tariffs, even in free trade, that she needed "to be reinforced in arguments on the right side." And on the day after the American presidential election in November 1884, with Grover Cleveland running against James G. Blaine, she went to the American exchange office in Berlin to get some news. "The young man announced with very gleeful tone that Cleveland was elected but on closer inquiry confessed that he had carried New York and New Jersey and it was certain he would be elected, that they would have another telegram tonight. As the exchange is a democratic institution we still allow ourselves to hope until tomorrow morning. . . ."[31]

Socially, too, she was still very much the product of her background and education. She was the Victorian young lady, the epitome of American feminine innocence that Henry James was so fond of depicting. She revealed in her letters to her sisters no sense of sexual identity, no interest in young men (as the Ellwood sisters did). Of course, she had her stepmother along as a chaperone, but more important she seemed not even to be tempted. She was one of those girls, described later by Ida Tarbell, for whom innocence came easily because they were "brought up as if no wrong doing were possible to them."[32]

She believed that the Sabbath should be a day of rest and she felt guilty about the one occasion during the entire trip that they traveled on Sunday. She also disapproved of drinking, not only for herself but also for others, but of course that was a typical attitude for someone from the Protestant, small-town, Midwest. At an American party in Dresden she did join in toasts to the King of Saxony and the President of the United States but remarked to her sister: "I do not approve of wine and since over here disapprove more gravely and surely than ever before, but this is the happy and jolly view of its use." In Munich she went to a Bauhaus. "There were about five hundred men in the room the day we looked at them and it was a disgusting sight that I should never care to see again. There is one side of the German beer drinking that is social and attractive to see, the entire family at a outdoor concert each with his huge mug etc., but here is the excess again and almost all of them show the miserable result."[33]

Yet, despite her puritanical nature and her innocence, she had a genuine interest in people, an impulse for fellowship. She met and talked to all kinds of men and women, and made many casual friends as she traveled. Despite many lessons she never mastered French and German, but she managed without them. It was not always easy, but she pushed herself. "I am more convinced all the time of the value of social life, of its necessity for the development of some of our best traits," she wrote George.[34]

Jane was happy traveling about Europe, studying the museums and the palaces; but occasionally there was a note of impatience in the letters she wrote home. She admitted that "sometimes we get so tired of sight seeing that we wish as Sarah put it, 'never to see another picture as long as I live." Jane had always thought of the trip as something more than sightseeing and acquiring "general culture," "There is every temptation while abroad to play the dilettante, she admitted to George, "and many of the people we meet are disappointing on that very account. You doubt whether any good is accomplished in placing yourself as a mere spectator to the rest of the world." Again a few weeks later she wrote: "It is easy to see how a light headed American traveler grows conceited from a foreign tour, you gain a great deal of showy knowledge, but after all it is not the kind that satisfyieth [sic]."[35]

She obviously did not want to be a spectator, or a lighthearted traveler, but the first winter when they settled down in Dresden for several weeks and she attempted some serious study she discovered that she had a return of "feelings of the old sort" and found it difficult to concentrate.[36] The second winter when the party was in Berlin she attended lectures at the Victoria Lyceum, and announced, "I am really becoming quite enthusiastic over music and fine concerts." "The German and French lessons go along smoothly," she reported in the same letter, "and between reading up for my lectures and writing the notes out in German afterward I seem to be about as busy as I was at school with this difference that there is no necessity about it . . ."[37] But that was a big difference, and there was no real purpose either. Jane could not recapture the sense of fellowship and commitment that she had felt in college. She was fascinated by Oxford and Cambridge and the other universities she visited in Europe. She inquired nostalgically about news from Rockford, and was envious of George, who seemed to have found his direction in his scientific studies at the Johns Hopkins University. "I have been idle for two years just because I had not enough vitality to be anything else," she admitted to Ellen, "and the consequence is that while I may not have lost any positive ground, I have constantly lost confidence in myself, and have gained nothing and improved in nothing."[38]

III

A Creative Solution

ILLIAM James once remarked that the people who became famous and did important things were likely to be a blend of "superior intellect and psychopathic temperament."[1] Jane Addams had psychosomatic illnesses, undefined depression; she was nervous and frustrated and had more than her share of family difficulties; but the important point to emphasize is that she, like William James, found a creative way to solve her problems. The solution did not come easily. It did not emerge suddenly in a kind of conversion experience at a bull fight in Spain, as she would later describe in her autobiography, nor was it simply the product of a rebellion against "the life her mother was trying to get her to lead," as one historian has argued.[2] In her search for identity and for something important to do, her relationship with her family was important, but the catalyst she needed to break away from the family claim and move out on her own was provided by the Christian social reform movements in London, and by the support and affection of Ellen Starr. Yet not even that is an adequate explanation of the complex motivation behind the founding of Hull House.

Perhaps Jane Addams came closest to an explanation herself when she wrote a few years after moving to Chicago that there were both "subjective" needs and "objective" reasons for the settlement movement. There were a great many young men and women, she argued, like herself "whose uselessness hangs about them heavily," and who had led over-cultivated and undernourished lives. They desperately needed something useful to do, but at the same time there was much that needed to be done to help those people trapped in poverty and cut off from culture. She also identified as part of the motivation "a certain renaissance going forward in Christianity" as well as an impulse to share the lives of the poor," and the "desire to make social service, irrespective of propaganda, express the spirit of Christ."[3]

Those compelling reasons, subjective, objective, and religious came together for her in the years between 1885 and 1888. How Jane Addams managed to escape the temptation to become a maiden aunt is important, for her example allowed many other young women to find an outlet for their creative energy, and a use for their carefully acquired culture.

As a young girl and as a college woman Jane Addams had many of the characteristics that Abraham Maslow defines as those of a self-actualizing individual or a growth-motivated person. She was self-directed, autonomous, independent, with a "special liking for privacy, for detachment and for meditativeness. . . . Growth-motivated people are the laws of their own inner nature," Maslow wrote, "their potentialities and capacities, their talents, their latent resources, their creative impulses, their needs to know themselves and to become more and more integrated and unified, more and more aware of what they really want, of what their call or vocation or fate is to be." But it was very difficult for a woman in 1880's to remain self-actualizing, much easier to become a deficiency-motivated person who was dependent, other-directed, and sensitive to other people's approval, affection and good will; to become, in other words, the very model of the genteel female. Practically every social pressure guided a young woman toward that model. Everyone is in a sense a mixture of these two types, as Jane Addams realized in describing the subjective and objective motives behind the settlement movement. She retained many characteristics of the growth-motivated person, though her upbringing and the years of self-doubt left her with a peculiar need to be reassured, left her dependent on honors, awards, and public approval. Yet one must take into account her self-actualizing personality, her determination to do something important, which survived eight years of questioning and self doubt.[4]

She returned from her first European trip in the summer of 1885 and did not set out on her second voyage until December of 1887. In her autobiography she cryptically summarized this interlude in her life: "Family arrangements had so come about that I had spent three or four months of each of the intervening winters in Baltimore, where I seemed

to have reached the nadir of my nervous depression and sense of mal-
adjustment, in spite of my interest in the fascinating lectures given there
by Lanciani of Rome, and a definite course of reading upon the United
Italy movement."

These two years between the European trips were years of depression
and frustration, but they were also years of groping and searching toward
a solution. She had failed at medical school and had given up finally on
her goal to continue her education at Smith College.

A large part of Jane Addams' difficulty in the years between her European trips was that she did not have a goal or an occupation, or anything
useful to do. As she searched during these years for her specialty she had
a vague understanding that it had something to do with learning more
about art and about European culture. She wrote several articles based
upon her European adventures, pored over her notebooks, and studied
the art books she had brought back with her. Even her essays written
during these years reveal her nostalgia for a happier time when she was
in college and her frustration with her life of indecision.

In an essay published in the *Rockford Seminary Magazine* she described a bout with seasickness during a cruise of the Mediterranean and
expressed some of her sense of guilt over her failure to act.

> An odor of camphor steals in the open door issuing from the state-
> room of my dear friend and comrade. She only uses camphor in ex-
> treme emergencies, she must be fainting, brought nigh unto death by
> the nausea. I ought to go to her rescue, but, as I cannot move, that is
> excusable, but what generous interpretation of law or mercy can
> pardon this diabolical apathy, even fiendish satisfaction which follows,
> I don't care if she does faint, let her faint! Every human soul has its
> moment of supreme test, and in a flash was revealed to me the perfidy
> and black selfishness of mine, as little was required of me as possible,
> no action, simply the breathing of a sympathetic thought. The appeal
> was made unobtrusively through the gentle medium of a particle of
> camphor gum upon the least sensual of the senses, and I had un-
> hesitatingly arrayed myself upon the side of evil. My soul is be-
> numbed by the revelation of herself. As the shadowy lion of De-
> Quincey's childish dream, before which he supinely laid himself down,
> forcast defeat in all the coming struggles of his manhood, so memory
> of this test will paralyze my powers forever and make moral attainment
> impossible.[5]

In another essay written about the same time, "Our Debts and How
Shall We Pay Them," she speculated on the possibility that college-
educated women were taking too much of the burden of the progress of

the human race upon themselves. "Whence comes this sweet delusion that has seized us that we are equal to anything and everything," she asked? "What spirit is it, which constantly impels us to *broaden* our field of usefulness and increase our responsibilities."[6] This was a far cry from the task of changing the world she had assigned to educated women in some of her college essays written just a few short years before. But time and circumstances had led her to question herself and the role of educated women. The conflict between her sense of responsibility to her family and her need to work toward a larger goal explained at least a part of her questioning and frustration.

In the fall of 1885 she stayed for a time in a little Illinois village with her sister Mary, whose husband was temporarily preaching in another town. "I have the 'study' fixed into a boudoir," she reported, "and with my framed pictures and books it is a very cozy room, much handsomer than I ever had at school or in a boarding house while we were away." But she was not able to get much studying done, "it is too selfish to shut myself off for hours at a time, and what reading I do downstairs I like to share with Mary. You know my experience in Philadelphia of trying to fullfill too many objects at once. I am afraid trying to study here would leave me with the same uneasy consciousness that I had not done what I came purposely to do, because I tried to do something else and failed in that."[7] She felt she had responsibilities to her studies, but her relatives and friends expected her to act like a woman, to cook and sew and wait on the infirm, the elderly or the young. To add to the frustration she did not have the skills or the competence in managing a household that some of the other women had. "Jennie McKee is here," she reported, "but leaves next week, she is wonderfully efficient, has been making comforters, doing over old quilts. I feel rather helpless when such work is going on . . . and I am afraid I will never be the typical old maid."[8]

Years later, writing a paper in which she used her own experience to shed light on a larger problem, she remarked: "It has always been difficult for the family to regard the daughter otherwise than as a family possession. . . . She is told to be devoted to her family, inspiring and responsive to her social circle, and to give the rest of her time to further self-improvement and enjoyment. She expects to do this, and responds to these claims to the best of her ability—even heroically sometimes. But where is the larger life of which she has dreamed so long? She has been taught that it is her duty to share this life, and her highest privilege to extend it. This divergence between her self-centered existence and her best convictions becomes constantly more apparent. . . . Her life is full of contradictions."[9]

Jane Addams worried and fretted but she moved dutifully to Baltimore with her stepmother in the fall of 1885, and again the next year but she was restless and depressed. "My faculties have been apparently paralyzed since I have been here," she reported the first winter, "I haven't studied 'worth a cent.' " But she did read; almost desperately she pored over Goethe, Ruskin, Tolstoy, Hawthorne, and George Eliot. She attended lectures, concerts, and fashionable parties, yet she found little satisfaction in all these activities. She also visited some of the charitable institutions in the city.

She went to a sewing school for poor children. "I found I couldn't make button holes very well myself but the children were very interesting, most of them patient and sick looking." On another occasion she inspected the "shelter," "a home for about 16 old colored women, who are so interesting I mean to go to see them often." In addition she visited "a little colored orphan asylum." "They take little colored girls and help them until they are 15, training them to be good servants, the children themselves expecting to be that and having an ambition for a good place. I heartily approve of the scheme."

She discovered that she felt better after visiting one of the charities than after a lecture or art exhibit. Later Ellen Starr recalled, in explaining the motives behind the Hull House idea, that Jane discovered in Baltimore that "after a lecture or a social evening she would feel quite exhausted. . . . but after a morning with the colored people in the Johns Hopkins home, she was actually physically better than if she had stayed in bed." But this insight was not so apparent to Jane Addams herself in 1886. "I have wasted time most shamefully this winter," she wrote her sister in March, "whether it is a reaction from fast traveling and exertion or simply the discovery of a natural indolence; I don't know." Yet in retrospect it seems apparent that her drive and determination to do something important, to study to a definite purpose, to aid the poor even in traditional ways was more remarkable and more significant at this point in her life than her failure to find a definite solution.[10]

Jane spent the summer of 1886 in Cedarville. Few letters survive from these months, and there is no indication, not even a hint, in them that she was aware of the Haymarket Riot and its aftermath in Chicago only a few miles away. She was concerned with family problems, and with finding her own sense of purpose. There were many family problems. Mary was pregnant again, and her husband, always unhappy and unsuccessful, was contemplating another move. Alice was ill and her husband Harry was having financial difficulties. Weber was still in the mental institution, and George Haldeman showed signs of a nervous breakdown himself. These things affected Mrs. Addams, who became more difficult than usual. It was no wonder that Jane felt nervous and unsure of herself, but she was the calmest of the lot and the one who usually made peace in the family.[11]

In the fall of 1886 Jane again accompanied her stepmother to Baltimore. She helped to organize an art club of six women. They studied Byzantine art, the Italian Renaissance painters, and Roman archeology, attended lectures and exhibits and wrote out essays on the topics that interested them. She even took drawing lessons: "I like it much better than I imagined and it does not make me nervous as I feared," she reported. But the drawing lessons and art classes did not provide the sense of purpose she was seeking.[12]

She returned to Cedarville in the spring of 1887 and discovered a possible solution to her dilemma. Her friend and former teacher Mary Blaisdell asked her to teach the French and German classes at Rockford College for a few weeks while she was away. Jane taught the classes for one day but then asked that they find someone else. "I enjoyed this day very much and if it were not that I had come to be constantly with Mary I should have been glad to take them." Perhaps this was the real reason: Mary was ill and needed help, and Jane enjoyed the children. "Stanley sleeps with me and is so sweet and charming that it will be harder than ever to leave him," she wrote. But was this enough to make her give up the chance of becoming a college professor even on a temporary basis? Teaching had never appealed to her, perhaps because it was so traditional an occupation for women and did not offer the opportunity she sought. Certainly she could have earned a Master's degree and been as well qualified as most of the teachers at Rockford, or she could have gone to graduate school to work for a Ph.D. and make her mark as a scholar, as a few women of her acquaintance were planning to do. But after her disastrous failure at medical school, and her inability even to enroll at Smith, she gave up on more formal education. Just before she left for Europe the second time she gave away her medical books and abandoned finally the one career that seemed worthy of an educated, ambitious woman.[13]

She invited Ellen Starr and Sarah Anderson to accompany her to Europe, and offered to pay half their expenses. The second European venture had been planned nearly a year in advance. The original idea was for Jane and Ellen to go directly to Spain, then to Rome and southern Italy in order to collect art reproductions for Rockford College and for the school where Ellen taught. Ellen, however, was impatient to get to Europe; she sailed in the fall, while Jane and Sarah Anderson, and Sarah's brother-in-law, Mr. Buckle, sailed in December and planned to meet Ellen in Germany.[14]

They arrived in England just before Christmas. Stopping there only a few days they went on to Paris, where they attended the opera and looked up a former teacher of French and German at the Rockford Seminary, "such a bright, brave, little woman living in the students' quarters attending lectures at the Sorbonne and the College de France and holding her own way with economy and self reliance." Again Jane envied a young woman who was working toward a definite goal, while she had none. But she was more independent and self-reliant on this trip than on the previous one. Sarah decided to do the north German cities, so that in the spring they could go from Paris to Spain and directly to England. Jane traveled with Mr. Buckle to Stuttgart, where she visited some of his friends, and then went on alone to Munich. "I am quite impressed with the difference in my age and dignity between this trip to Europe and the one before," she wrote her sister. "Then I was Mademoiselle and Fraulein and I felt like a young girl. I went to this hotel and ordered a room for the night, and was obliged to spend a night alone at the hotel in Munich. Everywhere it was 'Madame' with the utmost respect and I felt perfectly at my ease and dignified all the time." There was another difference too, when it came to museums and cathedrals. "I am enjoying it all so much better than before," she wrote. "Have lost that morbid thirst for information and doing that simply consumes American travellers and certainly did me the last time." She visited the Cathedral at Ulm, and was impressed by the stone carvings, the stained glass and by the way the church itself summed up the history of man's religious quest from Socrates to Christ to Luther. Her letter home, however, gives little indication that the Cathedral inspired her to dream of someday founding a "Cathedral of Humanity," as she later revealed in her autobiography.[15]

Then two blows struck in quick succession.

While she was traveling news came from home that her sister Mary's little girl had died. Jane felt very close to Mary's children, had cared for them frequently, and she felt a sense of responsibility toward Mary who had been her own "mother" for several years. "My heart is full of love and sympathy for dear Mary," she wrote to her sister Alice. "I have had a touch of genuine homesickness and longing for her as I have not had for years, a little girl's feeling who is away from home at night." Then Jane herself was struck down by an attack of sciatica. It would be easy to argue that her illness was caused by the bad news from home. The impression that emerges from the contemporary letters, however, is not that of a neurasthenic young lady taking to her bed at the least crisis, but rather of a strong-willed person who resisted the attempts of many around her to make her an invalid. Her doctor gravely lectured her on the impropriety of " 'so delicate a person an invalid one might say' travelling in Europe without a member of the family. He hasn't the remotest idea of the toughness of my constitution and was very much surprised by my rapid recovery."[16]

Jane recovered rapidly from her bout with sciatica, in part because she had Ellen and Sarah there to nurse and to comfort her. "Ellen is a great help to Jane," Sarah wrote to Mrs. Addams, "She is so devoted to her and I think one can take so many things, so many kinds of assistance from one that they are fond of, when they could not from an ordinary person. I am good at lifting and moving and waking up, but so is any strong person, but Ellen in invaluable and I am so glad that Jane has her."[17]

Jane's friendship with Ellen had started in college, but after Ellen dropped out it flourished largely through long letters written faithfully under many different circumstances. There were also occasional meetings in Chicago, or Cedarville, or in the little Illinois village where Ellen lived. It was a highly intellectual relationship with long discussions of books read, lectures heard and new theories expounded. It was also a sentimental relationship with both girls celebrating September 11, the day they met for the first time, even when they were apart. They exchanged pictures and got pleasure and comfort from the other's image. "Nothing has pleased me so much for a long time," Jane wrote. "I have stationed it where I can see you almost every minute. . . ." Even writing to each other became a ritualistic experience. "I have thought about you almost every day lately," Ellen confessed, "and tried to find a quiet time to write to you. I think I shall do it on Christmas day. The other day I found two old letters of yours, and read them. I think they gave me even more pleasure than the first time and I wished so much for more of them. I enclose a little reminder of my ever increasing love and friendship." At first they addressed each other as "Dear Friend," or "Beloved Friend," but then they became "Dear one" or "Dearie." In the beginning Ellen was more romantic and sentimental. "My dear I wish to say I admire you most for that is a cold word and you have too little vanity to care for admiration, but I love you more the longer and more I know you." Or again, "I wish you would write me one of your old-fashioned letters and talk about yourself and just let me look at you once more." But especially after the trip to Europe together Jane could be just as sentimental and dependent. "Lets love each other through thick and thin and work out a salvation," she wrote just before joining Ellen in Chicago, in 1889. "Of course, I miss you all the time and never wanted you more than the last few days when everything seemed to be moving at once," she admitted when they were separated shortly after Hull House opened.[18]

The months in Europe together made Jane and Ellen closer and more intimate. "I do believe her to be . . . the dearest, sweetest, preciousest girl the world contains," Ellen wrote to Mrs. Addams. "I have loved her dearly for eleven years, but I never knew how much she deserved to be loved till I saw her every day for weeks together and under all sorts of circumstances, irritated and in pain. I wish I could paint her or write her or put her into music to do the whole world good, as she does me; but I can only keep her in my heart to try to be just a little like her, with very limited success." "Ellen always overestimates me," Jane remarked to her stepmother, but it was Ellen's habit of loving and overestimating her that gave her confidence.[19]

It would be easy to misunderstand the relationship and affection between Ellen and Jane. As Gordon Haight has written: "the Victorians' conception of love between those of the same sex cannot be fairly understood by an age steeped in Freud—where they saw only beautiful friendship, the modern reader suspects perversion." In both England and America in the nineteenth century it was not uncommon for women, especially women of a literary bent, to develop a romantic attachment with another woman. Henry James describes such a friendship between Olive Chancellor and Verena Tarrant in *The Bostonians*, and there must have been countless thousands of girls who found a kindred spirit to correspond with, to discuss literature and religion and to dream with about the future. For after all who else could a young woman interested in literature and worried about religion pour out her heart to except another woman. Certainly one could not talk about these things with a man, even a minister, and few were lucky enough to have a sister or mother that they could confide in. Obviously Jane could not confide her innermost thoughts to her stepmother or to her sisters. She came closest to having an intimate relationship with Alice, but Alice was not especially fascinated by religion or literature and had fits of jealousy and temper. Ellen provided the ideal of a pure friendship for Jane. With Ellen's devotion and emotional support she was able to throw off her doubts and finally to commit herself to action.[20]

Jane stayed behind in Rome to recover from her illness while Ellen and Sarah traveled to Pompeii and Naples. She was well enough to spend Easter with the others in Florence. Here they were also joined by Helen Harrington, another college classmate, and by Mrs. Rowell from Freeport, a friend of the family. Most of the party went on to Venice, but Jane and Mrs. Rowell set out for the Riveria, hoping that the sun and the sea would restore Jane's health completely. They visited the casino at Monte Carlo. She was fascinated but at the same time horrified by the gambling, and she decided very quickly that she had seen enough of "depraved Vanity Fair."[21]

Jane and Mrs. Rowell spent a week or so sightseeing along the Riveria and then took the train from Nîmes to Barcelona, where they were joined by Sarah and Ellen. They continued on to Madrid, where they admired the buildings, the tapestries and the paintings by Velasquez, had tea with an American lady who had married a Spaniard and then went to a bull fight. In her autobiography Jane remarked that it was here she finally realized the folly of her search for culture "for going on indefinitely with study and travel."[22] But in the letters she wrote at the time there is little to hint that the bull fight was this important.

> The great event of our stay in Madrid after all was the thing we are all rather ashamed of," she wrote her sister-in-law, "and that was a bull fight or Festa del Toros, as we rather prefer to call it. The ring or amphitheatre itself was an immense affair with stone seats for eight or ten rows and the upper rows of wooden seats with a covering where we sat. Mrs. Rowell decided not to go finally, and we took as protector and guide, one of the men from the hotel who wore a gorgeous Spanish cloak and regarded it all in a true Spanish light. We got there just as the first grand procession was in the ring and just as they went out the bull came rushing in. He was a beautiful creature as lithe and active as a cat and as fleet and graceful as a deer with nothing of the awkwardness

one associates with a bull. The picadores are the two men mounted on horses who irritate the bull with long wooden lances until he rushes into them and kills the horses. The first bull killed four horses two under each picadore, he made a wild rush followed by a grand melee of horse and rider, the rider invariably being pulled out unhurt and the horse lying dead. That was the worst part of it. The second act of six men tiring and bewildering the bull with their bright red cloaks was graceful and brilliant with no suggestion of danger. The *banderilleros* who struck the victim with the gaily decorated little swords were in apparently greater danger than the *Matador* himself who did not come in until the bull was so tired out that it was a comparatively easy matter to kill by one clever stroke into his spinal cord. There were six bulls killed that afternoon but we did not stay until the bitter end although we were rather ashamed and surprised to find that we were brutal enough to take a great interest in it.[23]

Jane obviously was fascinated by the bull fight and though she did feel a sense of guilt at enjoying the spectacle, her description of it was similar to her description of the depravity of the casino at Monte Carlo, except she seems to have enjoyed the brutality more than the gambling. Her mixed feelings were more apparent in a long letter to her stepmother two days later:

It was one of the first of the season and the most brilliant affair . . . that I have ever seen. The excitement and interest were so great as to throw the cruelty and brutality quite into the background, and if it had not been for the suffering of the horses I am afraid the rest of it would scarcely have seemed reprehensible to me, so much does skill and parade do toward concealing a wrong thing.[24]

There is no contemporary evidence that the experience of the bull fight caused her to change her plans or alter her thinking. It seems more likely that she embellished the event for dramatic purposes when she was writing the autobiographical account. At least the letters she wrote home at the time indicate no dramatic shift in her perspective. They describe her reactions to Granada, Seville, and Tangier and reveal the leisurely pace of the tour. She even lingered in northern France and reported that she was "too much in love with the Gothic" to hurry off to England. But sometime late in May she decided to go to the International Congress of Protestant Missions in London which was scheduled for mid-June. Why she decided to go to this missionary convention is not clear; probably it was the same impulse that led her to seek out the sewing school for poor children in Baltimore, or to visit the insane asylum in Jacksonville, Illinois, while she was in college, or an English missionary hospital in Tangier. She had a rather undefined sympathy for the poor and unfortunate, and in regard to missionaries, something of a guilty feeling that she had not been more concerned with the movement when she was in college. But her decision to attend the conference had no sense of urgency about it.

When she arrived in England she went directly to Canterbury to visit and study the Cathedral. Here she met an English woman who invited her and her companions for tea. Their hostess turned out to be the wife of the Bishop of Dover. Among the guests was Canon W. H. Freemantle, and it may have been from him that Jane Addams first learned about Toynbee Hall, the pioneer English settlement. Canon Freemantle was a close friend, adviser, and former pastor of Samuel A. Barnett, the founder and warden of Toynbee Hall. In any case Freemantle invited the young women to his home for dinner and gave Jane Addams a letter of introduction to Canon Barnett.[25]

In London, Jane and Sarah attended a number of the meetings of the World Centennial Congress of Foreign Missions. Jane was particularly excited by an evening session devoted to the opium trade in China and the liquor traffic in the Congo. "I have become quite learned in foreign missions and ashamed of my former ignorance," she reported to her sister. But the most interesting and important thing they did in London was to visit Toynbee Hall. "It is a community for University men who live there, have their recreation and clubs and society all among the poor people, yet in the same style they would live in their own circle. It is so free from 'professional doing good,' so unaffectedly sincere and so productive of good results in its classes and libraries so that it seems perfectly ideal." Here was a way of serving, of helping the poor without the clowing paternalism, the "professional doing good" of the various charities she had tried or observed in the last few years. The Toynbee Hall experiment also provided a way to use her knowledge of art and culture, so arduously acquired over the years, and allowed the residents to live the way they would ordinarily live. In fact the settlement had much of the charm and fellowship of a college dormitory.[26]

Toynbee Hall, however, was only one of several influences on Jane Addams. London in 1888 was filled with reform spirit and a new awareness of the poor and their plight. She inspected the People's Palace, a large philanthropic institute which had opened just a year before, and contained meeting rooms, workshops and clubrooms for the working class. She also read two of Walter Besant's novels, *The Children of Gibeon* and *All Sorts and Conditions of Men*.[27] The first is the story of Valentine and Violet, two girls brought up in a wealthy English family who discover that one of them had been adopted as a young girl from the family of a poor woman from East London. The novel is filled with descriptions of life in the East End, of the working class, the paupers and various schemes to aid them, but the heart of the novel concerns Valentine who "feels an irresistible force to be among her people" and goes to live with a family in the East End. There she learned "the one lesson most worth learning, namely that the People are, in all essentials, exactly the same as the Other People. There are not, in fact, in this any more than in any other country, two races, but one; and the best way of acquiring an exhaustive and scientific knowledge of that one race is to sit before a looking-glass for a long time and look at it."[28] *All Sorts and Conditions of Men*, subtitled "an impossible story," is the tale of Angela Messenger, the young heiress who inherits a brewery and a large number of tenements in the Whitechapel section of the East End of London. Dissatisfied with her life of leisure she goes to live in a boarding house near the brewery and discovers the misery and drabness of life in the slums. Gradually she forms a plan; she would build a palace of delight in Whitechapel: "She would awaken in dull and lethargic brains a new sense, the new sense of pleasure; she would give them a craving for things of which as yet they knew nothing. She would place within their reach, at no cost whatever, absolutely free for all, the same enjoyments as are purchased by the rich." It was on the plan outlined in this novel that the People's Palace was modeled.[29]

"The mission side of London is the most interesting side it has," Jane decided. "I am glad to have had the two weeks here . . . which were not sightseeing," she wrote to her sister.[30] It was during these two weeks in June of "not sightseeing" in London, that Jane Addams probably made the decision to live in a working class neighborhood in Chicago. Her decision had deep roots. It was influenced by her relationship with Ellen Starr, by her earlier reading in Ruskin and Tolstoy, by her long search for something useful to do, by her vague interest in a variety of missions and charities, by her haunting sense of frustration and uselessness as she acquired more and more knowledge about art and history and culture. This frustration may well have reached a climax at the bull fight in Spain, as she describes in her autobiography, but to give all credit to this "conversion experience" is to make Jane Addams' decision to found

Hull House too personal and unique. It was during her stay in London, her visit to Toynbee Hall, the People's Palace, and reading the Besant novels that she became finally conscious of the modern movement to bridge the gulf between classes, not through charity or alms but by going to live in a poor section of a great city.

Other Americans were also influenced about the same time by the various English movements which sought to solve the problem of the industrial city. They read pamphlets like the Reverend Andrew Mearns' *The Bitter Cry of Outcast London*, while books like John Ruskin's *Unto This Last* became almost the Bible of an idealistic generation. Stanton Coit, a young graduate of Amherst with a Ph.D. from the University of Berlin, had visited Toynbee Hall two years before Jane Addams arrived and had returned to New York to found the Neighborhood Guild. Vida Scudder, Jean Fine, Helen Rand, and several other young graduates of Smith College had also been influenced by Toynbee Hall, by their reading of Ruskin and Walter Besant's novels, and in 1887 had organized the College Settlement Association, which would open a settlement in New York just a week before Ellen Starr and Jane Addams moved to Hull House.[31]

To be influenced by the stirring movements of social and religious change in England in the 1880's was not unusual. But for Jane Addams it was important; it provided a solution to her quest for something useful and meaningful to do. It also meant coming to terms with family problems and with years of questioning and doubt. She had always attended church regularly, but, like her father, she had never joined a church, even resisting the pressure put upon her at Rockford to take that step. But on the second trip to Europe, stimulated by conversations with Ellen Starr, inspired by the artifacts and monuments to the early church that she visited, but most of all influenced by the English social gospel movement, "the mission side of London" she decided to join a church. Her decision to establish a settlement in a poor section of Chicago was essentially a religious commitment, but the kind of Christianity she witnessed at Toynbee Hall and the People's Palace was a religion of social action, a version of religion that solved her doctrinal difficulties and doubts, which demanded only a desire to serve. Soon after she returned home, on October 14, 1888, she was baptized at the Presbyterian Church in Cedarville, and on September 2, 1889, less than three weeks before she moved to Hull House, she was admitted as a member in full standing.[32]

In her autobiography Jane Addams states that she joined a church sometime during the years between her European trips while she was at the lowest point of her morale and purpose, but she remembered inaccurately. Her decision to join the church was not the product of depression, nor was it the result of a conversion experience. It did not even finally settle her religious doubts, but by joining a church she was reaffirming the importance of the institution, and underlining her commitment to live in a working class neighborhood as essentially a religious act—a part of a larger movement toward social reform and a "Renaissance of Christianity."

IV

Founding a Social Movement

ANE Addams and Ellen Starr decided to move to a poor section of Chicago during the spring or summer of 1888. They talked vaguely of their "scheme," but some of Jane's dedication and commitment faded as she faced another series of family crises on her return from Europe. Her stepmother and other members of the family assumed that she would resume the familiar role of maiden aunt, ministering to the needs of relatives in trouble.[1] She had agreed to meet Ellen in Chicago early in January 1889 to get seriously to work on their plan. She was staying with Mary over Christmas; a child was ill, and Jane was overcome with sympathy. "I owe so much to Mary in so many tender ways that I feel now as if I ought to stay," she wrote wistfully to Ellen. But Ellen pushed and prodded, and this time Jane broke away forever from the family claim. If it had not been for the love and support of Ellen Starr at this crucial moment she probably never would have made the break with her past.[2]

The two young women took rooms in a boarding house at 4 Washington Place in late January 1889, and began to make plans in earnest for what they called "the scheme." Ellen, who had taught at the fashionable Kirkland School in the city, knew many prominent people who might help, and both girls had Rockford friends and acquaintances living in the city and the suburbs. But the inspiration for their plan had come from Toynbee Hall, the People's Palace and the "mission side of London," so it was natural that the two young women should look for support first from the missions and churches in the city. Jane began attending the prestigious Fourth Presbyterian Church and went to Bible classes and religious lectures wherever they were offered in the city. She even found time to write a long essay on the Bible lectures which she faithfully attended. Soon she had opportunities to teach Sunday School, give lectures at various church groups, and most important, chances to meet those people who were leaders in philanthropy and mission work in the city.

The two young women explored the Clybourne Avenue Mission and the Armour Mission, nonsectarian but religious institutions which provided kindergartens, libraries, lectures, and other services for the poor. At both places they got a warm reception and offers of assistance, though some of the older men thought they were "vaporizing." At the Armour Mission, founded by meat packing magnate, Philip Armour, Jane spoke before a meeting of the board, and Allen B. Pond, a young architect, was especially enthusiastic about the plans she described. He offered to introduce the young women to others who might be interested and to give them guided tours of some of the poor sections of the city.[3] They also talked to William M. Salter, head of the Chicago Ethical Cultural Society, and met Dr. Frank W. Gunsaulus, pastor of the Plymouth Congregational Church and one of the most popular ministers in the city. He became their "first convert" after they convinced him that they did not want to found another nursery school, or a training school where young ladies could be taught to "deal with the poor." He told them to avoid two types of people, the kind that went out "harpooning for souls trying to collect as many as possible," and the "men who buttoned up their coats formed committees and wrote out laws."[4] They also met the Reverend David Swing, pastor of the Central Church on State Street, where many Chicago millionaires, including George Pullman, were members of the congregation. They visited evangelist Dwight L. Moody's church and met the minister, Mr. Goss, who immediately became one of their most loyal supporters. They enrolled for lessons in industrial arts and volunteered to teach a class at the training school which, only a few weeks after Hull House opened, would become the Moody Bible Institute.[5]

Within a few weeks they had met some of the most powerful religious figures in the city and got their promise of support. It was an impressive beginning and was indicative of their ability to attract attention and get a hearing. It was an ability that went a long way toward making their plan a success. Their conscious attempt to meet and impress the religious leaders in the city was also an indication of the religious motivation behind their plan. In discussing a young woman who they hoped would "come into residence," Jane remarked: "It would have much weight with church people and be a good object lesson for us—she embodies the best of the missionary spirit." It was ironical, but Jane, who had so ardently resisted any attempt at making her into a missionary while she was in college, now thought of herself as almost a missionary to the poor in Chicago.[6]

One of their new friends gave them a tour of the Bohemian district. There they met a former missionary to Prague who had discovered the plight of the Bohemians in Chicago while home on furlough and had decided to become a missionary to the immigrants in America. Jane was impressed with his work, flattered that he considered their plan "immensely Christian," and not a little startled to find there just as " 'foreign' an atmosphere as I ever felt in Europe."[7] In her search for the underside of Chicago Jane even investigated an anarchist Sunday school. She was greeted with great suspicion and told that " 'Americans' never came up there except the reporters of the capitalist newspapers and they always exaggerated." She found about 200 children in a hall back of a saloon "with some young men trying to teach free thought without any religion or politics. The entire affair was very innocent," she decided.[8]

Visits to the anarchists, the Bohemians, and the various slums of the city were important in trying to determine a site for their work. Just as important, however, was the need to win support for their venture from the wealthy and socially prominent in the city. Before many weeks, however, they found themselves overbooked with teas, luncheons, receptions, and speaking engagements. They presented their plans before the Philanthropy Committee of the Chicago Woman's Club, where they were received with enthusiasm. One of the powerful members, Mrs. J. D. Harvey, wasted little time in asking Jane if she would like to become a member. Knowing that the club only took one new member a year she replied that it seemed rather impossible. "That doesn't make any difference," Mrs. Harvey responded, "if *I* want you, I am a pretty important member of that club."[9]

The Women's Christian Temperance Union was not very enthusiastic about their plan, but that was an exception. All over Chicago, as they talked and outlined their scheme, the response, especially from the younger women and men, was overwhelmingly favorable. Allen Pond told Jane that she "voiced something hundreds of young people in the city were trying to express, and that he could send me three young ladies at once who possessed both money and knowledge of Herbert Spencer's *Sociology*, but who are dying from inaction and restlessness."[10] They got the support of the local branch of the Association of Collegiate Alumnae, and talked to several graduates of Smith, Vassar, and Wellesley who seemed eager to join them. Indeed they made a special point of trying to appeal to the college women who in growing numbers had no creative outlet for their energies and no way to use their training. When one of the ministers at a reception denounced "the modern fashionable young ladies" as the most hard-hearted creatures in existence and predicted that they would never be interested in the plan, Jane defended the modern young woman and announced that "it was time someone did something for them if their very pastor talked about them like that."[11]

Both Addams and Starr knew from first-hand experience the sense of uselessness and frustration that many young women felt. "Jane's idea which she puts very much to the front and on no account will give up is that it is more for the benefit of the people who do it than for the other class," Ellen wrote to her sister. "She has worked that out of her own experience and ill health. She discovered that when recovering from her spinal trouble that she could take care of children, actually lift them and not feel worse but better for being with them. While an effort to see people and be up to things used her up completely. . . . Nervous people do not crave rest but activity of a certain kind."[12] But this insight was not based entirely on her own personal experience. Most of the college graduates she knew had similar difficulties. Helen Harrington, a college friend and traveling companion on the second European voyage, had floundered aimlessly for several years and had several bouts with illness before taking a job as a teacher at Rockford College. "This year's work has made me more sure of myself, sure that in common with all others I have a certain amount of energy that I can employ in doing what I have a certain conviction is a thing that needs to be done. . . ."[13]

Action did wonders for Jane Addams as well. Her letters to her family in 1889, while she and Ellen were in Chicago getting organized, enlisting support, and preparing the way for their scheme, are filled with a confidence and exuberance that is absent from her European letters and is only present in some of her letters written home while she was in college. She was busy every moment, attending teas and giving receptions, delivering speeches on Toynbee Hall, the missions of East London, and of course on the plan itself.

She read all the available literature on social movements in Europe and America, and discovered that their idea was not unique. She learned of the Neighborhood Guild in New York, the Denison Club in London, and especially of a group of Smith graduates who had organized the College Settlement Association and were planning to move into a house on the Lower East Side of New York. She immediately began to correspond with them about their plan but quickly decided "We are modest enough to think that ours is better." Any spare moments were spent looking for a place to settle. What they had in mind was a flat or a house to rent, large enough to have "classes or lectures or whatever we may wish," and to provide space for the other people they confidently expected to join them, but small enough to be homelike. Jane planned to spend several hundred dollars on furniture in addition to what she already had, and she decided that she could afford $100 a month toward the house expenses. They hoped that with diligence and economy they could manage on that.[14]

What exactly they would do after they had moved to the house in the "slums" they were not quite sure, but Toynbee Hall was their model, and they often referred to their venture as "a Toynbee Hall experiment." "After we have been there long enough and people see that we don't catch diseases and that vicious people do not destroy us or our property," Ellen explained, "We have well-founded reason to believe that there are at least a half dozen girls in the city who will be glad to come and stay a while and learn to know the people and understand them and their ways of life; to give out of their culture and leisure and over-indulgence and to receive the culture that comes of self-denial and poverty and failure which these people have always known. There is to be no organization and no institution about it. The world is overstocked with institutions and organizations. . . ."[15]

From the very beginning there was a dual purpose in the experiment. They were interested in providing an outlet for the talent and energy of college-educated young people, but they also sincerely wanted to help those trapped by poverty. They felt a sense of adventure and mission, a feeling of getting back to the basic elements of life. But at the same time they both betrayed a sense of paternalism, a feeling of *noblesse oblige* as they viewed the crowded slums.

Jane went from the Woman's Club to the anarchist Sunday school, from elegant receptions in the palatial townhouses of Chicago's Gold Coast to safaris through the worse slums, from lecturing to some of the wealthiest women in the city to teaching poor and dirty children how to model in clay and cut out Greek vases from colored paper. Her sympathy for the poor in those first months, albeit a traditional and somewhat paternalistic sympathy, can be illustrated by her experience with one of the old philanthropic agencies in the city. She learned about the Maurice Porter Memorial Hospital in her travels and made arrangements for a nine-year-old blind Italian boy to enter. "I took him this morning," she reported. "His father went with me and was delighted with the house and the assurance that the child would always have enough to eat. The hospital was built by Mrs. Porter as a memorial to her little son. It is free but they have had vacancies all spring because no one has applied. It is a curious instance of the need of communication between the benevolent people at one end of the city and the poverty at the other."[16]

They neglected very few possibilities in their attempt to learn about the city. They began with the churches and missions, but quickly branched out to talk with people from the Charity Organization Society, with a philanthropist interested in newsboys, and with many others including an attendance agent for the Board of Education, who took Jane on a tour of the Italian quarter of South Chicago. "It was exactly as if we were in a quarter of Naples or Rome, the parents and children spoke nothing but Italian and dressed like Italian peasants. They were more crowded than I imagined people ever lived in America, four families for instance of seven or eight each living in one room for which they paid eleven dollars a month, and constantly afraid of being ejected. Yet they were affectionate and gentle, the little babies rolled up in still bands and the women sitting about like wild eyed Madonnas. They never begged nor even complained, and in all respects were immensely more attractive to me than the Irish neighborhood I went into last week. . . ." It was a curious and paradoxical reaction.[17]

Jane favored settling in an Italian neighborhood, but Ellen leaned toward an area where there were German and French immigrants, because there were a great many more college girls who knew French and German than who knew Italian. "Jane seems to think that Chicago is swimming in girls who speak Italian fluently, which I happen to know is not the case . . . ," Ellen reported. There were other considerations as well.

The Woman's Club wanted the project to be under their auspices; the Armour Mission and several church groups offered to sponsor the enterprise. And even those who wanted no control were eager to suggest the perfect location in the city. But Addams and Starr, encouraged by many offers of financial support, determined to be independent of any official organization, and somewhat by accident they discovered their house on the corner of Halsted and Polk streets.[18]

The house, dilapidated and run-down, was the former Charles J. Hull mansion, built in 1856 by the Chicago real estate dealer in what was then the suburbs of the city. It was one of the few buildings in the area to survive the fire of 1871, but by the mid-seventies the growing city had engulfed it. In 1889 when Jane and Ellen discovered it there was a saloon, an office, and a storage room for a furniture company on the first floor, rooms for let on the second floor, with an undertaking establishment and another saloon next door. The house, along with many others in the neighborhood was owned by Helen Culver, Charles Hull's cousin and secretary. After careful and diplomatic negotiations with Miss Culver, who in the beginning did not entirely trust the two young women, they arranged to sublet the second floor of the old house with use of a large reception room on the first floor. The two young women managed the necessary business negotiations with skill and dispatch. Jane reported to her mother, "Dr. McPherson remarked the other day that we were not so unworldly as we looked."[19]

The two young women moved into the house on September 18, 1889, with Mary Keyser, a young woman whom they had engaged as housekeeper. "Probably no young matron ever placed her own things in her own house with more pleasure than that with which we first furnished Hull House," Jane later recalled. In a sense they were furnishing their first home. No living arrangement since they had left the college dormitory had seemed ideal. So they thought of the settlement house as a home rather than an institution, and they lavished great love in making it as attractive as possible. Despite the fears of friends and relatives that all their possessions would be stolen Jane placed her inherited silver in the elegant side board just as any bride would do.[20]

Even before they moved into the house, their idea had become well known in Chicago. They had organized carefully and advertised well. Offers of support came even from those whom they had never met. "If we don't succeed after all this help we will deserve to fail," Jane remarked.[21] A number of articles appeared in newspapers and magazines during the spring and summer of 1889. The story of two young, well-educated women going to live in the slums was, of course, a good human interest story. They became in Jane Addams' words, "a fashionable fad" before they even began. She occasionally seemed to regret the published accounts, which were not always accurate and gave a misleading impression, but in fact she worked very hard to advertise the venture. Indeed the major reason that Hull House became the most famous of many settlements was that Jane Addams worked constantly to promote it.[22]

Vague news items about "A Project to Bring the Rich and Poor Closer Together" began appearing in March. Jane Addams was characterized as "a young lady of independent means and generous culture," and the plan as "a mutual exchange of the advantages of wealth and poverty."[23] Jane and Ellen cooperated with the reporters who wanted to do stories and worked on accounts of their own, but before they were able to publish anything a number of full-length articles appeared. In May *The Woman's Journal*, Lucy Stone's feminist magazine, carried an article entitled "A Chicago Toynbee Hall." The article was flattering and foreshadowed the praise that would be heaped on Jane Addams as the years went by. "The moving spirit in this novel philanthropy is Miss Addams. . . ," the article announced, "She is a young lady, still young enough to make her choice of such life-work, with all the sacrifices which it involves, a seven-days wonder to all who know her. It is evident to every one that she goes into the work from no desire for notoriety, for she is the physical expression of modest simplicity itself; nor as an employment for remuneration, for she gives not only her time but generously of her means, of which she possesses sufficient to place her beyond the need of remunerative occupation. . . . Miss Addams' rarest attraction—although possessing a generous share of physical beauty—is her wonderful spirituality. One cannot spend much time in her presence without wondering by what processes she has attained to such remarkable growth of soul. . . ." The article was read before a women's convention in Freeport and then republished in its entirety in the Freeport newspaper. Jane was chagrined; she had talked to Leilia Bedell, the author of the article, but did not expect anything quite like this. "I positively feel my callers peering into my face to detect spirituality" she remarked to Ellen.[24]

Even before Hull House had opened some of the themes by which she became identified by press and public were already established. Perhaps the most important was the idea of spirituality, the conception that she was somehow different, that she had a quality of soul that made her close to God with special saintly powers. Even Ellen noted this quality in Jane when she commented a few days before they moved to Hull House. "It is as if she simply diffused something which came from outside herself of which she is the luminous median and I suppose that is precisely what she does do. . . ."[25] It is difficult to say what created this impression. It is true that she was calm, even gentle in appearance and action but she was hardly spiritual, certainly not nearly as concerned with the spirit as Ellen. It was, in fact, Jane's business acumen, her well-organized mind, her ability to get along with all kinds of people, her penchant for compromise, her worldliness, that would eventually make Hull House a success. But the news reporters and others mentioned the quality of spirituality, perhaps because they assumed that any young women who went to live in the slums must be spiritual and filled with piety, and the God-given feminine impulse to help the less fortunate. Ironically Jane Addams who wanted to break away from the traditional role of woman as wife, mother, or teacher, as pious, submissive, frail lady, and finally found a way to do so by going to live in the slums of Chicago, was viewed by the press and public and even by her friends in traditional terms. To explain her actions by the impetus of a special spiritual quality was to deny the break she was attempting to make with the past and to interpret her innovation in the context of the old ideas of the genteel female.[26]

Another theme that ran through the first articles on Hull House was the self-sacrifice of the founders. "To them it means something to forego the fascination of fashionable society life, for which they are remarkably well adapted." In truth it was this very life of society and culture, of nothing to do, that had caused years of frustration and unhappiness. Far from sacrificing anything, they were reaping great rewards in physical and mental well being through the excitement of activity and purpose. An article by the Reverend·David Swing, one of their minister friends, despite the air of incredulity was nearer the truth: "Instead of containing any monastic idea, that of seclusion from the world, these two sisters of good works have in mind the building of some additional bridges across the gulfs in the social world. They do not intend to be nuns. They do not with sad face take up any vow of self-abnegation. It seems to be their feeling that the woman of possible leisure and fashion should not accept of the leisure or the fashion as being an end worth the constant seeking." They did not intend to be nuns, but the comparison with "nuns" and "sisters" was constantly used by reporters as they tried to define the new experiment.[27]

Most of the early articles gave more attention to Addams, but *The Woman's Journal* characterized Starr as "full of vivacity, a rare conversationalist. . . . She is a great favorite in society, with young and old men and women. Petite, graceful, brilliant, even to sparkling, she adds to the combination what could by no means be left out." But very soon most of those who wrote about Hull House left her out of their accounts or gave her only a brief mention. It was Addams who made more speeches, wrote more articles, and somehow seemed the more commanding personality, and she got most of the credit. In addition Ellen consciously pushed Jane into the foreground. "Of course I know who has done the thinking although she resents my putting myself out of it in a way. Still I am unwilling to let people suppose that I would have worked it out."[28] Yet Ellen Starr was indispensable for the venture. She did balance Jane's personality, but not quite in the way the reporter for *The Woman's Journal* suggested. She was more artistic and religious, more emotional, and more committed to causes than Jane, who was inclined to be calm and business-like. More important, Ellen was completely devoted to her friend.[29]

The devotion and love between Addams and Starr was noticed by the reporters who wrote stories on the experiment, but they had some difficulty explaining why the two young women were going to live in the slums. Leila Bedell, in her article in *The Woman's Journal* made an attempt by suggesting that they were "answering affirmatively with all their powers, physical and spiritual, the question which is ringing in many of our ears, 'Am I my brother's keeper?' " she also mentioned rather vaguely that they hoped to act as "a chemical force to bring about some sort of union between two elements having some affinity for each other." She compared the needs of the poor to "the needs of the colored people, they both lack aspiration," and it was this she thought the two young women, mostly by example, planned to give them. David Swing thought their motive was to demonstrate that "there is a wide and beautiful bridge between the two sides of society." Mary Porter, in an article in *Advance*, a liberal Congregational journal, in April 1889 suggested that "the ladies fully believe with Tolstoy that 'Enlightment is not propagated by pictures,' not 'chiefly' by the spoken word, or the medium of print, but by the infectious example of the whole life of men." Others noticed that they had modeled their experiment on Toynbee Hall, and an article in the *New York World* for June 16, 1889, reported that "Jane Addams, a wealthy young Chicago woman, heard of the plan of the College Settlement and was so pleased with it that she went over to Europe a few months ago to examine the original model herself. She studied it carefully by the light of the modifications which the College Settlement thought necessary to make in the American institution, and she has now got back to this country with all the details of the scheme perfect." Another article announced that "Miss Addams doesn't purpose to play the part of Lady Bountiful but means to do what she can toward the elevation of society of the people among whom she is shortly to take up her residence. Her friends are awaiting the outcome of her experiment with interest but confidently predict she will weary of her new friends." Despite the denials, the image of "Lady Bountiful," of self-sacrificing missionary to the poor, came through in the early accounts, and Jane Addams, conscious from the first of the importance of publicity and concerned and impressed by her public image, carefully clipped each article, even the most ludicrous and inaccurate, and began a scrapbook made up of what other people thought of her and of Hull House.[30]

One part of the settlement idea which confused but fascinated the reporters was the concept that the settlement would provide an education and occupation for the young, well-educated men and women who chose to live there, and that they expected to gain more than they gave. "One of its chief aims," the writer for *The Woman's Journal* noted, "will be to make it also a retreat for other young women, who need rest and change or who desire a safe refuge from the inordinate demands of society, and in whom it is believed that a glimpse of the reverse side of life, of the poverty and struggles of half the people, will beget a broader philanthropy and a tenderer sympathy, and leave less time and inclination for introspection, for selfish ambition, or for real or fancied invalidism."[31]

This was not a particularly original idea, for it was part of the settlement idea in England as spelled out by Canon Barnett and before him by John Ruskin. Leo Tolstoy also postulated that young men had much to gain in physical and mental well-being by forsaking the life of polite society, and thus to see life whole and appreciate its meaning. What Jane Addams did was to take this "back to the people" idea that was being suggested by a number of others, and apply it specifically to the college-educated woman in America. Again and again in her career she would take an idea or a theme that was current, and give it meaning and direction by relating it to the everyday experience of a large group of people. It was this ability to apply and popularize and sharpen an idea that was her particular genius.

A Chicago club woman later recalled the first time she met Jane Addams in the spring of 1889. "I was hurrying from one committee to another when someone came to walk beside me and began to talk. I paid very little attention until I caught the words: 'a place for invalid girls to go and help the poor.' I turned in my astonishment to face a frail, sensitive girl. She looked anything but the reforming type. 'Suppose we sit down and talk about it,' I said. And we did."[32] A way for invalid girls to help the poor—an exaggerated way to put it, but Jane Addams did make a great deal of what she would later call the "subjective" side of the settlement impulse in her speeches in and around Chicago during 1889 and 1890. It was newsworthy and different to talk about what residence in a settlement house could do for nervous young girls, and it put the idea apart from the familiar philanthropies and charities of the day, though the listeners and reporters did not always comprehend the difference. "We need the thrust in the side, the lateral pressure which comes from living next door to poverty," Jane Addams announced again and again. "Nothing so deadens the sympathies and shrivels the powers of enjoyment as the persistent keeping away from great opportunities for helpfulness, and the ignoring of the starvation struggle, which makes up the life of at least half of the race." She described the glimpses of another way of life that one got in a variety of ways, such as arriving early in the morning a stranger in a great city and watching the stream of working people going by outside. "Your heart sinks with a sudden sense of futility . . . you pray . . . that the great mother breasts of our common humanity, with its labor and suffering and homely comforts, may never be with-held from you." The images are perhaps not very precise, but the startling concept that the most privileged and highly educated young people were themselves deprived and cut off from life's problems and opportunities came through.

"It is inevitable," she went on, "that those who feel most keenly this deprivation and partial living, are our young people; our so-called favored, educated young people who have to bear the brunt of being cultivated into unnourished, over-sensitive lives . . . young girls feel it most in the first years after they leave school. In our attempt, then, to give a girl freedom from care we succeed, for the most part, in making her pitifully miserable. . . . There is nothing after disease, indigence and guilt so fatal to life itself as the want of a proper outlet for active faculties. . . . Our young people hear in every sermon, learn in their lessons, read in their very fiction, of the great social mal-adjustment, but no way is provided for them to help. They are left in a maze of indecision. They come back from college and Europe, and Wagner operas and philosophical lectures, and wherever else culture is to be found . . . many of them dissipate their energies into ill health, or are buried beneath mere mental accumulations with lower vitality and discontent." The answer, she maintained, was to give these educated and pampered young people something to do that was related to the fundamental facts of life. This was the same impulse that she identified in 1892 as the "Subjective Necessity for Social Settlements," and she continued to use it in her speaking and writing for the next decade. Once she hit upon a seminal idea she exploited it to its fullest.

She always pointed out, in her early speeches and articles, that there were dual reasons for the Hull House experiment. Not only did one large group of people desperately need something to do, but there were, in American cities, many tasks to be done. There were thousands of immigrants—"Germans and Bohemians and Italians and Poles and Russians and Greeks and Arabs in Chicago, vainly trying to adjust their peasant habits to the life of a large city. . . ." But she always emphasized that initially those who came to live in the slums would benefit more than those they sought to help. "I hope it will never be forgotten in Chicago," she remarked, "at least where Hull House feels somewhat responsible for the Toynbee Hall idea, that Toynbee Hall was first projected as an aid and outlet to educated young men. The benefit to East Londoners was then regarded as almost secondary, and the benefit has always been held as strictly mutual."[33]

Of course, the message did not always get across to the various audiences who heard Jane Addams explain her project. And the press, instead of reporting her concept of the impulse behind the venture, often emphasized the "self-sacrificing work among the lowly," the "lifting up those whom fate has not smiled upon." The press and the public often misunderstood or distorted the reasons why two well-educated young women planned to go to live in the slums in 1889, but in general they approved the idea. It did not seem radical or dangerous, indeed it seemed benevolent and Christian.[34]

✗   Henrik Ibsen's A *Doll's House* opened in Boston the same year that
Hull House was founded. Most American critics did not approve of the
ending of the play in which the heroine, Nora Helmer, decides to leave
her husband and children in order to find her own role in the world and
escape a home where she was treated as a doll, a bird, an object. The
"ending can never be liked by American audiences who will be loath to
believe that a woman owes a higher duty to the development of her own
nature than to the young children she has brought into the world," one
reviewer decided.[35] Ibsen's play challenged the traditional conception of
woman as submissive, innocent, and devoted only to her family. In the
beginning Hull House and the settlement movement did not seem to
threaten the feminine ideal. Of course, the reaction would quite probably have been different if Jane Addams had abandoned husband and
children to take care of the poor. For most Americans in 1889 the role
of mother and homemaker was still the ideal for women, but in the transitional period when some of the old stereotypes were breaking down,
when a few women were going to college and beginning to assert themselves. Jane Addams' action in breaking away from the claim of family
and going to live in the slums to help the helpless, seemed a benign and
praiseworthy alternative to becoming wife and mother.

V

Early Years at
Hull House

FTERWARD, Jane Addams always insisted that when she and Ellen Starr moved to the dilapidated mansion at 335 Halsted Street, September 18, 1889, they had no planned activities in mind, and were "without preconceived social theories or economic views."[1] But, of course, they did have the English model to follow, and they were convinced that they could help by sharing their knowledge of art and literature with the neighbors and by opening their house for receptions, and for clubs and classes and lectures. They began by inviting some of their neighbors, mostly Italians, to come in during the evening to hear George Eliot's *Romola* read aloud in Italian, and to see slides of Florentine art. Perhaps some of the Italian women appreciated the lecture and enjoyed the novel, but more probably they were baffled by these two cultured young ladies and their big house. One visitor shook his head in amazement and said it was the "strangest thing he had met in his experience."[2]

Some of the neighbors came to the house out of curiosity, and some because there was such a desperate need in the overcrowded West Side of Chicago for a place to sit and talk and meet one's friends. Neighborhood women came in great numbers and they brought their children. Immediately it became obvious that there was need for a kindergarten and a nursery. Addams and Starr knew vaguely about the new educational theory of Friedrich Froebel which argued that children should be treated as human beings and helped to learn through "creative play," but it was the need of the moment, not their theory, that caused them to organize the kindergarten. Jenny Dow, a vivacious and attractive girl, the daughter of a prominent Chicago family, volunteered to run the kindergarten, and paid all the expenses. Every morning she traveled from her fashionable home on the near North Side to take up her job. Within three weeks after the opening of the settlement there were 24 "little people" enrolled, half of them Italian, with 70 more on the waiting list.[3]

Other activities quickly followed, some planned, some spontaneous. The two young women began a boys' club with Jane taking one section and Ellen the other. There were twenty boys in Jane's group all about sixteen years of age; they worked as errand boys, telegraph boys, or in machine shops. "They all are so anxious to come and very respectful," Jane decided, though the boys' habit of wearing their hats indoors and spitting tobacco on the floor exasperated the young Victorian ladies.[4] They managed better with the women and children in the neighborhood who came to a club for working girls, to classes in cooking and sewing, and to the special Italian and German evenings. In fact they discovered that the women came more eagerly if the men were not invited. "It seems to scare them to have 'him' invited," Ellen decided. "They aren't used to it apparently and get embarrassed over it." She did not mention the embarrassment of the young settlement residents, but they also seemed to prefer that the men stay at home.

One idea which they had conceived before the settlement was organized was to bring art to the people. Influenced by John Ruskin and William Morris they believed that they could bring meaning and purpose into the drab lives of their immigrant neighbors by introducing them to great art. They had collected reproductions of paintings in Europe, and these were hung in the various rooms in the settlement. Ellen organized art classes, and exhibitions, and provided pictures which the neighbors could borrow. "Within a short walk from Hull House a little parlor has been completely transformed by the Fra Angelico over the mantel and the Luca della Robbias on the walls, from which walls the picture scarfs and paper flowers have fallen away," Jane Addams explained. "A few doors down the street a tiny bedroom has been changed from a place in which a fragile factory girl slept the sleep of the exhausted, into one where she 'just loves to lie in bed and look at my pictures; it's so like art class!' " Ellen was careful only to exhibit pictures which combined "an elevated tone with technical excellence," and Jane was sure that the paintings provided "a strong impulse toward the heroic and historic."[5] There is something pathetic about little immigrant girls hanging copies of Fra Angelico angels on the dreary walls of their tenements and all the emphasis on bringing art to the masses in the early days at Hull House; but the people flocked to see the art, and the settlement founders, for all their esoteric nature, had hit upon a basic truth: those who lived in the slums of Chicago did crave to see and touch and make things of beauty.

Just as impractical as the early emphasis on art were the carefully organized lectures on a wide variety of scholarly topics offered free by a visiting faculty of university professors, college women, and protestant clergymen. Indeed in the beginning the founders tried to create a "college-like atmosphere" and even recruited college boys and theological students to entertain the neighborhood boys by teaching them college songs. More successful were the Italian Evenings and German "Klatches" with games for the children, and talk, singing, dances, and pictures for the women. Sometimes the residents would plan an evening and no would come, and on other occasions people would drop in unannounced. An Italian woman presented them with a bottle of olives, and a mother came to leave her baby for the day, while a young man dropped in to invite them to his wedding. All of which indicated that the young upper-class ladies were being accepted by at least some of those who lived in the neighborhood.[6]

During the first few months Hull House was a place of constant activity and enthusiasm, with clubs and classes, lectures on art and literature, receptions and teas multiplying almost every week. "Of course we are undertaking more than we ourselves can do, that is part of the idea," Jane explained to her sister.[7] And from the beginning they got plenty of volunteers to help, not only with money but with time and talent. The two young women had done their preliminary work well. They advertised widely and they preached an idea whose time had come. The friends they had made during the spring and summer of 1889 did not fail them. Allen and Irving Pond, both architects, came to offer advice on remodeling the old house and on planning new additions. Ellen Henrotin and other members of the Woman's Club volunteered their support. Other prominent Chicago women such as Mary Wilmarth, Mrs. Coonley Ward, and Mrs. Russell Wright, the mother of architect Frank Lloyd Wright, dropped in to call, and remained loyal supporters of the settlement. Jenny Dow, Mary Rozet Smith, and several other young society women, tired of trips to Europe and the usual round of parties and charity work, offered to help in any way they could. Not all the socially prominent women who came to Hull House during the first months proved useful. Some came only out of curiosity, others betrayed their disdain for the immigrant neighbors, and others simply wanted to put in a token appearance in order to make the society pages of the newspaper. A few like Mrs. Potter Palmer withdrew their support as soon as Hull House became controversial. But a remarkable number of those prominent in Chicago society remained loyal. In many ways the most important of this group was Louise De Koven Bowen, a strong-minded and determined woman, just a year older than Jane Addams. She did not discover Hull House until 1893 when she joined the Hull House Woman's Club. But from that time until her death in 1953 she devoted a considerable amount of her energy and money (both of which she possessed in abundance) to Hull House projects. She was often difficult, demanding, and unpredictable, but without her Hull House might well have collapsed during a number of crises. It certainly would have been less innovative and important. It was Jane Addams' ability to get along with strong-willed, aristocratic women like Mrs. Bowen, to sooth their anger, to tolerate their idiosyncrasies, that was a major reason for the success of Hull House.[8]

There were others besides society women who came to visit the settlement during its first months. There were ministers like Jenkin Lloyd Jones, a liberal Unitarian, editor of *Unity* and pastor of All Souls' Church. He came to Hull House to lecture on Emerson and other topics, to talk about the need for labor unions and to debate on almost any topic with anyone who would listen. He cooperated with the settlement workers in giving aid to the most destitute in the neighborhood, and publicized their activities among the intellectual, political, and religious mavericks in the city.[9] Professors and students from the colleges and theological schools stopped out of curiosity and a few volunteered their services. There were even some like the young man described by Ellen Starr as "a youth of wealth who is inspired by the Holy Ghost to build model tenement houses."[10] Then there was A. Mastro Valerio, editor of *L'Italia*, who became a warm friend, and did his best to get his countrymen to come to the settlement. On one occasion in the spring of 1890 he sent out invitations to a concert and reception at Hull House to 228 Italians in the neighborhood. "The room was packed and people were in the halls. It was a very good thing . . . ," Ellen Starr reported. "The sight was very interesting. There was a great many babies and even some of the women wore bright kerchiefs on their heads. The rich and vulgar Italians are taking to coming, sporting diamond crosses. I hope something will come of it. We put them on the back seats, & the peasants to the front. One of the ladies of the diamond cross recited a patriotic poem with great spirit. I missed it . . . I was awfully glad things went off so well. Poor Mr. V had toiled so, & was so nervous."[11]

Not all the Italians enjoyed the affair as much as Signor Valerio, indeed it was usually the educated immigrants, those with particular talents and interests who learned most from the cultural programs, the lectures, and the classes. The young man who had started art lessons in Italy and had been unable to continue his painting in America until Hull House opened; the woman who had gone to high school years before but had no chance to pursue her interests until she had a chance to go to a class at the settlement; the young German Jew who had grown up in Russia who prided himself on his English and his gentlemanly manners and found at Hull House a sympathetic place to practice both —all of these appreciated the experiment and had something in common with the young well-educated men and women who were trying to help. But there were thousands of others with whom the settlement had no connection and no communication.

Yet Jane and Ellen were also shocked by the conditions they found in the neighborhood, and they soon lost their coyness and modesty, at least part of it. They knew in a general way before they moved to Halsted Street, about the poor housing, the filth, and the overcrowded conditions in that part of the city, but the reality was even worse than their first superficial view had shown. "One is so overpowered by the misery and narrow lives of so large a number of city people, that the wonder is that conscientious people can let it alone." Jane wrote to her stepbrother two months after she moved to Hull House. The poverty she observed caused her to reexamine some of her earlier assumptions. She looked at the elegant and expensive furnishings in the house and had second thoughts. She returned the handsome curtains to her sister because "the moral effect of them down here is not good."[12]

Even with misery and poverty in abundance she was not depressed, for she believed that the situation could be improved. She was also convinced that Chicago was more fortunate than most European cities, or even than New York. The sanitary conditions were better, the houses simpler and there were fewer tenement houses. "New York is struggling with the question of how to rid herself of huge houses and begin over again. We at least have a fresh start. . . ." Another advantage that Chicago and other American cities had over those in Europe was the fact that most of the poor were foreigners. At first glance that would seem a disadvantage, but she concluded that "it is much easier to deal with the first generation of crowded city life, than with the second and third. It is more natural and cast in a simpler mould. Italian and Bohemian peasants who live in Chicago still put on their bright holiday clothes on a Sunday and go to visit their cousins. They tramp along with at least a suggestion of having once walked over plowed fields and breathed country air. The second generation of city poor have no holiday clothes and consider their relations a 'bad lot.' "

She betrayed a romantic and naïve admiration for the European peasant. "We go to Europe and consider our view incomplete if we do not see something of the peasant life of the villages, with their quaint customs and suggestive habits," she wrote. "We can see the same thing here." She assumed that plowed fields and country air, were superior to city streets, but she had committed herself to help those who lived in the city. Before she had been at Hull House many months one thing seemed clear, that the object of the settlement programs should be to help the foreign-born conserve and keep "whatever of value their past life contained and to bring them into contact with a better class of Americans."[13]

Preserving the best of the immigrant tradition obviously did not include their habit of drinking wine and giving it to their children. Jenny Dow, the kindergarten teacher, one day returned a child of five to her mother because she felt she was intoxicated from her breakfast of bread soaked in wine. "The mother, with the gentle courtesy of the south Italian, listened politely to her graphic portrayal of the untimely end awaiting so immature a wine bibber; but long before the lecture was fin: ished, quite unconscious of the incongruity, she hospitably set forth her best wines and when her baffled guest refused one after the other, she disappeared, only to quickly return with a small dark glass of whiskey, saying reassuringly, 'See, I have brought you the true American drink' " Substituting whiskey for wine was not the kind of Americanization the settlement had in mind. Jane Addams never overcame her Mid-western Protestant disdain for alcoholic beverages, though she did eventually learn to appreciate the social importance of drinking for many of her immigrant neighbors.[14]

There was often pathos even in successful attempts to help the neighbors. The case Jane Addams cited as a shining example of what could be accomplished was that of an old woman, "straight from the fields of Germany," who had spent her two years in America "carrying water up and down two flights of stairs and in washing the heavy flannel suits of iron-foundry workers." For this she got paid thirty-five cents a day. Her daughters, according to Jane Addams, had "fallen victims to the vice of the city," but Hull House came to the rescue, aided the daughters and arranged for the woman to move to the country. "This woman is now living with her family in a little house seventeen miles from the city. She has made two payments on her land and is a lesson to all beholders as she pastures her cow up and down the railroad tracks and makes money from her ten acres." Jane Addams held out the American dream of ten acres and a cow as the ideal solution for the immigrants trapped in the slums, but it was a dream unattainable and unwanted by most of those who lived in the city. "She did not need charity, she had an immense capacity for hard work," Jane Addams concluded, "But she sadly needed leading." The old woman was not poor because she was inferior or lazy, but because she was a victim of the city, all she and the thousands of others needed was help and direction. It was not long before Addams would decide that the problem was more complicated than that, but in the early days at Hull House she was optimistic about the possibilities of moral regeneration.[15]

Part of her optimism, in the first years, came from her religious faith. In the face of abject poverty she found solace and courage from her new-found Christian convictions. "The movement toward Christian Socialism is certainly becoming more general from the very stress of the misery," she wrote two months after moving to Hull House. A year later she reported:—"We have seen a great deal of suffering and want this winter, and the comfort of Christ's mission to the world, the mind of the Messiah to the race, has been impressed upon me as never before. It seems sometimes as if the race life, at least the dark side, would be quite unendurable if it were not for that central fact."[16]

She never went all the way with the Christian Socialists, who argued for a radical transformation of society, using Christ rather than Marx as a guide; her optimistic Christian faith was more like that of the moderate social gospel ministers, such as Washington Gladden, who wanted to promote the Kingdom of God on earth by improving working conditions, building better housing and sewerage systems, and eventually eliminating poverty. Like some of the social gospelers, she was ambivalent about the role of Christian social reform, was it to transform society, or was it to adjust the poor to their lot? Yet in the beginning she thought of Hull House as a religious institution, and prided herself on its being more distinctly Christian than the college settlement in New York. She approved some of the early articles which defined the purpose of the settlement in explicitly religious terms, and she wrote herself that "a simple acceptance of Christ's message and methods is what a settlement should stand for."[17]

There were no religious services held at Hull House; in a neighborhood that was about 90 per cent Catholic that would have been foolish indeed. But she often attended a Congregational Church nearby or Jenkin Lloyd Jones' Unitarian All Souls' Church. At the settlement she encouraged regular evening devotions and even "led in evening Bible and prayers with everyone on their knees."[18] Time eroded the religious atmosphere at Hull House and altered Jane Addams's personal faith until she became an agnostic, but the early years at Hull House were dominated by the conviction that she was engaged in furthering Christ's mission on earth.

Jane Addams never became a radical in religion, in economics or in politics, but she did become a social reformer, a defender of organized labor, and she did come to believe that her main task was to eliminate poverty rather than to comfort the poor. One of her greatest strengths, one of the major reasons for her influence, was this ability to grow and develop and change her mind. She changed for many reasons—the poverty she observed, the utter dispair she witnessed during the depression of 1893; but a major cause of change was the people attracted to Hull House. An especially able group came to the settlement; in part this was accidental, the settlement house in the 1890s and the first decade of the twentieth century provided a needed outlet for an altruistic generation intent on solving the massive problems of urban America, or determined to gain new experience and training as writers, social investigators, or social workers. Many other settlements had impressive and colorful groups of residents. South End House in Boston, University Settlement and Henry Street Settlement in New York, as well as Chicago Commons occasionally rivaled Hull House as exciting and intellectually stimulating places to live or visit, but none of them surpassed the powerful and impressive list of residents at Hull House, and for this Jane Addams was largely responsible. Many came explicitly because she was there and others stayed because of her ability to create a sense of unity, a sense of purpose among the residents.

The Hull House group shifted and changed over the years. There was diversity, yet at the same time there was a harmony and sense of commitment. There were men as well as women. Edward Burchard, a young college graduate who later became the Secretary of the National Community Center Association, was the first male resident; there were also George Hooker, Director of the Chicago City Club and expert on city planning, Francis Hackett, a writer and editor, Gerard Swope, later president of General Electric, and many others including Charles Beard, the historian, and William Lyon MacKenzie King, the future Prime Minister of Canada. Burchard, very early was elected to guard the paintings at the art exhibit at night, and even was enlisted to march around the neighborhood as a sandwich man advertising the affair. Hooker, because he was both an ordained minister and a lawyer, as well as an expert on city planning, was invaluable in many ways whether it was lobbying in Springfield, or putting pressure on a member of the city council. The presence of the men at Hull House, many of them able, aggressive, and articulate, prevented the settlement from becoming dominated by unmarried or unattached women, and saved it from becoming like a sorority house or a convent.[19] Yet for all their usefulness, it was the remarkable group of women at Hull House that made it famous and influential. The most important during the first few years were Julia Lathrop and Florence Kelley.

Julia Lathrop came from very much the same background as Jane Addams. Her father was a successful lawyer and politician in Rockford Illinois; her mother, a member of the first graduating class at Rockford Seminary, was an early and forceful advocate of woman's suffrage. Like Jane Addams, Julia went to Rockford Seminary, but she stayed only a year then transferred to Vassar where she graduated in 1880. Then, because she needed something to do, she studied in her father's law office while also acting as his secretary and assistant, but she was not altogether satisfied with her life of living at home and working for her father. Impatient with her inability to live up to the hopes and dreams of her college years she was vulnerable to Jane Addams' appeal for Hull House, which she heard even before the settlement opened. She moved to the settlement in 1890 and quickly became an important fixture. She was a small, slender woman with plain features and an almost mournful expression, but she had burning eyes and a flashing wit, and boundless energy. "Her brown eyes so sincere, but with a sparkle lurking in them, her slow redolent voice, her flavor of Illinois, gave her a richness which was valued by colleagues who had less vitality," one of the young residents at Hull House remembered.[20]

Julia Lathrop was a talented executive who was appointed a member of the Illinois Board of Charities in 1893. She helped organize the first Juvenile Court, the Immigrants' Protective League, and in 1912 became the first head of the Children's Bureau. Her organizing ability proved valuable at Hull House, but even more important in the beginning was her sense of humor. Jane Addams had a tendency to take herself and her work very seriously, even Ellen Starr joked and laughed more frequently, but it was Julia Lathrop who taught Jane how to appreciate the comic side of her experience and to laugh at her own predicament. She did not offer the love and devotion that Ellen provided, but she called her "J. A." and with a humorous prod or a subtle suggestion she encouraged her to become more active and involved, whether it was helping an expectant mother in a tenement flat or approaching a New York publisher with the draft of an article.

Florence Kelley forced Jane Addams to grow in other ways. Daughter of William D. Kelley, a Philadelphia judge and congressman who earned the nickname "Pig-Iron" from his aggressive support of high tariffs to protect the iron and steel industry, Florence grew up in an upper-class home, graduated from Cornell University, and then went to the University of Zurich for graduate study. There she was converted to socialism, married a Polish-Russian doctor, and translated one of Friedrich Engel's books into English. She and her husband joined the Socialist Labor Party, and, after a move to New York, she spent her time working for the party, lecturing, writing articles on the abuses of child labor, and translating an essay by Karl Marx on free trade. She also had three children, but her marriage was never happy. In 1891 she left her husband, and moved with her children to Illinois where the divorce laws were more lenient. She had lectured at the College Settlement in New York and had heard of Hull House; it seemed like a convenient place to stay. Years later she described her arrival:

One snowy morning between Christmas 1891 and New Year's 1892, I arrived at Hull-House, Chicago, a little before breakfast time, and found there Henry Standing Bear, a Kickapoo Indian, awaiting for the front door to be opened. It was Miss Addams who opened it, holding on her left arm a singularly unattractive, fat, pudgy baby belonging to the cook, who was behindhand with breakfast. Miss Addams was a little hindered in her movements by a super energetic kindergarten child, left by its mother while she went to a sweatshop for a bundle of cloaks to be finished. We were welcome as though we had been invited. We stayed.[21]

Florence Kelley had a background and experience quite foreign to Ellen Starr, Jane Addams, and Julia Lathrop. She had not only been married and had children, but she had broken almost every tenet of the genteel code. She had taken part in radical politics, published her political views, and was in the process of getting a divorce. While the other women had searched desperately for something meaningful to do in life, she had lived. She was a large woman, energetic and outgoing. "No other man or woman whom I have ever heard so blended knowledge of facts, wit, satire, burning indignation, prophetic denunciation—all poured out at white heat in a voice varying from flute-like tones to deep organ tones," one of her friends remembered. "Explosive, hot-tempered, determined, she was no gentle saint," another added. She was a "smoking volcano that at any moment would burst into flames."[22]

She immediately challenged Jane Addams and the others. She was not playing at life, not trying to escape boredom; she needed a job to support her family. She tried running an employment service; she taught school at night, but in the spring of 1892 she was appointed a special agent for the State Bureau of Labor Statistics to conduct an investigation of the sweating trade in Chicago. From that moment on she became a social investigator and an agitator for reform, and to a certain extent she pulled the rest of the group in that direction. She laughed at the "Reading Parties" and hooted at the evening prayer sessions, and more than any other single person she was responsible for making Hull House a center for social reform, rather than a place to study art and hear lectures on Emerson and Brook Farm. Both kinds of activity remained, but Florence Kelley, blustering, angry, and impetuous, helped redress the balance. She loved to argue with anyone who would take her on, and Julia Lathrop and Jane Addams often waited up for her to listen, to talk, and to debate over a cup of hot chocolate far into the night. Florence Kelley had great respect and admiration for Jane Addams, like Julia Lathrop she called her J.A., but she was the only one of the group who could laugh at her, poke fun at her, or even criticize her; and Jane took it from her. More than anyone else Florence Kelley turned Jane Addams from philanthropist into reformer.

These three—Addams, Kelley, and Lathrop remained very close. Different in personality, in approach, even in point of view, they addressed each other in their letters as "Dear Sister," or "Dear Lady," and they developed a sense of camaraderie, of dedication to an ideal that was based on respect and committment and love. A few others came along later to enter almost to the inner circle—Grace and Edith Abbott, the two sisters from Nebraska, Alice Hamilton, a young doctor from Fort Wayne Indiana, who became an expert on industrial medicine, and a few others. But these three were the most important in the early years.

Ellen Starr was, of course, in the beginning a part of the inner circle, but she was more of a loner than the others, more religious and much less interested in the give and take of argument. After the first few years she drifted away from the center of activity at the settlement. While Jane Addams and the others became public figures, occupied with committee meetings, speaking tours, and writing, Ellen stayed at the settlement and performed hundreds of small acts of kindness, even on occasion gave up her room to a sick neighbor. She continued to teach her classes and to devote her time to art and literature in which she was much more passionately interested than the others. She was a disciple of William Morris and in 1895 she went to England to study book binding with T. J. Cobden-Sanderson, and returned to construct a bookbindery in the settlement where she spent hours making beautiful books. Yet she found time to join the picket lines during the strikes in the neighborhood. After the first years her path diverged from that of Jane Addams, but she still exerted a powerful influence on many of the younger residents.

There were others that helped in the education of Jane Addams, however, and two of these were Mary Kenny O'Sullivan and Alzina Stevens. Mary Kenny, a tall, red-haired, and determined Irish girl four years younger than Jane, grew up in Hannibal, Missouri, dropped out of school after the fourth grade, and began work as an apprentice dressmaker to help support her invalid mother. But soon she moved from dressmaking to bookbinding and printing. She practiced her trade in Keokuck, Iowa, but after the plant there closed she moved with her widowed mother to Chicago, arriving about the same time that Ellen and Jane took an apartment to begin work on their scheme. She was employed by several binderies, and very quickly became a leader in the labor movement. She knew little about unions, but a lot about working conditions. With the kind of perseverance that marked her whole career, she sought out one of the few women's unions in the city and began to organize the first women's bookbinders union in Chicago. Mary Kenny was aggressive, quick witted, and somewhat defensive with Jane Addams and the other upper-class ladies at Hull House. When she was invited to come to the settlement she went very reluctantly. She was overwhelmed by the expensive furnishings and the rich visitors. But Jane Addams quickly disarmed her, by asking about trade unions and by inviting her union to meet in the settlement and by offering to work with her to improve conditions of labor. Years later Mary Kenny recalled. "It was that work 'with' from Jane Addams that took the bitterness out of my life. For if she wanted to work with me and I could work with her it gave my life new meaning and hope."

Mary Kenny and Jane Addams were never equals, but they became good friends. Through her Jane met other working girls, learned about the labor movement, and about the realities of life in a large city in a way she had not appreciated before. Together the two young women launched a boarding cooperative for working girls which became known as the Jane Club. Mary lived at Hull House for a time and then in 1892 at the age of 28 she became an organizer for Samuel Gompers and the A.F. of L. After a brief stay in Boston she was back in Chicago helping the Hull House residents lobby for the state's first factory act and she became a deputy inspector under Florence Kelley. Even after she married Jack O'Sullivan, a former seaman and labor organizer and moved to Boston, she was a frequent visitor at Hull House where she captivated everyone with her enthusiasm. She decked herself happily in a dress donated by Jane Addams or Mary Smith, flung herself into political campaigns, social investigations, or whatever was the activity of the moment. Mary Kenny, perhaps more than anyone, except Florence Kelley, broadened Jane Addams' perspective and made her sympathetic to organized labor, and helped her move from a position of wanting to comfort the poor—to one of a determination to eliminate poverty.[23]

Another woman who helped transform Jane Addams from a Christian philanthropist into a social reformer was Alzina Stevens, who like Mary Kenny had a background of experience quite different from those women who had been raised in upper-class homes, gone to college, and traveled abroad. Alzina was born in a little town in Maine eleven years before Jane Addams. At thirteen she was forced to go to work in a textile mill, and there in an industrial accident she lost her right index finger. That missing finger became a perpetual reminder for her of the need to improve working conditions and regulate child labor. She had little formal education, but she had drive and ambition. After her marriage failed, she learned the printing trade in order to support herself; she became a proofreader and typesetter, then a writer. She became active in the labor movement in Chicago, first president of the Working Woman's Union Number One and a leading spirit in the Knights of Labor. She was matronly and roundfaced, and she had had a wealth of practical experience. She was quick to join the picket line, and to defend the cause of organized labor. At the same time she was just as quick to denounce the young idealist at Hull House who defended a notoriously corrupt labor leader. Mrs. Stevens informed her sharply that it was "the worst kind of snobbishness to assume that you must not have the same standards of honor for working people as you have for the well to do."

Not as flamboyant as Mary Kenny or as impetuous and overpowering as Florence Kelley, Alzina Stevens, until her untimely death in 1900, was an important member of the Hull House group. She also worked closely with Florence Kelley as an assistant factory inspector, and co-author of an article for *Hull-House Maps and Papers*. In 1899 she became the first probation officer for the newly established Juvenile Court. Like Florence Kelley she had been married unhappily, and she had had experiences that Jane Addams, Julia Lathrop, Ellen Starr, and the other unmarried young ladies could not match or even imagine. Their experience and the presence of men at the settlement prevented Hull House from becoming a protective sanctuary for the "sexually unemployed," to borrow a phrase from Francis Hackett.[24]

For many Hull House residents, especially for the women, the settlement became a training ground for new professional careers as experts and administrators in government, industry, and the universities. Florence Kelley went on to become head of the National Consumers' League. Julia Lathrop was a member of the Illinois Board of Charities before becoming the first head of the Children's Bureau. Grace Abbott was the director of the Immigrants' Protective League before becoming director of the Child Labor Division of the Children's Bureau, and then replaced Julia Lathrop as head of the Bureau in 1921. Alice Hamilton became the first woman professor at Harvard Medical School and an expert on industrial medicine. Sophonisba Breckinridge and Edith Abbott were professors at the Chicago School of Civics and Philanthropy, one of the first schools of social work in the country. Many other young men and women left the settlement to fill the growing number of positions demanding professional training and experience. While Hull House became a training ground for the first generation of professional women, Jane Addams refused to become professionalized, and never took a salary. She played the role of expert and administrator but she was always more. She presided over Hull House and became a priestess and sage.[25]

Hull House attracted brilliant, aggressive, and talented men and women, many of them the equal of Jane Addams in ability and experience, but there never was any question about who was in command. She presided at the evening meal; often in the early days, she handed out mail to be answered or listened to reports from the various residents. She also gathered the flock together in the evening for meetings. Even after the prayers and Bible readings were given up, the meetings went on. "I had a long and solemn talk with the residents last evening," she wrote a friend. "I hope we are going to be more intimate and internally responsible on the financial side." Occasionally she shook her head in despair over the failure of one of the residents. Dr. Rice refused to treat the sick neighbors and Jane was afraid she did not have the "settlement spirit." Mr. Waldo spent too much money in relief work, but she forgave him because he seemed to be near a nervous breakdown. She treated everyone kindly and patiently; her influence pervaded the settlement. Francis Hackett, who was a resident in 1906-1907 exaggerated, but only a little when he wrote: "The essential fact of Hull House was the presence of Miss Addams. This is strange, because while one was living there she was away a good deal of the time, and when she was there one did not have a great deal to do with her; yet Hull House, as one clearly felt at the time, was not an institution over which Miss Addams presided; it was Miss Addams around whom an institution insisted on clustering."[26]

During the first months at Hull House, even during the first few years, Jane Addams played many roles, from leading the evening prayers, to raising money, speaking at the woman's clubs, and responding to neighborhood crises. One afternoon a young woman rushed through the door and announced that a girl in a tenement house down the street was having a baby all by herself, and none of the women would help her because she was not married and she was disgracing the neighborhood. Jane Addams and Julia Lathrop responded somewhat nervously to the cry for help and delivered the baby. On another occasion a call came at three in the morning from an insurance company requesting that two of the "ladies" go to a nearby transportation company where a barn was burning, and report how many horses were injured. Again Julia Lathrop accompanied Jane and later recalled that "J.A. walked bravely into the stable full of groaning, screaming horses, but could not open her eyes after she got there."[27]

Such adventures became increasingly rare for Jane Addams as time went on. The younger residents responded to the neighborhood crises, and she became the executive, the organizer, and the public figure. Yet through the first decade at least she played her many roles with an energy and commitment that sometimes exhausted the other residents. Gertrude Barnum, a young woman from Evanston who had dropped out of the University of Wisconsin in 1891 to join the Hull House group, reported in the summer of 1899 on Jane Addams' activities to Mary Smith who was in Europe:

> She is very tired . . . of course she did not let [that] deter her from tearing about. She preached for the Methodists last Sunday, entertained the Colored Women of the National Council (Mrs. Booker T. Washington et al) yesterday & later went to Winnetka . . . she runs over to Mrs. Jones—around to Mrs. Fiellras . . . up to Mrs. Kenyon—off with Mrs. Halderman, down to inquiring strangers & in and out & around about to Italian Fiestas, forced marriages, rows between scabs & unions etc. etc. etc. until my head spins & I sink exhausted while she poses to Mr. Linden [a portrait painter] & discusses the questions of the day with freshness & calmness that put the finishing touches on my amazement.[28]

Jane Addams often baffled and amazed the casual observer, and the resident alike. To Florence Kelley and to Julia Lathrop she was J.A., and to Ellen Starr she was "Jane" but to everyone else she was "Miss Addams," and for the younger residents there was not only respect, but a considerable amount of awe, even reverence in the use of that title. Jane Addams for her part accepted the title and played the part of *mater familias*. She spoke of the "settlement household," and the "settlement family." To a large extent Hull House was her home, and the residents her family; she accepted their praise, but continued to learn from them.

While her settlement family prospered and she became a national celebrity, her real family was engulfed by continuing tragedy and bitter-

ness. She had broken away from the "family claim," from the temptation to become a maiden aunt and nursemaid for brothers and sisters,
nieces, and nephews, but she did not give up her sense of responsibility
to her family. She wrote frequent letters, even while she was exceedingly
busy, to all her family. She knit sweaters and mittens and socks for the
children, even though she was never very proficient at the task. It was
one of those womanly skills she had learned as a young girl, that she felt
some strange obligation to continue even though in other ways she had
rebelled against the traditional role of women. She also gave money
and advice in a seemingly endless stream, but neither prevented tragedy
and conflict from overwhelming her family. George Haldeman grew
worse and he spent most of his time just sitting silently. Mrs. Addams
became bitter, somehow blaming Jane for her son's illness. "I have the
most helpless, bewildered feeling about them." Jane admitted to her
sister. For years her frequent visits to Cedarville triggered angry and
irrational outbursts from the embittered old lady. In order to avoid difficulty Jane often stayed at her brother Weber's farm rather than at
her old home, but she conscientiously wrote to her stepmother and
went to see her frequently. "I came here a week ago," Jane reported to
her sister Alice from Cedarville in August 1891, "Ma left for Mt. Carroll two days afterwards. Today is her birthday and I have just written
her. She is very thin but I think quite well as she has been for a long
time. Twice I have been here there has been no outbreak which seems
to me to indicate that she is better."[29]

Jane was partly responsible for the bitterness and animosity. She angered the old lady by suggesting that if Mr. Addams had lived he would
have given some of his money to Hull House, something Mrs. Addams
always refused to do. There was jealousy and resentment on both sides
and a clash of very different personalities and temperaments. Jane's
brother Weber also suffered from acute depression and spent long periods in mental institutions, though at other times he was well enough
to manage the farm. "Weber is so blue and depressed it quite breaks
my heart," she wrote to Alice in 1894. Two years later she reported: "I
took Weber home last Saturday and spent Sunday at Cedarville. He is
quite restored and I feel as if a great sorrow was gone. I am so much
happier when he is at home."[30]

No member of the family, however, caused more worry than Mary,
Jane's older sister. She was often ill, but in 1894 she got much worse.
After three months in a sanatorium in Kenosha, Wisconsin, she died,

leaving four children and a husband incapable of supporting them. Jane paid most of the expenses of the last illness and over the next few years devoted a considerable portion of her income to helping the Linn children. She became the legal guardian of the youngest, Stanley, and for a number of years she was "mother" as well as celebrity. She stepped in when Esther, her niece, was expelled from Rockford College, she lent money to John, the oldest, and watched over James Weber when he was at the University of Chicago. Settling the Linn estate, selling off some of the land in Dakota, and some of the property in Cedarville, paying taxes and sharing expenses for the children. All caused endless disagreements and arguments with Alice, who felt that her sister should pay more of the expenses and do more for the family, and who was often jealous of Jane's growing reputation. The disagreements extended to Alice's husband, Harry Haldeman, who had no use for Hull House or for its founder. Through it all Jane remained devoted to her sister, writing an endless stream of letters, making special purchases and frequent visits, always remembering Alice's daughter, Marcet. "My heart aches for you and I am homesick to see you," she wrote. "I do wish you would write me oftener; I get very anxious sometimes. I wake up in the night with a great longing for you." "I think about you so often, dear and hope and pray that no harm will come to you or Marcet."[31] It is easy to imagine, however, that Jane could be exasperating at times especially when she remained calm and reasonable while her sister became angry. In any case the relationship remained strained. "What is in your mind and why are your letters so reproachful?" Jane asked at one point. "I cannot imagine why you say 'that I fear that the children and finances are cutting you off from your natural sister.' Why do you feel cut off? It seems to me that I deserve an explanation." And then she asked, "why are you so suspicious of me, is there a new story afloat?" And on another occasion Jane wrote: "I have my faults, but I am sure I am not snobbish and it is always hard for me to comprehend why you imagine me sensitive about my relatives. I was really a little hurt by your first letter when you said you took pains not to say you were my sister." Yet the pull of family ties was very strong. Jane felt a sense of loyalty and obligation. She could rejoice over the birth of nieces or nephews and eventually grand-nieces and nephews, and she was saddened by the constant tragedy and conflict. At the same time she could take a step back and analyze her situation almost objectively. "Alice and Marcet leave this week," she wrote to Mary Smith. "We have really had a very nice time the last of the visit and I

am ashamed when I think of myself the first week, I have even been reduced to an elaborate theory in regard to it which I shall add to my
'Family Lecture.' " "It has always been difficult for the family to regard
the daughter other wise than as a family possession," she wrote in her
essay on the "The College Woman and the Family Claim," and that
was certainly true of her relationship with some members of her family.[32]

At least a part of Jane Addams' ability to see her family difficulties in
perspective, even to reduce them "to an elaborate theory," was her friendship with Mary Rozet Smith. In a real sense Mary Smith, who was gentle,
self-effacing, and content to devote herself to Jane's every need, to love her
without question and without criticism, gave Jane the confidence, encouragement and love she craved. Mary replaced the need for a sister,
the need for family, even the need for the affection of Ellen Starr.

Jane and Ellen drifted apart after the first years. Their commitment
to Hull House took them in different directions, and as their paths
diverged, they began to lose something of the closeness of that ideal
feminine friendship that had made Hull House possible. Years later
after reading through some old letters Ellen wrote to Jane: "I can see
by the way you overrate me in these letters that it was inevitable that I
should disappoint you. I think I have always, at any rate for a great
many years, been thankful that Mary came to supply what you needed.
At all events I thank God that I never was envious of her in any vulgar
or ignoble way. One couldn't be of anyone so noble and generous and in
every way fair-minded as she, and so humble; really self-depreciating."
One difficulty with Ellen in the first Hull House years was that she was
not humble, certainly not self-depreciating. She had her own ideas, and
she could be critical of Jane's actions and inactions. Jane functioned
best when she had an uncritical, loving disciple and that she found in
Mary Smith. But as Ellen Starr in her old age remarked, "Human relations are complicated affairs. . . . I remember an amusing thing you
said to me once," she continued. "I had said I suppose of somebody,
that I *liked* and respected her thoroughly [but] didn't love her, 'and,'
said you, 'you respect me and love me, but you don't *like* me.' I think I
was able to laugh. I certainly am now and hope you are." Jane demanded
not only that she be loved, but liked as well, and she found that kind
of a relationship with Mary Smith.[33]

In the beginning Mary Rozet Smith was one of several upper-class
young ladies attracted to Hull House because it offered something more

real and exciting than life in Chicago society. She fitted exactly Jane Addams' description of the young well-educated women, "whose uselessness hangs about them heavily." She was a friend of Jenny Dow, and came with her one day to the settlement. She returned to attend a lecture and to help out in the kindergarten, and she stayed a lifetime. We can follow the development of the relationship between the two women, at least one side of it, because Mary carefully preserved all of Jane's letters. Jane, on the other hand, seems to have destroyed most of Mary's letters. In the early summer of 1890, Jane wrote: "Jenny Dow is to spend next week here and probably Miss Trowbridge [another friend] will be here for part of the time. It would give us great pleasure to have you come on Monday prepared to stay for the rest of the week and share our homely fare and destiny obscure."[34]

The early letters are addressed to "My dear Miss Smith," or "My Dear Friend," and are signed "always Affectionately Yours." Most of them are thank you notes for gifts to the children in the Hull House classes, where Mary Smith served as a volunteer, or acknowledgements of money given for various programs. But very soon a note of real affection emerges. In February 1891 when Mary was going on an extended trip Jane wrote: "I am sure you know that we will miss you, not only for what you do, but for the interest and friendship which has come to mean a great deal to me." At first it was always "we," and Ellen Starr was included in her messages of thank you, but soon the letters became more personal. "My heart swells with a good deal of gratitude for all you have done for the nursery. I hope you won't let the children worry you. I am always your loving friend, Jane Addams." Mary Smith soon became a confederate with whom she could discuss her problems at Hull House and her family difficulties. She also became a traveling companion on many lecture tours, the first in 1893, and a valued confidante on financial matters. From her she got confidence and reassurance. "Miss Smith . . . is so good to me that I would find life a different thing without her," she admitted to her sister.[35]

Mary's family became a second family for Jane, more affectionate and comforting than her own, and their big house at 19 Walton Place was a warm and comfortable refuge from the confusion and disarray at Hull House. "Your good letter warmed my heart," she wrote while Mary was abroad in 1893. "Indeed it has warmed it several times after several readings. I called the other day to see your mother and inquire of your welfare. . . . I miss you very much and had a positive pang of homesickness as I went up the steps." Frequently Jane dropped in to see the family and occasionally when Mary was away she even went on trips with Mr. and Mrs. Smith.[36]

Sometimes Jane addressed Mary as "Sister" just as she referred to "Sister Kelley" and "Sister Lathrop" or she called her "Dearest Lady," also a term of affection used among the inner circle of settlement pioneers. Mary Smith was very much a part of the closeknit fellowship of the settlement; although she was never officially a resident, she was, after 1895, a trustee. She was loved and respected by all, not least because she loved and protected Jane Addams. Florence Kelley called her "Dearly Beloved," and remarked: "The Lady misses you more than the uninitiated would think she had time for." Mary Smith was also a constant source of money for settlement projects. She built the "Children's Building," sometimes called the Smith Building, in 1895, and she could always be depended upon, not only for a yearly contribution, but also to write a check when a crisis arose. "The check came this afternoon," Jane wrote in 1894. "It gives me a lump in my throat to think of the round thousand dollars you have put into the prosaic bakery and the more prosaic debt when there are so many more interesting things you might have done and wanted to do. It grieves me a little lest our friendship (which is really a very dear thing to me) would be buried by all those money transactions."[37]

The money transactions did not interfere with their friendship, though sometimes Jane had to wrestle with her conscience before she took the money. "I went to bed quite determined not to do it, but after a three o'clock vigil found myself weakly accepting it," she wrote. The gifts were not only for Hull House programs and buildings, but also included personal items, dresses, coats, and other things that Jane did not take the trouble to buy for herself. "I have been homesick for you, and have meditated much on your unfailing goodness to me," she wrote while away on a trip. "I put on the blue dressing gown the other night on the cars thinking that I had accepted it too much as a matter of course and when I put on my black dress and fine new jacket in the morning both which you had given me, I concluded that I had reached the limit of taking whatever you gave me without even so much as telling you how much I cared for them because they came from you." Their relationship could have become that of benevolent philanthropist taking care of the famous celebrity but each came to respect and trust the other. Mary seemed perfectly content to stay in the background while Jane played the role of famous lecturer, writer, and founder of Hull House. She got pleasure from supporting, comforting, and loving Jane and did not need public acclaim. "You can never know what it is to me to have had you and to have you now," Mary wrote in one of the few letters that Jane saved, "I only hope I am thankful enough. I'm given to turning sentimental at this season, as you know, and I feel quite a rush of emotion when I think of you. . . ."[38]

Jane wrote Mary none of the troubled, probing, intellectual letters she had earlier written to Ellen Starr; her relationship with Mary was more emotional than intellectual. In her letters at least she rarely discussed the ideas and theories she was dealing with in her lectures, articles, and books, only that she was speaking to a particular group or writing on a specific topic, or she wrote about practical and everyday matters. She did not need someone to test her ideas against; there were plenty of men and women like that at Hull House; she needed someone who accepted her and wanted her the way she was. That is the kind of relationship she had with Mary Smith. They became closer during a four months' trip to Europe in the spring and summer of 1896 when Jane was the guest of Mary and her mother and father. Aylmer Maude, a disciple of Tolstoy, mistook their relationship when they traveled in Russia on that trip. He thought Jane was Mary's aunt, and the way Mary deferred to Jane and at the same time kept a "watchful eye over her aunt's well-being" gave him that impression.[39]

Occasionally Jane addressed her as "Dearie, or "My Ever Dear," but usually it was "Dearest Friend" or "Dearest Sister." She signed off one letter with: "I miss you dreadfully and am yours 'til death," and on another occasion she gave her a book as a "token of my 'fondest love' and a feeble expression of my gratitude for our affection and friendship which has made life a very different thing for me during the last three years and has transformed the future." Yet when Robert Woods, of South End House, seemed to be interested in a romantic relationship with Mary, Jane encouraged it and urged her not to be "too frigid." Again a few months later she wrote: "please don't be an iceberg nor a tombstone when the seige begins." There never seems to have been anyone of the settlement group who had a romantic interest in Jane Addams; she was too much the reserved and saintly figure even as a young woman. Although when she was at the Paris Exposition in 1900, Robert Ely of the Cambridge Prospect Union accompanied her to all the meetings and on Bastille Day they wandered around the streets of Paris together from "4 p.m. to 1 a.m."[40]

Finding men to have a romantic and sexual relationship with was never a real possibility for either Mary Smith or Jane Addams, at least after they became mature women. Instead they came to think of themselves as married to each other—in a sense. "You must know, dear, how I long for you all the time and especially during the last three weeks," Jane wrote in the spring of 1902 while Mary was in Europe. "There is reason in the habit of married folks keeping together." At another time when Jane was away on a lecture tour she wrote. "Maybe I am not homesick for you . . . I almost cry for your ministrations at night when my conscience is bad and my spirits low." About 1904 they purchased a house together at Hull's Cove, near Bar Harbor, Maine, just a short distance from Mrs. Bowen's big summer house. Jane wrote of " 'Our House'—it quite gives me a thrill to write the word, it was our house wasn't it in a really truly ownership." Again about the same time she remarked: "Dearest you have been so heavenly good to me all these weeks. I feel as if we had come into a healing domesticity which we never had before, as if it were the first affection had offered us."[41]

The "healing domesticity" and "affection" meant a great deal to her, and it grew deeper and more important as both women grew older and Jane became famous—a public figure whose image as a benevolent saint took on a life of its own. When the world came crashing down and the saint became a villain, she always could depend on Mary's love. Once she tried to write a poem about her feelings for Mary. It was not a very good poem, but the fact that she tried to write it was an indication of the depths of her feeling.

> One day I came into Hull House,
> (No spirit whispered who was there)
> And in the kindergarten room
> There sat upon a childish chair
> A girl, both tall and fair to see,
> (To look at her gives one a thrill).
> But all I thought was, would she be
> Best fitted to lead club, or drill?
> You see, I had forgotten Love,
> And only thought of Hull House then.
>
> That is the way with women folks
> When they attempt the things of men;

They grow intense, and love the thing
　　Which they so tenderly do rear,
And think that nothing lies beyond
　　Which claims from them a smile or tear.
Like mothers, who work long and late
　　To rear their children fittingly,
Follow them only with their eyes,
　　And love them almost pityingly,
So I was blind and deaf those years
　　To all save one absorbing care,
And did not guess what now I know—
　　Delivering love was sitting there![42]

Jane Addams' close relationship first with Ellen Starr and then for 40 years with Mary Smith was not unusual for her time. Only about half of the first generation of college women ever married. Many of them formed emotional, romantic, and practical attachments with other women. Carey Thomas, three years older than Jane Addams, and for many years the president of Bryn Mawr College, had two close companions, first Mary Gwinn, a girlhood friend, and than Mary Garrett, who lived with her in the college "deanery" after 1906 and made large and frequent gifts to the college. Vida Scudder, Wellesley professor and one of the founders of the College Settlement Association, was a close companion of Florence Converse and Helena Dudley. Lillian Wald, head resident at Henry Street Settlement, found comfort and a loving relationship with Lavina Dock, an associate at the same settlement. Carrie Chapman Catt, suffragist and peace leader, lived with her close friend Mary Garrett Hay after her husband George Catt, died. Agnes Repplier, a popular writer formed a close relationship with Elizabeth Robins Pennell, another writer. Even Eleanor Roosevelt, married with five children, found her companionship with other women important. For a time she owned a cottage on the Hyde Park estate jointly with two women friends; their love and devotion was important to her when her family and the outside world seemed sometimes to be filled only with tension and difficulty.[43]

Frances Willard, the temperance leader, had a number of romantic attachments with other women, with whom she exchanged sentimental love letters. In her autobiography she wrote: "The loves of women for each other grow more numerous each day, and I have wondered much why these things were. That so little should be said about them surprises me, for they are everywhere . . . In these days, when any capable and careful women [sic] can honorably own her own support, there is no village that has not its examples of 'two heads in counsel' both of which are feminine. Often times these joint-proprietors have been unfortunately married, and so have failed to 'better their condition' until thus clasping hands, they have taken each other 'for better or worse.' These are the tokens of a transition age. Drink and tobacco are today the great separatists between women and men. Once they used these things together, but woman's evolution has carried her beyond them; man will climb to the same level some day, but meanwhile he thinks he must have his dinners from which woman is excluded and his club house with whose delights she intermeddleth not. Indeed the fact that he permits himself fleshy indulgences that he would depreciate in her, makes their planes different, giving him a sense of larger liberty and her an instinct of revulsion."[44]

Man's vulgar habits and woman's superiority do not account for the presence of so many women with companions of the same sex in that era in both the United States and England, though a sense that women were superior formed a part of the reason. Convenience explained a great deal for if one did not marry and preferred not to live alone, and if one rejected the role of maiden aunt, living with another woman was often the solution. There were also, doubtlessly, sexual reasons, latent or expressed, for many women living together, but whether or not these women were actually lesbians is essentially irrelevant. The romantic words, the love letters, the terms of endearment can be easily misinterpreted, but it is important that many unmarried women drew warmth and strength from their supportive relationships with other women.[45]

Jane Addams' relationship with Mary Smith was crucial in her development and continued growth. She was a complex person who held herself aloof from most people, who preferred to be called Miss Addams, rather than Jane, who enjoyed and depended on the fantastic praise that was showered upon her. But underneath the calm exterior she was not a saint, but a human being filled with doubts and insecurities related to the tension and conflict within her family, and the long hard struggle to break away from the family claim and to create a new role for herself. As she became a celebrity and played the role of saint, the solace and love of Mary Smith allowed her to throw off her doubts and fears and devote all her energies to her public role.

VI

A Wider Influence

HE settlement movement expanded rapidly in the decade after the establishment of Hull House. In 1891 there were six settlements, by 1897 there were 74, and in 1900 there were well over 100. Almost before she realized it Jane Addams was not just the head of one institution on the West Side of Chicago, but the leader of a national movement.[1]

In the summer of 1892 she gave two lectures at the School of Applied Ethics in Plymouth, Massachusetts. Among the others participating in the conference were Robert A. Woods, the young graduate of Andover Theological School who was the head resident of Andover House (later South End House) in Boston, Father J. O. S. Huntington, an Anglican Christian Socialist and founder of the Order of Holy Cross, Franklin Giddings, a sociologist and economist at Columbia University, and Bernard Bosanquet, an English advocate of scientific charity who had practiced his theories in the slums of East London. But it was the young woman from Chicago who got most of the attention. Her lectures were finished in a great rush at Hull House, the last part dictated to Edward Burchard on a hot Sunday afternoon before she caught a train. The lectures were similar to the speeches she had been giving in and around Chicago, though they were more polished, and a little better organized. She explained the impulse behind the settlement movement, the subjective necessity she called it. In her second paper she outlined the activities of Hull House and described the conditions in the neighborhood which demonstrated the objective need for settlements.[2]

In addition to the formal papers there was time for discussion, for getting acquainted. Vida Scudder, Helena Dudley, Emily Balch, and Jean Fine represented the College Settlement Association. Jane Addams and Julia Lathrop came away exhilarated by the realization that they were part of a national settlement movement, and involved in a still larger trend in the churches and the colleges concerned with getting back to the people. "To be identified with the common lot," to do something to solve the pressing problems of poverty and injustice, seemed terribly exciting in 1892 in America. With her two impressive papers and her leadership role in the discussion following them, Jane Addams established herself at the Plymouth Conference as the dominant figure in the new settlement movement.[3]

On the way back to Chicago she stopped in New York to try to find a publisher for her essays. At Julia Lathrop's suggestion she approached Walter Hines Page, the editor of *The Forum*, and to her surprise he accepted both for immediate publication. The articles appeared as "Hull House, Chicago: An Effort toward Social Democracy," and "A New Impulse to an Old Gospel." The next year the articles, along with the others from the conference were published in a book entitled rather prosaically, *Philanthropy and Social Progress*.[4] The book had only a small sale; the articles were probably read by a rather limited audience though they were reported in the liberal protestant journals. The important thing, however, was that Jane Addams was launched as a writer. Until she founded Hull House she did not have anything unusual to say and her chief outlet for her essays before this had been the *Rockford Seminary Magazine*. Now she had a subject and a national audience.

Her leadership in the national settlement movement was solidified the year following the Plymouth conference when the settlement workers from Boston, Chicago, and New York met in Chicago during the Columbian Exposition. She presided and led the discussion at the sessions. Many of the early settlement leaders were intense and ambitious young ministers, but Jane Addams, who might have been overawed by them, quickly became their leader. They treated her not just as an equal, but as a spiritual adviser. Robert Woods referred to her as "the gentle Jane," and Graham Taylor, founder of Chicago Commons and perhaps the most sentimental of the ministers in the movement, wrote to her in appreciation: "Personally your generous friendship has been to me one of the *three* sources of inspiration, courage and hope through the three years of the most serious spiritual conflict, severe struggle and incessant toil which have fallen to my lot." By transforming Jane Addams into a spiritual leader the young ministers discovered a way to deal with the young, attractive and aggressive woman without feeling threatened by her.[5]

After a trip in 1893 in which she visited settlements in Boston, New York, and Philadelphia she wrote to her sister: "I find I am considered quite the grandmother of American Settlements." It was a role she enjoyed playing, but she also served as the informal executive secretary of the movement as well. She was a constant source of information about the various settlement houses. She recommended head residents, placed young workers, and gave advice to the struggling houses.

The settlement workers had a strong sense of being pioneers during the first decade. They passionately believed that their methods and ideas were superior to those of the charity organizations, and the other social movements that were springing up around the country. They acted almost as if they belonged to a religious order. They called each other "Brother Woods," "Sister Kelley," and "Sister Addams," though very quickly Addams was treated as something special and called "Lady Jane." Lillian Wald, of Henry Street Settlement, in trying to express how much her friendship with Jane meant said: "We want to be good and like children look up to you for guidance." And Mary McDowell who had gone from Hull House to become head resident at the University of Chicago Settlement wrote: "The Love I have for you has grown stronger every day since I first knew you and Hull House, and is a motive power in my life. . . . It seems always that you reflect for me the Christ spirit as no one else does and I am braver after I have thought of you." She accepted the honors and thrived on them. When she was at the Paris Exposition in 1900, she discovered that she was considered a veteran by all the settlement people, "and [I] find myself a little assured by it."

Even with honors of all kinds bestowed upon her she needed this reassurance; she was happiest and did her best work when she was confident that she was surrounded by adoring disciples.[6] But not all of the settlement workers saw her as a mother-figure; some even resented her special position in the movement. Some of the leaders in Boston and New York feared what they saw as the undue dominance of Chicago, especially after *The Commons*, a journal published at Chicago Commons, became the unofficial magazine of the settlements. There were occasional arguments over when and where settlement conferences should be held, whether or not the workers should meet with the National Conference of Charities and Corrections or separately, whether they should meet on a country estate or in the city, and over what role religion should play in their deliberations. They even argued and debated whether or not to use the name "university settlement" or simply "social settlement" and whether a settlement should appeal primarily to one neighborhood, or to the whole city.[7]

Jane Addams had her own opinions and at one conference she interrupted Robert Woods, who was preaching his idea of neighborhood revival, by blurting out, "Mr. Woods, I do not believe in geographical salvation." Usually, however, she avoided the appearance of taking sides in a debate, and because of her unique position and talents for conciliation she was looked to by all sides to solve difficulties, to calm the angered factions. She was most often effective. Mary Richmond, General Secretary of the Baltimore Charity Society, and a pioneer in social case work, attended a settlement conference in 1899. She was shocked that some of the "gushing clergymen" persisted in calling Jane Addams "a nineteenth-century saint," but she was impressed with her skill as a compromiser and mediator.[8]

These same skills proved useful in the hustle and bustle of the daily activities at Hull House. As its reputation spread, the settlement became a favorite place to visit. It was, Henry Demarest Lloyd once remarked, "the best club in Chicago," and its guest book soon read like a *Who's Who*. In the first few years, settlement workers from other cities were frequent guests: Robert Woods, Lillian Wald, Jean Fine, James Reynolds, Helena Dudley, and many others came for a long or a short time. Social gospel ministers, like George Herron, and municipal reformers like "Golden Rule" Jones stopped for a few days. There were also foreign visitors. William Stead, the British editor and journalist, came to Chicago for the Columbian Exposition, but stayed to inspect the rest of the city. He visited the tenements, brothels, and flop houses and dropped by Hull House late at night to sip hot chocolate and talk to the settlement workers about his experiences. Later he went home to put some of his indignation into a book that became an immediate best seller, *If Christ Came to Chicago*. "The best hope for Chicago is the multiplications of Hull Houses into all the slum districts of the city," he decided.[9]

Many others came to visit during the first decade. Canon and Mrs. Samuel Barnett from Toynbee Hall; British Labor leaders Kier Hardie, and John Burns; Sidney and Beatrice Webb, the British Fabian Socialists, Aylmer Maude, the translator and disciple of Tolstoy; and Prince Kropotkin, the Russian anarchist. William Hard wrote that, "through the Hull House drawing-rooms there passes a procession of Greek fruit venders, university professors, mayors, aldermen, club-women, factory inspectors, novelists, reporters, policemen, Italian washerwomen, socialists looking hungrily for all persons yet unconverted, big businessmen finding the solution of the industrial problem in small parts, English members of Parliament, German scientists, and all other sorts and conditions of men from the river wards of the city of Chicago and from the far corners of the five continents." He called Hull House Jane Addams' "salon of democracy." She was always the gracious hostess; other residents were assigned the task of "toting" the visitors around the house or around the city, but she presided with charm and efficiency at the head of one of the long tables in the dining room, dispensing soup and salad and scintillating conversation. She treated the great, the near-great, and the unknown with the same spirit, and she organized receptions and lectures with skill and ease. Not all of the visitors appreciated her efforts. While Beatrice Webb found Jane herself "gentle and dignified [and] shrewdly observant," she characterized the group she met at Hull House as "all those queer, well-intentioned or cranky individuals."[10]

It was not quite an accurate picture. The settlement did attract its share of cranks, but it also became the meeting place for a new kind of scholar interested in studying the city. Jane Addams had consciously rejected a career in college teaching, and when she came to Chicago she carefully cultivated connections with clergymen and religious leaders in the city. But colleges were changing rapidly in the 1880's and 1890's. From her vantage point in the slums of Chicago she found herself a witness to the emergence of the first American universities, and a participant in the development of the fields of sociology and political economy. She preferred the term "social settlement" to "university settlement," but Hull House, within the first few years became a social laboratory for several universities, and she became almost an adjunct professor.

Hull House was founded three years before the University of Chicago was established, but within a few months after William R. Harper's institution on the South Side opened for its first semester a number of the distinguished professors there discovered the settlement. John Dewey, already a distinguished philosopher and psychologist in 1892, stopped for a few days even before he agreed to accept a position at the university. "I cannot tell you how much good I got from my stay at Hull House," he wrote to Jane Addams. "My indebtedness to you for giving me an insight into matters there is great. While I did not see much of any particular thing I think I got a pretty good idea of the general spirit and method. Every day I stayed there only added to my conviction that you had taken the right way." After he moved to Chicago, he became a regular visitor; he lectured at Julia Lathrop's Plato Club, and spoke to the University extension classes. Sometimes he came just to have dinner and to talk with the exciting mixture of people that always gathered there. In 1897 he became one of the trustees of the settlement. When his eight-year-old son died unexpectedly while he was abroad, the memorial service was held at Hull House and Jane Addams officiated. His daughter, named after Jane Addams, once remarked that "Dewey's faith in democracy as a guiding force in education took on both a sharper and deeper meaning because of Hull House and Jane Addams."

Dewey himself repeatedly used Hull House and a few other settlements as models for what he hoped schools would become, but it was a reciprocal relationship and Addams and the other residents learned a lot from him. He made them realize the implications of some of their programs and experiments.[11]

Not many of the scholars and professors who visited Hull House became as important to the development of the settlement as Dewey, but he was not alone. Sociologist Albion Small and economist Edward Bemis as well as George Mead, Charles Henderson, and others from the University of Chicago, were among those who came to visit or to take part in the discussions or lecture series. There was also Charles Zueblin, social gospel minister and pioneer sociologist, who was inspired by his contact with Hull House to found Northwestern University Settlement not far away.[12]

The two most important scholars, however, who participated in making Hull House a center for urban research and social reform were Henry Demarest Lloyd and Richard T. Ely. Each man in a different way introduced Jane Addams to a wider world of scholarship and reform. Lloyd was a brilliant journalist and muckraker, a crusader against special privilege, and a political activist. He had married the daughter of one of the owners of the *Chicago Tribune,* which gave him financial security as well as contacts among the wealthy and social elite in the city. But he preferred the company of labor leaders, radicals, and reform politicians. He quickly became interested in Hull House and proved a valuable friend and ally until his death in 1903. He introduced Jane Addams to

Clarence Darrow and to Governor John Peter Altgeld, but he also made sure that she met labor leaders, radicals, and an assorted group of writers and politicians. Lloyd's home in Winnetka became almost an annex to the settlement; there a temporary home for Florence Kelley's children was found when she moved to Chicago, and there, too, a number of residents repaired for a weekend of relaxation away from the turmoil and excitement of the neighborhood around Hull House. Lloyd could be depended upon to support a research project, to give money for the working girls' cooperative residence, to deliver a speech, or to make a key visit to a politician. He helped move Jane Addams and the other residents into the arena of politics and labor.[13]

Richard T. Ely, political economist, persuasive advocate of the social gospel, and academic entrepreneur, had graduated from Columbia and Heidelberg and had been a professor at Johns Hopkins University until 1892. At that time he went to the University of Wisconsin. He was one of the founders of the American Economic Association, and a prolific writer and lecturer on economic and social problems. He had become acquainted with Florence Kelley as early as 1890 while she was living in New York. They began a lively correspondence that covered the range of social problems, but was primarily a running debate over socialist theory and practice.[14]

When Ely moved to Madison, Wisconsin, in the fall of 1892, Florence Kelley was quick to introduce him to Jane Addams and the rest of the Hull House group, and Ely urged them to begin systematic social investigations and to publish their findings. Florence Kelley, however, had plunged into the work of social investigation almost from the moment she had arrived in Chicago. It was her investigations and Ely's encouragement that led to the first of many books produced at the settlement—*Hull-House Maps and Papers.*

In the spring of 1892 Mrs. Kelley was appointed a special agent for the State Bureau of Labor Statistics to conduct an investigation of the sweating trade in Chicago. "The greater part of the investigation is now completed and there remain 10,000 schedules to be filled in by 'sweaters' victims' in the clothing trades," she wrote to Friedrich Engels in May 1892. "They are Poles, Bohemians, Neapolitans, Sicilians and Russian Hebrews, almost excluding all other nationalities. . . . The municipal arrangements are so wretched that the filth and overcrowding are worse than I have seen outside of Naples and the East Side of New York. In the ward in which I live, the Nineteenth, with 7,000 children of school age (6-14 inclusive), there are but 2579 school sittings, and everything municipal is of the same sort. This aggrevates the economic conditions greatly, making possible child labor in most cruel forms and rendering the tenement house manufacture of clothing a deadly danger to the whole community."[15]

Jane Addams' letters from the same period do not report on social conditions, except for vague mention of the poverty in the neighborhood. She was more interested in art exhibits, lectures and the building plans for the settlement. But Florence Kelley had a different background and different concerns, and she gradually influenced the Hull House founder. In July 1892 Carroll D. Wright, the Commissioner of Labor, appointed Mrs. Kelley special agent to take part in a national investigation of city slums, and in January 1893 the State of Illinois appointed another commission to study the situation in Chicago. "The Commission had been intended as a sop to labor and a sinecure, a protracted junket to Chicago for a number of rural legislators," she explained years later. "Our overwhelming hospitality and devotion to the thoroughness and success of their investigation, by personally conducted visits to sweatshops, though irksome in the extreme to the lawgivers, ended in a report compendius, so readable, so surprising that they presented it with pride to the legislature."

This report, plus some shrewd lobbying by Florence Kelley and some of the other members of the Hull House group, led to the passage of the Illinois Factory Act of 1893, and the newly elected governor, John Peter Altgeld, appointed her the Chief Factory Inspector. The drive to eliminate sweating labor and to limit the employment of children in industry was exhilarating at first, though it ultimately failed. But out of the various investigations came the idea for a book patterned after Charles Booth's *Labour and Life of the People of London*, the first scientific and systematic attempt to study a poor section of a great city. The Hull House residents' plan was to survey the neighborhood block by block, house by house, to determine nationality and income. The project was a cooperative one, with most of the residents working on it in one way or another, but Kelley rather than Addams was the driving force behind the idea. Most of the work was done in the summer of 1893, and built on the surveys and investigations already conducted by Mrs. Kelley.[16]

Multi-color maps depicted the results of the door-to-door survey of the population living in a third of a square mile near Hull House. "The Italians, the Russians and Polish Jews, and the Bohemians lead in numbers and importance," the settlement workers explained. "The Irish control the polls; while the Germans, although they make up more than a third of Chicago's population, are not very numerous in this neighborhood; and the Scandinavians, who fill northwest Chicago are a mere handful. Several Chinese in basement laundries, a dozen Arabians, about as many Greeks, a few Syrians, and seven Turks engaged in various occupations at the World's Fair give a cosmopolitan flavor to the region." The wage maps covered the same areas indicating income per dwelling place. Six categories ranging from $5 a week to over $20 were used, and they discovered that most of their neighbors fell in the $5 to $10 range. There were also articles on the Bohemians, the Italians, the Chicago Ghetto. Ellen Starr had an essay on "Art and Labor," Julia Lathrop contributed a piece on "Cook County Charities," and Jane Addams had an article on "The Settlement as a Factor in the Labor Movement." The best and most hard hitting articles were the two by Florence Kelley on the "Sweating System," and with Alzina Stevens as coauthor, "Wage Earning Children."[17]

Some of the residents jokingly called the project, "the jumble book" and there was a certain amount of truth to the charge, but it was a pioneer effort, the first attempt to study a working-class neighborhood in an American city. Ely was impressed enough with the articles and the maps to urge his publisher, Thomas Y. Crowell, to publish *Hull-House Maps and Papers* as one of a series, the Library of Economics and Politics, which he edited. The book, however, had a difficult birth. There were delays while the various authors finished their articles, and then when the editors saw the complicated maps they balked. In November 1894 when the proofs were finally received, Kelley wrote in anger to Ely: "I am, of course, disappointed at the delay in getting out the book after I held back my essays from the *Archiv fur sozial Gesetzgebung* because you wrote me in May that the book would be in the market last Sept. But the disappointment over the delay is trivial in comparison with the dismay which I felt when you suggested cutting the maps. This I positively decline to permit. The charts are mine to the extent that I not only furnished the data for them but hold the sole permission from the U.S. department of labor to publish them."[18]

Ely apparently exploded in anger, for Jane Addams stepped in to play her familiar role as conciliator. "I am very sorry indeed that you were subjected to any annoyance," she wrote, "for I assure you that we all appreciate very highly the generous amount of time and care you have given to the editing of the work. Mrs. Kelley has been getting out her an-

nual report and has been very much driven by her work. In addition to
this she is having her annual struggle with the small pox and the apathy
of the manufacturers in regard to it. I have no doubt that accumulated
annoyances appeared in her letter to you, which I regret more than I can
say . . . but I assure you that our feeling of gratitude to our Editor has
never changed. It would doubtless have been impossible to have induced
Crowell or any other publisher to take the book without your name and
aid."[19] A few days later she wrote another conciliatory letter to Ely and
doubtless calmed the irate Kelley as well. The book finally appeared in
1895, with the maps expensively reproduced and folded in the covers
just as Florence Kelley had demanded. It was well received by the few
reviewers who noticed but it sold very badly, less than a thousand copies,
and it soon went out of print.[20]

Hull-House Maps and Papers stimulated further research on Chicago
and other cities, and although Jane Addams was only one author in a
cooperative venture, it helped her see herself as a writer and scholar, and
part of the newly developing field of sociology. Urban sociology especially was closely related in its inception to the social gospel movement,
the social settlements, and social reform. Hull House became a sociological laboratory where young instructors and graduate students could
combine research with social work. When Albion Small began the
American Journal of Sociology in 1895 he announced the connection
between thought and action, between scholarship and reform. It was no
accident that Jane Addams had an article in one of the first issues and
that other essays researched and written at Hull House found their way
into the early volume.[21] Addams read the books in her field as they
came out, Woods' book on *English Social Movement*, Amos Warner's
American Charities; Henry Demarest Lloyd's *Wealth Against Common-
wealth*, books and articles by Ely, and the stream of material being produced by British scholars and social critics—Beatrice and Sidney Webb,
John Hobson, Octavia Hill, Patrick Geddes, and many others. She welcomed all kinds of scholars and reformers to Hull House and eagerly
visited with many experts and writers when she traveled to Boston, New
York, or Madison on speaking engagements. When she and Mary Smith
were in London in 1896 she planned carefully to see all the important
scholars and reformers. "We buy a good deal of literature and 'cram up'
before we meet the folks who have written the books," she admitted to
Ellen Starr, but she managed to impress the likes of James Byrce, John
Hobson, John Burns, the Webbs, and Mrs. Humphrey Ward."[22]

Jane Addams learned from those around her; she had the ability to change and develop, and she had some truly outstanding teachers. She was influenced by Dewey and Ely, John Ruskin, Leo Tolstoy and Patrick Geddes; but essentially she learned from her own observation and experience. She became convinced that environment was more important than heredity. She believed that if you provided decent housing, better parks and playgrounds, and good schools it was possible to produce better citizens, although occasionally, like Dewey, she was not clear whether she wanted to help the immigrants and workers to adjust to their environment and their jobs, or whether she wanted to transform society. She was optimistic about the future of the country; she had a romantic faith in immigrants and ordinary citizens, although, like everyone else of her generation, she occasionally fell into the habit of using racial stereotypes. She fit Henry May's description of those progressives "who wanted to make a number of sharp changes because they were so confident in the basic rightness of things as they were." After the first year she gave up her emphasis on Christian social reform, but she kept the sense of mission and a secularized version of the goal of building the Kingdom of God on earth. She became a social justice progressive, more concerned with passing child labor laws, improving housing, and making the city a better place to live, than with regulating trusts. She was less interested in a search for order than in a quest for peace and justice, less interested in a cult of efficiency, than in a search for community.[23]

She came to think of herself as a scholar, even as a sociologist. She liked to speak on college campuses, and even agreed to give a series of lectures at the University of Chicago and another at the University of Wisconsin, but she resisted all attempts to make her a permanent member of any university faculty. Ely encouraged her to work on her material and to publish it in book form. She referred to him on one occasion as her "sociological grandfather," and in many ways he was responsible for making her a published scholar. She was certainly a sociologist by the rather loose definition used during her time, but although she carefully cultivated her scholarly contacts and reputation, she was always more than a sociologist, always more than a scholar. Jenkin Lloyd Jones appreciated this—he called Jane Addams "the sage of the Hull House," and "the Sanest head among students of sociology on the American Continent."[24]

Her national reputation was based not so much on her scholarship as on her position as sage and saint. In the beginning it was her speaking more than her writing which publicized Hull House and extended her influence. She had begun to speak in and around Chicago even before moving to Hull House, but she soon extended her field of action and by 1894 was accepting engagements from Boston to San Francisco. She spoke at Vassar, Wellesley, Smith, Mt. Holyoke, Wisconsin, Indiana, Knox, and gave the commencement address at Western Reserve University in Cleveland. *The Springfield Republican* proudly announced, after her speeches at the Plymouth Conference, that it was "good to see Chicago thus instructing the wise women of the East" and suggested that she was "essentially and characteristically an Illinois woman, with the quiet force of her sex, but also with the invincible energy for which Chicago is noted."[25]

Most of those who heard her early speeches emphasized not so much her forcefulness as her gentleness, her sincerity, her femininity, and her conviction. "The name of this woman stands as the synonym of the best type of womanhood," The *Philadelphia American* wrote. "Miss Addams is a sweet-faced, low-voiced woman, slight in figure with clear, tender eyes and a quiet dignified manner. . . ." "Jane Addams is a woman of indomitable energy and persistence, of enthusiasm and adaptability; intellectually she is strong and possesses a keen sense of humor . . . she is a slender, delicate, pink-cheeked woman with a face as fine as a cameo and a manner unassuming and attractive."[26]

Most of the writers and reporters, trying to describe Jane Addams, and to explain her popularity and purpose, came up with some combination of practicality and spirituality. The 1890's witnessed the gradual emergence of the "New Woman" whose image of boldness, radiant vigor, and interest in athletics contrasted dramatically with the languor, gentleness, and submissiveness of the genteel Victorian lady. The image of Jane Addams in the 1890's and well into the twentieth century was a combination and an accommodation of the two images, the new woman and the Victorian lady.

Although, as a young woman in the early days of Hull House Jane Addams was slender and attractive, no reporter described her as sensuous or sexually desirable or hinted that she might make someone a good wife. She was the epitome of the nineteenth-century heroine who had "never had a selfish thought," who was "wonderfully gentle" and sexually pure and innocent, and thus in a sense superior to men. Her public image in the 1890s became part of what Leslie Fiedler has called the Sentimental

Love Religion which taught that women, especially a few unusual
women, were absolutely pure and could themselves do Christ's work in
this world.[27] Some observers saw in her an "almost indescribable personal magnetism." Or they commented that "The girls at Hull House
buy photographs of Botticelli's pictures because his madonnas bear a
striking resemblance to their beloved Miss Addams." Some as early as
1893 were calling her "Saint Jane." A writer in the *Christian Union*
described a man so impressed with her sympathy and understanding for
the poor that he wanted to "touch the hem of her garment and gain a
little of that spirit."[28]

The praise and adoration came not only in the newspapers and magazines, but also in letters from friends and from women she had never
met expressing "love and admiration and gratitude for you and your
life," suggesting that she stood for Christ and for goodness in a "narrow
and selfish and artificial life."[29] Some of the neighborhood women
treated her as if she were a saint. Many of the immigrants living
near Hull House during the first decade, especially those from Italy,
had come from a peasant society where primitive myths and ceremonies
mixed with Catholicism to form a religion filled with superstition and
the worship of saints and madonnas. The madonna cult interpreted the
Virgin not so much as the mother of God as a miracle worker. In southern Italy, for example, there were hundreds of local madonnas each protecting a particular village or having a special power to cure a headache
or bring a good harvest. Many of the peasant women in the neighborhood, cut off from their native land and desperately searching for help
in adjusting to the strange city, viewed Jane Addams as a miracle worker.
Not all Italians, of course, treated her as a madonna. Indeed, one Italian
newspaper, disturbed that an anti-clerical club met at Hull House, denounced her as "Mother Jane Addams, the professional humanitarian
and patron saint of anti-Catholic bigotry in the city."[30]

There was always some criticism and a great deal of indifference, but
there was also praise and adoration, and that was important, for the
public approval gave her confidence and a sense that what she was doing
was important. She carefully preserved the most laudatory letters, and
clipped the sentimental and fawning articles, putting them in envelopes
which she carefully marked "Articles about J. A." She kept a scrapbook
of the early accounts about Hull House and about her own activities,
and assigned one of the young residents to keep it up to date. Very soon
after the founding of the settlement she subscribed to a clipping service

(paid for by Mary R. Smith) so that she might not miss any of the articles or newspaper accounts of her accomplishments. Within a few years the volume of clippings was overwhelming, and she enlisted her sister Alice to keep them in some order.

All celebrities and public figures in a sense become victims of their public image, and inevitably the public image affects the real person. But Jane Addams seems to have been especially dependent on the news clippings and the assurances of friends and strangers that she was doing well; that she was somehow special, even saintly. One would have expected that she might have laughed at the idea of her special "spirituality," but except at the very beginning there is no evidence that she did. Florence Kelley said to her on one occasion, "Do you know what I would do if that woman calls you a saint again? I'd show her my teeth, and if that didn't convince her, I would bite her." She revealed no inclination to bite those who called her "Saint," no desire to discourage the adoration.[31]

Another related role she came to play increasingly as time went on was that of priestess, and teacher. Very soon after the opening of Hull House she was frequently invited to fill in for Protestant ministers and she occasionally accepted, replacing men like Jenkin Lloyd Jones in his pulpit on Sunday morning. She was also constantly called upon to officiate at funerals and at weddings. In her autobiography she confessed that she was "constantly bewildered" by these requests and by the "curious confessions" made to me by total strangers. She did not act bewildered, however, but seemed comfortable in her role of teacher-priestess. She talked and wrote of the mysteries of life, the terror of death, and even published late in her life, a collection of her funeral orations. But it was not so much what she said as who she was. She decided that "for many people without church affiliations the vague humanitarianism the settlement represented was the nearest approach they could find to an expression of their religious sentiments." But it was not so much the settlement as it was its head resident who for mysterious reasons seemed to satisfy the desire of many different kinds of people who had lost faith in religion, and perhaps in American democracy. She fulfilled the need for a female religious figure—a saint, a madonna, even a Protestant virgin.[32]

The image of a self-effacing, self sacrificing, spiritual woman helping the poor with gentle compassion from her post in the slums, an image of herself which Jane Addams did not resist, is especially ironic because it left out the very habits of mind and traits of personality that led Hull House to success and made of its founder, in addition, a practical reformer and celebrity. In actuality Jane Addams was an expert executive with a shrewd business sense, an able organizer and fund raiser, a persuasive writer and public speaker who also had a genius for compromise and conciliation. She had carefully cultivated the ability to listen, to remember names, to give her undivided attention to the person she was speaking to at the moment. Throughout her life this carefully trained ability won her many friends. But perhaps most crucial in her success at Hull House was her upper-class background. She was able to obtain gifts of money and service from the well-to-do and social elite in Chicago in part because she was one of them. She was just as persuasive, although perhaps not as much at ease with the business and professional men who became important supporters of Hull House.

One of those supporters was Helen Culver, the owner of the building. She contributed a large amount of money and property to Hull House, and became one of the most ardent backers of the settlement. But she was a forceful woman with a shrewd business sense and there were inevitably moments of misunderstanding and disagreement that required Addams' most careful diplomacy. The original agreement entered into on May 16, 1889, called for rent of $60 a month, but Miss Culver also contributed some money as well as repairs and a new furnace to the venture. In the spring of 1890 Jane asked her if she would not contribute two bathrooms and also make repairs to the porch and basement, but instead she sent a check for $100. "I am somewhat embarrassed by the receipt of the check you sent the other day," Jane wrote, "I asked for the bathroom as a contribution to our work, but hoped you would repair the piazza and cellar in your capacity as landlord. We have appealed to Mrs. Field for the bathroom, but you doubtless understand how impossible it is to ask other people to repair property which does not belong to them. Our friends are extremely generous to us in regard to the money we use for pleasure and benefit of our neighbors, but we found when we asked them to put in the furnace how differently they felt. Twice those who gave liberally insisted that they were playing the part of landlord and not of philanthropist." After explaining all that she herself had spent on the house she said that she could use her own money to repair the cellar, and have the porch torn down as the cheapest way of dealing with the problem, even though it would "sacrifice the new roof they had put on last fall and destroy the character of the house." Miss Culver responded sharply. She cited the terms of the lease which provided that the "party of the second part is to pay water tax and make all repairs," and then continued: 'I regret that my benevolent purpose represented by gifts amounting to about $350.oo have been productive only of disappointment, and judging from your note, of an impression among your acquaintances that I sustain toward your enterprise the relation of delinquent landlady."[33]

Jane immediately responded, trying to pacify her: "Our relations have always been so frank that it seemed to me possible to tell you just what I was able to do and hope you would help accomplish it," she began. "The entire office of asking for money is new to me and I am afraid I do not do it well. . . . I regret being obliged to trouble you once again but of course we will do nothing to the piazza until we know your pleasure concerning it. I hope you will not consider me ungrateful for the one hundred dollars because I somewhat frankly showed I had hoped for something else."

The careful diplomacy, the patient cajoling worked, for a few weeks later Miss Culver not only made the repairs, but extended the lease rent free. Ellen reported the good news to her sister: "Miss Culver has given us the house rent free for four years, amounting to $2,800, & we have decided to call the house Hull-House. Connect those two facts in any delicate way your refined imagination suggests.[34]

Helen Culver continued to extend the lease, turned over much of the adjacent property and finally gave it all to Hull House, but she had to be pampered and persuaded. She would hold out for a high price for a piece of land; Jane would go to see her and after a long talk she would usually come down to a reasonable price or give it away. In 1895 she gave a million dollars to the University of Chicago and the newspapers carried the story that the land and buildings leased to Hull House would become the property of the University, and that had to be laboriously straightened out. Over the years Helen Culver was an important if sometimes exasperating benefactor, but it was the tact and patience of Jane Addams which sustained the difficult relationship.[35]

There were other important donors. Mary Rozet Smith provided money for the children's building and was always ready to make up a deficit or start a new program. Mrs. Joseph Bowen, the largest single donor, provided nearly three quarters of a million dollars over a period of years. Then there were the Colvins, the Cranes, the Wilmarths, Edward Butler, Julius Rosenwald, and many others. The settlement grew and expanded, in fact, like a medieval manor house, it was always in a state of metamorphosis. At first there was only one building, but soon additional structures were errected, and the existing one remodeled. An art gallery was added in 1891, a coffee house and gymnasium in 1893, a special building in 1898 for the Jane Club—a cooperative girls' residence, and a new coffee house and theatre in 1899. The Hull House complex was not completed until 1907. There were thirteen buildings sprawling over a large city block. Two alleys divided the buildings into one large and two small groups. The maze of structures which bordered Halsted Street were all interconnected, though it took some experience to negotiate the labyrinth of halls, corridors, and stairs without getting lost. A central heating plant, installed early in the century, served all the buildings, and a courtyard lent charm and a parklike atmosphere.

The complicated and expensive task of building, maintaining, and operating the buildings and running the settlement programs, which ranged from clubs and classes to a music school, a pottery, a bookbindery, and a summer camp, required funds which were provided largely by gifts. The residents, who in the early twentieth century sometimes numbered as many as 70, all paid for their room and board, but there was always a constant need for money. In 1903 Jane Addams estimated that she would need $26,554.10 to run the house and its programs; $12,634.94 would come from income, from the coffee shop, rents, etc. The remaining $14,119.16 would have to be raised through contributions; of this $9200 was pledged leaving $4919.60 to be secured, most of it from small donors.[36]

Not all the other donors required the careful handling of Helen Culver, but each had his own foibles and vulnerable spots. Over the years Anita McCormick Blaine, the daughter of Cyrus McCormick and the widow of the son of James G. Blaine, and a active reformer in her own right, gave a large amount of money to the settlement, but each year she had to be reminded, by letter and phone. "I am embarrassed to ask for your annual contribution so early in the year," a typical letter from Jane Addams went, "but owing to some changes in our shops and the need of more equipment we are facing the new term with a deficit and would be most grateful if you could find it possible to send your generous five hundred dollars this month." Finally she discovered that the most effective way to get the contribution from Mrs. Blaine was to send a telegram. All of this took an immense amount of time, of course; she wrote hundreds of letters soliciting money and thanking people for their contributions. There was a standing joke among her friends that they never received more than a one-page letter from her. Part of the reason was that she wrote so many one-page letters to strangers asking for money or thanking them for contributions.

As the settlement grew its programs became more complex and so did its finances. There were constant negotiations with builders and architects, continuing problems with hiring help for the coffee shop, supervising the purchase of supplies, keeping the relief account separate from the playground account, and the kindergarten money from being confused with the rent money paid by each resident. "I feel a little like a battered business agent," she admitted at one point.[37]

In 1895, Hull House was formally incorporated and a Board of Trustees appointed, including Mary Smith, Allen Pond, and William Colvin; very soon John Dewey and Mrs. Bowen were added. Yet even with the board Addams still managed things. She was re-elected President of the Hull House Association year after year, as well as head resident of the settlement. For years she served as treasurer as well. Although she was able to delegate some matters, a great many details and decisions she kept in her head. John Dewey was only exaggerating a little when he remarked much later that the chief responsibility of the board was to say to Miss Addams, "You are all right: go ahead."[38]

And go ahead she did balancing and manipulating, organizing and conciliating.

The public image of Jane Addams as a gentle angel of mercy, a lady bountiful bent on aiding the lowly, had some remote basis in fact, but an accurate picture of her must include the shrewd business woman, the expert fund raiser and publicity agent, as well as the careful compromiser. Without these talents Hull House would have been a failure and Jane Addams would not have become a national celebrity.

VII

Jane Addams — Reformer

HAT is perhaps the most outstanding fact in the temperament of Miss Addams is revealed only indirectly in her autobiography: it may be called the passion of conciliation," Floyd Dell declared. "No one would call Miss Addams 'implacable'. . . . "She has never ceased to be supremely reasonable."[1] It was this habit of mind deeply ingrained in her personality from her childhood and family background and her college experience that prevented her from becoming the impassioned advocate of any cause; she was too accustomed to see both sides as partly right, and to spend her energy seeking an accommodation between them. Or she would take a step back from the heat of the conflict and explain the significance and implication of events. She became a publicist and a philosopher of reform, but because she sought the reasonable middle ground she never became a radical and she left herself open to attack, from both sides.

Her attitudes and action toward organized labor are a case in point. She knew nothing of the problems of working men and women, nothing of the horrors of child labor, before moving to Hull House. She had never heard of scabs and lockouts and blacklisting, but she was quickly educated by Mary Kenny, Alzina Stevens, Florence Kelley, Henry Demarest Lloyd, and by the events that erupted in her neighborhood. She had great sympathy for the workers. She defended their right to organize, yet she deplored strikes and violence, and hated the pettiness and corruption which she detected in some labor organization. "It is only occasionally that I get a glimpse of the chivalry of labor," she admitted to Lloyd, "so much of the time it seems so sordid."[2] She rejected class conflict, and saw labor unions as an instrument to promote brotherhood. She stood for arbitration, for compromise, for the passage of legislation to improve the worker's lot. Although she defended labor in many speeches and articles she never followed the logic of her position to march in the picket lines as did Ellen Starr, nor was she as aggressive and consistent in support of labor's cause as Florence Kelley. Still she was denounced as a socialist or an anarchist by many because she dared to speak out in defense of labor, and to suggest that the working man and woman had some basic rights that were being denied them by American business.

Several unions met at Hull House with her blessing, and labor leaders of all kinds were frequent visitors at the settlement. She learned from them and she tried to teach the American people what it was like to be a laborer, to sell one's strength by the hour. When she spoke of the problem of domestic servants it was not to denounce their inefficiency, or to comment on the difficulty of finding servants who were loyal (the topic of many tea time conversations among society women in the 1890s). Instead she explained to her upper-class audience why most girls preferred employment in a factory to working in a home. As a domestic servant "she is isolated from the people with whom she has been reared, with whom she has gone to school, with whom she has danced and among whom she expects to live when she marries. . . . she is naturally lonely and constrained."[3]

Jane Addams had greater difficulty establishing a feeling of empathy for the workingman than she did for working women and children, but she tried. She explained the resentment of the striking worker for the scab. "Let us put ourselves in the position of the striking men who have fallen upon workmen who have taken their places," she suggested. "The strikers have for years belonged to an organization devoted to securing better wages and a higher standard of living, not only for themselves, but for all men in their trade. . . . They honestly believe, whether they are right or wrong, that their position is exactly the same which a nation, in time of war, takes toward a traitor who has deserted his country's camp for the enemy . . . we regard the treatment accorded to the deserter with much less horror than the same treatment when it is accorded to the 'scab', largely because in one instance we as citizens are participants, and in the other we allow ourselves to stand aside."[4]

But when a violent strike broke out, Jane Addams preferred to stand aside and interpret rather than to get involved in the fray. The first major strike which interfered with the daily routine at Hull House was the Pullman Strike of 1894. The employees of the Pullman Palace Car Company lived in a model town nine miles south of Chicago. The head of the company, George M. Pullman, was proud of the town which had a library, churches, stores, recreational facilities, and landscaped parks, but rents and services were high, most of the apartments had no bathtub, there was only one water faucet for every five units, and the workers had no choice but to live in the feudal domain.[5]

During the depression of 1893 a number of employees were laid off and those remaining saw their pay reduced, with no corresponding drop in their rent. Pullman refused to listen to the grievances of the workers, but the American Railway Union, newly organized by Eugene Debs, listened and began to organize the Pullman workers. In June when three members of the grievance committee were laid off, the union called a strike. They demanded arbitration within five days, and when that failed to materilize, they called a boycott ordering all members to "cut out" Pullman cars from trains. The railroads retaliated by firing any railway employee who took part in the boycott, but the American Railway Union was not easily put down by the threats. When someone was fired for cutting out a Pullman Car the whole train crew quit. The entire national rail system was brought close to a standstill. Eugene Debs, the tall, gaunt, young leader of the Railway Union was catapulted into national prominence. He was denounced as a criminal, anarchist, and lunatic. *The New York Times* called him a "lawbreaker at large, an enemy of the race." Class warfare seemed eminent in America.

Several groups and individuals tried to mediate the differences, to restore order and peace. The newly organized Civic Federation of Chicago appointed an investigating committee which it hoped would find out the facts and arbitrate the strike. Jane Addams was one of the six members of this committee. When the managers refused to see the whole group, she went to Pullman on her own and discovered that there were some real causes for the discontent, that among other things rents were too high, and the cost of services exorbitant. She suggested that an impartial board be appointed to investigate the grievances. The Pullman officials, however, would not even consider the suggestion, and told her it was none of her business.

Meanwhile the Managers Association imported strikebreakers from Canada and convinced United States Attorney General Richard Olney to swear in 3400 deputies to keep the trains running. Clashes between strikers and deputies occurred and some railway property was destroyed. An appeal to President Cleveland brought four companies of federal troops. Still the strike continued, and violence and looting spread, although the newspaper headlines such as the *Washington Post*'s "Chicago Is at the Mercy of the Incendiary's Torch," or the *Chicago Tribune*'s "Strike is Now War," were greatly exaggerated. On July 2, 1894, Olney obtained a blanket injunction forbidding any person from interfering with the mails. Debs and three of his assistants were arrested on a charge of conspiracy to obstruct the mails. They were released on bail but within a week rearrested for contempt of court and Debs was sentenced to six months in prison.

Hull House was immediately involved in the strike and its aftermath. While Debs was out on bail Alzina Stevens and Florence Kelley shielded him from the press and public while he went on a colossal drinking spree. Kelley also set out to organize a mass meeting to raise money for his defense. "Debs is in jail," she wrote to Lloyd, "and his courage, while not failing needs all the bracing it can get. And the length of his imprisonment may, perhaps, be modified by the degree of public interest shown in the present injunction outrage." She discovered, however, that most people did not want to be associated with Debs. They refused to give money or to appear publicly in his behalf, or they begged off with one excuse or another. Then she learned that the Central Music Hall, the best place in the city to hold a meeting, was mysteriously under repair and unavailable.[6]

Florence Kelley makes no mention of Jane Addams' reaction to the idea of a mass meeting or to Debs' imprisonment. Jane's sister, Mary, died during the middle of the crisis so she was otherwise occupied. But mass protests were not her style. Instead, after her attempt at conciliation failed, she wrote a speech on the implications of the strike. She gave it at the Chicago Woman's Club, the Twentieth Century Club of Boston, and at several other places. Her protest was not as direct or as dramatic as was Florence Kelley's; it was subtle and oblique, but she did protest. She also tried to educate the American people about the meaning and implications of the conflict.

To illuminate the crisis she compared the industrial situation to the family relationship, the indulgent employer with the indulgent parent. (Almost all her early essays in one way or another relate to family conflicts.) Then she suggested a similarity between the tragedy of Shakespeare's King Lear and George Pullman. Just as King Lear thought he was giving a great deal to his daughter, so Pullman thought he was a generous benefactor to his employees, but the "end to be obtained became ultimately commercial and not social," for the benefit of Pullman not his workers. Pullman could not appreciate why his workers were not satisfied with what he had provided for them. Of course the labor movement also had its faults; "that the movement was ill-directed, that it was ill-timed and disastrous in results, that it stirred up and became confused in the minds of the public with the elements of riot and bloodshed, can never touch the fact that it started from an unselfish impulse."

There was blame on both sides, she argued, and both labor and management needed in the future to learn that they must work together, "the new claim on the part of the toiling multitude, the new sense of responsibility on the part of the well-to-do arise in reality from the same source. They are in fact the same "social compunction; and in spite of their widely varying manifestation logically converge into the same movement." Despite the mild nature of Jane Addams' message, despite the fact that she did not deal with the role of the Debs in the strike, or the rightness or wrongness of his imprisonment nor the controversial use of the injunction, she found no one who would publish her essay. *The Forum, North American Review, Century,* and *Atlantic Monthly,* among others, turned it down. Horace Scudder of *Atlantic Monthly* disliked the assumption that he found in the essay that "Pullman was in the wrong," and decided that because he was still alive they had to proceed with great caution.[7]

Jane Addams did chair mass meetings during later crises (though always reluctantly); she collected money, wrote articles, and made many speeches trying to educate the public. She went to great length to make sure that the workers involved in the remodeling of Hull House were not scabs. She protested when she discovered that one of her books was printed by a non-union shop. She spoke out on the side of the striking workers in the Building Trade Strike in Chicago in 1900, in the National Anthracite Strike in 1902, the Chicago Stockyards Strike of 1904, and the great Textile Strike of 1910, but she always advocated conciliation and arbitration, and she almost always saw fault on both sides. Often she served on arbitration committees, and in 1904 during the stockyard strike, she went with Mary McDowell on an unsuccessful visit to Mr. Armour to present the strikers' demands.[8]

Her position in the textile strike of 1910 was perhaps typical. The strike began as an unorganized walkout of workers at the Hart, Schaffner, and Marx factories in Chicago, and spread to other plants. The original grievance was the reduction in the piece-work rate, but as the strike spread a more general discontent with wages and working conditions became the issue. With 40,000 workers on strike, Jane Addams' first action was to organize a relief fund to help the men and their families. She met the young and aggressive leader of the textile workers, Sidney Hillman, who later became a close friend of Hull House. She also knew many of the leading businessmen involved, for Joseph Schaffner and Harry Hart had been generous donors to the settlement and its programs. They were upset by her support of the workers, and especially by her entertaining strikers and labor leaders at Hull House. She tried to communicate to them the way the workers felt; and she went around to Harry Hart's house during the strike to have dinner and explain her stand. The strike ended with a partial victory for the strikers. Though they failed to win the closed shop, the agreement did include the appointment of a permanent board of arbitration to settle difficulties in the future before they reached the crisis stage. Jane Addams played an important role in bringing the two sides together, but when the arbitration board was appointed her name was missing because there were those on both sides who felt she was too committed to the other.[9]

Ellen Starr, who accused her of retreating to her study to write whenever a crisis occurred, once remarked: "Jane if the devil himself came riding down Halsted Street with his tail waving out behind him, you'd say, 'what a beautiful curve he has in his tail.'"[10] Ellen was much more willing to take an aggressive stand in defense of labor. When a group of tailors in the Hull House neighborhood went on strike in 1896 Addams convinced the Chicago Civic Federation to call for arbitration in the dispute, and presided at two mass meetings to collect money and support for the strikers. "The object of the meeting is to bring out clearly the issues of the strike," she wrote to Lloyd, "to insist further upon arbitration, and at the same time to increase the esprit-de-corps of the tailors by getting them all together under one roof." But to Starr and a few others fell the task of organizing the relief funds and providing transportation out of town for the blacklisted leaders after the strike failed. "I feel like a funeral, but let us hope it will count for something in the next fight," Ellen remarked.[11]

Ellen Starr continued to come to the defense of striking workers in a direct fashion. While Jane Addams and many others at Hull House recoiled from the violence of the labor struggle, frail and artistic Ellen joined the picket lines. In 1914 she was arrested for disorderly conduct for picketing with the striking waitresses of Henrici Restaurant. "I maintain the right of free speech," she said in her testimony. "I maintain the right of organization for working people. I was there in front of Henrici's on March 2 to see fair play, to prevent brutality if I could by my presence, and to make formal protest against illegal arrest. All I said was, 'As an American citizen, I protest against the arrest of these persons who are doing nothing contrary to the law.' I did not jump into the air or shake my fists about, as was charged, nor did I shout or make any commotion. I spoke in as even a tone as I could command. My act was a formal protest born of my sympathies and my desire to do what I believed was for the right. I said what I said for the benefit of whomever it might concern. I should do so again if I felt so inclined." She was released, and she did indeed go on protesting.[12]

Jane Addams preferred to work behind the scenes. Even so she was still attacked for being too pro-labor. "Jane Addams is no longer a safe leader to follow, she is becoming too socialistic in her tendencies," a Chicago businessman reported in 1900. "If Miss Addams really wished to put herself upon the record forcibly she should have said emphatically that violence practiced by the labor unions has made them infamous and that none of them should again meet at Hull House," a Chicago newspaper charged, and went on to argue that Hull House was "sowing seed which must inevitably ripen in another Haymarket catastrophe." Another Chicago businessman in refusing to give money to the Hull House summer camp, remarked, "If Hull House would confine its activity to work like this, it should meet the approval and support of all good citizens, but to my mind it has been so thoroughly unionized that it has lost its usefulness and has become a detriment and harm to the community as a whole."[13]

Closely related to the charges that Addams was pro-labor were the accusations that she was a socialist or anarchist or worse, which was ironic because she consistently rejected the radical position and sought the middle ground. She was, however, a consistent advocate of freedom of speech and that position was often misinterpreted by her critics. Hull House welcomed all kinds of people, allowed them to speak and present their point of view, even if it was unpopular. Free speech and radical ideas became more difficult, however, after the assassination of President McKinley by Leon Czolgosz, an avowed anarchist.

In Chicago, where the memory of the Haymarket affair was still vivid, the police rounded up and arrested hundreds of people, most of them immigrants suspected of holding radical views. One of those arrested was Abraham Isaaks, a Russian immigrant and leader of a society of philosophical anarchists. Isaaks was a thoughtful, sensitive, well-educated man in his mid-fifties who was married and the father of a sixteen-year-old daughter and a twenty-two-year-old son. He edited a paper called *Free Society* and regularly attended the lectures and discussions at Hull House and Chicago Commons. On the night the President was shot officers of the Detective Bureau entered Isaaks' apartment and arrested him and his family. They destroyed his presses and confiscated his books, including his volumes of Shakespeare, on the excuse that they were radical and dangerous literature. Raymond Robins, a young settlement worker at Chicago Commons was the first to realize Isaaks' plight. He appealed to Jane Addams and together they rushed to his defense. They attempted to get him freed on bail, and when that failed they went directly to Mayor Carter Harrison, Jr., to protest his use of police power. He allowed them to obtain legal counsel for those arrested. The Isaaks family was quickly released from prison, and within a short time the others who had been rounded up in the police raids were freed as well.[14]

The incident received a lot of coverage in the Chicago newspapers and naturally Jane Addams got a large share of the attention even though it was Robins who had initiated the protest and the rescue operation. Not everyone was favorably impressed. *The Central Christian Advocate*, a Methodist journal, remarked that Addams' support of an anarchist, "does small credit to her judgement and will do less to increase her influence for good. . . . she will not help the laboring classes by rushing to the aid of a 'fire brand.'" Another paper argued that Isaaks was out of "the pale of charity or benevolence" and "Miss Addams can find plenty to do for the lowly classes without bothering herself with the defense of avowed anarchists." Some critics took more direct action and threw stones through the windows of Hull House and Chicago Commons.[15]

Jane Addams along with other Chicago settlement workers joined with other groups in 1908 to challenge the threatened deportation of an obscure Russian carpenter. He was finally granted political asylum in the United States, but the *Chicago Inter-Ocean* attacked the defenders of the immigrant as identical with those "always expressing 'sympathy' for the murderers and would-be murderers who call themselves 'anarchists.'" *The Chicago Chronicle* which took particular pleasure in pointing out what a dangerous radical Jane Addams was, remarked that "It is a cruel fate which guides the ignorant immigrant into the socialist precincts of Hull House and Chicago Commons. It is a sad misuse of Chicago money which maintains these alluring pitfalls for the trustful and helpless." The same year Jane Addams again joined settlement workers in protesting the gunning down by the police of a feeble-minded youth who called himself an anarchist. In all of these incidents she was one of several who took a public stand, in most cases she was not the most important, but because she was the most famous settlement worker in Chicago, she got more than her share of publicity. She immediately began to make speeches, and soon rushed into print with an article defending the right of the settlements to allow even anarchists and other radicals to speak, and trying to make sense out of the irrational impulse which caused some people to charge that "he who knows intimately people among whom anarchists arise is therefore an anarchist."[16]

Hull House and Jane Addams were also charged with being opposed to religion (synonymous with socialism in many quarters). "The fact that Hull House conducts its great work for the uplifting of humanity without religious teaching of any kind will be news to many people who as Christians or as members of Christian organizations have given support to that enterprise," the *Chronicle* announced. In 1904 Cornell College, in Mt. Vernon, Iowa, considered awarding Jane Addams an honorary degree and inquired of several prominent clergymen in Chicago regarding the propriety of a Methodist institution honoring the founder of Hull House. The corresponding secretary of the Home Missionary and Church Extension Society replied that he could not pass judgment on her intellectual attainments, but "I exceedingly regret to be informed that the Hull House over which she presides and exercises authority, permits on the Sabbath day the playing of cards, billiards and other amusements. . . . The general opinion of moral standards among Chicago people is sufficiently low without giving additional influence to those who are in a position to make them lower. I do not think that the cause of Christ would gain any advantage by giving such a degree." Not all the correspondents were as negative, but Jane Addams was not awarded the degree.[17]

There were also critics who found that Jane Addams was too conservative, that her reforms had not gone far enough. "Miss Addams is an excellent and well-meaning woman," the socialist *New York Call* announced. "In fact 'gentle Jane is as good as gold.' For her good intentions and desire to elevate humanity we have the sincerest respect. . . . If the self-sacrifice of an individual could accomplish anything of value, her work should have told effectively. But what has her effort accomplished? We will not say it has accomplished nothing. Some of her handiwork remains, but what does it amount to? A speck in an ocean of misery, suffering and poverty."[18] Margaret Dreier Robins, president of the National Women's Trade Union League, chided her on one occasion for writing that the anthracite strike might have been settled faster if violence had not been perpetuated by the miners, though acknowledging that ". . . in all America I know of only one person who can reach the honorable conservatives of this country and rouse for them a rallying cry and that is you." Others echoed the same sentiment. Walter Rauschenbush, the social gospel minister remarked. "You are one of the invaluable people who combine velocity and stability, so that conservatives have to remain respectful toward you even while they are being dragged along."[19]

She was conscious of her role in arousing honorable conservatives and keeping peace with all groups. Some radicals misinterpreted her stand and suggested that if it were not for her need to appeal to the wealthy she would have been more radical. "It is a safe conclusion," said the *National Single Taxar*, "that she accepts the entertaining not for the sake of being entertained, but because she needs the money . . . for the poor beggers to whom she is the only rock of shelter."[20] The single-tax magazine did not realize that she enjoyed being featured in the drawing rooms of the wealthy, and she would not have become a single taxer or a socialist even if she had been absolved of the responsibility of collecting money for the Hull House programs. Occasionally she talked like a radical. When she visited John Brown's grave in 1904 she remarked: "I always had a secret sympathy with his impatience and his determination that something should happen about it. I suppose the first martyrs of economic slavery will come from the city, if it depends on impatience I might be one." But she contained her impatience; and she had almost nothing in common with John Brown.[21]

She did become an expert practical reformer. She learned how to lobby for bills in Springfield and Washington, how to marshall evidence and statistics, how to mobilize support in order to influence elected officials. But she was the general who planned the campaign rather than the lieutenant who led the troops into battle, and she sometimes received credit for what others accomplished. She worked hard to win a better child labor bill for Illinois, but it was Florence Kelley who was the driving force behind the venture. Addams appealed to President Theodore Roosevelt in 1905 to support a systematic investigation of women and children in industry, but it was Lillian Wald and Mary McDowell who did the major task of organizing the investigation. She presided at the meeting that led to a campaign for the appointment of an Industrial Relations Commission in 1911, and at a crucial time she raised money to keep the campaign alive, but it was a large group of young settlement workers and social researchers who did most of the leg work and made the campaign a success. She supported the movement to found the Women's Trade Union League, but it was Mary Kenny O'Sullivan and William English Walling, both influenced by her during their stays at House, who did the hard work to get the organization started in 1903. Her position as vice-president of the National Women's Trade Union League, her membership in the executive committee of the National Child Labor Committee, the National Playground Association, and a great many other national reform organizations formed in the first decade of the twentieth century was a recognition of her general influence and reputation. She was the strategist, the propagandist, rather than the tactician of reform.[22]

She usually avoided partisan politics for she did not want to limit her influence to one party or faction. The situation in the Hull House neighborhood, however, finally convinced her that a partisan stand in local politics was necessary. Nothing bothered the residents more than the incredible filth of the streets, and the overwhelming smell, especially in the summer months. Bakeries, slaughterhouses, fruit peddlers, livery stables, and ordinary citizens dumped their refuse into the streets which were already clogged with dirt and obstructed by an occasional dead horse. There were garbage boxes, but the collection was erratic and soon the boxes were overflowing with their odorous mixture of wastes. The settlement workers conducted campaigns to educate the people in the neighborhood on the importance of keeping the area clean; they protested to City Hall (700 times in one summer) about the inadequate collection system. They even set up an incinerator at Hull House and tried to burn the debris, but that just added to the smell in the neighborhood. Finally in desperation Jane Addams, with the support of two businessmen, submitted a bid for the garbage removal in the ward. One of her ideas was to pay one cent a bushel for clean ashes, in order that the garbage could then be taken to an incinerator rather than to the city dump. Her bid got a great deal of publicity, after all it was not every day that an upper-class lady sought to become a scavenger. The bid was finally thrown out on a technicality, but because of the publicity, the Mayor appointed her as the garbage inspector for the ward, at a salary of $1000 a year. Again the newspapers had a field day. One reporter described the proper uniform for the new street inspector, "how fetching she would look in a trim uniform of cadet gray, with a jaunty military cap set upon her well-poised head, a stunning tailor-made coat liberally adorned with gilt, a proud star on the breast, a short shirt and—shall we say?—the daintiest of knickerbockers beneath." Another writer insisted that no special exceptions should be made because she was a woman. "If women accept public office they must expect to hold it precisely as men hold it." But he continued, "Miss Addams understands this and is a model officer."[23]

She kept the job for less than a year, but nothing she had done in six years at Hull House won her so much national attention. The image of the brave little woman battling the establishment and following the garbage carts to make her neighborhood safer and cleaner established her reputation as a practical and determined reformer, and very few accounts of her life from this time forward failed to mention the story. It became part of the legend that surrounded and obscured her life.

But the streets did not get much cleaner, and the death rate in the nineteenth ward remained one of the highest in the city. One of the reasons, Addams decided, was the presence in the Hull House ward of a powerful and corrupt boss, Johnny Powers, or "De Pow" as he was known locally. This short, stocky Irishman was no ordinary ward politicians, he was one of the most powerful men in Chicago. He was chairman of the Finance Committee of the Chicago City Council, the boss of the caucus that distributed the chairmanships of the other committees. He had personally been responsible for giving away millions of dollars in street railway franchises to Charles Yerkes and his associates. "He is coolheaded, cunning and wholly unscrupulous," one reporter decided. "He is the feudal lord who governs his retainers with open-handed liberality or crushes them to poverty as it suits his nearest purpose."[24]

Jane Addams and her colleagues first became aware of Powers when they tried to convince the Chicago School Board of the need for a new public school in the ward, only to have Powers' henchman Billy O'Brien, who was chairman of the City Council Committee on Education, quietly reject their plea in favor of a new parochial school. The Hull

House reformers never learned to accept a Catholic school as a possible alternative to a public school. They also blamed the filth and disease in the ward on Powers, and as garbage inspector Jane Addams came to appreciate the extent of his control. She decided that he should be defeated. The campaign against Powers was organized by the Hull House Men's Club. The club met regularly at the establishment for lectures and discussion; its membership came mostly from the neighborhood though there were also a few male residents of the settlement who belonged. In 1895 with Jane Addams encouragement they nominated one of their number, Frank Lawler, to run as an independent candidate for alderman. In a four-way contest Lawler won without much difficulty, but within a matter of months the Hull House reform alderman had been bribed by Powers and became his most loyal supporter.

The Hull House campaign began in earnest in 1896 as they tried to unseat Powers himself. The campaign was really a cooperative effort involving most of the residents of the settlement, and many other reformers in the city, yet in the press Jane Addams got most of the credit. It was much easier to contrast the gentle, upper-class garbage collector with the corrupt ward boss than to try to describe the complexity of the settlement group. Of course, Addams, like most of the residents, had no chance to vote against Powers because she was a woman. Yet in a real sense she was the mastermind behind the campaign. "I really believe that if we could get an investigation in the 19th ward against our corporation alderman, it might extend to the city," she wrote to Henry Demarest Lloyd.[25] She made no campaign speeches, but she did invite Hazen Pingree, the reform mayor of Detroit, George Cole, chairman of the Committee of One Hundred of the newly organized Municipal Voters' League, and Judge Murray F. Tuley to come into the ward in an attempt to influence the voters. The young settlement workers together with some neighborhood youths saturated the ward with posters and placards denouncing "Yerkes and Powers, the Briber and the Bribed." They bombarded the citizens with handbills listing Powers' contributions to the ward: "filthy, ill-paved, and snow-laden streets, high rates, low services, double fares . . . scant public school accommodations, lack of small parks and playgrounds . . . taxation that favors the corrupt and oppresses the honest." They paid little attention to their own candidate, William Gleeson, a forty-two-year-old Irish immigrant and member of the Hull House Men's Club, all of their fire was directed at Powers, "the prince of the boodlers."

Gleeson lost, but the settlement reformers were encouraged that he had reduced Powers' usual margin of victory. They set to work to prepare for an all-out campaign in 1898, and Jane Addams characteristically began to formulate and to ponder what she had learned from her experience in practical politics. She decided that the situation was much more complicated than just good against evil, reformer against corrupt politician. Powers, she learned, served many useful functions in the ward. When a death occurred in the neighborhood, he provided a stylish burial, indeed he had a standing account at the undertakers. When a man lost his job, Powers provided work; he boasted that 2600 residents of the ward were on the city's payroll. When a resident of the ward got into trouble Powers was always there to bail him out of jail and fix things with the judge. At Christmas time there was a free turkey, and if needed, passes for the railroad. In fact after the election was over those who had supported the Hull House candidate expected the settlement to be as generous as the ward boss and Jane Addams was beseiged with requests for favors. Despite many attempts to discredit him the reformers could not shake Powers' image as a good friend and neighbor. "He isn't elected because he is dishonest," Addams decided. "He is elected because he is a friendly visitor." By contrast the reformers seemed like cranks to most of the citizens of the ward, "their goodness is not dramatic; it is not even concrete and human." One of the campaign posters showed Gleeson in working clothes eating from a dinner pail while Powers was shown in a dinner jacket drinking champagne. "To the chagrin of the reformers," she wrote, "it was gradually discovered that in the popular mind a man who laid bricks and wore overalls was not nearly so desirable for an alderman as the man who drank champagne and wore a diamond in his shirt front. The district wished its representatives to stand up to the best of them." Still she could not forgive Powers or condone his tactics. "The positive evils of corrupt government are bound to fall heaviest upon the poorest and least capable," she argued. He gave turkeys at Christmas time, but he refused to be concerned with the filthy streets; he bailed people out of jail, but his corrupt bargains raised the cost of using the street railways.[26]

Jane Addams opened the campaign against Powers in January 1898 with her careful analysis of the forces at work in ward politics. This was one of the first attempts to explain the source of boss power, and at the same time a thinly veiled attack on Powers. The essay was published in the *International Journal of Ethics,* condensed in the *Outlook,* the *Re-*

view of Reviews, and *Public Opinion*, widely summarized in the newspapers and praised by many experts. More than anything else she had written up to that time, it put her in the national eye.[27]

Powers, meanwhile, was annoyed by the publicity he was getting because of the Hull House campaign. "The trouble with Miss Addams," he told a reporter, "is that she is just jealous of my charitable work in the ward." "Hull House will be driven from the ward, and its leaders will be forced to shut up shop," he predicted as he opened his campaign against the settlement workers.[28] He was joined in the attack by the *Chicago Chronicle*, a newspaper with a vested interest in street railway franchises. And some of the Catholic priests in the neighborhood charged that Hull House was anti-Catholic and anti-immigrant. Posters and placards appeared in the ward denouncing "petticoat government," and Jane Addams received many critical letters, some of them obscene, denouncing her entry into politics. One which she carefully saved was signed "a voter," and praised "that good, noble and charitable man, John Powers . . . His hand is ever outstretched to assist the helpless, his pocketbook ever opened to the needy. . . . Now what has Jane Addams done?" the annoymous writer asked:

> Nothing. But because Mr. Powers is a man of principal who loved a woman, in a woman's place, not as a female politician, he has been subject to newspaper notoriety by you Jane Addams, who has long since forgot the pride and dignity so much admired in a beautiful woman. When a man prepared to take unto himself a wife will he go into an alleyway among the rubbish and filth to find a good true virtuous woman? No, a woman with pride and virtue would shrink with horror from such a life. . . .[29]

From this point, the letter degenerates from criticism to obscenity, and one wonders why Jane Addams preserved it. She was undoubtedly hurt by it, as she was hurt by any criticism, even irrational and sick criticism, and in 1898 she had not yet sorted out all the problems relating to women's proper role and her own sexual identity. She did not let her doubts interfere with the campaign against Powers, however.

This time the reformers found an appealing candidate who would not sell out to Powers, Simeon Armstrong, an Irish Catholic and member of the Democratic party who had lived in the ward for 30 years. But the inevitable happened; Powers won by an even larger margin than he had mustered in 1896. He had too much power. A threat here, a bribe there and much of the opposition disappeared. "I may not be the sort of man the reformers like," Powers gloated, "but I am what my people like, and neither Hull House nor all the reformers in town can turn them against me."

After defeat in 1898 the reformers had to decide if it was worth all the time and effort to oppose Powers again in the next election. To Florence Kelley there was only one answer. To admit defeat, to withdraw from politics, she argued, would be to accept the conventional ethics of too many organizations that preached reform in theory but failed to practice it in fact. "True to its avowed purpose, 'to provide a centre for a higher civic and social life,' Hull House entered the campaigns of 1896 and 1898 to make its protest on behalf of municipal honesty," Florence Kelley maintained "and from that task it cannot turn back." But Jane Addams had little interest in wasting her energy opposing Powers when it seemed a futile task; she was more pragmatic than Kelley, less interested in standing for principle. She had learned something about the limitation of reform in one ward, but she was ready to move on to the next task, to tell the world something about the lessons she had learned.[31]

The next few years were among the busiest of her life. Her health was good, her spirits high. She criss-crossed the country speaking constantly and with growing confidence, glorying in the parties, the adoration, the money she made, even finding excitement and meaning in a train-wreck —"the jar, the moment of panic, the thrill of rescue." She gave a series of lectures at the University of Chicago in the summer of 1899 on social ethics, and although she claimed that the first one went badly, she soon "got in the swing" and all of them were well received. She signed a contract to bring the essays out in book form in a series edited by Richard T. Ely. In February 1899, she went on a typical lecture tour—leaving Chicago on February 13, she spoke at Wells College in Aurora, New York, on the 14th; at Auburn Seminary the next day; at Wells again on the 16th; then to New York for a quick stopover; then to Boston where she made two appearances at woman's clubs on the 18th; two more appearances on Sunday; on to the University of Vermont on Monday; back to Boston for two more appearance on Tuesday; two more on Wednesday, and two on Thursday; then she was off to Meadville, Pennsylvania; to Harrisburg, Richmond, Virginia, and Columbia, South Carolina, before returning home. "I am going to make clear about $350 on this trip which is a great satisfaction and much relief financially," she wrote to her sister.

She was usually accompanied on her speaking tours by Mary Smith, Florence Kelley, or Mrs. Bowen. While she disliked being alone and became dependent on the companionship of other women, she also needed privacy, as Mrs. Bowen discovered when she shared a hotel room with her and another women in a small Illinois town.

> When we arrived at the crowded hotel we were given a room for three with a closet and bath. Miss Addams said that she would undress first. She went into the closet, which was unlighted, disrobed, went into the bathroom and took her bath, came out and got into bed. We other two went through the same performance. In the morning Miss Addams got up first, shut herself in the unlighted closet and emerged fully dressed, with her hair neatly arranged—in spite of no light. I thought to myself, "Will I have to do that every time I go out with a social worker?[32]

Despite her busy speaking schedule, she also found time to manage the settlement, supervise the constant remodeling, and institute several new programs. She went to the Paris Exposition in the summer of 1900 where she was a juror in social economy. Her duties were mostly judging the various exhibits, but she also went to lectures, gave some herself at the invitation of Patrick Geddes, the Scottish biologist and sociologist, and mingled with social reformers and intellectuals from around the world. "My poor old emptied-out mind is getting filled up," she reported to Mary Smith. Returning home she continued her gruelling schedule, and seemed to thrive on it. During a lecture tour in 1902 she wrote her friend; "I will confide to you alone that I have never spoken so well and so many times as during this trip. It has altogether been successful socially and financially and in ideas . . . I expect to go home prepared for valiant deeds."[33]

Somehow during this constant movement she found time to write her first book. Even though she admitted that she got very little writing done on her lecture trips (there were too many parties, teas, and receptions), she did rework her lectures, smooth out the transitions, include another example here, and add a human story there. The lectures, most of them first published as articles in the *American Journal of Sociology*, *Atlantic Monthly*, and other magazines, became *Democracy and Social Ethics*.

Her roles as reformer and author were of course related. But she was not only interested in spreading reform ideas, she was also concerned with increasing her own reputation. Very early she discovered how to get the maximum use of her material. She kept apologizing to Ely for not getting the manuscript done, and he kept gently encouraging and prodding her to get it finished. "It is surprising that you are able to accomplish so much. I do not at all wonder that you find it hard to write your book. I am so confident, however, that your book is going to be helpful that I hope you will steal the time from other things, important as these other things are." To his publishers he wrote: "It is my belief that there are, from the publisher's point of view, and, for that matter, from many other points of view, great possibilities in Miss Addams."[34]

The book came out in 1902. The subject was democracy, but not simply the franchise, for she argued that most people interpreted democracy too narrowly. She was concerned with the relationship of human beings to each other, and she asserted her optimistic faith in the essential worthiness of every person, regardless of background or occupation. She wrote of the relationship of the charity agent to his client, and argued that each was the equal of the other. "Formerly, when it was believed that poverty was synonomous with vice and laziness, and that the prosperous man was the righteous man, charity was administered harshly with a good conscience; for the charitable agent really blamed the individual for his poverty, and the very fact of his own superior prosperity gave him a certain consciousness of moral superiority." But now that we know that there are social causes of poverty and standards of success other than financial ones, she went on, the relationship between those who are in need of help and those giving the aid should be democratic. In the other essays she argued the same point for the employer and his employees, for the parent and his children, especially his unmarried daughters. In the last chapter, which is a reworking of her essay on the ward boss she seemed, at least for a brief moment to perfer the boss to the reformer. "Would it be dangerous to conclude that the corrupt politician himself, because he is democratic in method, is on a more ethical line of social development than the reformer, who believes that people must be made over by 'good citizens' and governed by 'experts'? The former at least are engaged in the great moral effort of getting the mass to express itself, and of adding this mass energy and wisdom to the community as a whole."

The book was filled with a glowing optimism, as if accepting democracy and affirming the humanity of all people were reform enough. "As the acceptance of democracy brings a certain life-giving power, so it has its own sanctions and comforts. Perhaps the most obvious one is the curious sense which comes to us from time to time, that we belong to the whole, that a certain basic well being can never be taken away from us whatever the turn of fortune."[35] There is never any indication of how we are to reach this wonderful state, except that presumably all classes and all people, workers and employers, teachers and students, parents and children, even the political boss and the reformers, would cooperate to promote democracy. There was no sense of class conflict, no sense that there was anything fundamentally wrong with the American system. "She sees nothing of the great class forces which are not at all waiting for the coming of some benevolent reformer, but will move of their own initiative, to the discomfiture of reformers and boodlers alike," a reviewer in a socialist journal noted and went on to charge her with writing from the point of view of the ruling class. Edward T. Devine criticized her with holding up an archaic picture of the charity worker in order to attack it. A few others found the book sentimental. But in general it was well received. It sold well for a book of this sort, 4500 copies in the first year and a half, and about 10,000 over fifteen years. William James called it "one of the great books of our time"; Edwin Seligman found it "sane and inspiring" and added, "no other book by a woman shows such vitality, such masculinity of mental grasp and surefootedness." Oliver Wendell Holmes called her a "big woman who knows at least the facts and gives me more insights into the point of view of the working man and the poor than I had before"; a college girl wrote that just reading a few pages of the book made her feel better.[36]

Her influence and her reputation came in large measure from her genius for putting herself in the place of other people, of appreciating and interpreting their problems, and her ability to diffuse even the most controversial matter and write and speak in a style of calm reasonableness. Her empathy and her rational, logical stance enabled her to communicate to the American people some of the problems and difficulties facing the immigrants in American cities. Her own family background prepared her to understand the exaggerated generational conflict that took place in many immigrant families where the normal rebellion of youth against parents was complicated by a simultaneous reaction against the language, clothes, and customs of the old country. She encouraged the preservation of customs, dress, and language in order that the process of Americanization would not be so harsh as to rip out the older heritage that each group brought with them. It was partly for this reason that she established the Labor Museum at Hull House in 1900. Here, she hoped, could be preserved some of the ancient skills of weaving, pottery making, and handcrafts that seemed to be threatened by industrialism. She also hoped that by employing the older skilled artisans as teachers she could restore some of their pride and confidence and perhaps give the younger generation some pride in their parents' skills and national heritage. She also hoped that by showing the history of the textile industry, for example, that some lost pride in workmanship could be restored, and that a young man or woman employed in a textile factory might get a glimpse of how his job related to the ancient process of making cloth. Unfortunately it was often a forlorn hope and a romantic dream, but it was an example of her sympathy and understanding for the process of change.[37]

Her sympathy and understanding of immigrants extended also to blacks. She did not entirely avoid the racist attitudes of her day, but she came much closer to overcoming them than most of the reformers of her generation. There were few blacks in the Hull House neighborhood until the 1920's, but she cooperated in the founding of Wendell Phillips Settlement, which served a mixed neighborhood. When the National Association of Colored Women met in Chicago she invited them all to lunch at Hull House. She also entertained many black leaders including Mr. and Mrs. Booker T. Washington. At the National Convention of Women's Clubs in Los Angeles in 1902 she spoke in favor of the inclusion of the Negro clubs, although one newspaper reported that she spoke "in language that was at once diplomatic and persuasive." She was a close friend of both Mary White Ovington and William English Walling who, along with Henry Moskowitz, founded the National Association for the Advancement of Colored People in 1909. She was made a member of the executive committee even though she was not present at the original meeting because, as Mrs. Walling put it, "you are one of the few whom we felt we can lean upon." She also was a member of the Chicago Urban League and on many occasions spoke out against lynching, offering the special perspective of a woman:

> To those who say that most of these hideous and terrorizing acts have been committed in the name of chivalry, in order to make the lives and honor of women safe, perhaps it is women themselves who can best reply that bloodshed and arson and ungoverned anger have never yet controlled lust. On the contrary, that lust has always been the handmaid of these, and is prone to be found where they exist; that the supression of the bestial cannot be accomplished by the counter exhibi-

tion of the brutal only. Perhaps it is woman who can best testify that the honor of women is only secure in those nations and those localities where law and order and justice prevail; that the sight of human blood and the burning of human flesh has historically been the signal for lust; that an attempt to allay and control it by scenes such as those is as ignorant as it is futile and childish.

And if a woman might venture to add another word on behalf of her sex, that the woman who is protected by violence allows herself to be protected as the woman of the savage is, and she must still be regarded as the possession of man. As her lord and master is strong or weak, so is the protection which she receives; that if she takes brute force as her protection, she must also accept the status she held when brute force alone prevailed.[38]

Addams had experienced little lust and brutality in her own life but she tried to understand. She spoke for equal opportunity for the black man and woman even though she believed that the breakup of the Negro family during slavery and the obliteration of the African heritage made the Americanization process more difficult for blacks than for immigrants. Sometimes she was put to great inconvenience by her conscience and her reasonableness. She tried to hire only union labor at Hull House, but at one time she hired a black cook, and there was no union in Chicago that would allow him to become a member. She could have protested loudly about discrimination, but instead she allowed Grace Abbott to arrange for the cook to join a union in St. Louis, while she continued to work quietly and calmly to expand the rights for both blacks and organized labor.[39]

Jane Addams was able to accomplish much with her policy of conciliation and compromise and her basic sympathy and understanding for all people. But occasionally she got herself into a situation where compromise was impossible, and where the middle ground was the most difficult to stand on. She found herself in such a position during her brief tenure on the Chicago school board.

From the beginning Hull House was an educational institution. Central to its early goals was a desire to extend the advantages of a college education to the working men. There were University Extension classes taught by volunteers from the local colleges, together with an extensive summer program held at Rockford College, but she soon realized that another kind of educational fare was needed by the neighbors, and she became disillusioned with the early educational goals of the settlement. "The academic teaching which is accessible to workingmen through

University Extension lectures and classes at Settlements, is usually bookish and remote, and concerning subjects completely divorced from their actual experiences," she wrote in 1902. "The men come to think of learning as something to be added to the end of a hard day's work and to be gained at the cost of toilsome mental exertion." Many of the Hull House programs, from vocational classes to the Labor Museum were designed to relate directly to the experience of those who lived in the Hull House neighborhood. Borrowing a phrase from Dewey she argued that the Labor Museum "concentrates and dramatizes the inherited resources of a man's occupation, and secondly, that it conceives of education as 'a continuing reconstruction of experience.' "[40] The influence of Dewey, and her own observations enabled her to appreciate the woeful inadequacies of the Chicago public schools. She served on an ad hoc committee formed in 1893 after a muckraking article by J. M. Rice appeared in *The Forum* criticizing the schools of the city. Through the work of the committee she met Colonel Francis Wayland Parker the principal of the Cook County Normal School, who was experimenting with new teaching and learning methods, and whose practice school was the model for John Dewey's laboratory school at the University of Chicago. She also met Margaret Haley, a petite but fiery elementary school teacher, who became the leader of the Chicago Teachers' Federation and a tireless fighter for better schools and higher salaries for teachers.

Jane Addams was known as a progressive in education so it is not surprising that Mayor Edward F. Dunne in 1905 made her one of his reform appointees to the school board. The school system and the school board had been embroiled in controversy for years. Part of the conflict was political, involving tax assessments, the struggle of the teachers for professional status as well as a controversy over teaching methods, pensions, tenure, and many other things. In 1902 the Chicago Teachers' Federation had won a court order requiring five Chicago utility companies to pay back taxes that they had been avoiding because of fraudulent assessment practices, but the school board had not used the extra money for teacher salaries. There were also rumors about other unfair assessments, and charges that the *Tribune*, whose building was on land leased from the board of education was paying ridiculously low rent. The school board was the center of complicated, but emotion-laden controversy. In addition to Jane Addams, Mayor Dunne's reform school board appointees included Raymond Robins, Anita McCormick Blaine, Louis Post, the editor of the *Public*, a single-tax journal, John J. Sonsteby, a liberal attorney and Dr. Cornelia De Bey, a young physician and friend of the settlement workers in the city. The newspapers generally hailed Jane Addams' appointment, the exception was the *Chronicle* which announced, "She is openly at war with the existing constitution of society. Her mind is a nest of sociological vagaries. Her associations are revolutionary. We can regard her appointment as nothing more than a compliment to the socialism of the mayor and the insubordination of the Teachers' Federation." But before many months the reform board, by investigating the coal and book contracts, the leases of land held by many Chicago businesses, approving higher salaries for teachers and holding hearings on the pension and promotion plans, had angered most of the newspapers in the city. They were denounced as "tools of labor" "subservient to Roman Catholic interests" and by the *Tribune* as "freaks, cranks, monomaniacs, and boodlers."[41]

Jane Addams was made chairman of the School Management Committee, which had responsibility for teacher promotion, curriculum, supplies and salaries. She immediately got into trouble. Her ability to manipulate, compromise and conciliate were of little use, and she proceeded to anger one group after another in her attempt to steer a middle course. Teacher promotion was one controversial issue. Under the existing system a teacher got small automatic raises for six years, then the raises stopped and the only way that he could advance was to take a special examination, and the only ones eligible for this exam were those who had been given a high efficiency rating by the principal. The Teachers' Federation, led by Margaret Haley, had been pushing for a fair system, one that would remove the evaluation of teachers from politics. Most of the recommendations were included in a new plan submitted by Louis Post, which called for a three-year probationary period, at the end of which the teacher would be given a certificate of release, pay raises for those kept would be automatic for seven years, and then the teacher would be observed by his superintendent, another superintendent, and the principal of the Chicago Normal School or someone she would designate. Jane Addams appeared to approve this plan, or something close to it, in a speech given shortly after she was appointed to the board. But a massive controversey raged about the proposal; to many observers it seemed like the opening wedge to socialism. When the showdown came Addams voted for a compromise proposal that kept the promotional exam.

Margaret Haley was horrified. She wrote to Dr. DeBey and expressed her "deep regret and sorrow that Miss Adams [sic] had so disappointed those of us who had built our hopes on her as a believer in democracy and as one who had the courage to stand by her convictions in action." DeBey sent the letter to Addams who called Haley to explain. She began by saying the measure was a compromise and that she believed in compromise. "I told her I did not believe in any compromise that compromised a principle," Haley later recalled, "and that I feared that she had compromised more than one fundamental principle which she herself had annunciated and defined in her public speeches. . . . As a matter of principle and not of policy I felt and I still feel that Miss Adams made a mistake and a serious one. Miss Adams if she is anything to Chicago is an ethical and moral leader not a compromiser. It was as such that the people of Chicago looked up to her . . . and this incident simply demonstrates the difference between my view of Miss Jane Adams and her function in Chicago and her view of her place in the activities of the city."[42]

Haley was not the only one upset with Jane Addams. Margaret Robins, whose husband was also a member of the board, was disturbed by her failure to stand for principle. Thinking that she was influenced by the attacks on the board in the press and by the fear that her position would lose contributions for Hull House, Mrs. Robins offered to pay up to $20,000 to Hull House for any money lost directly or indirectly because of Addams' stand. But it was not fear of losing money that made Jane Addams' equivocate. She did believe in compromise, as she told Margaret Haley. She did on occasion stand for a principle, but she preferred compromise, disliked conflict, and those who believed with all their hearts in an idea, as Robins and Haley did, were always disappointed in her.[43]

Jane Addams got into further difficulty with the reform members of the board when Mayor Dunne was defeated for reelection in the spring of 1907 by Fred Busse. The first thing Busse did when he assumed office was to demand the resignation of twelve of the twenty-one members of the school board, almost all the reform members except Jane Addams. Several of those ousted were later legally reinstated, but by then their terms were up and it was irrelevant. Raymond Robins and several other of the group fully expected Jane Addams to come to their defense or to resign in protest. As chairman of the temporary pension board she had a chance to recognize the dismissed board members, but as one of the newspapers put it, "She diplomatically avoided a sharp clash by announcing that she would adopt the course of the board's executive head and say a quorum was present." The ousted members protested loudly, but "again she took the middle ground."[44] "What a dreadful backward step has been taken because of St. Jane," Mary Dreier, wrote her brother-in-law, Raymond Robins, without the usual reverence. "[t]here could not have been a greater blow to the cause than she has given." But Florence Kelley had a slightly different view of the situation. "Did you ever hear of anything so loony as Raymond Robins' systematic attack upon Miss Addams because she did not resign from the Chicago school board when he was dropped from it?" she asked Lillian Wald, "Did you ever hear of a man resigning because a woman was dropped?"[45]

Florence Kelley, of course, appreciated Jane Addams' penchant for compromise and conciliation, but even though she often disagreed with her, Kelley continued to have respect for her position. More casual acquaintances often misunderstood. Margaret Haley, not long after the school board affair, reported what she considered the Addams' betrayal to Anna Garlin Spencer, the feminist and reformer. "We had made the mistake in Chicago of considering Miss Addams as a moral leader and treating her as such and expecting her to do in very difficult positions what a William Lloyd Garrison would do . . ." she remarked. She characterized Addams as a sensitive plate that reflected the feeling of those around her, she had the power of putting herself in the other person's place to an unusual degree but that she was not a great moral leader. It is true that Jane Addams was not a William Lloyd Garrison; William Hard was closer to the truth when, referring to her role on the school board controversy, he called her "The Harry Clay of Chicago."[46] She was by nature a compromiser who preferred the middle ground. But through her writings and her speaking she created the image of being a great moral leader, indeed she was credited with being the feminine conscience of the nation.

VIII

A Moral Equivalent for War
and Juvenile Delinquency

ANE Addams became a pacifist gradually over a period of years. Her peace activities and her search for a moral equivalent for war were closely related to her experience in an immigrant neighborhood in Chicago. Her attitude was also influenced by her reading of Tolstoy and by the problems raised by the Spanish-American War. Her opposition to war had nothing to do with her Quaker heritage, a convenient explanation cited in many popular accounts of her life. In fact, her father's Quakerism was so vague that he was not even a pacifist, and helped recruit a regiment during the Civil War. There is no indication that when Jane was a child or in college that she was troubled by the thought of war, and her letters written during her two European adventures reveal a lively interest in the military displays and marching soldiers she saw all across Europe. She was especially fascinated as were many Americans, by exploring the battlefields, monuments, and other artifacts relating to Napoleon. Certainly when she moved to Hull House in 1889 she was in no sense a pacifist, but on the other hand war and peace were not especially vital issues in the world of the 1880's.

She discovered the writings of Leo Tolstoy during the interlude between her two European trips, but it was not until after she had moved to Hull House that some of the implications of his theories began to take effect. In the beginning it was not so much his doctrine of non-resistance to force and violence, as his courage in acting out the logic of his ideas, that attracted her. Tolstoy's decision to give up the life of a celebrated writer and live like a peasant, to wear peasant garb, work in the fields, eat coarse and simple food, and to spend his spare time making boots with his own hands, had a particular attraction to many Americans in the late nineteenth century who were worried about their own idleness and luxury. Clarence Darrow, William Jennings Bryan, John P. Altgeld, Ernest Crosby, Brand Whitlock, Samuel Jones, William Dean Howells, Hamlin Garland, and many others felt the influence of Tolstoy. Garland noted how his generation received "utterances of such apolostolic austerity that they read like encyclicals from the head of a great church—the church of humanity . . . We quoted Ibsen to reform the drama and Tolstoy to reform society. We made use of every available argument his letters offered."[1]

Tolstoy's Christian vision of a better world, and his anger at the contrast between wealth and poverty impressed the American reformers. The shock of this contrast, of course, had been part of the impulse behind the settlement movement, both in England and America. It had inspired John Ruskin and William Morris to try to preserve handicrafts and to build something beautiful in the age of the machine. It was the same impulse that caused Jane Addams to write about the need of her generation of young college women to "recapture the race life," to do something real, to savor the primitive aspects of life, to go "back to the people" after years of literature, aesthetics, and theory. But Jane Addams had never had any idea of giving up her upper-class values and life style when she founded Hull House, no more than had Ruskin and Morris and the other social reformers in England. Tolstoy's action in actually living like a peasant, not just living among the peasants, seemed very appealing to Jane Addams (in moments of despair) and made her feel at least a little guilty about her life of comfort and ease. Especially she felt guilty and unsure of her next step in the early 1890's because of the constant pressure she got from Florence Kelley and a few others to become more radical and have greater concern for the horrors of poor housing, sweating labor, and abject poverty. The suffering of the poor during the depression of 1893 increased her doubts and made her more fascinated by the example of Tolstoy, though she was also critical of him. "I do not believe that Tolstoi's position is tenable," she wrote to a friend in 1895, "a man cannot be a Xtian by himself."[2]

In 1896 while traveling in Europe with Mary Smith, she made a short excursion into Russia. After visiting St. Petersburg and Moscow, she sought out Aylmer Maude and with his help arranged for a visit to Yasnaya Polyana, the estate about 130 miles from Moscow where Tolstoy lived. It was not quite a trip to Mecca for Jane Addams though her curiosity was mixed with awe. Maude, who had himself never visited Tolstoy, was not too pleased to have uninvited guests, but Tolstoy welcomed them cordially. He had never heard of Hull House, but Maude sketched the purpose of the settlement as he understood it, and Addams described the poverty of the immigrants who lived near by. "Tolstoy standing by clad in his peasant garb listened gravely," she later recalled, "but, glancing distrustfully at the sleeves of my traveling gown which unfortunately at that season were monstrous in size, he took hold of an edge and pulling one sleeve to an interminable breadth, said quite simply that 'there was enough stuff on one arm to make a frock for a little girl,' and asked me directly if I did not find 'such a dress' 'a barrier to the people.' I was too disconcerted to make a very clear explanation, although I tried to say that monstrous as my sleeves were they did not compare in size with those of the working girls in Chicago and that nothing would more effectively separate me from 'the people' than a cotton blouse following the simple lines of the human form, even if I had wished to imitate him and 'dress as a peasant,' it would have been hard to choose which peasant among the thirty-six nationalities we had recently counted in our ward."[3] She did not mention the incident in any of the letters she wrote home at the time, but Maude recalled that Tolstoy was not very much impressed by her argument.[4]

But Jane Addams was impressed by her host. "We have just come back from a visit to Tolstoy on his country place," she wrote to one of the Hull House residents. "We were entertained to supper, taken at ten o'clock outdoors under the porches, and were almost as much fascinated by his family as himself. One of the daughters had been working in the field all day, they took us over their village to make calls and were charming in every way. Tolstoi himself is one of the gentlest and kindest of human creatures I ever saw. He was tired so that the actual conversation did not amount to so much as his presence and spirit."

When she returned to America she talked enthusiastically about Tolstoy with friends and the press. "He is a wonderful personality, you cannot come near the man without feeling his genius," she reported. She was also fascinated by peasant life in Russia. "The manner of life among them takes one back almost to the beginning of history," she decided, and expressed the naïve hope that Russia, presumably led by the peasants, would avoid the problems of industrialism that the more advanced nations were suffering through.[5]

She continued to mull over the implications of Tolstoian ideas in the context of her situation in Chicago. A few weeks after her return she wrote to Maude:

> The glimpse of Tolstoy has made a profound impression upon me—not so much by what he said as the life, the gentleness, the Christianity in the soul of him. . . .
> A radical stand such as Tolstoy has been able to make throws all such effort as that of settlements into the ugly light of compromise and inefficiency—at least so it seemed to me—and perhaps accounts for a certain defensive attitude I found in myself. . . . I am sure you will understand my saying that I got more of Tolstoy's philosophy from our conversations than I had gotten from Tolstoy's books. I believe so much of it that I am sorry to seem to differ so much.

She could not accept Tolstoy's view that the state was anti-Christian and therefore should be rejected. She differed with him on the interpretation of non-resistance, and was not willing to accept his extreme position that no physical force should be used to compel any man to do what he did not want to do, and to condemn any government that used force to command obedience to law. "It seemed to me that he made too great a distinction between the use of physical force and that moral energy which can override another's differences and scruples with equal ruthlessness," she later recalled. To her non-resistance had nothing to do, at least initially, with war and non-violence.

"Our effort at Hull House," she told Maude, "has always been to seize upon the highest moral efforts we could find in the labour movement or elsewhere, and help them forward. To conserve the best which the community has achieved and push it forward along its own line when possible.

"We have always held strongly to the doctrine of non-resistance, select the good in the neighborhood and refraining from railing at the bad. Gradually I have come to believe even farther than that in non-resistance—that the expectation of opposition and martyrdom, the holding oneself in readiness for it, was in itself a sort of resistance and worked evil or at best was merely negative." Yet within months of her return from her visit to Tolstoy, she was railing at Powers, the ward boss, and some years later when Maude published her letter in his biography of Tolstoy, she admitted that "non-resistance was clearer to me then than it is now."[6]

Jane Addams had felt guilty as she ate the elaborate and carefully prepared food at Tolstoy's table, while he ate porridge and black bread. She was also impressed that he worked in the fields and made his own boots— that he worked with his hands in an age when most people of his class did not have to. She felt guilty enough about her idle hands, her lack of labor, that when she returned to Hull House she spent a few hours baking bread in the settlement kitchen, a skill she had learned as a child. But the business of the day, the visitors, the correspondence, the phone calls, even her own writing waited while she preformed her symbolic "bread labor." After a time she gave up her effort to bake bread, and compromised with the Tolstoian ideal.

Yet the example of Tolstoy continued to haunt her. She lectured on his ideas frequently after she returned from her visit; she worried about her investments and vowed to live on her lecturing alone. She kept up a correspondence with Maude who was trying to establish a community in England based on Tolstoian ideas; she had a great respect for the Dukhobors, a religious sect which took the Christian message, and Tolstoy's non-resistance literally. She admired their courage, but found that for her, compromise and conciliation was more effective. She probably agreed with George Herron, the controversial Christian Socialist who, after a visit to Hull House summed up their discussion in a letter: "How to make one's life a true witness that is the question. I do not see that Tolstoi has rightly answered it. At bottom his is an egoistic peace. There is a better way. My wishes go with him, it is the simple solution, but my *voices* tell me that after all it is not the noblest or selfless one. It is peace for one's self, but not for the world."[7]

In 1897 Jane Addams was searching for an inner peace, and for the right relationship with the neighborhood and the world. She was not at this point, however, particularly interested in world peace, nor in international affairs. She belonged to no peace societies; she may have attended some of the sessions of the World Peace Congress held in connection with the World's Fair in Chicago in 1893, but she was not a participant. For her, Tolstoy's doctrine of non-resistance had little to do with international disagreements, but with forces at work in the neighborhood and the city.

Then in the spring of 1898 the Spanish-American War broke out.

It was a lightning war, over within three months, but the issues raised by the war and the peace settlement were to be debated for years to come. They brought to a climax the controversy over American expansion abroad. There is no evidence that Addams had any interest in American foreign policy in the 1890's. She does not seem to have followed the Venezuelan Crisis of 1895-1896, or the events in Cuba that eventually precipitated the war, at least she mentioned none of these developments in her letters, or in her public addresses. After the war came, however, she became a participant in the controversy. Although she was not a prominent anti-imperialist, the debate over imperialism, and her own experiences, helped her bring together some of the ideas aroused by Tolstoy and made her a full-fledged advocate of peace.

Her first reaction to war was not so much shock and horror, as it would later be with the outbreak of World War I, but rather a realization that a far-off event was changing life in the Hull House neighborhood. Speaking at a meeting of the Academy of Political and Social Sciences in December, 1898, a few days after the signing of the peace treaty, in the middle of an address on the function of the social settlement, she noted that there had been an increase in murders in the neighborhood since the outbreak of war. Children were "playing war" in the streets. "In no instance . . . were they 'freeing Cubans,' but with the violence characteristic of their age, they were 'slaying Spaniards.' The predatory spirit is so near the surface in human nature," she added "that the spectacle of war has been a great setback to the development and growth of the higher impulse of civilization."[8]

In citing the "predatory spirit," the primitive instincts that lay close to the surface, especially in young people, she was borrowing from the thinking of psychologists G. Stanley Hall and William James. She was also taking the first halting steps toward formulating a theory for a substitute for the war spirit, for a "moral equivalent for war." She was not alone in this search; William James, always ambivalent about war, hating it yet appreciating its attraction, had also been searching for a way to sublimate the predatory spirit of man. As early as 1888, James, in trying out ideas for the prevention of war, and the settling of international disputes had written cryptically in notes for a lecture in one of his classes. "But how decide conflicts? . . . Follow the common traditions, Sacrifice all wills which are not organizable and which avowedly go against the whole. . . . Find some innocent way out, Examples: savage virtues preserved by athletics; warlike by organized warfare. . . ."[9]

Jane Addams, however, did not have the benefit of hearing James' college lectures. She worked out her ideas about a moral equivalent for war from her own experience, though later she was to profit from hearing him speak, and he in turn learned from her. She agonized over the war and the problem of keeping the peace. "I sat in Mrs. Porter Palmer's box at the Peace Jubilee and otherwise exposed myself to its fascinations," she reported to a friend in October 1898, "but can do nothing but feel a lump in my throat over the whole thing. I have been really quite blue, not play blue but real depths and will have to be more of a Tolstoyan or less of one right off." She and James both appeared on the same platform in Chicago for a discussion of Tolstoy's ideas, but both rejected his doctrine of non-resistance, and instead took a milder path of protest by joining the anti-imperialists.[10]

Addams was not among those who organized the Anti-Imperialist League in Boston in June 1898, but she did support its action and later she joined the Chicago branch. She was always a minor figure in the anti-imperialist movement which was led by such mugwumps as Andrew Carnegie, George Hoar, Edward Atkinson, E. L. Godkin, Charles Eliot Norton, and Carl Schurz. She could agree with their opposition to President McKinley's policy of annexing the Philippines and forcibly destroying the nationals led by Aquinaldo. She could agree with their rejection of American expansion and imperialism, but she must have had some difficulty with their racist rhetoric, which depicted the Filipinos and other Orientals as inferior people not equipped for self-government.[11]

She was in the audience in Chicago on October 17, 1899, when Carl Schurz delivered his stinging address attacking the McKinley administration for its actions in the Philippines. He denounced "the slaughter by American arms of a once friendly and confiding people." "I confidently trust," he announced, "that the American people will prove themselves . . . too wise not to detect the false pride or the dangerous ambitions or the selfish schemes which so often hide themselves under that deceptive cry of mock patriotism: 'Our country, right or wrong!' They will not fail to recognize that our dignity, our free institutions and the peace and welfare of this and coming generations of Americans will be secure only as we cling to the watchword of *true* patriotism: 'Our country—when right to be kept right; when wrong to be put right.' "

"Carl Schurz was so fine last night that I feel uplifted in spirit," she wrote Mary Smith, "that straight intellectual clearness that inevitably leads to uprightness appeals to me as nothing else does. He was fair and reasonable."[12]

In her own speaking, she avoided direct attacks on the administration and instead took a broader view. She decried the narrow interpretation of patriotism in time of war; "patriotism as taught in our schools is fast becoming an abstraction," she argued, "to be patriotic is to salute a flag or to sing 'America,' rather than to feel responsible for the condition of the public school and its grounds, which may later lead to the same sense of responsibility in regard to the public streets and community duties." Peace as well as patriotism must be made meaningful, she argued; it must be more than the absence of war. "Peace is not merely something to hold congresses about and to discuss as an abstract dogma," she told an anti-expansion meeting at the Central Music Hall in Chicago on April 30, 1899. "It has come to be a rising tide of moral feeling which is slowly engulfing all pride of conquest and [is] making war impossible." She cited the Russian peasants who were refusing to drill and fight and the opposition of organized labor to imperialism. She did not, however, underestimate the appeal and fascination and horror of war. "The appeal to the fighting instinct does not end in mere warfare, but arouses these brutal instincts latent in every human being." "Let us not make the mistake of confusing moral issues sometimes involved in warfare itself," she warned, "Let us not glorify the brutality. The same strenuous endeavor, the same heroic self-sacrifice, the same fine courage and readiness to meet death may be displayed without the accompaniment of killing our fellowmen," she argued, in anticipating the thesis later made famous by William James.[13]

The next year, speaking in St. Louis, she continued to explore some of the implications of peace and war, of "patriotism and duty." "The great pity of it all is that war tends to fix our minds on the picturesque," she announced, "that it seems so much more magnificent to do battle for the right than patiently to correct the wrong. A war throws back the ideals which the young are nourishing into the mold of those which the old should be outgrowing. We allure our young men not to develop but to exploit. We turn their imagination from the courage and toil of industry to the bravery and endurance of war. We incite their ambitions not to irrigate, to make fertile and sanitary the barren plains of the savage, but to fill it with military posts and to collect taxes and tariffs." But she also realized how difficult it was to find a substitute for the military virtues. She recalled how, some years before, she had tried to convince some of the boys from a Hull House gymnasium class that it was just as exciting to use long, narrow, sewer spades instead of rifles and bayonets in the military drill they so eagerly organized, but they soon pretended that the spades were guns and went back to their military tactics. "I honestly doubt," she decided, "if now I could even get them to touch a spade, so besotted have we all become with the notion of military glory."[14]

She appeared at an anti-war, pro-Boer rally in Chicago and appealed for contributions to the Red Cross to help the wounded, as one positive action those who opposed war could take. "War in all its horror is a terrible thing," she announced. "It is the law of the jungle elaborated. It is the old story of the rulers of Persia and Rome, when they conquered other peoples and forced them into slavery to work for them and no longer for themselves alone. We are taken in once more . . . and go back again to where the Romans were a thousand years ago." She gave a series of lectures in the summer of 1902 at Chautauqua, New York, on Leo Tolstoy, and in an address before the Ethical Culture Society of Chicago in the spring of 1903 she talked on "A Moral Substitute for War."[15]

William James and Jane Addams appeared on the same platform in Boston in the fall of 1904 at the thirteenth Universal Peace Conference. "The meetings are pretty courteous and some of them filled with platitudes, but on the whole it is a fine group of people trying to do a real thing and I rise up from time to time," she reported. In fact she gave three formal addresses and in one she spoke of the need for "a moral substitute for war." William James also spoke. "Our permanent enemy is the rooted bellicosity of human nature. Man, biologically considered and whatever else he may be into the bargain, is the most formidable of all beasts of prey and indeed, the only one that preys systematically on his own species. We are once for all adapted to the military status. A millennium of peace would not breed the fighting disposition out of our bone and marrow, and a function so ingrained and vital will never consent to die without resistance, and will always find impassioned apologists and idealizers." Therefore he argued, in much the same terms that Jane Addams had been stressing, we must find a way to absorb and sublimate the natural bellicosity of human nature.

William James formulated his ideas in their final form in his famous essay, "The Moral Equivalent for War," first written as a pamphlet for the American Association for International Conciliation in 1910 and then published as an article in *McClure's* and *Popular Science Monthly*. Jane Addams put her ideas in more permanent form in a book, published in 1907, which she called *Newer Ideals of Peace*. James' essay was more dramatic, with its plans for conscription into a peacetime army designed to preserve "the military ideals of hardihood and discipline."[16] He appreciated, more than Jane Addams did, the appeal of the manly virtues and was convinced that warlike tendencies were deeply imbedded in human nature. On the other hand, she maintained that only the longing for adventure, for group approval, and the desire to do useful work were deeply ingrained, primitive instincts.[17]

Jane Addams' book was not easily written even though she had used most of the material many times in articles and speeches. She first mentioned the possibility of a book in the fall of 1902, just after the publication of *Democracy and Social Ethics*. She would call it "Newer Ideals of Peace," "Dynamic Peace," or "War and Labor." Richard Ely was enthusiastic and so were the editors at Macmillan. She signed a contract in January 1903 for the book to be published in the Citizen's Library, the same series in which her first book had appeared. The royalty rate was a little better than in her previous contract, 13 per cent from the first copy sold, and she was to get $200 in advance on the date of publication. But in May 1903 she wrote, "The book moves slowly, but I hope to get at it a little later. Hobson has really said it all in his 'Imperialism' which seems to me to be a very masterly presentation of moral and economic claims." Hobson had not said it all, but her letter indicated that she was reading, and stumbling around trying to formulate and strengthen her own views on peace and war. Of course, she was busy with other matters, collecting money, serving on dozens of committees, making speaking tours, and lobbying for legislation. She found time to write only by spending a few days at a time at the congenial and relaxed Smith residence, or during summers at Bar Harbor.[18]

In the fall of 1904 she wrote to Ely: "The book is moving slowly but after all is in motion. I think it would be safe to announce it for the spring, if that means that I need not have the manuscript ready before February." But February came and went and she missed her deadline. By the spring of 1905 Ely was patiently trying to convince her that she should finish the manuscript. "I felt that you had a real message and a very important one," he wrote, as you yourself intimated, there is danger that by delaying you will lose your viewpoint, or at any rate lose something of the spirit that you had when you planned out the book."

Another deadline was set to assure spring publication, but that too was missed, in part because she spent much of the summer editing a manuscript that Henry Demarest Lloyd had left unfinished when he died. Finally in desperation Ely offered her a chance to lecture on "Newer Ideals of Peace" at the summer session of the University of Wisconsin. He was willing to pay her $250 for twelve lectures, and she accepted because "It will be the only way to get my book out." She finally delivered the manuscript in September 1906. "I am sorry that it isn't better," she wrote, "but I do not believe that I will improve it by writing on it any longer." Ely thought on the whole it was acceptable though he was unhappy with the style of the first part, and he added semicolons and commas and shortened many of her sentences. "Generally speaking I would say that you do not punctuate sufficiently," he suggested. She continued to revise and improve the manuscript at every stage, changing many things even in page proofs to the despair of her editors. But at last it was finished.[19]

Newer Ideals of Peace, finally published early in 1907, was a muted, and optimistic book. It was even in spots naïve and sentimental. Continuing the theme of finding a substitute for war and the military spirit, and giving explicit credit to William James, she began by attacking the "older dovelike ideal" of peace as represented especially by Tolstoy. For Tolstoy's non-resistance, which suggested "passivity, the goody-goody attitude of ineffectiveness," she would substitute "more aggressive ideals of peace." But it quickly became apparent that these ideals were not very aggressive. They were already present in the "poorer quarters of a cosmopolitan city where men and women of many different nationalities mixed and mingled." These people were in the process of forming a new internationalism which would supplant the old national loyalties, and make war obsolete "for after all the things that make men alike are stronger and more primitive than the things that separate them." Of course, the "fighting rabble," the "quarrelsome mob" did not yet know that they were leading the world to peace; they still shout for war. Yet, she continued hopefully, "we care less each day for heroism connected with warfare and destruction and constantly admire more that which pertains to labor and the nourishing of human life. The new heroism manifests itself at the present moment in a universal determination to abolish poverty and disease, a manifestation so widespread that it may justly be called international." While some peace advocates, Elihu Root and Nicholas Murray Butler, for example, argued that it was the irrational masses who drove the leaders to war, Jane Addams found the hope for the prevention of war in the peaceful instincts of working men and women.

She described the survivals of the old military spirit, that had not yet faded away. The cities depended too much on "penalties, coercion, compulsion, remnants of military codes, to hold the community together." It was not by accident, she argued, that the police department, "the most vigorous survival of militarism to be found in American cities" was responsible for the greatest amount of corruption. Much of the corruption ironically was caused by the breakdown of the military discipline, by the policeman's kindness, for "all kindness is illicit on the part of the military sentinel on duty but to bring that code over bodily into a peaceful social state is to breakdown the morals of both sides, of the enforcer of the ill adapted law, as well as of those against whom it is so maladroitly directed."

Much of the book was not about peace and war, but about the plight of the cities—the immigrants, the working women and children. She defended organized labor and saw in its communal spirit and loyalty to a larger ideal, a hope for universal peace. "Workmen have always realized, however feebly and vaguely they may have expressed it," she argued, "that it is they who in all ages have borne the heaviest burden of privation and suffering imposed on the world by the military spirit, but she criticized employer and trade unionist alike for resorting to the use of brute force, "to the method of warfare."

Throughout the book she demonstrated a great faith in the industrial process and in the American free enterprise system, though she advocated more social legislation. She hoped that the industrial factory could somehow utilize some of the *esprit de corps* that children naturally had in their spontaneous games, the force of cooperation of an athletic team or the thrill of martial music and the common cause of the arms. Just how this industrial "spirit," the "sense of endurance and discipline," were going to aid the average factory worker, or become a substitute for the appeal of the military, she did not explain.

She was also not entirely clear about how exactly woman's new role in industry and government was going to promote peace. Woman's work had traditionally been that of taking care of the family, its health and education, she argued. But now that industrialism and the modern city had usurped some of her traditional role, woman should be given the vote so that she could regain some of her old function as nurturer through participating in the government. "She will bear her share of civic responsibility because she is essential to the normal development of the city of the future, and because the definition of the loyal citizen as one who is ready to shed his blood for his country, has become inadequate and obsolete." Women, Addams believed, could restore a larger meaning to citizenship through their maternal instincts, but how this would preserve world peace she was not entirely clear.

Throughout the book there is the idealistic assumption that the new industrial age, especially with the growth of democracy and woman suffrage, was in the process of making war impossible, that "constructive labor" was replacing destructive warfare. There would come a time very soon when we would all appreciate the truth which Ruskin had stated many times, "that we worship the soldier, not because he goes forth to slay, but be slain." And very soon all men would be like the Russian peasant, a member of the Dukhobors, who refused to enter the army. He was brought to trial and the judge "reasoned with him concerning the folly of his course and in return received a homily upon the teaching of Jesus. 'Quite right you are,' answered the judge, 'from the point of abstract virtue, but the time has not yet come to put into practice the literal saying of Christ.' 'The time may not have come for you, your Honor,' was the reply, 'but the time has come for us.' "[20]

William James was one of the first to receive a copy of the book. He wrote enthusiastically, but somewhat cryptically, "I soothed myself by the perusal of your book. I find it hard to express the good it has done me in opening new points of view and annihilating old ones. New perspectives of hope! I don't care about this detail or that, it is the new *setting of questions*. Yours is a deeply original mind, and all so quiet and harmless! Yet revolutionary in the extreme, and I should suspect that this very work would act as a ferment these long years to come. I read precious little sociological literature, and my opinions in that field are worth nothing, but I am willing to bet on you." He also said that the publisher had sent him an extra copy and suggested sending it to George Bernard Shaw, assuming that she had not sent him a copy. "I *bet* (again) that it will stimulate his genius in the most extraordinary way . . . B.S. is a fanatic moralist of the new type and will some day be cared for as such."[21]

Jane Addams had not sent a copy to Shaw, but he was one of the few men and women of prominence in England and America that she had forgotten. She sent complimentary copies to more than 50 college professors hoping they might use the book in their classes. In addition she sent the book to social workers, friends, and acquaintances. The legend of Jane Addams portrays her as modest and self-effacing, but in reality she was ambitious and eager for publicity.

The book did not sell as well as some of her later studies, not even as well as *Democracy and Social Ethics*. Peace was not an especially popular subject in 1907, but nearly 2800 copies sold the first year, and over 6000 copies had sold by the time the United States entered World War I. Not everyone was as enthusiastic as William James about the book. Florence Kelley thought the title was misleading. "The book was not so much about peace," she maintained, "as a curious commentary on the fact that we have not yet attained self government," but in a personal letter she wrote, "it is whole and wise, and parts of it are beautiful."[22] Others commented on the lack of unity in the book. "It is disappointing to pick up a self-professed monograph and discover that it is only a collection of somewhat miscellaneous essays," the *New York Tribune* decided. "I think in logical organization this book suffers more than her earlier writing," George Mead wrote. A few critics disagreed with her basic idea that there was a need for a substitute for war. "Unfortunately one has a fixed conviction that as the world is now constituted circumstances may arise in which it is necessary for a nation to go to war and when not going to war is national dishonor," a Chicago newspaper suggested. "One is also of the opinion that one of the best guarantees of immunity from attack is the ability successfully to withstand that attack." Theodore Roosevelt, as might have been expected, did not like the book. He called her "Foolish Jane Addams," and implied that she did not have the "strength, training, and natural ability" to withstand the naïve and sentimental theories of Tolstoy. Shortly after he left the White House in 1909 he wrote an essay for the *Outlook*. Without mentioning her name, he used her as an example of the comic and evil effects of Tolstoy's teachings on his American followers. "One of these disciples, for instance, not long ago wrote a book on American municipal problems," he noted, "which ascribed our ethical and social shortcomings in municipal matters in part to the sin of 'militarism.' Now the mind of this particular writer in making such a statement was influenced not in the least by what had actually occurred or was occurring in our cities, but by one of Tolstoy's theories which has no possible bearing upon American life." She did not reply to him; she merely clipped and filed the article, but Francis Hackett, Hull House resident and editor of the *Chicago Evening Post* responded for her. "*Newer Ideals of Peace* is a profound and searching, as well as practical, analysis of American tendencies," he wrote. "It has nobility, without the demerits of egoism and extravagance, whereas Mr. Roosevelt's sneer is egoistic and extravagant, without a trace of nobility."[23]

At least Roosevelt, flippantly and in passing, dealt with her thesis, and that was something that most of the reviewers failed to do. Unlike the former President they were enthralled by Jane Addams and devoted their space to her rather than to her book. Richard Watson Gilder, the journalist and novelist, was inspired to write a poem which he dedicated to her. "No one else could have written it because no one else could have felt it," *The North American Review* announced. "Miss Addams is not primarily a writer of books," another reviewer suggested, "she is a woman who has sought to realize to the fullest extent of her great ability and her great spirit the capacity of social sympathy." The reviewer for the *Chicago Tribune* compared her to Catherine of Siena. "Her temperate, judicious, infinitely kind utterance seems to furnish the nuclei around which the drifting star dust of our souls gathers, shining thence forth with a radiance new and strange . . . Back of it lies illimitable sympathy, immeasurable pity, a spirit as free as that of St. Francis, a sense of social order and fitness that Marcus Aurelius might have found similar to his own."[24]

Such praise and adoration obscured the message she was trying to convey. But it was difficult to get the American people excited about the problems of peace and war in 1907, or to get them to consider seriously any substitute for the military virtues. To be against war was not a radical position or a subversive idea despite Roosevelt's blustering diatribe, indeed opposition to war was easy to ignore. One newspaper called her "the little handmaiden of peace," but in general her opposition to war and militarism did not lend itself to saintliness quite the way aiding the poor did, and so many of those who saw her as a saint ignored her pacifism.

Jane Addams' efforts to promote peace did not occupy a great portion of her time in the years before 1914, but her major insight (borrowed in part from William James and G. Stanley Hall) that it was possible to sublimate and redirect basic human drives informed her thinking and writing about the other problems she observed in the Hull House neighborhood. It influenced her attitudes toward the young people she saw growing up and getting into trouble in the city, and resulted in the book which she always claimed was her favorite, *The Spirit of Youth and the City Streets.*

Concern for children and youth in the city led the Hull House residents into a variety of activities and reform movements. They began a kindergarten, and a playground, they started all kinds of clubs and classes and recreational activities and they tried to improve the schools. They worried about the widening split between immigrant parents and their rapidly Americanized children. They tried to preserve the customs of the old country to ease the conflict. The Labor Museum, the theater, the festivals, the woodworking and pottery classes, even the Hull House basketball team were all designed, at least in part, to ease the burden of growing up in the city.

Yet all these activities did not keep the young people who lived in the Hull House neighborhood from getting into trouble with the law. The settlement workers were disturbed that many juvenile offenders were picked up for minor offenses and then were thrown together with hardened criminals. The spirit of adventure, the impulsive action, which would be of little consequence for the rural youth, often resulted in a prison term and a life of crime for the city youngster. Concerned about this situation, the Hull House group agitated for a new law which, in 1899, provided for the first Juvenile Court in the nation. The Juvenile Court was not a criminal court, and was supposed to keep the rights and interests of the offender chiefly in mind. The judge could put the delinquent on probation, make him a ward of the state, or assign him to an institution. While the main idea was to help rather than to penalize the child, it did not always work out that way, for the judge had great power while the offender had none of the rights of due process. Not until 1967 did a U.S. Supreme Court decision recognize that even juvenile offenders were entitled to procedural rights. Still, at the time, the Juvenile Court represented a major breakthrough in the treatment of boys and girls in trouble. Alzina Stevens of Hull House was the first probation officer of the court, and Julia Lathrop and then Louise Bowen were successively chairmen of the Juvenile Court Committee. Through the cases that came before the court the Hull House residents had a chance to study systematically the problem of the juvenile delinquent, and to try to understand why he got into trouble. Jane Addams used material collected by the Juvenile Court to illustrate *Spirit of Youth,* and she dedicated the book to Mrs. Bowen, the chairman of the court committee. In 1909, the same year that Jane Addams' book was published, the Hull House reformers organized the Juvenile Protective Association, an outgrowth of the Juvenile Court Committee. One of its purposes was to control or eliminate poolrooms, bars, dance halls, theaters, and other institutions which the committee felt were breeders of crime and vice. Also in 1909 the reformers founded the Juvenile Psychopathic Institute at Hull House. Under the direction of Dr. William Healy it became a leading center for research into the causes of delinquency. Healy's careful studies resulted in such books as *The Individual Delinquent* (1915) which rejected the theory that delinquency and crime were primarily caused by heredity. He emphasized that while delinquency had many causes, environment was the most important. In a more informal way, without the scientific evidence, Jane Addams came to a similar conclusion in her book.[25]

She was influenced in her thinking by a large number of studies of childhood and youth in the nineteenth century. Some of this concern for "child study" was stimulated by Darwin and also by Friedrich Froebel, founder of the kindergarten movement in Germany and led to a conception of the child as something special, and not just a little adult. The concept of adolescence, of a special time between childhood and adulthood, developed gradually during the nineteenth century, but it was not until the first decade of the twentieth century that the idea became firmly planted in the national consciousness. In America the leading authority on childhood and adolescence was G. Stanley Hall, a leading psychologist and president of Clark University. In 1904 he published *Adolescence: Its Psychology, and Its Relations to Physiology, Anthropology, Sociology, Sex, Crime and Education.* This encyclopedic work contained an immense amount of information and had a large impact on thinking about adolescence in many fields, indeed it introduced the term "adolescence" into common usage. Perhaps his most important theory was his idea of "recapitulation," that a child in his growth and development "recapitulated" the history of the race, that babies in their need to grasp and small children in the urge to climb showed their kinship with the apes. Adolescence in this theory took on a crucial importance for it represented the most recent of man's great leaps, and the adolescent had the possibility of advancing beyond the present stage of civilization. But Hall also saw this transitional stage as a troubled time of contradiction and emotional stress. Not everyone accepted Hall's ideas, and his theory of "recapitulation" was repudiated within two decades, but his work did serve to focus attention on the child and especially the adolescent.[26]

Jane Addams was familiar with Hall's work, and she used his theories in arguing for more parks and playgrounds for the children who needed an outlet for their animal energies. The romantic belief in the civilizing possibilities of youth that permeates the *Spirit of Youth* also owes something to Hall as do constant references to primitive instincts. Yet she never once used the term "adolescence" in the book, preferring the older and more general phrase "youth." Her first thought was to call the book "Juvenile Delinquency and Public Morality," or "Juvenile Crime and Public Morals." She rejected these titles because they seemed too sociological, implied facts and figures and footnotes, and she had something more literary in mind, something that would appeal to a wide audience.

The greatest forces in Jane Addams' developing ideas were her observations in Chicago and the memories of her own childhood and youth. Part of her genius and success as a writer was her ability to adapt the theories of others and to make universal her own experience. Everything she wrote was in a real sense autobiographical.

Jane Addams wrote the *Spirit of Youth*, as she wrote most of her books, by first approaching a topic in a speech, then reworking it into an article, and finally arranging and rewriting the articles into a book manuscript. She revised constantly. The first time she gave a speech she often spoke from notes, talking quietly and calmly with a voice that could be heard easily throughout the auditorium. She illustrated her points with stories of people, sometimes pathetic, occasionally heroic, but always believable. As she gave the speech again and again the timing became better, the illustrations sharper, until gradually she developed a polished manuscript. Usually she wrote her material out by hand before giving it to a secretary to type. Then she would cut up the typed manuscript, putting it back together again with straight pins, while writing in transitions and new ideas. She had not only become a professional writer, but she had learned how to drive a hard bargain and get the top price for her articles and books. Her first two books had been published in a series edited by Richard Ely for Macmillan, but as she planned a new book she decided to negotiate the terms herself. In February 1909, she wrote Edwin Marsh, the Macmillan editor, suggesting she might have a manuscript on juvenile delinquency ready by October 15. Marsh was delighted, he realized what a valuable property she was. He offered her "a royalty of 13% on the retail price of the first 1500 copies sold and 15% on all copies sold thereafter." She replied quickly: "The terms you suggest are not as advantageous as those your company gave me for *Newer Ideals of Peace*. I have just looked over your account rendered April 30th, 1908, and find that I received 16¼ per cent upon 1112 copies of *Newer Ideals of Peace* and 16¼ per cent upon 497 of *Democracy and Social Ethics*, I am not able at this moment to lay my hand upon the original agreement, but I remember being paid an out and out sum when the manuscript was delivered. I think the sum was $100." As it turned out she was mistaken and had confused 16¼ cents per copy with the percentage, which had been 13 on the previous books, but this penchant for bargaining for every dollar, for getting the best possible contract, was very much a part of her personality.[27]

A determined pride and high professional standards motivated her as she prepared the book. It was to be composed of essays and speeches she had done over a period of two years, a speech before the National Society for the Promotion of Industrial Education, an article that had appeared in *Charities and the Commons* called "Public Recreation and Social Morality," an address given for the New York Playground Association, an article that had been published in the *Ladies Home Journal* called "Why Girls Go Wrong," and some other material. In the spring and summer of 1909 she spliced the pieces together, rearranging and rewriting until she had a finished manuscript—a manuscript which, unlike some of her other work, was changed very little as it passed from typescript to galley proofs to page proofs. The book was published in November 1909, with two excerpts appearing in the *Ladies Home Journal* in October and November. The Macmillan editor was not sure he liked the title of the book and was worried about confusion of copyright with the magazine excerpts and the book coming out so closely together, but he did appreciate the speed and efficiency with which Jane Addams worked. It had been barely nine months since she had suggested that she might have a book manuscript ready for fall, a marked contrast to the four years of struggle it took to finish *Newer Ideals of Peace*. Yet she could still write to a friend: "I am sending you a copy of the book which I regard with mixed emotions, one is gratitude that it is out at last, and the other regret that I did not fuss with it longer."[28]

Perhaps the most remarkable aspect of the book, given the time that it was written, was Addams' appreciation of the importance of sex and the basic erotic instincts, although she always assumed that the sex drive was more important for the male than for the female.) She referred to "the emotional force," the "fundamental instinct," "this sex susceptibility," and, although she knew nothing of Freud, she suggested that the sex drive furnished "the momentum toward all art." She argued that this natural instinct if repressed served as "a cancer in the very tissues of society" and resulted in all kinds of deviant behavior. A good portion of the book is taken up with descriptions of how the modern city overstimulates the adolescent.) "The newly awakened senses are appealed to by all that is gaudy and sensual, by flippant street music, the highly colored theater posters, the trashy love stories, the feathered hats, the cheap heroics of the revolvers displayed in the pawnshop windows," as well as movie theatres, dance halls, prostitution, and drugs. The rural youth of another age, and of her memory, never had to face these temptations. In rural America the quest for adventure led to harmless pranks, but in the city the same impulse resulted in arrest and jail. She never argued for turning the clock back, for returning to the world of the small town, but rather she insisted on the need to channel and sublimate the natural drives of youth into creative and socially acceptable paths. She suggested Mollière and Shakespeare to replace the cheap movie, chaperoned parties to compete with the dance halls, recreation centers and settlements to substitute for the saloon, parks and playgrounds and competitive sports to replace the spirit of adventure associated with drugs and liquor. She realized how difficult it is to find a "moral equivalent" for juvenile delinquency, and yet she revealed a certain naïve optimism in believing that her substitute would work. She was much more convincing in describing the irresistible attraction of the train, the movies, and the dance halls than in defining the alternatives. There is an assumption throughout that the lower-class, urban environment of saloon, dance halls, and street life needed to be changed and made more like a middle- or upper-class neighborhood. And yet the book was amazingly free of an attitude of moral superiority and of puritanical preaching.

There was, however, another and more fundamental cause for the discontent of youth in the city—the industrial system which employed them for long hours in meaningless jobs.) The city youth was not able to expend his energy in a worthwhile job as the rural youth could, for factory work tired only the nerves and the senses, not the body. She understood the dullness and the monotony of factory work, but her solutions seemed to beg the question. She accepted the industrial revolution and realized that the machine was here to stay, but she had no great faith in technology. She wanted to control the machine so that it would not destroy the man who was forced to run it. She also wanted to preserve the art and skill of the craftsman. She put great faith in a practical industrial education to train young men and women for the real jobs they would be doing. She argued for a team spirit (for a kind of giant Labor Museum) so that 39 men all working on the same product would appreciate that they were actually a meaningful part of one operation. It was the same industrial *esprit de corps* she hoped would replace the military virtues. She supported a revolt against shoddy, poorly designed products, and against dehumanizing working conditions. But never did she carry her arguments to their logical conclusion and suggest that there is something fundamentally wrong with the industrial system. In the end, although she carefully documented the destruction being wrought by the factory, the best she could offer was to help adjust the young people to the system and make them a little happier in the process.

Jane Addams sent a copy of her book to Vida Scudder, a Christian Socialist who was an English professor at Wellesley College, and one of the founders of the College Settlement Association. After praising the "rare and lovely tenderness" of the book, Miss Scudder continued: "I rebuke myself, but I grow heavy of heart as the years pass on, 'save the children,' was our cry when the settlements started twenty years ago. Those children are men and women now, fathers and mothers and still we raise the same cry and hold the new generation under the same stupid and criminal conditions as the old. How long, O Lord how long." But Jane Addams, like most of the progressives, was more optimistic, for unlike the socialists she still had faith that the system could be patched and made to work; that the right legislation would solve the difficulties.[29]

It was probably the calm optimistic answer to the problem of juvenile delinquency that made *Spirit of Youth* a success, that, with her faith in the potential, in the civilizing and regenerative power of the young. It sold 7000 copies the first year, and a total of 18,000 to 20,000 during her lifetime, and many more people got the message through her articles and speeches. There was praise from sociologists, psychologists and from ordinary citizens. William James wrote in the *American Journal of Sociology*: "Certain pages of Miss Addams' book seem to me to contain immortal statements of the fact that the essential and perennial function of the Youth-period is to reaffirm authentically the value and the charm of Life. All the details of the little book flow from this central insight or persuasion. Of how they flow I can give no account, for the wholeness of Miss Addams' embrace of life is her own secret. She simply inhabits reality, and everything she says necessarily expresses its nature. She *can't help writing truth.*

A few years later Walter Rauschenbusch, re-reading the book, took the trouble to write and express his admiration. "You have a womanly and a poetic comprehension of human nature which enables you to see its nobility even in the most ignoble expressions. I have often said in public that I know of no one among contemporary writers in this whole field who has so much power of interpretation as you have. You make us see what we have always seen and never seen."[30] She added to her reputation and lent credence to the myth of special spiritual powers, by publishing her autobiography the next year.

IX

Twenty Years at Hull House

N the preface to *Twenty Years at Hull House*, published in 1910, Jane Addams gave two reasons for writing her autobiography at that time. "Because settlements have multiplied so easily in the United States," she explained, "I hoped that a simple statement of an earlier effort, including the stress and storm, might be of value in their interpretation and possibly clear them of a certain charge of superficiality." Her second reason, she maintained, was to start a "backfire" to extinguish two biographies already under way, one of which "made life in a settlement all too smooth and charming."[1] These are possible and reasonable explanations, but we must ask, as Erik Erikson asks of Gandhi's autobiography, why it was written at the precise time it was, what sense it makes in the context of her earlier life, what community it was written for, and how much of the book was truth, how much illusion?[2]

Twenty Years at Hull House, like all autobiographies, bears a close resemblance to fiction. Especially in writing of her early years, but to a large extent throughout the book, she organizes her vague memories into a pattern, reflecting on incidents, even on dreams, that may or may not have happened as she remembered, but which take on a new reality in the writing and in the brooding over the recollections. "The act of writing about oneself brings together the personal, unassimilated experiences of the writer and the shared values of his culture," one study of American autobiographies suggests. "The act of recollection becomes an act of creation and an act of self-evaluation at the same time."[3] Like most American autobiographical literature (and American literature is especially rich in autobiographies and thinly disguised autobiographical fiction), *Twenty Years at Hull House* tries to probe the essence of the American experience, and both consciously and unconsciously attempts to fit one life into the American dream.

X Jane Addams, even as a young girl, was introspective. Her letters were often filled with self-evaluation, and her college writing constantly sought to understand her own experience and to make it universal. This autobiographical habit of mind increased in the years after college—the years of self-doubt and search for a career. After the founding of Hull House she suddenly had more to write about, but whether she was defining the impulse behind the settlement movement, or describing the poor housing and the child labor abuses in Chicago, she was quick to deal with each situation in personal terms. Her insight that well-educated young ladies needed activity rather than rest to cure their nervous illness came from probing her own experience and her observation of her friends. Her ability to describe the pathos of the child working in a factory from dawn to dusk and then playing in the streets, came in part from her ability to relate this experience to her memory (and the memory of her readers) of a different kind of rural childhood.

She thought autobiographically in part because she was by nature introspective and in part because she was in constant need of establishing her own identity and place in the world. She started writing her own story during the summer of 1905, and she published three articles early in 1906 in the *Ladies Home Journal* which contained most of the key incidents of the book.[4] She was not quite 45 when she began the account of her life, but she was already a celebrity, and had reached a pinnacle of success and popular approval. She was awarded an honorary degree by the University of Wisconsin in June 1904, delivered the convocation address at the University of Chicago in December 1904, and she was appointed a member of the Chicago School Board in 1905. Her personal life had settled down to what she called a "healing domesticity." With Mary Smith she had purchased a cottage near Bar Harbor, Maine, in 1904 and their relationship continued to be a source of strength and support. Her book, *Democracy and Social Ethics*, published in 1902, had received extravagant praise and was going into a new edition in the summer of 1905. Magazine and book editors clamored for her work, she was in constant demand as a speaker, and was already treated by the public as a spiritual leader and saint. A feature article on her in *Harper's Bazar* in October 1904 ran to six full pages and dwelled at length on her sad face, her "divine inquisitiveness" and how "her patriotism took to itself an exquisite feminine and spiritual form." "Miss Addams has walked a long road," the article continued, "and she has come at last to a beautiful and windless place, a plateau of high altitude, where a wonderful peace lies brooding. Her melancholy eyes behold much—behold the pageants of earth and the long terrible processions of the poor. The friendship she pours out upon them is the essence of friendship—something spiritualized and made universal. It related itself not to one person nor to a group of persons, but to the whole world. . . . She walks in the paths which only the great-spirited may tread."[5]

Success, adoration, and growing confidence led Jane Addams to begin her autobiography. She wanted to tell her version of her life because she was confident it would help those who read it. She chose to publish the first excerpts in the *Ladies Home Journal,* which had one of the largest circulations of any American magazine, because she wanted to reach the widest audience possible, not just a community of social workers or those interested in settlements. Here was a chance, in the face of publicity and honors, to rediscover and confirm her own sense of identity, and to give a new creative shape to her life. She sought to reinforce her role as priestess and feminine spiritual leader in America.[6]

Henry Steele Commager, in the foreword to a 1961 paperback edition of *Twenty Years at Hull House,* wrote: "She never thought of herself; even her autobiography is the story of Hull House. Was there ever a more impersonal autobiography? Miss Addams does not ask us to consider her, but only the society she served . . . ," he decided.[7] But she did think of herself, and her autobiography is a conscious attempt to focus the reader's attention on Jane Addams. Her motives were not entirely selfish, of course, she did want to promote her reform ideas and to publicize Hull House, but what better way to accomplish these goals than to write of herself as a heroine?

If she had been concerned primarily with telling the story of Hull House she could have done so without writing at such length about her childhood and youth, but most of the people who wanted to know about Hull House, who wanted to understand its function and its beginnings, were interested in the life of its founder. Like most popular writers describing the settlement, she began at the beginning and reconstructed her life. But writing about oneself, especially about the childhood years is difficult. How does one organize and select from the memories and to what purpose?

She began the first article in the *Ladies Home Journal* with a sentence left out of the book. "I have been asked many times to recall, if possible, my first impulse or determination to live among the poor, and have always found myself at loss for a reply." The key incidents of her first chapter were published in the magazine version in 1906, and are organized around the influence of her father. She says quite honestly that of course she had other memories, "but because my father was so distinctly the dominant influence and because it is quite impossible to set forth all of one's early impressions it has seemed simpler to string these first memories on that single cord." Even though her father was a strong influence, she distorts the true picture of her childhood by concentrating on him. Her stepmother—Anna Haldeman Addams, who had a great impact on her formative years, is not even mentioned in the autobiography. Much later her niece, Marcet Haldeman-Julius, the daughter of her sister Alice, asked her "if it were not true that grandmother had been a constructive force in her life—in some ways even more than had my grandfather." She answered " 'yes,' but added that it was 'all too complicated.' "[8]

It was not only too complicated it was also much more natural and believable for a young girl to admire her father and by putting the emphasis on the father-daughter relationship she was describing a situation that was familiar to all who had read American fiction. "Mother died so long ago that I only cherished a memory . . . Since her death I had been my father's all, as he had been mine," a nineteenth-century heroine confessed. Henry James in *The Golden Bowl* wrote of a daughter who was "passionately filial" and a father who was "peculiarly paternal." Indeed many of the most impressive young women in nineteenth-century fiction have an intense affection for their fathers. It was somehow assumed that such a relationship prepared a girl for marriage. One critic has suggested that writers in the genteel tradition sought "to idealize the affection between a tender daughter and a solicitous father in order to please a sentimental society. Placing a girl within her father's orbit was first of all good politics and only incidentally acute psychology. Yet the relation provided a kind of shorthand through which the two most perplexing qualities in a woman's character—her virtue and her accessibility—were rendered graphic: it guaranteed her lure and did not discredit her honor."[9]

Jane Addams was probably not consciously aware that she was patterning her first chapter after the fiction of her day or that she was using a genteel shorthand for a special relationship between father and daughter. But when she described how as a young girl she desperately wanted to have a smooth miller's thumb like her father or how she would confess to him that she had told a lie, her readers understood.

By creating an image of a strong, purposeful, stern, and honest father she was also able to picture herself as motherless, weak and unsure, indeed she became "an ugly duckling" a "pigeon-toed little girl, whose crooked back obliged her to walk with her head held very much upon one side," and who avoided walking with her father as they left church so that strangers would not connect "this ugly child with this fine gentleman." But almost all heroes and heroines from classical myths to American tales of self-made men start out life with a handicap. They are weak or crippled or poor. They must have something to overcome before they achieve success and fame.[10]

At the same time that she pictured herself as physically weak and handicapped she also (again in the tradition of heroes and heroines of all times) endowed herself with special precocious powers and foresight, and implied that the decision to found Hull House came from a childhood experience.

I recall an incident which must have occurred before I was seven years old, for the mill in which my father transacted his business that day was closed in 1867. The mill stood in the neighboring town adjacent to its poorest quarter. Before then I had always seen the little city of ten thousand people with the admiring eyes of a country child, and it had never occurred to me that all its streets were not as bewilderingly attractive as the one which contained the glittering toyshop and the confectioner. On that day I had my first sight of the poverty which implies squalor, and felt the curious distinction between the ruddy poverty of the country and that which even a small city presents in its shabbiest streets. I remember launching at my father the pertinent inquiry why people lived in such horrid little houses so close together, and that after receiving his explanation I declared with much firmness when I grew up I should, of course, have a large house, but it would not be built among the other large houses, but right in the midst of horrid little houses like these.[11]

The origin of this legend is not clear, though there is some indication that it is based on a family story and it was recounted in one version as early as 1892, in an article published in a Chicago newspaper. "She was a gray-eyed slender, little creature, full of daydreams. She had a passion for beautiful things. She built air castles, had lively plans of what she would do when she was a woman. 'I shall have a splendid house!' she said, 'I won't have it in a row with all other houses. I shall have books and pictures, and I am going to have it just right in the midst of dingy, dreadful houses, streets and streets of them so that people who don't have much can come and enjoy my things.' " This article may have been based on an interview (although it differs from Jane Addams' version in almost every detail), and the story may have some basis in fact, but in telling it in her autobiography she gave an explanation for the founding of Hull House—a childhood plan, a dream carried out many years later. This story of childhood foresight would be told in almost every account of Jane Addams' life from that time forward and the story distorted the real reason for the founding of Hull House, but it was believable and contributed to the folk lore and legend which collected about her name.[12]

Some kind of childhood plan or dream or decision is quite common in the autobiographies and the legends of the famous as an explanation for their later acts and deeds of glory. Sarah Grimké in explaining why she became an abolitionist recalled that when she was four years old she saw a slave whipped and instantly resolved to fight against the evil institution. The Lincoln legend also explains his opposition to slavery by citing a childhood incident. And the Washington myth depicts the greatness of the man through the boyhood story of the cherry tree.[13] Universally the hero or heroine is endowed with extraordinary powers from childhood, or even from the moment of birth, although he has handicaps to overcome and a long period of obscurity to live through, he is endowed with precocious strength, cleverness and wisdom. In addition to the "big house among small houses" story, Jane Addams indicated her early sense of fear and responsibility by relating how she had a dream "night after night" that everyone in the world was dead except herself and that upon her rested the responsibility of making a wagon wheel.[14]

The image of an ugly duckling with a precocious wisdom and dreams of great responsibility came through in the early part of the autobiography, but that was not all. She not only connected her story with the great myths of all heroes and heroines and thus made it believable, but she also appealed to the nostalgia of those who, like herself, had grown up in rural, small-town America. She recreated the childhood experiences filled with dreams and nightmares; but she also recalled the world of the mill, the blacksmith shop, the Sunday school, and one-roomed school, the woods and the hills. "The intimate fellowship of my boyhood with loving and thoughtful parents made your first chapter very dear to me," one man wrote. Other readers recalled their own experiences around mills and streams, or reading Mazzini, or hearing Lincoln speak. "I am surprised that your conclusions and inner experiences should have been so similar to my own," a woman wrote from Kentucky.[15]

Her second chapter "The Influence of Lincoln" continued the nostalgia for a past which could never be recaptured. "I suppose all the children who were born about the time of the Civil War have recollections quite unlike those of children who are living now," she began, and recalled how she felt on that day, even though she was only four and a half, when her father told her that "the greatest man in the world had died." She recounted how the children in her tiny village were fascinated by the picture of the one armed soldier, who had survived the war, how they liked to drive by the house of a gentle old lady whose son had died a hero and had died at home because his mother had overcome Army red tape and rescued him from the military hospital where he lay. But, despite their intense interest in war heroes they always fell silent as they approached an isolated farm house outside the village where two people lived alone. "Five of their sons had enlisted in the Civil War, and only the youngest had returned alive in the spring of 1865. In the autumn of the same year, when he was hunting for wild ducks in a swamp on the rough little farm itself, he was accidentally shot and killed, and the old people were left alone to struggle with the half-cleared land as best they might." These incidents and stories connected with her home town had always fascinated her. She had used them in slightly different form in an essay written shortly after she had graduated from college. She changed a line here, a word there, or condensed a paragraph, and then in the autobiography she added a moral. On the injustice of one family losing five boys she remarked: "It was well perhaps that life thus early gave me a hint of one of her most obstinate and insoluble riddles, for I have sorely needed the sense of universality thus imparted to that mysterious injustice, the burden of which we are all forced to bear and with which I have become only too familiar." *Twenty Years at Hull House*, like most American autobiographies, taught a lesson, preached a sermon.[16]

But there was more than moral lessons and nostalgia for the time of the Civil War when American democracy met its greatest test—and survived. Jane Addams also connected herself to the great American folk hero and symbol of the best of American Democracy. She told of how her father would show her a small packet of letters in his desk marked "Mr Lincoln's Letters"—written by Lincoln to Addams while both were engaged in Illinois politics. The letters always began "My dear Double D'ed Addams," (and they have never been discovered by two generations of avid searchers). She recalled a trip to Wisconsin to see an eagle named "Old Abe," mascot of a Wisconsin regiment, and told how the eagle and Lincoln seemed to her symbolic of "all that was great and good." She also described how years later in Chicago, when she was worried and perplexed, she would walk several miles to Lincoln Park where the St. Gaudens' statue of Lincoln somehow gave her courage to go on. She felt chagrined because she was offered a bribe and her father (and Lincoln) had the reputation of not only never having taken a bribe, but of never having been offered one. The result of her chapter was to connect herself to the Lincoln ideal. After her stories appeared in print most of the popular accounts of her life mentioned the connection; indeed she became the female counterpart of Lincoln. Born, like Lincoln, in rural Illinois, she came to represent, as he did, the best of the old-fashioned American virtues, hard work, humility, integrity, honesty. They both possessed a pensive brooding quality; they were compassionate and spiritual, but good natured, and they believed in equal opportunity for all.[17]

A few months after *Twenty Years at Hull House* was published, she was in Boston for a speech and one of the Boston newspapers made much of the occasion:

> Miss Addams comes to Boston when the citizens of the United States are recalling reverently the personality of that great American father, Lincoln, the Emancipator. There are living a very few men and women in this city, who heard Lincoln on his trip to Boston more than sixty years ago. Sixty years hence, if history repeats itself, others will recall the visit of that mother Emancipator from Illinois—Jane Addams.
>
> Lincoln stood alone for the right when it took a man of courage to make that stand. The forces of race prejudice and ignorance and darkness, which he battled with, were not unlike the foes which have engaged Jane Addams for twenty years. She, too, has fought to free the unfortunate men, women and children of Chicago from their inherited shackles of discrimination, prejudice, ignorance.[18]

Not everyone depicted her as "the mother Emancipator" but nearly all saw her as the symbol of American woman at her best—the new woman, educated and taking her place as a leader in society. She added to this impression in her autobiography especially in her chapter called "Boarding School Ideals" where she told her version of her college years —the intellectual striving, the Christian atmosphere, the self-conscious desire that was probably similar to, if not typical of, the experience of many other women who were going to college. Her essay on her college years, which suggests a little less stridently than Henry Adams, that she really did not get a very useful education in college, struck an authentic note for many who read the book. But the way she distorted the facts, altered the story, or simply failed to remember can be illustrated by one incident as she described it at the time and as she wrote about it later in her autobiography.

One of the high points of her senior year was a trip in the spring to the interstate oratorical contest at Jacksonville, Illinois.

In line with this policy of placing a woman's college on an equality with the other colleges of the state, we applied for an opportunity to compete in the intercollegiate oratorical contest of Illinois, and we succeeded in having Rockford admitted as the first woman's college. When I was finally selected as the orator, I was somewhat dismayed to find that, representing not only one school but college women in general, I could not resent the brutal frankness with which my oratorical possibilities were discussed by the enthusiastic group who would allow no personal feeling to stand in the way of progress, especially the progress of Woman's Cause. I was told among other things that I had an intolerable habit of dropping my voice at the end of a sentence in the most feminine, apologetic and even deprecatory manner which would probably lose Women the first place.

Women certainly did lose the first place and stood fifth, exactly in the dreary middle, but the ignominious position may not have been solely due to bad mannerisms, for a prior place was easily accorded to William Jennings Bryan, who not only thrilled his auditors with an almost prophetic anticipation of the cross of gold, but with a moral earnestness which we had mistakenly assumed would be the unique possession of the feminine orator.

I so heartily concurred with the decision of the judges of the contest that it was with a care-free mind that I induced my colleague and alternate to remain long enough in "The Athens of Illinois," in which the successful college was situated, to visit the state institutions, one for the Blind and one for the Deaf and Dumb. Doctor Gillette was at that time head of the latter institution; his scholarly explanation of the method of teaching, his concern for his charges, this sudden demonstration of the care the state bestowed upon its most unfortunate children, filled me with grave speculations in which the first, the fifth, or the ninth place in an oratorical contest seemed of little moment.

However, this brief delay between our field of Waterloo and our arrival at our aspiring college turned out to be most unfortunate, for we found the ardent group not only exhausted by the premature preparations for the return of a successful orator, but naturally much irritated as they contemplated their garlands drooping disconsolately in tubs and bowls of water. They did not fail to make me realize that I had dealt the cause of woman's advancement a staggering blow, and all my explanations of the fifth place were haughtily considered insufficient before that golden Bar of Youth, so absurdly inflexible![19]

But she described the same incident quite differently in a letter to her father a few days after her return.

My dear Pa,

. . . I have been on a journey since my last letter and have a long story to tell. I have some times doubted the wisdom of it and I hope it won't seem to you sudden and erratic. The editors of the Magazine received an invitation to the Inter-State Oratorical Contest held at Jacksonville last Wednesday evening and, at the same time there was to be held a conclave of the college editors from the same six states viz. Wis. Iowa, Ill. Minn. Ind. and Ohio. Miss Sill has been anxious for some time to have Rockford Semy enter the State Contest so she was very desirous to have two of the editors go to open negotiations, and likewise to bring forward the institutions by bringing forward the magazine. The Priscian Union raised $20 & delegated Hattie Wells and myself to go and we forth with started on Wednesday morning on the C. and I. road. We expected to change at Aurora for Peoria to Galesburg, but found after we started that we could not make connections at Galesburg and so went on to Chicago & took the Chicago & Alton, this brought us into Jacksonville in the morning and so we missed half of the contest but were in time to hear the successful orator from Indiana, he took the first prize a gold medal $75., and to share all the excitement in the decision of the judges. I never realized before what a bond of sympathy college & state ties represent. The second prize was taken by Minn, the Iowa orator was a lady who stood 3rd, her subject was Hypatia & criticism offered was that she was over oratorical almost theatrical. Much to our disappointment Ill. stood last. The Ill. orator was very kind to us indeed gave us all necessary directions in our arrangements for next year. He was very cool over his defeat but seemed to feel very much disgraced. Of course after Ill. we were interested in Beloit College and that orator stood next to the last to our disgust. He was Mr. Salisbury you have probably heard George speak of him as the boarder at Mr. Greenleaf's. I never saw anyone more despondent than he was after the contest & all the time he was talking about it. We could hear the Indiana men outside singing college songs of triumph. The committee of entertainment had us in charge and showed us every possible attention and politeness. The next day we met the officials most of the orators & a great many of the editors and accomplished our business satisfactorily, received more compliments on the magazine than we had ever dreamed of & only hope they were all sincere. Visited two deaf and dumb asylums and two of the colleges & Thursday evening attended a contest between the two societies of Knox & Ill College escorted thither by two editors of the "College Rambler," the committee of entertainment provided entertainment for all the editors that is paid our hotel bills & we could not possibly have been better provided for. It was an experience entertaining and decidedly different from anything I ever had before, we got more into the spirit of college life than I had ever dreamed of. We wanted to stop at Springfield but thought we ought to get back on Friday, the Chicago train Friday morning was three hours late but even then we would have made connections with the north-western if the Wells St bridge had not been turned & we missed it.

Hattie Wells home is in Geneva and as we were tired she insisted on our going out there all night—about an hours ride—& taking the train next morning. Her father & mother are very pleasant indeed, we rested splendidly & came on Saturday as fresh as could be. Miss Sill & the Priscian Union seem perfectly satisfied with our report & we certainly had a good time, Jacksonville seems to me one of the prettiest towns I ever was in. Of course I would have felt much better satisfied and comfortable if there had been time to write home & see what y u & Ma thought of such an undertaking—but unfortunately there was no time. I know a great deal more about the colleges in the six states & the internal workings of the oratorical ass. than I ever did before, and I hope the added experience & information will make up for the lost time here. . . . Ever your loving daughter,

Jane Addams[20]

There are several crucial differences in the two versions. Jane was not a participant in the contest, but merely an observer and William Jennings Bryan, who was a senior at Illinois College at the time, did not speak because he had lost out in an earlier contest to the young man who eventually finished last. The great debate between Jane Addams and William Jennings Bryan as college seniors, an incident told and retold hundreds of times by those recounting the life story of the founder of Hull House, was simply the figment of the imagination of the enthusiastic autobiographer. There are other discrepancies as well; the letter indicates a greater concern for the social side of the occasion than for the sight seeing trip to the state institutions, and there is no indication that what she saw had any great impact on her. Nor is there any clue that her college friends berated her for her performance or that she had "dealt the cause of woman's advancement a staggering blow." But after all one should not expect autobiographies to be exact in fact, or to recapture the mood and thinking of the past.[21]

"The snare of preparation," a phrase from Tolstoy, is the title of her fourth chapter in which she describes her years of depression and inactivity. She stresses her melancholy and insecurity. But at the same time, in describing her first European venture, she gives too much weight to the sights and sounds of East London, in the final decision to found a settlement house, at least if one compares these accounts with the letters she wrote at the time. Of course, the letters may not have revealed her innermost thoughts, but neither does the autobiography recreate them. She does mix up the date on which she was baptized and joined the church, making it seem a product of her melancholy rather than part of her discovery of a meaningful religious faith—a faith directly connected with her decision to found Hull House. But by the time she came to write her story she had moved away from her belief in a social Christianity and so she quite naturally de-emphasized religion as a motivating factor in her account. The chapter and the book move toward a climax with the bull fight in Spain; she recalls how the revulsion was mixed with fascination as she viewed the spectacle.

> We had been to see a bull fight rendered in the most magnificent Spanish style, where greatly to my surprise and horror, I found that I had seen, with comparative indifference, five bulls and many more horses killed. The sense that this was the last survival of all the glories of the amphitheater, the illusion that the riders on the caparisoned horses might have been knights of a tournament, or the matadore a slightly armed gladiator facing his martyrdom, and all the rest of the obscure yet vivid associations of an historic survival, had carried me beyond the endurance of any of the rest of the party. I finally met them in the foyer, stern and pale with disapproval of my brutal endurance, and but partially recovered from the faintness and disgust which the spectacle itself had produced upon them. I had no defense to offer to their reproaches save that I had not thought much about the bloodshed; but in the evening the natural and inevitable reaction came, and in deep chagrin I felt myself tried and condemned, not only by this disgusting experience but by the entire moral situation which it revealed.

It was suddenly made quite clear to me that I was lulling my conscience by a dreamer's scheme, that a mere paper reform had become a defense for continued idleness, and that I was making it a *raison d'être* for going on indefinitely with study and travel. It is easy to become the dupe of a deferred purpose, of the promise the future can never keep, and I had fallen into the meanest type of self-deception in making myself believe that all this was in preparation for great things to come. Nothing less than the moral reaction following the experience at a bull fight had been able to reveal to me that so far from following in the wake of a chariot of philanthropic fire, I had been tied to the tail of the veriest ox-card of self-seeking.[22]

Her letters at the time, however, revealed no such moral reaction, nothing remotely resembling a crucial career decision. But every book needs a climax, and every life, especially the life of a heroine, needs a dramatic, conversion experience.[23]

Joseph Campbell, writing in *The Hero with a Thousand Faces*, suggests that all myths in all times are variations on a monomyth—that all heroes go through a process of separation, initiation, and return. "A hero ventures forth from the world of common doings into a region of supernatural wonder, fabulous forces are then encountered, a decisive victory is won, the hero comes back from this mysterious adventure with the power to bestow boons on his fellow men."[24]

Jane Addams' experience at the bull fight is not as dramatic as St. Augustine's conversion to Christianity, or Gandhi's discovery of the Truth. It is not even as emotional as Emma Goldman's reaction to the death of the anarchists in Chicago, the experience she claimed in her autobiography turned her into a radical. "I was in a stupor," she wrote, "a feeling of numbness came over me, something too horrible even for tears. . . . I was entirely absorbed in what I felt was my own loss." And the next morning she awoke with "a great ideal, a burning faith, a determination to dedicate myself to the memory of my martyred comrades. . . ."[25] No, Jane Addams' description of her conversion—of the experience which led her to found Hull House—was not especially dramatic, but it sufficed and it lent itself to more emotional and sentimental accounts as the story of her life was reduced to a formula by the popular writers. She had traveled to a land of mystery—and been transformed. She returned to found Hull House and began her work to aid all mankind.

The reading public got its first look at Jane Addams' story in March, April, and May 1906 when her articles appeared in the *Ladies Home*

Journal. The response was immediate. A housewife from Illinois wrote, "My March number of *Ladies Home Journal* is just in and I have just finished 'Fifteen Years at Hull House' and as I have admired *you* and your soul-saving work, for so many years this article appeals to me so strongly that I feel I must simply tell you how greatly it pleases me to have you tell us all about your very human work, and how you did it. You will never live to know the good you are doing." A high-school teacher wrote from Nebraska to praise the article: "some of its lines vibrated in such perfect accord with the longings in my own soul that I am now writing to ask a favor. Is there any thing one could do to help relieve the burdens of . . . the poor in the large cities . . . ?" Another young woman wrote that after reading the articles she felt "impelled to write you and tell you something of myself and what I would like to do with my life," and then she went on for seven pages. There were other letters from high-school students wanting help with themes and housewives seeking information or money or a job.[26]

The *Ladies Home Journal* in 1906 had a circulation of well over a million and was read avidly by women in all parts of the country. These articles helped to increase Jane Addams' fame and extend the myth of the gentle, saintly woman who sacrificed all to aid the poor. Other magazines picked up the story. *Current Literature* carried an article entitled "The Only Saint America Has Produced," a characterization conferred on her by John Burns, but the article suggested "The enthusiasm is not peculiar to Burns. Wherever social reformers congregate the name of Jane Addams elicits a feeling that has a touch or something more than a touch of the adoration which the devout Catholic bestows upon the name of a saint."

The outpouring of letters especially from women indicated the reverence and respect they felt for her, but another kind of reaction came from the editors who saw in the articles the basis for a successful book. She finally did admit to the editor of Doubleday that she had made an outline for several more chapters, but insisted that she was not yet ready to sign a contract for the publication in book form. The pressure of other activities and the task of finishing *Newer Ideals of Peace* (1907) and *The Spirit of Youth and the City Streets* (1909) intervened, and it was not until 1910 that "Fifteen Years at Hull House," became *Twenty Years at Hull House* and with Macmillan rather than Doubleday as publisher.[27]

In completing the book, she added a considerable amount of material

John Addams

Anna Haldeman Addams, Jane and George Haldeman, *ca.* 1876.

Jane Addams' home in Cedarville, Illinois.
Anna Addams on balcony

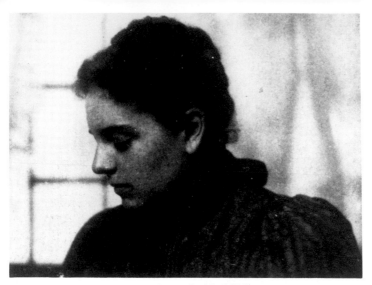

Mary Rozet Smith, 1896

Jane Addams, 1896

Neighborhood family, near Hull House, *ca*. 1892

Hull House, *ca*. 1892, much the way Jane Addams
and Ellen Starr found it in 1889

Ellen Starr and Jane Addams in Hull House, *ca.* 1902

Reception room and library, Hull House

Hull House, *ca.* 1915

Hull House, *ca.* 1930

Neighborhood boys, *ca.* 1930

The American Delegation to The Hague, 1915. Jane Addams, front row, second from left

Jane Addams, *ca.* 1911

Jane Addams and Mary McDowell, *ca.* 1932

...ieth Anniversary of Hull House, 1929. Seated left to right: Dr. Alice Hamilton, Rose Gyles, Jane ...ams, Enella Benedict, Edith de Hancrede. Standing left to right: Jessie Binford, Rachel Yarros, Esther Kohn, Victor Yarros, Ethel Dewey, George Hooker, Adena Miller Rich.

Jane Addams and Louise De Koven Bowen, *ca.* 1934

Jane Addams in the Hull House dinning room, *ca.* 1930

on the operation of the settlement, on reform campaigns, work with the immigrants, and human incidents relating to people in the neighborhood. She changed transitions and strengthened and unified certain themes, but essentially she took over the early version without major alterations and the theme of the early articles remained. The tension and drama are in the first part of the book, the story of how a sickly little girl who had lost her mother overcomes her handicaps, works hard, and achieves success. This part of the book was in the tradition of the American success story and *Twenty Years at Hull House* was quickly compared to the autobiographies of Helen Keller, Clara Barton and Booker T. Washington, who also struggled against handicaps to become successful and then, in the best American tradition, went on to help others. These Americans did not, like John D. Rockefeller or Henry Ford, make their fortunes, but they represented the other side on the American success myth, that of benevolence, public works, and self-sacrifice.

Jane Addams dominates the early part of the book; it is a personal story of how she came to found Hull House, but then in the last part she moves to the background and becomes the calm, humble, self-effacing and self-sacrificing leader, with very little reference to personal problems or motivations. It is a book filled with human stories of triumph and tragedy. But unlike *The Education of Henry Adams* (written about the same time, but not released to the public until 1918), which moves from unity to multiplicity, from relative happiness to despair, *Twenty Years at Hull House* is an optimistic book. There are tales of lonely desperate people, of pathos and poverty, but the tone is optimistic and the message is that all problems can be solved with patience, understanding and hard work.

She told the story of the shipping clerk who had lost his job during the depression of 1893, and who came to the relief station set up at Hull House for help. "I told him one day of the opportunity for work on the drainage canal and intimated that if any employment were obtainable, he ought to exhaust that possibility before asking for help. The man replied that he had always worked indoors and that he could not endure outside work in winter. I am grateful to remember that I was too uncertain to be severe, although I held to my instructions. He did not come again for relief, but worked for two days digging on the canal, where he contracted pneumonia and died a week later. I have never lost trace of the two little children he left behind him, although I cannot see them without a bitter consciousness that it was at their expense I learned that life cannot be administered by definite rules and regulations; that wisdom to deal with a man's difficulties comes only through some knowledge of his life and habits as a whole; and that to treat an isolated episode is almost sure to invite blundering."

To illustrate the point that to suppress the instinct of workmanship often leads to disastrous results she told the story of a little Bohemian girl who had attended classes at Hull House. One day the child was almost choked to death by her drunken father, then a few days later the father committed suicide.

> His poor wife, who stayed a week at Hull-House after the disaster until a new tenement could be arranged for her, one day showed me a gold ring which her husband had made for their betrothal. It exhibited the most exquisite workmanship, and she said that although in the old country he had been a goldsmith, in America he had for twenty years shoveled coal in a furnace room of a large manufacturing plant; that whenever she saw one of his "restless fits," which preceded his drunken periods, "coming on," if she could provide him with a bit of metal and persuade him to stay at home and work at it, he was all right and the time passed without disaster, but that "nothing else would do it." This story threw a flood of light upon the dead man's struggle and on the stupid maladjustment which had broken him down. Why had we never been told? Why had our interest in the remarkable musical ability of his child, blinded us to the hidden artistic ability of the father? We had forgotten that a long-established occupation may form the very foundations of the moral life, that the art with which a man has solaced his toil may be the salvation of his uncertain temperament.[28]

Each incident taught a lesson, preached a sermon. Each tragedy led to greater humility, but also renewed hope that the mistake would not be repeated, that poverty and human sorrow and suffering could be abolished.

One writer shrewdly called his review of *Twenty Years at Hull House,* "The Sermon of the Deed"; another defined the subject of the book as, "The Pursuit of the Holy Grail,"[29] There was about the book a sense of religious quest. Indeed it was an affirmation of American democracy and the American myth which bracketed democracy with Christianity, and made the search for the American dream a secular version of the Christian mission to save the world, and the doctrine of political freedom and opportunity for the individual, a secular version of the Christian idea of salvation for the regenerated man.[30]

Again and again throughout the book Addams affirmed the superiority of American democracy, of American innocence and virtue, when compared with the decadence and corruption of the old world. The bull fight in Spain, the climax of the book, becomes a symbol for the worst of European decadence and brutality, "the last survival of all the glories of the amphitheater," and the event which brought her to her senses and led her back to the land of innocence and opportunity. In describing Lincoln "who cleared the title of our democracy," she remarked: "He made plain, once for all, that democratic government, associated as it is with all the mistakes and shortcomings of the common people, still remains the most valuable contribution America has made to the moral life of the world." Again in describing the impact of the English movement of Ruskin and others to go back to the people, she asked "Why should an American be lost in admiration of a group of Oxford students because they went out to mend a disused road, inspired thereto by Ruskin's teaching for the bettering of the common life, when all the country roads in America were mended each spring by self-respecting citizens, who were thus carrying out the simple method devised by a democratic government for providing highways." In describing her confrontation with Tolstoy over her large sleeves she leaves the impression that the American way of trying to teach the peasant to live like the middle class is superior to the Russian way of trying to live like the peasants. She made the connection between democracy and Christianity explicit in describing her feeling when she finally joined the church.

> There was growing within me an almost passionate devotion to the ideals of democracy, and when in all history had these ideals been so thrillingly expressed as when the faith of the fisherman and the slave had been boldly opposed to the accepted moral belief that the well-being of a privileged few might justly be built upon the ignorance and sacrifice of the many? Who was I, with my dreams of universal fellowship, that I did not identify myself with the institutional statement of this belief, as it stood in the little village in which I was born, and without which testimony in each remote hamlet of Christendom it would be so easy for the world to slip back into the doctrines of selection and aristocracy?

But the democratic spirit of the frontier and the rural community, which she praised throughout the book, was severely challenged in an urban neighborhood such as that in which Hull House was located, with its dirt and filth, political corruption, and thousands of recently arrived immigrants from diverse backgrounds and traditions so alien to the American way. It was the message of the book, however, that democracy could survive this challenge, indeed could become stronger because of the diversity and the talents brought from other countries, that the new land could renew the lives, and make use of the ability of the immigrants from the old world. In describing how the Italian school children celebrated the hundredth anniversary of Mazzini's birth, and how the Chicago branch of the Society of Young Italy presented a bust of the Italian hero to Hull House, she remarked, "I found myself devoutly hoping that the Italian youth, who have committed their future to America, might indeed become 'the Apostles of the fraternity of nations' and that our American citizenship might be built without disturbing these foundations which were laid of old time."[31] *Twenty Years at Hull House* was not only the story of a quest for the Holy Grail and the American dream, but a triumphant tale of the discovery of that magic formula which would assure peace and prosperity for the American nation.

It was this optimistic message that contributed to the book's success. In her usual fashion of making the greatest possible use of what she wrote, she brought out about a third of the book in five articles in *The American Magazine* and one article in *McClure's*. She republished some of the same material she had used in the *Ladies Home Journal* four years before, but no one seems to have complained. But when a mix-up in scheduling at *McClure's* occurred, at least one editor worried about copyright confusion. She received $300 for the *McClure's* article and $500 for each of the *American* articles. The book came out in November and went through six printings and nearly 17,000 copies in the first year. It continued to sell in various editions to reach a total of at least 60,000 copies during Jane Addams' lifetime and many more since then.[32]

The reviews were overwhelmingly favorable. "The most important book of the year," wrote a critic in the *Baltimore Sun*. "It is more interesting than any literary confession. Before it Rousseau, Marie Bachkirtsoff, De Quincey, pale." "Twenty Years at Hull House . . . will long stand as one of the most helpful autobiographies in all literature," predicted the *Portland Evening Telegram*. "A book which breathes on every page the spirit of a dedicated life," a rewiever in *Sociological Review* decided. "It is an inspiring exhibit of what one brave and determined spirit has done and may still do in making rough ways smooth for sorcly beset humanity," the *Philadelphia North American* exclaimed.

It was translated into German, French, and Japanese. "You have enlarged the word 'American' for me," a woman from Germany wrote.[33]

Her friends and colleagues liked it too. Julia Lathrop thought "it was lovely and noble and sensible and appealing." Richard Ely wrote that "it is a great work, stimulating and encouraging. You have helped me as well as hundreds of others who have the privilege of coming in contact with you." Mrs. Robert Woods decided that "nothing has given the settlement idea more reality in the minds of large numbers of people." But Ellen Starr, after hearing Jane read the chapter on Arts at Hull House, made no comment at all, and Jane was hurt and angry. Graham Taylor decided that what was left out was just as important as what was included. Ella Flagg Young, Superintendent of the Chicago Public Schools, was disappointed that there was not more of Jane Addams' educational ideas in the book, and then, in a statement that could stand for almost any event described in the autobiography, she remarked, "So far as the School Board episode is concerned it is sketched true to life, but there was more."[34]

There was much more that Jane Addams might have included in the book, but it was written with a point of view and with a purpose. It was meant to define and consolidate her own position and identity, and it was designed to present herself as a symbol of Americanism. That she succeeded was a tribute not only to her ability to write, but also to her genius for relating her experience to the hopes and fears of ordinary Americans everywhere.

X

Prostitution, Woman Suffrage, and Progressivism

Y 1912 Jane Addams had come, for many, to symbolize the movement for social justice in America, the movement that sought to improve the working and living conditions for millions of Americans, especially those in the cities who had been unable to share in the American dream. She solidified that position further by seconding the nomination of Theodore Roosevelt, and by campaigning for the Progressive Party and for woman suffrage. In 1912 she also published a book on prostitution, and became a symbolic figure in the crusade to wipe out organized vice. At the same time she became for many a defender of feminine virtue, and a custodian of sexual purity.

The decade just prior to World War I witnessed a spectacular campaign of moral indignation against prostitution and the white slave trade. Americans suddenly became aware of the great sexual evils and exploitation in the cities. Twenty-one cities appointed vice commissions whose lurid reports provided the details for thousands of newspaper and magazine articles, and many books, including Reginald W. Kauffman's best-selling novel, *The House of Bondage*, the story of a small-town girl lured into prostitution. Of course there had been vice crusades before in America, indeed each generation seemed fascinated and appalled by the life of sin led by the street walker and the girl in the luxurious house of ill fame. Each generation worried about the moral effect of prostitution and its evils—drinking, swearing, gambling, illegitimacy, venereal disease, destroyed families, and ruined lives. Prostitution was usually blamed on the weakness of the individual, the moral deficiency of prostitute and patron alike. The argument, made famous by William Lecky in England, that the prostitute protected the purity and vritue of respectable ladies and provided an acceptable way for young men to "sow their wild oats" was rarely used in America. Instead, the reformers urged individual regeneration and held out chastity as an attainable ideal. In the twentieth century, attitudes changed somewhat. Just as poverty came increasingly to be blamed on the environment, rather than on laziness, drunkenness, and sin, so sexual exploitation was credited to social and economic forces rather than to individual weakness, though some of the old attitudes and fears remained.[1]

The progressive vice crusade attracted many different kinds of people. There were environmentalists who simply added the elimination of prostitution to the eradication of poor housing and child labor in their attempts to humanize the industrial city. There were hereditarians who envisioned prostitutes spreading venereal disease to unfaithful husbands, and thus to unsuspecting wives and unborn generations, leading eventually to moral degradation and race suicide. The crusade attracted immigration restrictionists and racists who maintained that it was the inferior people—blacks and East Europeans and recent immigrants—who became prostitutes and pimps. They were joined by social workers and others who argued that innocent immigrant girls needed to be protected from well-organized vice rings in America. There were also those connected with the social hygiene movement who denounced prostitution as part of their campaign to fight ignorance and prudery about sex, but there were others who joined the crusade with the apparent object of wiping out the threat of sex itself. Americans were just beginning to rid themselves of Victorian reticence about sexual practices and problems. Yet they were not quite ready to discuss sex openly, or to accept the theories of Havelock Ellis or Sigmund Freud. One acceptable way to learn about sex was to read the shocking reports of the vice commissions.

Contradictory motivations were present in every reform campaign, but the progressive vice crusade, unlike some earlier efforts, tended to focus more on the organized, commercial system of exploitation than on the individual prostitute and patron. Those who supported the movement included John D. Rockefeller, Jr., Charles Eliot, former president of Harvard, David Starr Jordan, president of Stanford, Edward A. Ross, the sociologist, Julius Rosenwald, the philanthropist, and psychologist

G. Stanley Hall, as well as many distinguished physicians, such as Abraham Flexner, and social workers Frances Kellor, Grace Abbott, Lillian Wald, and Jane Addams.

Jane Addams, of course, was no expert on vice and prostitution. But one could not live at Hull House and observe the neighborhood and be unaware of the problem. She also had read many of the case studies collected by the Juvenile Protective Association, and it was from these files that she gathered the examples and the tales of human pathos to illustrate the book she called *A New Conscience and an Ancient Evil.* Many of her friends were reluctant to have her write about the troubling and controversial topics of sex and vice, though Louise Bowen worked with her almost as a collaborator on the project. Alice Hamilton, who read some of the early drafts, approved the subject, but felt that the writing was "you only in spots." Norah Hamilton, however, who had done the wood cuts for *Twenty Years at Hull House,* decided that this was not the kind of book she wanted to illustrate.[2]

Despite the nervousness of some of her friends, Addams plunged ahead with the work. She believed that she had something important to say on a subject that both disturbed and excited many people. She was also aware that anything written on prostitution would sell. She tested the material first in the form of articles, which she sent to *McClure's,* the muckraking journal, rather than one of the more sedate or scholarly magazines. *McClure's* had for several years been running a large number of articles on prostitution and white slavery. Perhaps she wanted to correct some of the misleading impressions left by the other authors, but she also wanted to reach the largest possible audience. *McClure's* offered her $1,000 for five articles, a very good fee in 1911, but she held out for $1,500 and got it. Her Macmillan editor advised her against publishing the material in a periodical before the book came out but he quickly capitulated to her wishes. Both *McClure's* and Macmillan rearranged their schedules to allow the articles and the book to appear in the right sequence (the book coming out after the third article) and to permit her to use the same material in speeches while the work was in press. Her first essay in the magazine was the lead article, and was featured on the cover. In 1912, Jane Addams was a celebrity and the publishers treated her that way. They also realized that anything she wrote sold. She realized it too, and was enough of a business woman to take advantage of the situation and get the best terms possible.[3]

The thesis of her study was simple. There was an ancient evil, prostitution, which had always been with us, but which was more damaging and dangerous in an urbanized, industrial world. At the same time there was emerging a new conscience, a reform movement that would end the evil and destroy prostitution. She likened the attack on white slavery to the abolitionist movement, and again, as she had done in her autobiography, encouraged comparisons between herself and Lincoln. Throughout the book, despite a generally sympathetic treatment of the fallen woman, there is an assumption that once lured into prostitution, living a normal life, single or married, was next to impossible. She told the story of a young girl forced into prostitution, who gave it up when she was only seventeen. "Fortunately the poor child did not know how difficult that would be," Jane Addams remarked. She believed that no woman chose to become a prostitute voluntarily, and that no prostitute enjoyed her work, instead all were driven, usually by economic needs, into a life of sin. Once a girl had lost her virginity, prostitution seemed the next logical step, and Jane Addams assumed that it was the male who had the sexual desire and need, and the female who was always the passive recipient or victim of these needs. She specifically indicated that she was not making moral judgments about "illicit affection between men and women," and yet, like most reformers she believed that the best solution was chastity, and she sought to eliminate lust along with prostitution. She did not make her argument as extreme or as explicit as did reformers such as Alice Stone Blackwell and Charlotte Perkins Gilman who maintained that the answer to prostitution was to reform men and to teach them to have the same kind of self-control that women had learned to practice. But she did assume with these other reformers that women with an adequate salary would not become prostitutes, and women when given the vote would not tolerate prostitution.[4]

The book was filled with accounts of girls who had for one reason or another become prostitutes, their stories were told with a calm yet sympathetic detachment quite different from the lurid and dramatic detail of some of the more popular books on white slavery. Still there was enough information to titillate the minds of respectable readers. There was the "honest, straightforward girl from a small town in northern Michigan" who worked in a Chicago cafe and sent half her wages home to help her mother and her little sister who had tuberculosis. "The girl's heart grew heavier week by week as the mother's letters reported that the sister was daily growing weaker." In order to get home before she died, the girl agreed to accompany a local business man on the night boat, if he would pay her return fare. "She reached home twelve hours before her sister died, but when she returned to Chicago a week later burdened with the debt of an undertaker's bill, she realized that she had discovered a means of payment." Then there was the story of a "Milwaukee factory girl, the daughter of a Bohemian carpenter," who had met a young man at a dance and after a brief courtship had promised to meet him in Chicago and get married, but when she arrived the young man introduced her to an older woman who convinced her that she needed to work for a few weeks to earn money for a trousseau. It was only by accident that the "unsuspecting girl narrowly escaped a well-organized plot" for as it turned out the young man was an "agent for a disreputable house."

She described how a factory girl sometimes "yields in a moment of utter weariness and discouragement to the temptations she has been able to withstand up to that moment. . . . The long hours, the lack of comforts, the low pay, the absence of recreation, the sense of 'good times' all about her which she cannot share, the conviction that she is rapidly losing health and charm, rouse the molten forces within her. A swelling tide of self-pity suddenly storms the banks which have hitherto held her and finally overcomes her instincts for decency and righteousness, as well as the habits of clean living, established by generations of her forebears." The cheap dance halls and the saloons were even more dangerous than the factories and a job as waitress, domestic servant, or secretary had its own special risks.

The book is filled with pathetic stories, some of them believable, some of them incredible. She struggled to put herself in the place of the women she was trying to describe, but that was difficult, in this case, and some of her remarks sound naïve, others sentimental and condescending. On the habit among working girls of using makeup she remarked: "the poor girls could not know that a face thus made up enormously increased their risks." Or in discussing the dangers of dancing she suggested that "often the only recreation possible for young men and young women together is dancing, in which it is always easy to transgress the proprieties." And writing of young offenders: "one knows that whatever may be done for them later, because of this early neglect they will probably remain impervious to the gentler aspects of life, as if vice scarred their tender minds with red-hot irons." In discussing the prevalence of black prostitutes she revealed that she was not immune to the racist thinking of her day. "The community forces the very people who have confessedly the shortest history of social restraints into a dangerous proximity with the vice districts of the city," she explained. The assumption throughout that there is a well organized ring of white slave traders waiting to lure every unsuspecting girl into a house of ill fame, was at best grossly exaggerated —though it was an exaggeration made by all of the reformers in the progressive area.

The response to the articles and the book was overwhelmingly favorable, and probably because of the nature of the subject there was an unusually large outpouring of letters. Jane Addams was a priestess to whom men and women could write to explain their theories and reveal their fears and fascination with sex and prostitution. Of course, a few were shocked by the book. One woman from Long Island wrote that she was deeply grieved that Jane Addams who had compiled such a record of "*womanly worth* and *work* should stoop to use such a subject for publication." She accused her of inciting other women to sin, and urged her to withdraw the book from publication. "You have probably heard from many," she continued, "who would accept as *right* and *best* anything you had done. I do not question your motive, but I agree with the sentiment that 'Miss Addams is beginning to see the *world* through Hull House *windows!*' "⁵

Some of those who wrote to Addams about her articles and book objected to her thesis that it was primarily economic need that caused most girls to lose their virtue and be lured into prostitution. Charles Sheldon, author of *In His Steps*, suggested that it was only those who "had no religious principles underlying their definition of life" who fell prey to the evils of prostitution. A doctor from Missouri said it was all heredity, and "if a girl of good moral character 'strikes her flag,' then there is a defect in her family tree somewhere." A woman from Kansas argued that it was girl's habit of flirting that ultimately was to blame. Others suggested sterilization as the only answer to the problem of sex, and a man who signed himself "John Doe" defended the chivalry of the average man and urged that through the Boy Scouts and other organizations all boys be required to take a pledge that they "will never seduce an innocent woman or girl."⁶

A few men wrote her to defend prostitution. "Denial of their [men's] sexual desire whether practiced consciously or unconsciously is very likely to end in mental and physical breakdown, followed by either insanity or suicide," one man wrote; and another was critical of her assumption that women had less sexual need than men. But no one challenged her right to be an authority on sex and prostitution. By 1912 her reputation was so great that many middle- and upper-class Americans considered her an expert on all things pertaining to lower-class life in the city. The letters poured in; she couldn't possibly answer them all, but she carefully filed them and apparently read them. Her "fan mail," and the mountain of favorable clippings were important factors in her growing self-confidence and sense of identity. A few disagreed, but politely, and many more corroborated her stories of the evils of white slavery and sexual passion. Many told tales of young girls lured into prostitution or confessed that they had once been pimps or prostitutes.[7]

One day a letter arrived from a woman who admitted frankly that she was a prostitute still practicing her profession. She asked if she could correspond with Miss Addams, but she was out of town so Dr. Alice Hamilton answered the letter and offered to correspond with her. To the young doctor it seemed a "thrilling glimpse into a terrible, unknown world filled with helpless victims of man's lust." Jane Addams was not really interested in this world. She could write sympathetically about the life of prostitutes, but she did not care to meet or to correspond with one. The woman would write to Dr. Hamilton early in the morning before her clients arrived, and she pictured herself as a captive bird beating herself against the bars. Some months later Dr. Hamilton went to Toledo to see the unfortunate woman, though she first informed the Charity Organization Society where she would be and asked them to alert the police if she failed to return by five o'clock. "It was a sadly disillusioning experience," she reported years later, "I found a home luxurious but vulgarly ugly, and a woman of mature years, handsome, dignified, entirely mistress of herself. The pitiful little bird in the cage was a ludicrous picture." The woman had come into the house of her own free will and had no intention of leaving unless she found a man to support her (a possibility Jane Addams took no account of in her book). Dr. Hamilton came to a rather odd conclusion from the experience, that prostitutes were somehow more guilty than their customers, for the men it was only a momentary bit of pleasure and dissipation for which they paid, but for the prostitute "it was her sole preoccupation and at the same time it brought her money." Yet her curiosity led her to visit a brothel; something that Jane Addams probably never dreamed of.[8]

Most of those who wrote in response to *A New Conscience and an Ancient Evil* and the articles were not prostitutes but ordinary middle-class men and women, and the greatest numbers were filled with praise for what Jane Addams was doing and for the delicate way in which she described the problem. *The New York Times* pointed out that "there is nothing in the book that can offend an intelligent reader of either sex or any age." Walter Lippmann, almost alone among the critics, did not like the book. Writing in *A Preface to Politics*, he criticized her for not having an explicit philosophy, but more than that, "her book on prostitution," he decided, "seems rather the product of her moral fervor than her human insight. Compare it with *The Spirit of Youth*, or *Newer Ideals of Peace* or *Democracy and Social Ethics*, and I think you will notice a very considerable willingness to gloss over human need in the interests of an unanalyzed reform. To put it bluntly, Miss Addams let her impatience get the better of her wisdom. She had written brilliantly about sex and its 'sublimination,' she had suggested notable 'moral equivalents' for vice, but when she touched the white slave traffic its horrors were so great that she also put her faith in the policeman and the district attorney. *A New Conscience and an Ancient Evil* is an hysterical book, just because the real philosophical basis of Miss Addams' thinking was not deliberate enough to withstand the shock of a poignant horror." He also suggested that she had a good deal of sympathy for the prostitute's condition, but none at all for "lust in the heart of men and women."[9] Lippmann was right. *A New Conscience and an Ancient Evil* is an hysterical book, also sentimental and naïve, but few noticed it except Lippmann. The praise came from all sides and was out of proportion to her accomplishment, as if she singlehandedly upheld the purity of the American woman. "It certainly gives new hope to womanhood when a voice like yours is publically lifted and your pen dipped in sincerity, truth and wisdom, writes of this crying need for a betterment of that which takes the best life-blood of a Nation," a woman from Brooklyn wrote. A man admitted that he was impressed by "the fact that like Lincoln, you fearlessly attack a slavery that can only be uprooted by just such utterances and fearlessness as shown by graphic pen." "Miss Addams go on with every good work," a woman from Indiana wrote, "and perhaps the time will come when the evil will be no more."[10]

The *Knoxville* (Tennessee) *Sentinel* reviewed the book in glowing terms, but like many others the reviewer took the occasion to praise Jane Addams as the practical patron saint of American reform:

A noble book! What a grand creature is Jane Addams! One who had clasped her kind hand and looked into her good and beautiful eyes feels her personality in every line here written; her wisdom moderation and naturalness; her thorough acquaintance with modern world movements.

She pleads her cause without reserve, with plain speaking but refinement. And she draws from the treasury of facts she has gathered from a life-time of social settlement work.

As she gets older her heart seems to grow more and more tender, until now she has taken it into the cause of the most forlorn, most hopeless class in the work—her erring sisters, victims of the "ancient evil."

There is nothing of the fanatic, no railings, but much sane, common-sense, and an immovable conviction that conditions may and will be bettered.

Even more glowing and revealing was the tribute of a woman from a small town in Arkansas:

There are many women in the world today who are doing great things and for them I have a respect and a sort of impersonal affection. They are fighting my battles, of course, and those of my beautiful daughter, yes and the big son's too for we stand and fall together. And I myself know enough and have had the courage of my faith in a square deal to a sufficient extent so that the son looks at other boys' sisters with clean eyes and understands why he must do so in order to be a man. For them all I have respect and affection. But you, to me, have represented something holy and apart, yet active for good in the affairs of all the world. You do so still, and I am happy enough and selfish enough in the feeling to want to tell you about it. I can hear you saying the truths you place before us, in that quiet impersonal, gray tone of yours which yet suggests all the primary colors of the passions of man; I can see you standing with your hands together, a figure that looms into that greatness of the mother of all the women. . . .[11]

From symbol of purity, protector of womanly virtue, crusader against prostitution, "mother of all the women," she became before the year was out a symbolic figure in another crusade—the presidential campaign to elect Theodore Roosevelt. She became involved with the Progressive Party the way a number of social workers and social justice reformers got involved because at the time it seemed to be a legitimate way to restructure American politics and bring social justice to America. She also believed it was a way to help the cause of women and to promote woman suffrage.

It is impossible to recapture the exuberance, the enthusiasm and the hope that many social reformers felt in the summer and fall of 1912. One has to appreciate the years of struggle to prohibit child labor, to promote better housing and all the other measures designed to improve life in the city. There had been some successes at the state and local level, and even some national legislation, but the failures had been obvious and the work left undone overwhelming. And now a national political leader was listening to their reasoning, a political party was taking their social justice program seriously.[12]

The social and industrial planks of the Progressive Party platform were drafted by a committee on occupational standards of the National Conference of Charities and Correction. This committee included among its members Paul Kellogg, the editor of the *Survey*, the most important magazine of social work; Florence Kelley, former resident of Hull House and general secretary of the National Consumers' League, Margaret Dreier Robins, president of the National Women's Trade Union League, and Owen Lovejoy, secretary of the National Child Labor Committee. The committee had originally been appointed in 1909, the year Jane Addams was elected president of the organization, but in 1912, an election year, the committee decided that they should draft a minimum platform to help "direct public thought and secure official action." The "Social Standards for Industry," as the social workers called their minimum platform, included, among other things, the demand for an eight-hour day in continuous twenty-four-hour industries, a six-day week for all, the abolition of tenement manufacture, the improvement of housing conditions, the prohibition of child labor under sixteen, and the careful regulation of employment for women. They also called for a federal system of accident, old age, and unemployment insurance. The committee insisted that these were not long-range goals, but minimum standards for any community "interested in self-preservation."[13]

A group of the reform-minded social workers presented their platform of industrial minimums to the platform committee of the Republican National Convention, but it was immediately obvious that the Republicans were not interested. Jane Addams also made a brief appearance before the platform committee to make a plea for a plank supporting woman suffrage, as well as the other reform proposals, and she was virtually ignored.[14] A few days later, however, Roosevelt walked out of the Republican Convention and went to work to form a new party. A group of social workers traveled to Oyster Bay, New York, to confer with him; they also presented their program to the platform committee of the new Progressive Party. "Roosevelt took over the Cleveland program of standards of life and labor practically bodily . . . ," Paul Kellogg later remembered, and most of the specific proposals made by the social workers

found their way, almost word for word, into the Progressive Party platform. The Progressives also adopted a plank supporting woman
suffrage.[15]

The combination of the Progressives' stand for social justice and for
woman suffrage proved irresistible to Jane Addams, as it did to a large
number of social workers and social justice reformers. "Just think of having all the world listen to our story of social and industrial injustice and
have them told that it can be righted," one social worker remarked ex-
citedly. "The Progressive Platform contains all the things I have been
fighting for for more than a decade," Jane Addams announced.[16] She
was not being quite accurate, however, for the Progressive Party did not
stand for some things she believed in. There was the matter of the two
battleships they promised to build each year. "I confess that I found it
very difficult to swallow those two battleships," she admitted. There
was also Roosevelt's decision to prevent the seating of Negro delegates
from several southern states, despite the vigorous protests of Jane
Addams, Henry Moskowitz, and a few other progressives. But politics
was a matter of equivocation, of principles compromised, of bargains
made. Why did she expose herself to the inevitable criticism, and attacks
that participation in partisan politics would bring in 1912? Her position
was secure, her reputation at its highest; she was both a symbol and a
spokesman for many. Her usual style had been to avoid partisan stands
where possible, to compromise and keep the respect of both sides, but in
1912 the Progressive campaign seemed more like a moral crusade than
partisan politics, like a natural extension of what she had been doing at
Hull House, and she was swept along by the enthusiasm of the time.
"I never doubted for a moment that my place was inside, where there
was a chance to help on such a program, as this one," she wrote to Lillian Wald during the campaign.[17]

It was not just the Progressives' stand for social justice although that
was important; it was also their support of woman suffrage that influenced her entry into the political arena. She realized that to many people she represented the best of American womanhood, and that votes
for women was an issue of growing concern and urgency. Publically supporting the Progressives allowed her to be counted on the side of woman
suffrage. She came rather late to the suffrage movement. She advocated
votes for women as early as 1897, but she was more concerned with
women's rights and women's role in the world. Much of her writing and
speaking had dealt with woman's relationship to her family, her respon-

sibility to be more than an obedient daughter, her rights to an education and a creative role in the world outside the home. She had written most often of the special burdens and threats to the immigrant woman living in the city. Unlike some of the more militant suffragists, she did not claim that women were superior to men. "We have not wrecked railroads, nor corrupted legislatures, nor done many unholy things that men have done; but then we must remember that we have not had the chance."[18] But women were different from men, they had special temperaments and background and thus special responsibilities. One of women's traditional roles was that of housekeeper she was fond of pointing out, but the simple tasks of keeping a house clean and feeding children, became more complex in a modern city, and inevitably involved women in municipal housekeeping. "Women who live in the country sweep their own dooryards and may either feed the refuse of the table to a flock of chickens or allow it innocently to decay in the open air and sunshine," she wrote. "In a crowded city quarter, however, if the street is not cleaned by the city authorities no amount of private sweeping will keep the tenement free from grime; if the garbage is not properly collected and destroyed a tenement house mother may see her children sicken and die of diseases from which she alone is powerless to shield them, although her tenderness and devotion are unbounded. She cannot even secure untainted meat for her household, she cannot even secure fruit. . . . In short, if woman would keep on with her old business of caring for her house and rearing her children she will have to have some conscience in regard to public affairs lying quite outside of her immediate household. The individual conscience and devotion are no longer effective." Women, she went on to argue, should have the vote because they were specially qualified for modern municipal housekeeping. She also believed that women because of their empathy and intuition could lead a moral reform movement, by transferring their natural talents from the home to society.[19]

While many supporters of woman suffrage advocated votes for middle- and upper-class women, and approved votes for working women and immigrants reluctantly if at all, Jane Addams consistently maintained that the immigrant women would vote intelligently and, what was more important, they needed the vote to protect themselves and their families from being exploited by government and society. "The statement is sometimes made," she wrote, "that the franchise for women would be valuable only so far as the educated women exercised it. This statement totally disregards the fact that those matters in which woman's judgement is most needed are far too primitive and basic to be largely influenced by what we call education." She described how women from Scandinavia had voted in Europe and were now disfranchised in America, how an unschooled Irish woman who could not read still made intelligent and sensible choices on municipal issues after women were granted the franchise in Chicago. "It galls the men some to have us voting," she quoted the woman, "but from the questions put up to me it seems pretty much a woman's job."[20]

After 1906 Jane Addams spent more time speaking and working for suffrage. She joined the National American Woman Suffrage Association, she lectured frequently on college campuses, before women's clubs and in public lectures arguing for woman's right and responsibility to take a more active role in government and society. She campaigned for municipal suffrage for women in Chicago but to no avail. In 1911 she became a vice president of the N.A.W.S.A. and helped manage a more aggressive campaign in Illinois for woman suffrage in all elections. She boarded a train filled with over 300 women and traveled to Springfield where the group spent three days testifying before committees, stopping legislators in the halls, confronting them in their offices. But again they lost out. In 1912 she spoke at the meeting of the National American Woman Suffrage Association in Philadelphia, then, after the convention was over, she led a group to Washington to testify before the House Judiciary Committee in favor of a federal suffrage amendment.[21]

Roosevelt's conversion to woman suffrage had been recent, but he spoke in favor of votes for women during a speech in Chicago in 1911, and he assured Jane Addams in 1912 that he was "without qualification or equivocation" for woman suffrage.[22] She took him at his word although there were some who charged that she had been duped. In any case it was not so much Roosevelt as it was the platform that she had helped to draft that seemed important and the platform said: "The Progressive Party, believing that no people can justly claim to be a true democracy which denies political rights on the account of sex, pledges itself to the task of securing equal suffrage to men and women alike." And women suffrage was just one of many important issues. The sessions of the platform committee seemed much like the meetings of the Men and Religion Forward Movement, the American Sociological Association or the National Conference of Charities and Correction; there were so many old friends there. They had to compromise, of course, and these were many disappointments, but these were all forgotten when the convention itself opened. There was a sense of dedication, a feeling that this was the climax to years of struggle. The atmosphere was more like that of a religious revival than a political convention. The delegates waved flags and banners, they sang "Onward Christian Soldiers" and "Roosevelt Oh Roosevelt" to the tune of "Maryland My Maryland." They sang the "Battle Hymn of the Republic" and they ended each session with the doxology.

When Jane Addams rose to second Roosevelt's nomination, her name introduced by Senator Albert Beveridge, the permanent chairman, the cheers, applause, and feet-stamping rivaled that which greeted Roosevelt himself. She was dressed simply in white, and she spoke quietly and calmly. She spent most of her time praising the platform. "I rise to second the nomination stirred by the splendid platform adopted by this convention," she began. "Measures of industrial amelioration, demands for social justice, long discussed by small groups in charity conferences and economic associations, have here been considered in a great national convention and are at last thrust into the stern arena of political action.

"A great party has pledged itself to the protection of children, to the care of the aged, to the relief of overworked girls, to the safe guarding of burdened men. Committed to these human undertakings, it is inevitable that such a party should appeal to women, should seek to draw upon the great reservoir of their moral energy so long undesired and unutilized in practical politics. . . ." Only at the end did she get around to the candidate and then in guarded language. "I second the nomination of Theodore Roosevelt because he is one of the few men in our public life who has been responsive to the social appeal and who has caught the significance of the modern movement. Because of that, because the programme will require a leader of invincible courage, of open mind, of democratic sympathies, one endowed with power to interpret the common man and to identify himself with the common lot, I heartily second the nomination."[23]

As she stepped down from the platform the crowd erupted in cheers, not so much for Roosevelt, as for Jane Addams. A group of women grabbed a banner which read VOTES FOR WOMEN and stepped in behind her as she walked up the aisle to her seat, beginning a spontaneous parade that lasted for several minutes before the speaker could restore order. There were other nominating speeches for Roosevelt and for his running mate, Hiram Johnson of California, but the newspapers gave

ENLISTED FOR THE GREAT BATTLE

her speech the most attention. "Jane Addams seemed to be the most distinguished figure at the convention," one reporter decided. It was not so much what she said, few listened to the words, but it was what she symbolized. *The Boston Journal* printed a cartoon showing Roosevelt and Addams shaking hands surrounded by figures representing poverty, old age and child labor—the caption read "Enlisted for the Great Battle." *The Philadelphia North American* published an editorial, which was widely reprinted in other newspapers, entitled "The Bigger Meaning of Jane Addams": "When Jane Addams, the foremost citizen of Illinois rose in the Progressive convention and seconded the nomination of Theodore Roosevelt for President, it marked an important step forward in the cause of social and industrial justice. Jane Addams is not only the foremost citizen of her great state. She is one of the ten greatest citizens of this republic. She is, moreover, probably the most widely beloved of her sex in all the world." The writer went on to exclaim that her speech was "one of the greatest examples of pure oratory since Lincoln's address at Gettysburg," and to point out that her presence symbolized not only the coming of age of women in America, but more important the victory for the movement "for the aid of those who are now overwhelmed in the flood of economic error and social wrongs."[24]

Roosevelt also recognized the symbolic and practical importance of her support. He dashed off a note of thanks. "I prized your action not only because of what you are and what you stand for, but because of what it symbolized for the new movement." Others joined in the chorus of praise. "How great you were to carry off a political party at a strategic moment," Mary McDowell remarked. "Aren't you magnificent," Katharine Coman, a Wellesley economics professor wrote, "what a grand new service you have rendered the human race! thousands of women are blessing you this day because your leadership brings us perceptively nearer to the Kingdom of Heaven." The newspapers all announced that this was the first time a woman had seconded the nomination of a presidential candidate, but later some argued that Mary Lease had seconded James Weaver's nomination at the Populist Convention in 1892. It did not matter, for women all over the country viewed her action as signaling the coming victory for woman suffrage, and for women's rightful place in the world.[25]

Jane Addams realized the symbolic importance of her support of the Progressives. She was perfectly aware of the drama she was acting out by seconding Roosevelt's nomination, and convinced that no one could represent the cause of women and social justice better than she. She was not satisfied with the token appearance in Chicago; she flung herself into the campaign. She was a member of the National Progressive Committee, the Illinois State Progressive Committee, and the Cook County Progressive Committee. She also prepared a series of six articles, syndicated in newspapers across the country, to attract attention to the platform of the new party and to educate the people about the need for action to outlaw child labor, regulate hours and conditions for working women, etc. She also found time to write articles on the new party for the *Crisis, McClure's; Survey* and *American Magazine.*[26] Her seconding speech was reproduced and distributed widely especially among women's groups. But she did more than write for the cause. Beginning in September she was constantly on the move giving speeches. She spoke in Boston, and New York, debated Rabbi Stephen Wise, a Wilson supporter, in Worcester, Massachusetts, and then went on a whirlwind tour that included all the major cities in the Midwest. She went as far south as Oklahoma, talked in Wichita, St. Paul, Denver, Colorado Springs, even in places like Leadville, Colorado, and Fargo, North Dakota, and in the small towns of Iowa, Nebraska, and Missouri. Large and enthusiastic crowds greeted her everywhere, and there were many more requests for her appearance than she could fill. Anna Howard Shaw also on the campaign trail remarked: "Wherever I went I heard nothing but talk of Jane Addams, I suppose other political speakers had been out there, but you never would have guessed it from what people had to say." In Los Angeles a group of women organized a "Jane Addams Chorus" to sing at Progressive rallies, and the idea spread. Many other cities began choruses made up of hundreds of young women all dressed in white who sang "Roosevelt Oh Roosevelt," "Follow, Follow, We Will Follow Jesus," and other songs. There was a "Jane Addams Song Book" and a special certificate for those who joined a chorus with Jane Addams' picture and signature. The sale of these certificates brought in more than $5,000 to help the Progressive cause.[27]

Addams was such an effective campaigner that she was often chosen to make rejoinders to Democratic attacks, and her support of Roosevelt caused Democrats to attempt to persuade Lillian Wald to come out publicly in favor of Wilson to counteract some of her influence. But Jane Addams soon discovered that to enter partisan politics was to tarnish her saintly image, at least in the eyes of some of her former admirers. Mrs. Mabel Boardman, President of the women's advisory committee of the

Republican Party, attacked Jane Addams for supporting the Progressives, arguing that no one connected with "a great non-political work or organization" should permit the use of his or her name in support of a political party. "The great moral questions for whose furtherance the country owes a debt of gratitude to Miss Addams," she continued, "should not be handicapped by the limitations of party affiliation nor trammelled by becoming involved in the bitterness of controversies over candidates and utterly irrelevant policies." Jane Addams quickly replied that "an institution reveals its own weakness when it cares more for its position and influence than for the cause itself." But the truth of the matter was that the Progressive Party seemed to Jane Addams and many others a cause above politics (and Mrs. Boardman, despite her disavowal, played an important role in the Taft campaign).[28]

Even some of her social-work friends were critical of her entry into politics. Edward T. Devine of the New York Charity Organization Society, announced in *Survey* magazine that it is "the first political duty of social workers to be persistently and aggressively non-partisan, to maintain such relations with men of social good will in all parties as will insure their cooperation in specific measures for the promotion of the common good. . . ." Both Sophonisba Breckinridge and Graham Taylor were less than enthusiastic about Addams' political activity during the campaign and they remained neutral. A few years later Taylor decided that by taking part in a partisan campaign she had "lost the heeding if not the hearing of the whole city which she had before. . . ." Jane Addams, always sensitive to criticism, took Devine's article as a personal attack on her, though he denied that he meant it that way. The enthusiasm of the campaign and her belief that the Progressive campaign was a natural outgrowth of her work at Hull House, not just an ordinary political campaign, helped to sustain her, but she must have been distressed by the number of letters she received attacking her for supporting Roosevelt, and the editorial comment on "the strange political conjunction of the Gentle Jane Addams of Hull House with the Roaring Bull Moose of Oyster Bay."[29]

"With others of your friends and those who have long trusted in your sane judgment and clear-eyed vision of things as they are, I am bewildered and annoyed that anyone could so have pulled wool over your eyes," a woman wrote from Springfield, Massachusetts. "You may not be aware that you give your splendid reputation in aid to the cause of the most selfish man living . . ." a man wrote from Newark, New Jersey.

Others accused Roosevelt of being a drunkard and a supporter of white slavery. "As one who has felt a deep trust in your work in Chicago and elsewhere I greatly regret your action in publicly identifying yourself with Mr. Roosevelt and his principles," a woman wrote and went on to suggest that Jane Addams, like a minister, had a public responsibility to limit her statements and actions to those which were noncontroversial.[30]

She tried to respond to some of the criticism, to point out that the platform was more important than the candidate. But much more difficult to answer were her friends in the peace movement who reminded her that Roosevelt was a militarist and an imperialist. Charles Beals, Secretary of the Chicago Peace Society, remarked: "I am quite bewildered that the Big Sister has swallowed Bull-Moosism or been swallowed by it, I don't quite know which." Erving Winslow, Secretary of the Anti-Imperialist League, criticized her public stand for Roosevelt and reminded her that he had opposed Philippine independence, supported a big navy as well as "the fortification and appropriation of the Panama Canal." Baroness Bertha von Suttner, an Austrian pacifist and the only woman recipient of the Nobel Peace Prize, in an open letter accused her of joining an anti-peace organization which favors "the ancient and barbaric system of justice called war." And Jenkin Lloyd Jones, an old friend, asked her to remember that Roosevelt was the "arch-champion in the United States and perhaps in the world of the idea that armament contributes to the pacification of the world."

Jones, like many of her other friends, was also troubled by the refusal of the Progressive Party to seat the Negro delegates from Florida and Mississippi, and the failure of the platform committee to include a plank on Negro rights, even though she fought very hard to promote both causes. She considered leaving the party over this issue but decided to stay. In explaining her decision in an article in *Crisis* she argued rather weakly "the issues were those of political democracy and industrial justice—a merging of the political in the West and country districts with the social insurgency of the cities. Imbedded in this new movement is a strong ethical motive, and once the movement is crystallized, once as a body of people it gets a national foothold . . . it is bound to lift this question of the races, as all other questions, out of the grip of the past and into a new era of solution." She sent a copy of the article to Jones who replied, "I do not need your article to persuade me that you had thought your way out of the position you have taken. I never distrusted for a moment your sincerity, or integrity in the matter, but I am frank to say that after reading your article you are 'too big a man' to be identified with any *party* organization or as a leader of *party* enthusiasm, which under the best of all circumstances destroys the perspective and does violence to the proportions."[31]

Not all her friends were unhappy with her, in fact many blacks hailed her as a friend and protector of their race. The medical director of the Frederick Douglass Memorial Hospital in Philadelphia wrote to thank her "for the firm stand you have taken in the National Progressive Party for human rights, without discrimination of race or sex." The secretary and business manager of Howard University wrote "as one of the ten million to whom you referred in your speech seconding the nomination of Col. Roosevelt, and a Progressive, I want to thank you for your noble, just and admirable stand you took with respect to our people." But another correspondent who signed himself, "one of them," had a different reaction. "As I read of the enthusiasm of the great convention with which you have identified yourself," he wrote "the solemn hymns sung —the promises of consecration to the peoples' freedom—made by pious delegates and their leader the arch hypocrite I thought of the breaking hearts of my people—the Afro-Americans—and I shudder at the blasphemy of the farce. Away with sophistry! Is it right before God to do evil that good may come? Is woman suffrage more important in his sight than the right of the Negro to be treated like a man? Or are these views too old-fashioned for the Progressive Party. Oh woman of the warm heart and golden tongue, who has done so much for humanity do not identify yourself with those who have joined hands to crush the poor African. Come out from among them, and by doing and letting it be known, you will accomplish more for the race than has been done since the days of Lincoln and your name will go down to posterity linked with that of the great Harriet Beecher Stowe, and the thanks and prayers of the colored people will ever follow you."[32] It was a disturbing letter for one who liked to be acclaimed as a moral leader and compared to women like Harriet Beecher Stowe, even though she tended to compromise during moments of crisis. Yet there was enough praise and adulation during the campaign to counteract the critical letters and the unfavorable editorials.

The Progressive Party lost, as most of the leaders expected it would, but many had idealistically thought that it would cause a realignment of parties and that by 1916 it could replace the Republican Party as a major party, and move on to victory. After the campaign was over Addams continued to be active in the party for a time. She convinced the National Progressive Committee meeting in December to support the social workers' plan for a National Progressive Service. This organization, the brain-child of Frances Kellor, a social investigator and ardent Progressive, was designed to apply the principles and techniques of social work and social research to the organization of a political party. Jane Addams headed the Department of Social and Industrial Justice, served on the general committee as well as on the Legislative Reference Bureau, and cooperated with the attempts of Frances Kellor and others to draft bills, send out speakers, and keep the enthusiasm of the Progressive Party alive. But it was quickly obvious that the enthusiasm of the social workers could not keep the party together. They worried about the men Roosevelt seemed to be turning to for advice, especially they were concerned that George Perkins, a partner in J. P. Morgan and Company and a board member of U.S. Steel and International Harvester, had too much power in the party. A few days before Christmas some of the social workers active in the Progressive campaign met in New York to decide on strategy. They agreed that "The Colonel has become suspicious of the whole social worker crowd except Jane Addams and he is afraid of her, and we must depend on her to save the situation."[33]

Jane Addams, however, was unwilling to try to save the situation if it meant becoming involved in a factional struggle within a party which increasingly seemed like a lost cause. Several times in the next two years she tried to resign from her positions in the Progressive service organization and from the executive committee of the party. But the "extreme wing," or the social-work wing of the party, which felt she was "the greatest asset which the real Progressive cause has at this time" would not hear of her resignation. She remained on the various committees, but she devoted less and less time to the Progressive cause. Roosevelt wired her urgently when he discovered she was going to be in New York and did not plan to go to the Progressive Party Lincoln dinner. "I am afraid that your absence from the dinner were you in New York would give rise to serious misunderstanding." She did not put in an appearance at the dinner.[34]

She was not despondent and disillusioned over the defeat of Roosevelt and the Progressives. "I had expected from the beginning that Mr. Wilson was to be the next President of the United States," she told a reporter shortly after the election. "The candidacy of Mr. Roosevelt and the principles enunciated in the Progressive platform afforded the opportunity for giving wide publicity to the necessity for social and industrial reforms, and it is my belief that Mr. Wilson as President of the United States will give heed to the necessities of the people as they have been so plainly apparent." She was pleased with Wilson's early efforts to support social reform measures and by 1916, like a great many others who had supported Roosevelt in 1912, she came out publicly for Wilson. She did remain active in the cause of woman suffrage and of woman's rights. Traveling in Europe and Egypt with Mary Smith in 1913 she took time out to attend the Woman's International Suffrage Association in Budapest. When she returned to the United States, especially during 1914, she traveled extensively, testified before congressional committees, and spoke from New York to South Dakota, from Alabama to Kansas, arguing for the vote for all women, the poor as well as the well-to-do, the naturalized citizen as well as the native-born. Her foray into politics had not hurt her reputation, except for a few who did not forgive easily. Indeed on the eve of the outbreak of World War I she was at the peak of her reputation, internationally known as the best representative of American womanhood and symbol of the American spirit of equality and justice for all people.

XI

Practical Saint and the Most Useful American

ANE Addams reached the peak of her popularity and symbolic importance in the period from 1909 to 1915. There was an occasional critic who denounced her as being too friendly to radicals and labor leaders or who disagreed with her support of Theodore Roosevelt and the Progressives. There were also a few who charged her with being too much the compromiser, but she was almost universally loved and admired by the public, and in the period before World War I her critics were a small minority indeed.

Honors were heaped upon her. She became the first woman to be elected president of the National Conference of Charities and Corrections in 1909, the first woman awarded an honorary degree by Yale University the same year. She even had a chrysanthemum named after her. She helped spread her own reputation through her speaking and writing. She did not stick to the ordinary lecture circuit. She spoke in small towns, and at out-of-the-way colleges. She talked at women's clubs and settlement houses as well as in the largest auditoriums. And she was not afraid to experiment with new formats and techniques. In 1912 in order to publicize the cause of woman suffrage she performed a "witty monologue" on the stage of the Majestic, a vaudeville theater in New York, and she acted in a movie with Anna Howard Shaw. It was a suffrage melodrama whose message was that votes for women would eliminate sweatshops.[1] She played the role of celebrity and she enjoyed it. Her writing, even more than her speaking, led to her reputation as the most famous woman in America. Between 1907 and 1916 she published six books, including her autobiography, and more than 150 essays and reports.[2] Many of her articles appeared in the new mass-circulation magazines such as *Ladies Home Journal, The American Magazine,* and *McClure's;* indeed, in some ways, her national reputation was the product of the twentieth century when the more popular magazines aiming at a wide audience eclipsed such old standards as *Century, Harper's,* and *Scribner's.* The new magazines attracted more advertizing, used slick paper and more illustrations, sold for ten cents rather than twenty-five and often had circulations of five hundred thousand to a million copies an issue. Unrivalled by radio, television, or the movies, during the period just before World War I, these magazines were the only communication medium of national scope. They allowed Jane Addams to reach a much wider audience than was possible for Margaret Fuller or Frances Willard in the generation before. The newspapers, of course, had gone through a similar revolution and by the first decade of the twentieth century they reached an even greater audience than the magazines. Reporters discovered that Jane Addams was good copy; they summarized everything she wrote, and reported everything she did. Even the small town newspapers picked up stories of her books and speeches from the wire services and passed them on to their readers. She was an opinion leader, who not only made news, but influenced attitudes on a wide variety of subjects.[3]

She was given many titles by reporters seeking a dramatic touch, "The Lady Abbess of Chicago," "The Genius of Hull House," "The Only Saint America has produced," "Chicago's First Citizen." Ida Tarbell, the muckraker and journalist, called her simply "The First Lady of the Land." Her name became so well known that it was used generically. "Local 'Jane Addams' to found New Hull House," *The Los Angeles Tribune* announced in 1912; a young woman in Jersey City was dubbed "A New Jersey Jane Addams," and Kate Barnard became an "Oklahoma Jane Addams." "Jane Addams is synonymous with all that is charitable, ennobling, public spirited and good," *The Atlanta Constitution* announced.[4]

She was constantly winning popularity contests. A poll in Chicago in 1906 asked "Who is the best woman in Chicago?" The choice was limited to unmarried women because, the contest organizers explained, "unless a married woman ignores the wishes of her husband it is difficult for her to achieve the same degree of goodness that the unmarried woman does." Jane Addams ran first in the poll, with Mary McDowell of the University of Chicago Settlement, Harriet Van der Vaart of Neighborhood Settlement, and Julia Lathrop of Hull House following in order. In 1908 the *Ladies Home Journal* named her the "First American Woman," ahead of Helen Keller, Helen Miller Gould of the YMCA, Maud Ballington Booth of the Salvation Army, Julia Ward Howe, author of the Battle Hymn of the Republic, and Frances Folsom Cleveland, the wife of the former President. In 1912 the New York State Woman Suffrage Association took a poll of its members to determine the twenty-five "greatest women in history." Susan B. Anthony, Madame Curie, and Jane Addams led the list, but of those still alive, "Jane Addams was far in the lead." In 1913 the Twilight Club of New York sent out 3,000 ballots to representative Americans asking them to list the twelve most socially useful Americans, Jane Addams finished far in front and was listed first on more than 50 per cent of the ballots. Theodore Roosevelt was second and Thomas Edison third. Also in 1913 *The Independent,* a popular magazine, asked its readers to list the ten "most useful Americans." "In other words, who among our contemporaries are of most value to the community . . . ?" Jane Addams finished second to Thomas Edison and ahead of Andrew Carnegie.[5]

She was the subject of laudatory articles, and poems praising her accomplishments, and her biography was included in several children's anthologies with titles such as *Heroines of Modern Progress,* and *Famous Living Americans.* She was mentioned half seriously, as the first woman mayor of Chicago; not quite so seriously but still with respect, as the first woman President of the United States. She was the most famous woman in America, but she was more; she was treated with awe and reverence, as she had been by many from the very beginning of Hull House.[6]

Probably no other woman in any period of American history has been venerated and worshiped the way Jane Addams was in the period just before World War I. Certainly none of her contemporaries was treated with quite the same awe and reverence. It is true that Mary McDowell was often called the "angel of the stockyards," that Lillian Wald was sometimes referred to as saintly. Clara Barton and Helen Keller were acclaimed as heroines and praised for overcoming obstacles and working with the underprivileged. Mary Baker Eddy, the founder of Christian Science, was revered and treated like the female counterpart of Christ, and as "composite maiden-mother" by her followers. But the two women who came closest to matching the role played by Jane Addams were

Frances Willard in the generation before her, and Eleanor Roosevelt in the generation after.

In the years before the War, Jane Addams became a community symbol representing the American virtues of "benevolence," "disinterested conduct," and "redeeming love," the same attributes that George Bancroft in his *History of the United States* bestowed upon all his heroes, and a concept that became a part of American thought and folklore through school books, sermons, and patriotic biographies. These virtues were the opposite of "avarice," "self-love," and "greediness." Of course this still left room for hard work, perseverance, and thrift. But one should not be misled by all the emphasis on the Protestant ethic, and the idea of the self-made man in describing the American popular mind in the nineteenth century. Americans have always admired benevolence and the idea of disinterested virtue, and in addition to the successful soldiers, the self-made millionaires, and the lone adventurers, they have in every generation found a few idols of the other American virtues. Even Washington and Franklin, of course, were not admired simply because they were successful, but because they were public spirited, and Abraham Lincoln came to represent the highest ideal, a self-made man who became a humanitarian and suffered for his people. Perhaps it was a sense of guilt, that allowed Americans to praise a few for their benevolence, to admire their saintly and selfless acts, so the rest could be freed to scramble for the more immediate rewards. In any case, during the years just prior to World War I, Jane Addams came to symbolize the disinterested virtues and to be pictured as a benevolent saint. She represented, according to William Allen White, "the altruistic elements in a civilization that is on the whole too acquisitive."[7]

She was viewed as a saint, but a special American kind of saint, brooding and benevolent, self-sacrificing, giving her life to uplift the poor, but also practical and useful. "Jane Addams is a blend of the saint and the statesman," a reporter decided in 1910. "She had the purity of life and character and immense capacity for self-sacrifice of the one combined with the facility of looking at things in the large and the knack of securing results of the other."

"It is one thing to dream of things which might be done," another reporter announced. "It is another thing to do them. Though Miss Addams may, by her own confession, have been for long years a dreamer, she long since gave up dreaming for doing." One observer even put it into the American language of baseball. "Miss Addams has never fouled out, nor been retired to the bench for 'fanning'—she is a safe hitter."[8]

"Miss Addams is not the woman to see visions, to indulge in mysticism or to think of herself as a martyr or a spiritual leader," one writer decided. "Her compassion for the world takes a curiously practical and immediate form." "Chicago men approved of Miss Addams," a San Francisco newspaper suggested in 1909, "because she had a moderate generous point of view. She was not a fanatic, not rabid in any way. Her modes of going to work to better the city were sane and practical." Occasionally she was denounced as a friend of organized labor, or as a defender of the anarchists, but most popular accounts of Hull House in the years before World War I were quick to point out that she was not a socialist, she was too practical for that, indeed she was a comforting alternative to radicalism of all kinds. "Another element making for her practical success has been Miss Addams' ability to guard against the insidious approach of moonshine in the shape of theories reconstructing the universe," one account suggested. It was true that all kinds of radicals were welcome at Hull House "yet they never succeeded in doing the thinking of Jane Addams who was great enough to see her work in conditions rather than in utopias."

In 1909 Mrs. Annie Besant startled Americans, when in an interview with a Chicago newspaper she admitted that she had not even heard of Jane Addams. "This statement of the high priestess of theosophy . . . might be regarded as astonishing at first thought, the newspaper theorized, but after all it is not even surprising, Mrs. Besant deals with matters —not matter—entirely apart from this mundane sphere." Her specialty is the "superterrestrial consciousness and her study is in the vague and delightfully mysterious proposition of the reincarnation of souls. . . . But theosophy has nothing to do with bread and butter, how to make a living, how to keep clean, and how to make human environment as uplifting as possible. Jane Addams of Hull House is a leader in the work of improving social conditions, cleaning up the soiled places on the face of humanity, lifting men and women and children into better surroundings and inspiring them with healthy notions of life."

Jane Addams was often pictured as the practical philanthropist and woman of the world. In 1909 when Yale gave honorary degrees to both Addams and railway magnate James J. Hill, the newspapers were filled with comparisons suggesting that both had succeeded in the real world and both had a lot to teach the cloistered academic community. That neither Yale, the degree recipients, nor the news reporters saw anything anachronistic about simultaneously honoring a robber baron and the founder of Hull House, tells us something about the progressive era in which business efficiency and reform could both be praised with no sense of contradiction. "Have you noticed how colleges are beginning to prize the people who do things in the world?" a Holyoke newspaper asked. "It is only a short step from the recognition of the value of practical organization to the putting of such things into the college curriculum."[9]

She was compared to successful businessmen and praised for her practical approach to reform. Of course, much of what she said should have been disturbing. The horrors of child labor, the pathos and tragedy of life in the tenements which she described should have upset people and made them angry. But it was easier to praise Jane Addams for solving the problems of poverty and the slums than to do something about inequality in America. As a community symbol representing benevolence and self-sacrificing work for the poor, she helped to reassure the public and to make a terrifying world understandable and benign. She was in part responsible for the comforting image she projected. Everything she wrote, every speech she gave contained an optimistic message. "Under all the suffering and sordidness she sees the great, basic element of human-kindness," one observer reported. "You have such a crowning power of illustration, and such a judicial non-partisan tone," one of her friends decided, "that you can say quite fresh and 'shocking' things without frightening people." It was not only the way she spoke, however; her presence, her symbolic importance, became so overwhelming that it was easy to praise her, to worship her even, and to fail to listen to the implications of what she was saying. She diffused conflict and quieted fears. She was, according to William Hard, "the softened reflection of all the emotions that agitate the age, the center from which they radiate with their harsher colors all lost in the white purity of her thought. She is a prophecy for men as well as for women." She was a very comforting prophecy for most Americans. Her example demonstrated that Americans were not as materialistic, not as "sordid and shallow" as some European critics charged. "Her name marks an epoch, the era when a new social conscience began to reign."[10]

The image of Jane Addams was most reassuring to the middle and upper-class Americans who felt vaguely guilty about the presence of poverty, crime and disease in the city. Of course it was these same people, with the aid of the press, who helped to create the comforting image and who succeeded in diffusing Addams' criticism of American society. Only rarely and fleetingly does one get an impression of how the poor viewed the founder of Hull House. Among the great masses of poor around the country, Jane Addams was unknown; they did not read her books and articles, or listen to her speeches. In Chicago, however, especially on the West Side, she was known and apparently admired by thousands of humble men and women, as well as by a group of young and ambitious immigrants. Francis Hackett, speaking of Hull House remarked: "life began for me at a social settlement." Philip Davis, a Russian immigrant, called Hull House "The University of good will, good English, good citizenship, in brief everything good that America stands for." Neither seemed concerned that Jane Addams quite consciously tried to teach middle-class values to the poor. But there were many others in the neighborhood, especially the men, who came to hate and to resent Jane Addams. For all her work with the immigrants she was most comforting to those people who had never lived in an immigrant neighborhood.[11]

Jane Addams, despite her limited appeal to the under class, was the American heroine who symbolized feminine virtue and the best of American democracy. "Alert, a deep thinker, progressive, strong and tenderhearted, Jane Addams is a true type of useful American womanhood," *Leslie's Weekly* announced. "The heroine," Alfred Kazin has argued, "is a unique presence that composes and socializes our existence . . . she is the cementing element in our civilization. . . ." For a brief time at least Jane Addams was a unique presence who helped to preserve faith in the American dream.

The popular image of Jane Addams in the years before the First World War was built in part on an American tradition in popular culture and literature which pictured women as superior to men and by nature more benevolent. "The American writer for reasons profoundly rooted in our national life," Leslie Fiedler maintains, "has insisted that the female who in Europe symbolized the libido, stands instead for the superego, the conscience." In literature, another critic has suggested, "the chief result of this mystique of sex—women are better than men— is a preference for heroines rather than heroes." Whether or not it was uniquely American there was a tradition in the late nineteenth century that defined women as the principal agents of moral regeneration. Man saw in woman, as Henry James noted, "a diviner self than his own." Because of their special, gentle temperaments, and innate concern for humanity, women represented the hope for the salvation of the world. Jane

Addams not only symbolized this tradition, she expanded on it in some of her writing, arguing that women, because of their particular temperament and intuition, could lead the movements for municipal reform and world peace.[12]

Jane Addams' image had changed from the early days at Hull House. Then she was pictured as innocent, pure, and selfless—"the angel of Hull House." Now as she turned fifty in 1910 and grew heavier, and some thought sadder, she was characterized as motherly, even as the earth-mother protecting humanity. "With the gentleness of motherhood, the sweet tenderness of a good woman's love, she has investigated, collected and analyzed facts and statistics regarding the denizens of Chicago's slums, lifted them up, put them on their feet and taught them the lesson of self help and self respect," one newspaper decided. While Mrs. Ethelbert Stewart, wife of the labor leader and journalist, wrote: "I thank God for the intuitive motherhood that has made you see the needs so plainly, and the education and opportunity that has enabled you to express what you see, as we mothers of large families cannot." Or as one of the many poems dedicated to her expressed it:

> MOTHER of races fusing into one,
> and keeping open house with presence sweet
> In that loud city where the nations meet
> Around thy ample hearth when day is done,
> When I behold the wild tribes thou hast won
> And see thee wooing from the witching street
> By thy own saintly face the erring feet,
> I know Love still has power beneath the sun.[13]

An important part of her image continued to include the erroneous idea that she sacrificed herself to aid the poor and downtrodden, but self-sacrifice was a necessary ingredient for an altruistic hero or heroine who would serve society. "Jane Addams is to Chicago what Joan of Arc was to her people, she is sacrificing all for the masses," a newspaper reported. "She has attained the heavenly beauty of the Madonna for she has borne the suffering of the people," Professor Edward Steiner remarked. "Her life is a sermon in self-sacrifice and a parable of service. Well-born, well-educated, and with most unusual personal charms, she abandoned the world into which she had been born, and gave herself without reserve to good works," another observer remarked.[14]

Addams was often contrasted in the press with other American hero-

ines. "There are many people who call Jane Addams beautiful even
though she is homely," *The Milwaukee Leader* suggested. "There is a
difference, you see, between the beauty of Jane Addams and that of Lillian Russell. One of them depends on massage and the other doesn't."
In 1909, just as Jane Addams was elected president of the National Conference of Charities and Correction, Katherine Clemmons Gould, an
actress, made headlines by divorcing her husband and declaring that she
could not possibly live on less than $40,000 a year. A Pittsburgh newspa-
per editorialized on the contrast between the two women, and speculated on how many dresses Jane Addams needed, or how many inside
servants, or if she could spend $500 a month for automobile expenses.
"Miss Addams would probably be unable to furnish satisfactory answers.
Her experience is too limited. She has been too busy inspecting streets
and alleys in Chicago, helping our immigrants to become good American
citizens, teaching the poor how to improve their lot, bringing light and
love into the dark corners of humble lives. Her service has been to humanity, not self. When the newspapers parade the lives and opinions of
women like Mrs. Gould—which, to say the least, are useless and empty
of inspiration—it is well to remember that there are also women like
Miss Addams, whose example and evangel are given for the bettering of
the world, the healing of the hurts and the lifting up the lowly." And
again when Mrs. Melwin Drummund, the widow of Marshall Field, Jr.,
lost $130,000 in jewelry about the same time Jane Addams lost a hat
and refused to take $50 for it because she said she never paid more than
$10 for a hat, a Memphis paper editorialized: "Mrs. Drummond lost
$130,000 worth of jewelry, and is wildly excited. Jane Addams lost a $10
hat and does not fret about it. Mrs. Drummond's interest in life centers
in herself. Jane Addams' interest in life radiates from herself to all humanity. Who is the more useful of these women is not a debatable
question."[15]

Jane Addams may not have been everyone's idea of the ideal American
woman; some may have preferred the beautiful actress or the rich society
woman. But the image of the ideal woman had not remained static.
From the idea of true womanhood in the mid-nineteenth century which
emphasized piety, innocence, and duty to one's family and husband, the
ideal changed in the early twentieth century to stress duty not to one's
family, but to oneself, to approve active participation in the world. Freedom, not dependence, became the ideal for women, but with freedom
went a responsibility to act for the public good, at least that was the

opinion of Margaret Deland who charted the emergence of the "new woman" in a widely read article, "The Change in the Feminine Ideal," which appeared in the *Atlantic Monthly* in 1910. Another article put the change from the old ideal of weakness and dependence to the new sense of freedom and candor more dramatically when it contrasted "The Steel-Engraving Lady and the Gibson Girl." Of course the image of Jane Addams did not include the sexual freedom or the beauty and wit implied by the symbol of the "Gibson Girl." But the symbolic Jane Addams did include independence and public spirit and a special feminine mystique. Her image was not far removed from the heroines in the best selling novels of Winston Churchill, such as Victoria Flint in *Mr. Crewes' Career*, who represent "social morality, civic virtue, personal integrity," in the fight against the corrupt and the powerful. She is still a woman, but "aloof and coldly virtuous, this heroine insists not so much on being loved as being literally adored." Churchill was one of the first novelists to make the "new woman" a heroine and it is no accident that his novels were among the most popular of the progressive era, the very time Jane Addams reached the highest point of her public adulation.[16]

The image of Jane Addams in the decade before World War I symbolized feminine benevolence, saintly devotion and practical usefulness, as well as the best of American democracy. Her image challenged some of the tenents of the old feminine ideal, of the Steel Engraving Lady, or the ideal of true womanhood. She was a public figure, active reformer, author, lecturer, even political campaigner—the equal of men in many ways but still his superior in others. She personally had rejected the life of wife and mother, but her career did not challenge the conventional concept of marriage and motherhood, or for that matter the role of maiden aunt. Nor did she question the traditional sexual role of women as Emma Goldman did. In a sense the symbolic Jane Addams solved the dilemma of the Gibson Girl and the Steel Engraving Lady. She rebelled but in a way that was comforting not disturbing, at least that was the picture that came through for many who read and heard about Jane Addams in the years before the war.

Simone de Beauvoir remarked in *The Second Sex*, that no one is born a woman, one is born female, and one "becomes a woman according to the models and meaning provided by the civilization." During the middle ages, the Virgin Mary provided one model, and in the 1960's, according to Harvey Cox, Miss America served as a role model for millions of American girls. During the transitional years of the early twentieth century when the status of women was undergoing rapid change, a generation of women brought up on genteel novels and convinced that women were superior to men, found a model in the life of Jane Addams. Even if they were themselves submissive Penelopes, or tied to the home by husband and children, they could admire Jane Addams, write poems of tribute to her, and place her picture on their mantle. For many she came to represent what women could do. As Jill Conway has argued: "She was the model of feminine virtue which answered to every need of American women of her day. She embodied in her person a solution to the problem of the role of women which was acceptable for both men and women, for her active public career carried with it no threat to the accepted fabric of society."[17]

Jane Addams was also a role-model for young college women eager to do something about the world's problems. Rebecca Shelly, graduate of the University of Michigan who became an ardent suffragist and pacifist, described the impact of Jane Addams on her life. "In 1915 women were in a ferment of rebellion against political bondage. And strange as it now seems, in the life I then lived, Jane Addams was its visible symbol. During my senior year at the University of Michigan she was forbidden to speak on the campus because her subject was controversial! It was votes for women! How the Suffrage Club chairman's brown eyes flashed sparks of anger as she told us of the indignity to the great Jane Addams as well as to ourselves. On that day I became a militant suffragist. In my sociology seminar I learned of Jane Addams' pioneer social settlement work. Her *Twenty Years at Hull House* was a classic, and so as Frances Willard had been the heroine of my Puritan childhood, now Jane Addams embodied for me the best, bravest and wisest in American womanhood."[18]

Jane Addams was well aware that she served as a model and guide for a great many women, that she was viewed as a spiritual adviser. She enjoyed that role and she played it to the hilt. During 1913, and periodically for the next two years, she wrote a column for the *Ladies Home Journal* called "The Jane Addams Page." She wrote about child labor, white slavery, woman suffrage, the need for better public health, and other matters. Each article contained her picture, her signature and an invitation for the reader to write and ask her questions. She enjoyed writing the articles and she once told Paul Kellogg, the editor of the *Survey*, that when she wrote for the *Ladies Home Journal* she had the farmer's wife in mind and she imagined her sitting there beside a kerosene lamp placed on a table with a red table cloth. This kind of empathy

allowed her to communicate with all kinds of women. But it was significant that it was she who became the national heroine in the years before
World War I. Women such as Florence Kelley, Julia Lathrop, and
Grace Abbott might have been admired and emulated during these
years, for they were creating new careers for women as experts, and pro-
fessionals. They did not write as many books, or make as many speeches,
nor did they work as hard at promoting themselves, but they also challenged the stereotype of woman in a way that the image of Jane Addams
did not. By emphasizing woman's special intuitive powers, rather than
her capacity to compete with men, and by cooperating with her public
image as gentle and benevolent saint, Jane Addams helped to defend the
traditional role of woman even as she challenged it every day by managing Hull House, touring the country making speeches, and in other
ways acting as a self-possessed and independent woman.[19]

She was more than a symbol of what woman could do; she also served
as a priestess and sage. She was asked even more frequently as she grew
older to officiate at funerals, to preach at Protestant churches. Always
fascinated with ancient myths and symbolism, she read James Frazer's
The Golden Bough and other works in anthropology, and used them to
help explain the mysteries of life and death. "In the presence of a sorrow such as this . . ." she remarked solemnly at the funeral of Jenny
Dow, "it takes all of our steadiness and courage to face the mystery of
justice—to divine the path wherein lies fortitude and resignation." "The
craving to perpetuate the memory of one we love," she explained at another memorial service," to make tangible and enduring for yet, a human span, the personality which has passed from the region of daily in-
tercourse and beyond the reach of household affection is, perhaps, one
of the oldest cravings of the hungry human heart."[20]

While traveling in Egypt in 1913, Jane Addams was intrigued by the
ancient temples and tombs, and the Egyptian ideas about death, and a
life after death. When she returned she shared her insights and her own
early memories of death, in order to instruct her readers and listeners.
She assumed the role of priestess and Lincoln-like spiritual teacher with
ease. "We are scarcely prepared to find that the Egyptians were endlessly
preoccupied with death, constantly portraying man's earliest efforts to
defeat it, his eager desire to survive and to enter by force or guile into
the heavens of the western sky. The mind of the traveler is thus pushed
back into earliest childhood when the existence of the soul, its exact
place of residence in the body, its experience immediately after death

had so often afforded material for the crudest speculation. The obscure renewal of these childish fantasies reproduces a state of consciousness which has so absolutely passed into oblivion that only the most powerful stimuli could revive it." She recalled her own childhood experience with death, her childhood thoughts about immortality, and the vague feelings that she had lived before, thoughts and feelings that must have been shared by many of her readers. Then she taught her lesson, ended her sermon on an optimistic note. "Such ghosts of reminiscence, coming to the individual as he visits one after another of the marvelous human documents on the banks of the Nile, may be merely manifestations of that new humanism which is perhaps the most precious possession of this generation, the belief that no altar at which living men have once devoutly worshiped, no oracle to whom a nation long ago appealed in its moments of dire confusion, no gentle myth in which former generations have found solace, can lose all significance for us, the survivors."[21]

Another story she told which touched on the supernatural and exposed a primitive side of human nature, and taught a lesson as well, was the tale of the Devil Baby at Hull House. "The knowledge of the existence of the Devil Baby burst upon the residents of Hull-House one day when three Italian women, with an excited rush through the door, demanded that he be shown to them. No amount of denial convinced them that he was not there, for they knew exactly what he was like, with his cloven hoofs, his pointed ears and diminutive tail; moreover, the Devil Baby had been able to speak as soon as he was born and was most shockingly profane." There was an Italian version and a Jewish version and many variations, but the old women seemed most fascinated. "It stirred their minds and memories as with a magic touch; it loosened their tongues and revealed the inner life and thoughts of those who are so often inarticulate." One woman told how she got the twist in her face, after she saw her father kill her mother, another of how she had had fourteen children, of which only two had lived beyond childhood and they were both killed in the same explosion. Still another described how her son beat her up to get the money she earned scrubbing, but she did not blame him for "the ugliness was born in the boy as the marks of the devil was born in the poor child upstairs." Jane Addams decided that, "the vivid interest of so many old women in the story of the Devil Baby may have been an unconscious, although powerful testimony that tragic experiences gradually become dressed in such trappings in order that their spent agony may prove of some use to a world which learns at the hardest; and that the strivings and sufferings of men and women long since dead, their emotions no longer connected with flesh and blood, are thus transmuted into legendary wisdom. . . . In the midst of the most tragic recitals there remained that something in the souls of these mothers which has been called the great revelation of tragedy, or sometimes the great illusion of tragedy—that which has power in its own right to make life acceptable and at rare moments even beautiful."[22]

Jane Addams enjoyed her role of priestess and sage, of explaining the mysteries of life, and hearing the "curious confessions" of total strangers. It was not so much what she said, or her careful connections made with the myths and symbolism of the past, it was her very presence that was important. It was true of Jane Addams as Matthew Arnold remarked of Emerson, "Yes truly his insight is admirable, his truth is precious. Yet the secret of his effect is not . . . in *these*; it is in his temper. It is in the hopeful, serene, beautiful temper. . . ." Jane Addams, as Lillian Wald pointed out, was more important than what she did, more important than what she wrote. In the years before World War I, she was a symbol of the best American Democracy, the best of American womanhood, and a semi-religious figure who explained all mysteries and assured everyone that despite poverty and tragedy everywhere, in the end, right would prevail. "In America, the cult of personality is the faith of the outcast . . . ," a critic has recently written, "To be revered beyond reason, the cult-hero need not be particularly talented . . . nor especially commanding. . . . But he must express, however ambiguously, the unrealized hopes of the disaffected of his age for a new order of life. The only mandatory article of faith is the belief that the qualities of his personality can somehow become the values of their society." For a time before World War I Jane Addams served that need for many Americans.[23]

XII

A Pacifist in Time of War

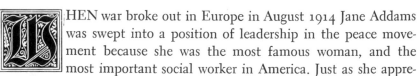HEN war broke out in Europe in August 1914 Jane Addams was swept into a position of leadership in the peace movement because she was the most famous woman, and the most important social worker in America. Just as she appreciated the symbolic importance of taking up the cause of the Progressives in 1912, she could not hold back in 1914 when most of those who had fought for woman suffrage and social justice instinctively revolted against a war that seemed to negate all they stood for. "War is the doom of all that has taken years of peace to build up," Lillian Wald announced. Jane Addams was equally discouraged for she had been arguing for some years that working men the world over would reject war, and that women's "nurturing instinct" should make them oppose the brutality of armed conflict. The outbreak of war seemed to contradict all her theories, but more than that, she was genuinely shocked by the irrational events 3,000 miles across the ocean. Child labor, even a 25 per cent infant mortality rate, seemed a "little thing" when compared to the "wholesale slaughter of thousands of men a day."[1]

Lillian Wald and Fanny Garrison Villard led a parade of 1200 women down Fifth Avenue in New York on August 29, 1914, to protest the war. Jane Addams took no such direct action in Chicago, but she was looked to for leadership by the social justice reformers. Paul Kellogg, editor of the *Survey*, and the master organizer of many progressive reform movements, wrote to her to ask her advice on the proper course of action. He reminded her that she had chaired a meeting at the Henry Street Settlement, a few years before, that had led to the formation of the Industrial Relations Commission. He suggested a similar round-table discussion "as a means by which in humbleness and quiet some of us who deal with the social fabric may come together to clarify our minds and, if it seems wise to act in concert." At first he had in mind a ringing message similar to Lincoln's Gettysburg Address which would "breathe the spirit of democracy," and "enunciate a world policy to take the place of commercial exploitation." The call issued by Kellogg, Wald, and Addams for a meeting late in September at Henry Street Settlement hardly lived up to that hope, but they suggested that even though the United States was and ought to be neutral "Americans should as freemen and democrats and peace lovers express themselves in some definite way." The meeting itself, chaired by Addams and attended by eighteen veterans of the social justice movement including Wald, Kellogg, Kelley, Emily Balch, John Haynes Holmes, Owen Lovejoy, and Samuel McClune Lindsay, led to the formation of an informal "Henry Street Group" to explore the possible ways they could influence the peace settlement after the war, and perhaps help to bring the war to a quick conclusion. There was no universal agreement even among this group, but they issued statements pointing out how war forced the abandonment of normal activities, and how it brutalized men. Jane Addams warned that war and a rise of national feeling endangered international cooperation. "To remain neutral is not to remain indifferent to this international sentiment," she argued. "The cultivation of this sentiment is our only hope." It was assumed from the beginning that Jane Addams would chair the meeting at Henry Street Settlement, and that she would play a prominent role in drafting the statements issued by the group. She had the prestige and the respect of all those who were invited. She had written *Newer Ideals of Peace*, lectured frequently on Tolstoy and on a moral substitute for war, and she had attended several peace conferences. But much of her reputation as a pacifist had been eroded by her support of Theodore Roosevelt. Her prestige in 1914 was related to her national reputation and her leadership in many progressive causes, and this was a meeting made up largely of social justice reformers. It was Kellogg who organized the meeting, with advice and help from many sources, but he used Jane Addams' name to draw attention to the statements, and to enlist others to support the cause.[2]

The Henry Street group, disturbed by the increasing clamor in the country for military preparedness, organized the American League for the Limitation of Armaments early in 1915 and appealed to the President to resist the pressure to make the United States an armed camp. The group added a few impressive people to their numbers: Frederic C. Howe, the Commissioner of Immigration, Oswald Garrison Villard, editor of the *Evening Post* and the *Nation*, and Hamilton Holt, editor of the *Independent*. Late in 1915 the group organized an "Anti-Preparedness Committee," to resist the President's National Defence Bill, and to enlist support for a League of Neutral American Nations. This committee changed its name in 1916 to the American Union Against Militarism from which eventually emerged the American Civil Liberties Union. Lillian Wald, Florence Kelley, Paul Kellogg, John Haynes Holmes, Crystal Eastman, and many other friends and associates of Jane Addams were very much involved with these organizations. They often asked her advice or sought her aid. She occasionally went to the meetings and signed their appeals, but her role in these important anti-military and civil libertarian organizations was peripheral. Her health was poor during the war years and it was a struggle for her to get to New York where these anti-military organizations were headquartered, but she was also deeply concerned with the special responsibilities of women in time of war.[3]

Most of her energy during these years was devoted to the Woman's Peace Party. Again she was swept into a position of leadership, because of her reputation and prestige established earlier as head of Hull House and as symbol of the feminine conscience in America. She was also genuinely upset by the outbreak of war, and she believed that women had a special responsibility to preserve the peace. But she was pushed into action by the arrival in the United States of two militant pacifists, Emmeline Pethick-Lawrence from England and Rosika Schwimmer from Hungary.

Rosika Schwimmer, a short, round-faced woman with black hair and brown eyes, was thirty-seven years old in 1914. She was a persuasive orator in several languages and an energetic and determined advocate of her cause. She was committed, militant, and implacable. Unlike Jane Addams, she had no interest in compromise, and no understanding or patience for those who sought conciliation. Before the war broke out she had devoted most of her time and energy to working for woman's rights. She helped to found the International Woman Suffrage Alliance at a meeting in Berlin in 1904. There she first met Carrie Chapman Catt, the American suffrage leader who was elected president of the new organization. She also helped to organize the Hungarian feminist and pacifist organization, Feministák Egyesülete. She wrote and spoke extensively, and edited a feminist-pacifist journal. In 1913 she organized the Seventh Congress of the International Woman Suffrage Alliance in Budapest and here she met Jane Addams for the first time. When World War I broke out Rosika was in Great Britain. Stranded away from home, she immediately began to organize European women to promote peace. She circulated a petition urging President Wilson to take the initiative to end the war through mediation. In September she arrived in the United States and was met by Mrs. Catt. She talked to William Jennings Bryan, the Secretary of State, and President Wilson. She then began a tour of the United States to arouse the women of the country to support the cause of peace, and to urge the United States to end the war through mediation.[4]

Often Rosika Schwimmer appeared on the same platform with Emmeline Pethick-Lawrence, a militant British suffragist, who had been jailed along with Emmeline Pankhurst for use of violent tactics in their suffragist campaigns. She had broken with Mrs. Pankhurst over the use of violence, but she remained a militant reformer. With the outbreak of war she turned her attention toward the cause of peace. She called for a "women's war against war" and argued that women should have a direct role in settling international disputes. Pethick-Lawrence's position was similar to Schwimmer's, except that she put her emphasis on a program for peace after the war's end, rather than on ending the war by mediation. She arrived in the United States on October 27, 1914, and in an interview the next day, announced: "If we are going to accept war as inevitable, women might just as well give up living at once, for under these circumstances it is not worth while to continue the race."[5]

Jane Addams made no such dramatic statement, but she was forced into action by her own conscience and the stir caused by the two crusading suffragists from abroad. After Mrs. Pethick-Lawrence's visit to Chicago in December an Emergency Federation of Peace Forces was formed with Jane Addams in her usual position as chairman. The founders of the organization sought to enlist all peace forces and organizations to exert pressure on the governments of the world, and to bring about an end to the war through a league of neutral nations. But it was Carrie Chapman Catt, not Jane Addams, who suggested calling a conference in Washington of all women's organizations, taking advantage of the enthusiasm for peace aroused by the foreign visitors. Actually a number of women seem to have had the idea about the same time but Catt wrote to Addams suggesting that they might jointly call the conference. At first Jane Addams was not too enthusiastic about a separate women's peace organization. She believed that "men and women work best together in these public measures," though she admitted that there was no doubt that "at this crisis women are most eager for action," and she had been talking for years about the special nurturing instinct that made women natural pacifists. With Mrs. Catt she drafted a letter which was sent to most women's organizations calling a meeting in Washington for January 10, 1915, "looking forward to the organization of women throughout the country into a peace movement." "I am undertaking all this with a certain sinking of the heart," she admitted to Catt, "knowing how easy it is to get a large body of women together and how difficult it is to take any wise action among many people who do not know each other well. The demand, however, has been tremendously spontaneous and widespread, which should give us confidence."[6]

About 3,000 women gathered on January 10, 1915, in the ballroom of the New Willard Hotel in Washington to try to unite women's efforts toward peace. In addition to Addams and Catt there were many other well-known American women: Lucia Ames Mead, a lecturer and writer on peace; Fannie Fern Andrews, secretary of the American School Peace League and a director of the American Peace Society; Alice Thatcher Post, vice-president of the Anti-Imperialist League; Anna Garlin Spencer, professor of ethics and sociology at Meadville Theological College; Charlotte Perkins Gilman, sociologist and feminist; Anna Howard Shaw, a veteran of the woman movement; Mrs. Joseph Fels, wife of the philanthropist and single-taxer; Mrs. Robert LaFollette, wife of the senator and progressive leader, and Fanny Garrison Villard, daughter of William Lloyd Garrison, in addition to the two European peace advocates, Schwimmer and Pethick-Lawrence. But even in this assemblage of important and accomplished women Jane Addams was looked to for leadership. She presided at the meetings and delivered the keynote address. There was some fear that particular organizations such as the National Union, a militant women's organization led by Alice Paul, would try to dominate the meeting, and that the woman suffrage groups would not get enough attention, but Addams, with her skill at running public meetings, steered a middle course and avoided the potential disruptions.[7]

The group adopted a Peace Platform with a preamble written by Anna Garland Spencer. "We, women of the United States, assembled in behalf of World Peace, grateful for the security of our own country, but sorrowing for the misery of all involved in the present struggle among warring nations, do hereby band ourselves together to demand that war be abolished. . . . As women, we are particularly charged with the future of childhood and with the care of the helpless and the unfortunate. We will no longer endure without protest that added burden of maimed and invalid men and poverty-stricken widows and orphans which was placed upon us. . . . We demand that women be given a share in deciding between war and peace in all the courts of high debate —within the home, the school, the church, the industrial order and the state. . . . So protesting and so demanding, we hereby form ourselves into a national organization to be called the Woman's Peace Party."[8]

Their platform contained eleven planks including the demand for an immediate convention of neutral nations in the interest of early peace. This plan for "continuous mediation" during the war by a conference of experts from the neutral nations was first suggested by Rosika Schwimmer, and then developed and refined by Julia Grace Wales, an instructor in English at the University of Wisconsin. The plan was not entirely original, but the Woman's Peace Party took as its special mission the idea of "continuous mediation." They tried first to sell the plan to Wilson, and then to the world.

Almost as a matter of course Jane Addams was made chairman of the Woman's Peace Party, but despite her presence and that of all the other prominent women in Washington, the newspapers paid almost no attention to the conference. Women organizing for peace was not an especially newsworthy event in 1915, but before many months they would receive more publicity than they needed. In February Addams received a cablegram from Aletta Jacobs, an ardent suffragist and one of the first women physicians in Holland, inviting the Woman's Peace Party to send delegates to an International Congress of Women to meet at The Hague, Netherlands, from April 28 to May 1. The idea for an international meeting of women from both the neutral and belligerent countries came primarily from the European women connected with the International Suffrage Alliance, which had been forced to cancel its biennial meeting scheduled for Berlin in 1915. "We feel strongly that at a time when there is so much hatred among nations, we women must show that we can retain our solidarity and that we are able to maintain a mutual friendship," the appeal for the conference announced. Also supporting the plan of a woman's conference in time of war were Emily Hobhouse, an Englishwoman who had attracted attention by sending a letter of

Christmas greeting to the women of Germany and Austria, Lida Gustava Heymann, the leader of German woman suffrage movement, and Chrystal Macmillan, a lawyer from Scotland. Jane Addams, as a delegate from the largest neutral nation, was invited to chair the conference, though Carrie Chapman Catt, better known in international suffrage circles, was the first choice of the conference planners. Along with Fannie Fern Andrews, Addams was also made a member of the executive committee.

There was only a short time to enlist the American delegates to go to The Hague. Addams was not overly enthusiastic. The trip sometimes seemed to her like a "fool's errand." She alternated between hope "that it may perhaps be the first negotiations leading ultimately to some result," to fear that it would be a "flat failure, and even do harm to the cause of peace." Yet she had little choice but to go; her role as symbolic leader of American women demanded it, and all her friends in the peace movement expected it. "The whole enterprise has about it a certain aspect of moral adventure, but it seems to me to be genuine," she wrote to Lillian Wald. "Don't you think that there is a certain obligation on the women who have had the advantage of study and training, to take this possible chance to help out?" she asked in trying to convince Emily Balch, a Wellesley economics professor, to go.[9]

Emily Balch did decide to go. She joined an impressive group which included Alice Hamilton, Grace Abbott, Julia Grace Wales, Madeleine Doty, a lawyer and juvenile court investigator, Elizabeth Glendower Evans, a trade union organizer, and many others. There were 42 in all (with five more joining them in Europe) and they sailed on the *Noordam*, a Dutch ship, on April 12. It was no vacation excursion; German submarines prowled the North Atlantic and those aboard realized that they were risking their lives. There were a few men on board as well; Louis Lochner, secretary of the Chicago Peace Society, Hamilton Holt, editor of the *Independent*, and a few journalists covering the conference or the war. The correspondent for the *Chicago Daily News* wrote sympathetically and somewhat sentimentally about the women and their mission: "These women had embarked because the cry from the women of Europe was too pitiful to be ignored, and because it is feminine nature to respond impulsively and completely. . . . It was a serious-minded party enough, but it was not a gloomy one. In the central group, where the women flocked around Miss Addams, there generally was laughter. But here could scarcely be hilarity, for the women bore in their memories the awful tidings they had received from their sisters abroad, tidings of sexual horrors, of naked children, of ruined generations, of racial peril. . . ."[10]

The ship became a seagoing classroom. "It is like a perpetual meeting of the woman's club or the Federation of Settlements, or something like that," Alice Hamilton reported. There were classes at 11 a.m., 3 p.m., and 8 p.m. Lochner lectured on the peace movement, Wales presented her plan on continuous mediation, Dr. Hamilton gave a gruesome talk on the medical aspects of the war, and Addams explained Tolstoy's ideas of nonresistance. There was a certain amount of tension and some disagreement; after all, nearly everyone on board was accustomed to leading not following. "There are people aboard who are lightweights, as far as one can judge, especially a DAR climber," Emily Balch decided, "but there are many who would count in any group." The tension already high on the ship mounted when they were stopped for four days off the coast of England. They were not allowed to land, to send messages, or to have anyone come aboard. They were permitted newspapers, but that did not encourage them for they discovered that they were being denounced in England as "Pro-hun peaceites." At one point a British gunboat came along side and trained a machine gun on the ship, as two stowaways were escorted off. "Think of Jane Addams with a machine gun trained at her," Alice Thatcher Post remarked. Jane did her best to calm the women and she appealed to the American ambassador to insist that the British government allow them to proceed. "Miss Addams shines," Emily Balch wrote in her journal, "so respectful of everyone's views, so eager to understand and sympathize, so patient of anarchy and even ego, yet always there, strong, wise and in the lead. No 'managing,' no keeping dark and bringing things subtly to pass, just a radiating wisdom and power of judgement. . . ."[11]

Not all the women were as enthusiastic about Jane Addams' abilities. Rosika Schwimmer, who was not aboard the *Noordam* but who would be at The Hague, was suspicious of Jane Addams almost from the beginning. She feared that Addams was under the influence of a Hull House clique, and that she was more interested in smoothing ruffled feathers, in compromising differences, than she was in taking an unequivocal stand for world peace. She called her "slippery Jane," because she claimed it was impossible to pin her down to a particular ideological position.

The meetings at The Hague were exhilarating. There were over 1,000 voting members at the Congress with twelve nations represented. "The great achievement of this congress," Jane Addams told a reporter, "is . . . the getting together of these women from all parts of Europe when their men folks are shooting each other from opposite trenches."[12] There were occasional clashes; Rosika Schwimmer denounced Alice Post for suggesting that some kinds of war might be acceptable, and there were moments of tension between delegates from the countries actually at war. Yet there was little difficulty, and there was a spirit of dedication and faith in the future among the impressive group of women gathered at The Hague. "What stands out most strongly among all my impressions of those thrilling and strained days at The Hague," Emily Balch recalled, "is the sense of wonder at the beautiful spirit of the brave, self-controlled women who dared ridicule and every sort of difficulty to express a passionate human sympathy, not inconsistent with patriotism, but transcending it."[13] The conference resolutions called for liberal peace terms, the establishment of a permanent international court, and a permanent international conference; no transfer of territory without the consent of the people, and the representation of women in both national and international political life.[14] Jane Addams managed the confusing resolutions and amendments in several languages with her usual skill. "Again and again, when she rose to speak and when she closed," Elizabeth Glendower Evans remembered, "the audience would stand and applaud—until one pitied her for this challenge to her gentle modesty."[15] She was not, of course, that modest, but modesty was part of the image she projected. In her presidental address the last night of the Congress she reached sentimental heights as she appealed to the women of the world to unite and stop the fighting.

But no one was as eloquent as Rosika Schwimmer. She was the only one who could sweep the Congress off its feet, Alice Hamilton decided and "she did it several times notably at the end when she succeeded in having them pass the resolution which filled most of us with dismay."[16] The resolution called for delegates from the Congress to carry the resolutions to the belligerent and neutral nations of Europe and to the President of the United States. Jane Addams was elected one of the delegates, but at first she thought the plan was "hopelessly melodramatic and absurd," but then she saw that it was important to some of the European women so she reluctantly consented to go. "I know how wild they [the plans] must sound in the U.S.A.," she admitted to Mary Smith. "You can never understand unless you are here, how I could be willing to do anything. . . . I don't think I have lost my head. There is just one chance in 10 thousand."[17]

While Jane Addams and Aletta Jacobs visited the warring countries, accompanied by Alice Hamilton and Frau van Wulfften Palthe as unofficial delegates, another committee made up of Chrystal Macmillan and Rosika Schwimmer, Mme. Cor Ramondt-Hirschmann, and Emily Balch visited the neutral countries. Jane Addams and Aletta Jacobs went to London, Berlin, Vienna, Budapest, Rome, Berne, and Paris. It was a strange and sometimes frightening trip for the four well-dressed, upper-class ladies from Holland and the United States. They crossed and re-crossed international boundaries and all around them they saw signs of the war—barricaded cities, bombed-out buildings, wounded and crippled soldiers. In most places they were treated courteously, and in many cities, peace groups or social workers arranged for Jane Addams to speak. In London they talked to Prime Minister Asquith and Sir Edward Grey only two days after the sinking of the Lusitania. They were received cordially but coolly by the British officials, who insisted that the war would have to be fought to the end. In each capital they talked not so much about the cause of the war, or even about the war itself, but about finding some substitute for fighting to solve the difficulties. They urged a conference of neutral nations to bring the war to a close. Jane Addams found it difficult sometimes to talk peace to people who had lost sons in the war, to imply that the cause they were fighting and dying for was not worth the sacrifice. "Your tongue cleaves to your mouth," she admitted.[18]

Their greatest success came in Austria during their interview with Prime Minister Sturgkh. After they had completed their presentation Addams said rather apologetically, "It perhaps seems to you very foolish that women should go about in this way. . . ." The minister banged his fist on the table and responded, "Foolish? Not at all. These are the first sensible words that have been uttered in this room in ten months." That remark sustained their courage when it was easy to lose faith. "I am awfully sorry to be away so long . . ." she wrote Ellen Starr, "but one thing makes the next imperative and we·go to the next. At moments it seems worthwhile and again it fades into nothing." In Germany they talked to Professor Hans Delbrueck, an ardent nationalist, who told them that the only way to end the war was for the United States to intervene. Wilson, he argued, "should tell England that he will place an embargo on munitions of war, unless she will accept reasonable terms for ending the war, and let him tell Germany that this embargo will be lifted unless Germany will do the same." But Jane Addams explained that Wilson would lose his moral influence if he used blackmail and coercion. She was convinced that rational persuasion was more important than the threat of force.

"We met with no molestation anywhere," she told a reporter on her return, "in fact, we found the officials ready to help us along. That does not mean that the officials gave the impression that they sympathized with the idea of bringing about a speedy peace, for they expressed only the idea that the war must be pushed to a decisive end."[19]

Meanwhile the other delegation traveled to Denmark, Norway, Sweden, the Netherlands, and Russia, talking to government officials, hoping to get a commitment from someone to call a conference of neutral nations or at least a promise to cooperate with the United States in calling such a conference. They got some encouragement from the leaders in the neutral countries, who implied that if the United States would take the lead; they would cooperate. The original plan agreed upon by the two delegations was to meet in Amsterdam after their separate missions had been accomplished, to discuss the next step they should take in promoting a neutral conference. But suddenly near the end of June, Jane Addams decided not to return to Amsterdam to consult with the others, but rather to sail immediately for the United States. She was probably convinced that only President Wilson could effectively call a neutral conference, and she doubtlessly believed that she could be most effective in the United States rather than in prolonging her stay in Europe. But she was also tired of traveling, and very eager to get home to America, to rest and relax at Bar Harbor. She had gone reluctantly on the mission in the first place, she knew that Mary Smith and other friends opposed her participation, and she was never as committed to the idealistic scheme as were some of the other women. Rosika Schwimmer, who believed much more passionately in the plan, never forgave Jane Addams for deserting the cause at a crucial moment. Even Emily Balch was surprised at her quick decision to return home, and Jane Addams herself was not sure she was making the right move. She felt somewhat guilty about leaving the mission, but her mind was made up, and she sailed for New York, arriving there early in July.[20]

There was a mixed reaction in America to Jane Addams' trip abroad to attend The Hague conference and her subsequent journey to the capitals of Europe. There was some pride that an American woman was picked to chair the conference. "The guiding spirit of Chicago's Hull

House has proven herself worthy of honors that come from beyond the confines of her own country, and the choice of Miss Addams as chairman is an indication that her fame has traveled across the seas into foreign lands." Except for those within the peace movement there was little faith that the women's mission to end the war would be successful. There were probably many who agreed with the editor who wrote: "They may not succeed in restoring peace, but they will at least have given voice to the humane instincts of the world and they will have been true to their own conception of duty. And that, in itself, will be an example of vast value." Or as a writer for the *New York Evening Mail* put it: "It may seem that their work has been in vain, but who shall make bold to call it a failure? Who can deny that they have sown seeds of conciliation that may take root even in hearts now stony and bear fruit in time, possibly before many months?"[21]

But there were also hostile voices, and the most prominent of those was Theodore Roosevelt's. In a letter written to Mrs. George Rublee of Washington, a member of the Woman's Peace Party, the former President denounced the "hysterical pacifists" and called their platform "both silly and base." He went on to compare the "peace at any price" group with the Copperheads of the Civil War, who "did all they could to break up the union and to insure the triumph of slavery, because they put peace as the highest of all good. . . . Let every wise and upright man and woman refuse to have anything more to do with a movement which is certainly both foolish and noxious, which is accompanied by a peculiarly ignoble abandonment of national duty, and which, if successful, would do only harm. . . ." The Colonel did not, on this occasion, single out Jane Addams in his attack, but in the next months he denounced her as "one of the shrieking sisterhood," as "poor bleeding Jane," and as a "Bull Mouse." Most newspapers gave Roosevelt's charges wide publicity and everyone noticed the split between the two partners in the Progressive crusade.[22]

In general, however, though there was criticism of or mild amusement over the idea of a group of women trying to end the war, Jane Addams' reputation as a practical embodiment of the best of American democracy survived. Not everyone would have agreed with the reporter who wrote just before she returned home: "Miss Addams was received by the war lords, greater and lesser, and must have impressed them not only with the justice of her cause, but with the strong good sense of her arguments. She is a fine example of American intellectual womanhood."

More typical was the reaction of the *New York Post* which remarked:
"There are ways of advocating peace that are irritating, there are ways
that are foolish, there are ways that are not only mischievous but per-
verse and dishonest; but with none of these ways is the name of Miss
Addams associated. That even those who, not recognizing this, think
that in point of fact her efforts were ill-advised and injurious speak of
her in tones of the highest personal respect, is a tribute to the quality
and value of her life-long work at home as rare as it is gratifying." A *New
York Times* editorial writer remarked on the day Jane Addams was due
back from her trip: "Everyone will be glad to welcome Miss Jane Addams back and this includes those of her admirers who were sorry to see
her go. These will hope that the next time there is to be a demonstration
of the folly of those who think peace can be brought by stopping a war
it will fall to the lot of someone less generally respected than she is to
make it. For Miss Addams is a citizen too highly valued for any one to
see her engaged in such melancholoy enterprises without a feeling of
pain." Some commentators were more blunt: "In the United States,
Jane Addams has some influence; in Europe she has none," the *Detroit
Free Press* announced, "The time she spent upon the continent has been
time wasted. . . . The trip of Miss Jane Addams abroad may have had
a sentimental value," The *Rochester Democratic Chronicle* remarked,
"but there never was any hope that anything directly in the interest of
peace would be accomplished by it."[23]

Jane Addams' ship docked in New York on July 5th, and she was met
by a group of about 50 people wearing white ribbons inscribed "Welcome Jane Addams." On the night of July 9th she spoke to a large audience at Carnegie Hall at a meeting sponsored by the Church Peace
Union. Anna Howard Shaw presided and Oswald Garrison Villard,
George Foster Peabody, Carrie Chapman Catt, Jacob Shiff, Oscar Straus
and Meyer London among others were on the committee of welcome.
She began tentatively and calmly using only a few notes. "It is difficult
to formulate your experience when brought face to face with so much
genuine emotion and high patriotism as Europe exhibits at the present
moment. You become very much afraid of generalizing," she began.
"The situation is so confused, so many wild and weird things are said
about it, that you are afraid to add one word that is not founded upon
absolutely first-hand impressions and careful experience; because for the
world, you would not add a bit to his already overwhelming confusion.
And you do not come back, at least I do not, from these various warring

countries with any desire to let loose any more emotion upon the world."
She described the conference at The Hague and the experiences she had
had in the European capitals, and reported some of the impressions she
had picked up along the way. "The first thing which was striking is this,
that the same causes and reasons for the war were heard everywhere.
Each warring nation solemnly assured you it is fighting under the impulse of self-defense." "Another thing which we found very striking was
that in practically all of the foreign offices . . . the men said . . . that
a nation at war cannot make negotiations and that a nation at war cannot even express willingness to receive negotiations, for if it does either,
the enemy will at once construe it as a symptom of weakness. . . ." But
she also discovered, she reported, a genuine desire on the part of both
sides to have a neutral nation lead the way to a negotiated peace. She admitted that they talked mostly to civilians, those naturally on the side of
ending the war, and not the military people, but one main thesis of her
speech was the presence in all the warring countries of a revolt against
war. It was not blatant, not obvious, for there seemed to be a united
front behind the fighting men, a patriotism that surmounted divisions—
yet there were people "quite as loyal as the military people, quite as eager
for the growth and development of their own ideals and their own standard of living; but believing with all their hearts that the military message is a wrong message, which cannot in the end establish those things
which are so dear to their hearts." Then she went on to document the
revolt against war that was present, she felt, on both sides of the line.
"Generally speaking, we heard everywhere that this war was an old man's
war; that the young men who were dying, the young men who were doing the fighting, were not the men who wanted the war, and were not
the men who believed in the war; that somewhere in church and state,
somewhere in the high places of society, the elderly people, the middle-
aged people, had established themselves and had convinced themselves
that this was a righteous war, that this war must be fought out, and the
young men must do the fighting. . . . Now, this is a terrible indictment," she continued, "and I admit that I cannot substantiate it. I can
only give it to you as an impression. . . ." But then she went on to cite
examples to prove her case. She told of a young soldier she had met in
Switzerland who told her that "never during that three months and a
half had he once shot his gun in a way that could possibly hit another
man. He said that nothing in the world could make him kill another
man. He could be ordered into the trenches; he could be ordered to go

through the motions, but the final act was in his own hands and with his own conscience." She told of the five young German soldiers who had recovered from their wounds and were ready to be sent back to the front but who committed suicide rather than go, "not because they were afraid of being killed, but because they were afraid they might be put into a position where they would have to kill someone else."

Near the end of her speech she warned against putting too much faith in the militant version of anti-militarism that was present in Europe. "The old notion that you can drive a belief into a man at the point of a bayonet is in force once more. It is quite as foolish to think that if militarism is an idea and an ideal, it can be changed and crushed by counter-militarism or by a bayonet charge." And then she said almost as an afterthought, "and the young men in these various countries say of the bayonet charges: 'That is what we cannot think of.' We heard in all countries similar statements in regard to the necessity for the use of stimulant before men would engage in bayonet charges—that they have a regular formula in Germany, that they give them rum in England and absinthe in France; that they have to give them the 'dope' before the bayonet charge is possible." Then she went on to conclude "The people say they do not want this war, they say that the governments are making this war. They say, "We will be grateful to anybody who would help us to stop the war."[24]

Jane Addams had dropped a bombshell, with her offhand remark about liquor and the bayonet charge. The newspapers the next day headlined the story: "Troops Drink-Crazed, says Miss Addams," and the main point of her talk got lost with all the attention focused on one sensational remark. She had struck at a sacred myth, the myth that the soldier fought and died because of his sense of duty and his love of country, and although it was the French and English and German soldiers that she was referring to, by implication she seemed to be attacking all soldiers and impugning their bravery and patriotism—the myth of the brave and gallant soldier was close to the heart of many Americans, as she was soon to find out.

A few days after her speech Richard Harding Davis, a popular novelist and war correspondent, wrote a letter to the *New York Times* defending the soldiers and attacking Jane Addams:

> In this war the French or English soldier who has been killed in a bayonet charge gave his life to protect his home and country. For his supreme exit he had prepared himself by months of discipline. Through

the winter in the trenches he has endured shells, disease, snow and ice. For months he had been separated from his wife, children, friends—all those he most loved. When the order to charge came it was for them he gave his life, that against those who destroyed Belgium they might preserve their home, might live to enjoy peace.

Miss Addams denies him the credit of his sacrifice. She strips him of honor and courage. She tells his children, "Your father did not die for France, or for England, or for you; he died because he was drunk."

In my opinion, since the war began, no statement has been so unworthy or so untrue and ridiculous. The contempt it shows for the memory of the dead is appalling; the crudity and ignorance it displays are inconceivable.

Davis then went on to announce that the French government had outlawed absinthe and one could not obtain it as a civilian, let alone as a soldier.

If Miss Addams does know that the French government has banished absinthe, then she is accusing it of openly receiving congratulations of the world for destroying the drug while secretly using it to make fiends of the army. If what Miss Addams states is true then the French government is rotten, French soldiers are cowards. . . . If we are to believe her, the Canadians at Ypres, the Australians in the Dardanelles, the English and the French on the Aisne made no supreme sacrifice, but were killed in a drunken brawl. . . . Miss Addams desires peace. So does everyone else. But she will not attain peace by misrepresentation. I have seen more of this war and other wars than Miss Addams, and I know all war to be wicked, wasteful and unintelligent, and where Miss Addams can furnish one argument in favor of peace I will furnish a hundred. But against this insult, flung by a complacent and self-satisfied woman at men who gave their lives for men, I protest. And I believe that with me are those women and men who respect courage and honor.[25]

The newspapers around the country gave a great deal of attention to this letter and most sided with Davis rather than with Miss Addams. "One feels instinctively that Mr. Davis is right in his protest and that Miss Addams was insulting in her attack," one newspaper remarked. Even the Socialist *New York Call* agreed with Davis.

We cannot positively settle this problem but, though it may seem unchivalrous to say so, we incline rather to the pro-Davis side, and regard the stimulants he speaks of as, on the whole, sufficient. Indeed, if Miss Addams were correct, there would be much hope of stopping the war by simply stopping drunkenness. But the problem is hardly as simple as that, though Prohibitionists may think so. If it were true, there would be no use for the commandment, "Thou shalt not kill!" It would be superfluous, and would be completely covered by another, "Thou shalt not get drunk!" No, Miss Addams. You mean well, but Mr. Davis is right. Patriotism, love of country and the desire for peace are far more powerful as stimulants to a bayonet charge than distillery products.[26]

Others quickly joined the fray. Everett P. Wheeler, a New York lawyer, founder of East Side House, a settlement patterned in part on Hull House, and a long time opponent of woman suffrage, also wrote to the *New York Times*. He praised Jane Addams as a philanthropist, but suggested that as a politician she was a "pitiful failure." Then he proceeded to refute her charge:

> Now I have a son in the French Army, and have been in the way during this war, of seeing letters from men at the front on both sides and I assert that the charge is false and shows a pitiful ignorance of human nature. Miss Addams evidently knows nothing of the joy of combat; whatever faults the soldiers have, they are not cowards. The Germans, the French, the English who are struggling from Alsace to the sea do not need any "dope" to stimulate their courage, or to drown their fears. Some one has told Miss Addams this gruesome tale and she believed it. . . . Let me add, that statements like this are characteristic of the suffragists. I have been debating with them for two years, and have met and heard their principal orators. They mean well, perhaps, but are always making positive statements which show ignorance of the fundamental facts of human nature. No fable is too gross for them to swallow if it reflects on the tyrant man.[27]

Editorial writers around the country took up the cry, and a great many irate ordinary citizens wrote angry letters to Jane Addams defending the honor and the courage of the soldier. There were a few who supported her charge including an occasional soldier at the front, but the great majority were critical. She preserved the favorable letters and apparently destroyed the critical ones for few of them survive in her papers. She remarked later that "it was at this time that I first learned to use for my own edification a statement of Booker Washington's. 'I will permit no man to make me to hate him!' " But it was obvious that the attack of the press and the public troubled her deeply, all the more because she had been accustomed to such adoration and praise.[28]

Jane Addams, of course, was not striking out blindly and innocently against the use of stimulants by the soldiers; she was simply trying to document what appeared to her as a revolt against war on the part of the young. She also wanted to discredit the myth, accepted by many Americans, that war was a glamorous and glorious affair. The extent and ardor of the reaction to her offhand remark indicated that the myth was an important one for many.

It was obvious that she, who had only recently been idealized as the finest example of American womanhood and a living tribute to the American way of life had stepped out of the mainstream. By challenging the part of the American dream that saw war as glorious and patriotic she had fallen from grace. The animosity of the attack can only be explained by the fact that she had been an important symbol for Americans.

"Jane Addams is a silly, vain, impertinent old maid, who may have done good charity work at Hull House, Chicago, but is now meddling with matters far beyond her capacity." "Poor Jane Addams" one newspaper headed its editorial. "The time was when Miss Jane Addams of Hull House, Chicago held a warm place in the hearts of the American people but she is fast losing the esteem, which her earlier efforts seem to merit. Her dabbling in politics, her suffrage activity and her ill-advised methods of working for peace have very materially lowered her in the esteem of hundreds of former admirers." "Somebody has been hoaxing Miss Addams," another writer suggested. "A Foolish, Garrulous Woman" the *Louisville Courier-Journal* called her. "Miss Addams, like many other worthy persons before her, has been misled." Other commentators suggested that Jane Addams knew nothing of war or of soldiers, but one who signed himself "H. D." in a letter to the *Rochester (N.Y.) Herald* went even further. "Miss Addams evinces an utter and amazing ignorance of the elements of human nature. In the true sense of the word, she is apparently without education. She knows no more of the discipline and methods of modern warfare than she does of its meaning. . . . If the woman conceded by her sisters to be the ablest of her sex, is so readily duped, so little informed, men wonder what degree of intelligence is to be secured by adding the female vote to the electorate. . . . The antis have made great capital out of Miss Addams' unfair reflection on brave men." In fact many critics who objected to Addams' statement attacked her not just as an opponent of war but as a woman. She was called a silly old maid while one editorial writer announced that her action and words denied her very claim to womanhood.[29]

Jane Addams was upset and confused by the irrational attack on her, but she defended her remark, at first in a statement to the press from her summer home at Bar Harbor and then in August at an address at Chautauqua, New York, when she announced that her informants in England, France, and Germany were soldiers, officers, and well-informed civilians. She cited though not by name, a German lieutenant, an official in a Paris war office, and an Oxford University professor. She also reemphasized that she was not questioning the soldier's courage but "When common talk in all countries among the women who have husbands, sons and sweethearts at the front tells the same thing, I begin to believe that the average soldier is not sufficiently brutish and beastly to fight with cold steel against his brother men unless primed with drugs or strong drink."

But then she got back to the main point of her Carnegie Hall address which had got lost somehow in all the controversy over rum and bayonet charges. "Every nation sincerely believes it is fighting for self-protection, for righteousness," she announced. "Each will hold out to the end of its strength unless some neutral power offers effective intervention. Everywhere civilians are dominated by militarists. America must lead the fight for peace and disarmament. No European country can solve the riddle and the muddle." But again the press concentrated their attention, with a few exceptions, on her defense of her original charge and not on her plea for calling a conference of neutrals.[30]

Through all the criticism and the attack in the press and the hordes of critical letters there were some who kept the faith. "I want to say to you that I think your Carnegie Hall address is simply a marvel of beauty and of wisdom." Elizabeth Glendower Evans, a Boston social worker who had been at The Hague conference, wrote, "to my mind it is the high water mark of utterance which you have yet achieved."

One woman compared her to Florence Nightingale and assured her that despite the criticism, history would vindicate her effort to stop the war. Ellen Henrotin, a long time Hull House supporter, commenting on her Carnegie Hall address remarked, "You were soul satisfying and great in your simplicity and I felt while listening to you how true it is 'that God does not leave himself without a mistress in this world.' " But these were only the faithful few, and many of her friends were silent. In the summer of 1915 the criticism, the derision and the attack were much more obvious and overwhelming than the few scraps of praise. One newspaper editor commented: "If Jane Addams is a careful reader of the newspapers, she must have discovered by this time that any popular idol can be knocked from its pedestal by talking too much." It was not because Jane Addams talked too much that she fell from her pedestal as one of the most admired, indeed worshipped, American women; it was because in the summer of 1915 she openly challenged a basic tenet of the American myth.[31]

XIII

From Saint to Villain

ANE Addams was not accustomed to vilification by the press and the public. She was much more comfortable with adoration and applause, and the knowledge that her actions and ideas were accepted by the American people. But it was more than personal attacks; she was disturbed that the American people seemed to misunderstand what she was trying to say—that there was more to patriotism and heroism than war and killing. She blamed the press, not only for distorting her meaning, but also for stressing the glories of war and giving no attention to the more subtle forces in the world which sought peace and understanding. She worried about how the spirit of retaliation and brutality spread in time of war, how the tales of atrocities became exaggerated, and how intelligent men and women lost all sense of reality in the face of the fanatical patriotism which the war fostered. The persistence of the irrational controversy was frustrating to her; it also helped her eventually to become a more militant pacifist. She went back in remorse and confusion, to one of the ideas she had expressed in *Newer Ideals of Peace*—that women had a special responsibility to promote peace and bring men to their senses. "It is possible," she wrote, "that the appeals for the organization of the world upon peaceful lines have been made too exclusively to man's reason and sense of justice quite as the eighteenth century enthusiasm for humanity was prematurely founded on intellectual sentiment. Reason is only a part of the human endowment, emotion and deep-set radical impulses must be utilized as well, those primitive human urgings to foster life and to protect the helpless, of which women were the earliest custodians, and even the social and gregarious instincts that we share with the animals themselves. These universal desires must be given opportunities to expand and the most highly trained intellects must serve them rather than the technique of war and diplomacy."[1]

Women's special role in promoting peace, together with the natural horror of war that she believed most working people felt, and the internationalism of the immigrant community, fused to form Jane Addams' special kind of pacifism. She also added the mystical dimensions of Tolstoian "bread labor," a subject that had fascinated her for years. But in the summer of 1915 she was not quite sure how to proceed to translate her ideas into action, and the personal attacks contributed to her lack of confidence and conviction. She had been a reluctant convert to Rosika Schwimmer's plan to send delegations from the Women's Congress to both the belligerent and neutral nations of Europe, but by the time she returned home, she sincerely believed that the only way to promote peace was through some kind of a neutral mediating committee or conference. Once back in the United States, however, she was suddenly confronted by pressures from all sides. Some of her close friends, especially Mary Smith and Louise Bowen, had little sympathy for her peace activities; they wanted to wisk her off to Bar Harbor where she could relax and they could protect her. She had been away from Hull House for some time, and the settlement residents were quick to point out the problems that had piled up in her absence. There were the usual demands for speeches, for interviews and for articles, increased now by the controversy over the bayonet-charge story. Her friends in the peace movement, especially those connected with the Henry Street group, looked to her for leadership, but she hesitated, hoping that President Wilson would solve her dilemma and take over the moral leadership of the peace movement himself.[2]

There were two basic plans for ending the war through mediation. One called for an international conference of neutral nations convened by President Wilson; the other envisioned a small, privately initiated conference of distinguished citizens from the neutral countries with no official governmental sanction. After a meeting of the Henry Street group July 19, 1915, Paul Kellogg reported to Louis Lochner, with some surprise, that "Miss Addams was, as a matter of fact, far from self-confident and cocksure that she knew the way to go about it to get together the agency which would be most effective."[3] Actually, she tended to favor the more informal conference made up of scientists, labor leaders, artists and others of a humanitarian viewpoint, but she agreed with the others that the most important first step was to convince Wilson to take the lead in calling a neutral conference of some kind. That meant that she had to get an appointment to see the President, and he had consistently refused to talk to the peace advocates since the fall of 1914 when he allowed an interview with Rosika Schwimmer.[4] But he had written to Lillian Wald and indicated that he would be delighted to talk to Jane Addams. Probably he changed his policy because he realized that Addams had been welcomed by the leaders of the belligerent countries of Europe and that he could hardly turn down an interview with her. The peace advocates, however, took it as a sign that Wilson was finally ready to cooperate with their plan to call a neutral conference and end the war.[5]

The hope for quick action on Wilson's part began to fade, when Jane Addams' interview was postponed again and again. Those close to her worried that the controversy which swirled about her after her New York speech and some of her public statements, might interfere with her ability to communicate with the President. Finally after waiting longer than she had at any European capital, she was granted an interview. The meeting was cordial, but Wilson was non-committal about the possibility of calling a neutral conference. In the next weeks she also talked with Colonel House and with Secretary of State Robert Lansing. Emily Balch also talked with both House and Wilson, and later in the fall, Aletta Jacobs, Louis Lochner, and Davir Starr Jordan all spoke with the President, but none of these peace advocates could get any kind of commitment from him.[6] Perhaps the peace advocates would have been more successful if their plans had been more carefully formulated, but in all probability no one could have pushed Wilson into a role of active mediator in the summer and fall of 1915. Since the sinking of the *Lusitania* his own attitudes had hardened and his advisers opposed any attempt at mediation at this point. Just before Jane Addams' interview with him she talked to Colonel House, who wrote to Wilson: "Jane Addams came on Monday. She saw Von Jagow, Grey and many others and for one reason or another they were not quite candid with her, so she has a totally wrong impression."[7]

Whether or not Jane Addams had a totally wrong impression of the European leaders, she doubtlessly misjudged Wilson. For despite the vague answers and equivocation the peace advocates got from him, they continued to believe that he would act, when he felt the time was right, to end the war through mediation. Addams, together with Wald, Kellogg, Lochner, Balch, Jordan, and most of the others who formed a peace coalition in 1914-16, were liberals who believed in the democratic process; they had the progressive's faith that elected officials could be moved by the evidence. Even though many of them, including Addams, had opposed his election, they believed that Wilson was a man of reason, a progressive like themselves, and that he could be persuaded. But they failed to realize that there were others, closer to the President, who were arguing for a different course of action. While he was exchanging pleasantries with the peace advocates, he was taking much more seriously the advice he got from Lansing who wrote to him: "I do not believe that it is true that the Civil leaders of the belligerents would at the present time look with favor on action by the neutral nations; and even if they did, the military branches of the belligerent governments dominate the situation, and they favor a continuance of the war. Holding these views I would strongly favor discouraging any neutral movement toward peace at the present time, because I believe it would fail and because, if it did fail we would lose our influence for the future."[8]

The European women pacifists, were not nearly as confident that Wilson would lead the world to peace. Even though Rosika Schwimmer remarked that she hoped Wilson would become "the great man whom this world needs so badly," she did not have the same faith that the American progressives had, and she also had different ideas about tactics. With Aletta Jacobs and Chrystal Macmillan she drafted a manifesto which Emily Balch and Jane Addams signed. The manifesto asserted that the belligerent governments, while opposing negotiations as a matter of pride and principle "would not be opposed to a conference of neutral nations." About the same time the Fifth International Peace Congress, meeting in San Francisco, commissioned David Starr Jordan to take a resolution to the White House urging the President to initiate a neutral conference for continuous mediation.[9] But the President did not respond any more favorably to the manifesto and the resolution than he had to all the letters and personal pleas. During the fall the women continued to badger House and Lansing and to pressure Wilson, with what House described in his diary as, "the same old story of trying to get the President to appoint a peace commission jointly with other neutral nations."[10]

The fall of 1915 was a difficult time for Jane Addams. Her health broke down, as it did periodically for the rest of her life. This time it was the recurrence of an old kidney and bladder ailment. She was no longer a young woman; her fifty-fifth birthday was in September. She tried to recuperate at Bar Harbor and at Mary Smith's home in Chicago, but there was constant pressure on her time. Visitors sought her out and tried to influence her ideas, or to enlist her influence in a particular cause. Her stand for peace caused some controversy among the members of the editorial board of the *Survey,* and echoes of the bayonet-charge story continued to reverberate. She desperately wanted to be right and to be approved. She grasped at the small amount of adoration left. A poem appeared in *Harper's Weekly* in August 1915 entitled "Jane Addams":

> It is a breed of little blinded men
> And wanton women who would laugh at her
> Because in time of war she sets astir
> Against the sword the legions of the pen
> To write the name of Jesus Christ again.
> And on this page, a swarming broken blur,
> Restore the word of the Deliverer
> Above the words of little blinded men.
>
> In time of peace, which is a time of war
> More subtle slow and cunning, she has brought
> Together enemies in armistice . . .
> Yet, in the face of what she did before
> Against the war that centuries have fought,
> We ban her from a little war like this!

She carefully clipped the poem, and filed it away in an envelope. Approval was important when she was being pressured from several directions. Friends like Louise Bowen, who believed the United States should support Great Britain, tried to get her to give up her peace activity. At the same time Rosika Schwimmer badgered her to take a more aggressive stand for peace and to do more to influence Wilson.[11]

"It is my experience that every *political* movement has to have two kinds of genius, before it becomes successful," Emmeline Pethick-Lawrence remarked to Jane Addams, "the genius for 'stirring the dust' and the genius for quiet administration." In the women's peace movement Jane Addams was the quiet administrator (though she was always more than that) and Rosika Schwimmer the dust stirrer; that is one reason the two women did not get along very well, but there were fundamental ideological reasons as well. In the fall of 1915, tired of quiet attempts to influence Wilson, Rosika took matters into her own hands. She talked Henry Ford into donating $10,000 to finance a mother's campaign for peace. Thousands of women all across America sent telegrams to President Wilson, urging a conference of neutral nations. The telegrams were timed to arrive on November 26, the day Rosika Schwimmer and Ethel Snowden of England had an appointment to see Wilson. Also timed to coincide with the arrival of the letters was a mass meeting called by the Woman's Peace Party and chaired by Alice Post, wife of the assistant Secretary of Labor. Jane Addams took no part in the demonstration though she did help solicit the letters.[12]

Even the show of public support did not change Wilson's mind about sponsoring a neutral conference, but Rosika Schwimmer had not yet played all her cards. She had talked to Henry Ford about another plan. In fact, two days before the mass meeting in Washington, Ford had startled a group of reporters by announcing that he had chartered a ship and was going to get the boys out of the trenches by Christmas. Henry Ford had announced his conversion to pacifism on August 22, 1915, and was quoted in the newspapers as saying he would give half his fortune if it would shorten the war by one day. Rosika Schwimmer, who had only recently arrived in the United States, took Ford at his word and went to see him in Detroit. Louis Lochner also talked to him, and on November 21 Ford conferred with a group of peace advocates in New York, including Paul Kellogg, Oswald Garrison Villard, and Jane Addams. Originally the pacifists were interested in having Ford subsidize an informal and non-official neutral conference in Stockholm. Wilson and his advisers had made it clear that the President was not going to promote an official conference. Why not let Ford help pay for an alternative plan? Jane Addams had always favored an unofficial commission or conference which would "act as negotiators, going back and forth in the same way that negotiators have settled strikes." But Ford had no understanding or appreciation of the thinking that had gone into the idea of a neutral conference. He simply translated all the complicated discussion into a simple idea. Within hours he had chartered the *Oscar II* to take the group overseas. "We are going to get behind the work done by The Hague Peace Conference and carry that work forward," he announced. "It is my earnest hope to create a machinery where those who so desire can turn to inquire what can be done to establish peace and begin relations with those who also desire peace." A few days later

he told a large group in New York, "I simply want to ask you to remember the slogan, 'Out of the trenches never to go back.' "[13]

The Ford Peace Ship immediately became the target of newspaper
writers and cartoonists. It was easy to heap ridicule on a venture led by
the American industrialist who announced that he was going to set out
in early December and get the boys home for Christmas. One cartoon
depicted the *Oscar II* as a sinking tugboat with a sign on the bow asking:
"Have you seen our 1916 model?" Another pictured three women in a
tub with their bonnets labeled, "faith," "hope," and "charity," and the
caption read, "We don't know where we're going, but we're on the
way."[14] Jane Addams was horrified that the idea of a neutral conference
was being lost in a flamboyant showman's scheme. She was even more
upset by the guest list which included a great many college students,
businessmen and others who had no experience in the peace movement.
Most of the distinguished citizens invited—William Jennings Bryan,
Thomas Edison, Colonel House, Anna Garland Spencer, Lillian Wald,
William Howard Taft, Rabbi Stephen Wise, John Wanamaker, and
many others—refused to go. There were a few well-known people who
accepted the invitation, Jenkin Lloyd Jones, the liberal clergyman; Ben
Lindsey, the judge of the Denver Juvenile Court; Mrs. Joseph Fels, the
wife of the philanthropist and single-taxer; but most of these had little
experience with the peace movement. Many of her friends urged Jane
Addams also to decline the invitation, but she insisted on going, even
though she realized that she was leaving herself open to "ridicule and
social opprobrium." She felt a compelling obligation to go on the Peace
Ship. But three days before the sailing date she became seriously ill,
with what was later diagnosed as tuberculosis of the kidney, and the
Oscar II sailed without her. Why Jane Addams, usually cautious and
careful and opposed to militant protests of all kinds, decided to sail on
the Peace Ship is difficult to explain. Her own account of the incident
suggests that she was convinced by Lochner and others that the antiwar
movement had been "too quietistic and much too grey and negative,"
and that there was need for a spectacular and symbolic action. There
seems to be a large amount of truth in her explanation. She understood
the value of symbolic action. After all she had seconded the nomination
of Theodore Roosevelt in order to dramatize the social reform measures
in the Progressive platform, and she had allowed herself to be pictured
as the feminine conscience of America. She had also become a more
ardent and committed pacifist because of the events of the past year. She

had been hurt by the attacks on her, but she still had the confidence, based on years of adoration and praise, that her presence on the *Oscar II* and at the neutral conference would help end the war. She may have been right about the symbolic importance of her presence, at least for a few people. Vachel Lindsay, the poet, wired Henry Ford that he could not go even though he approved the expedition. "Am particularly in favor of anything that has the endorsement of Miss Jane Addams, our best woman and queen."[15]

The Ford peace mission was a debacle from the very beginning. The newspapermen on board did not help matters by filing stories which emphasized the bizarre and exotic—the marriage performed by Jenkin Lloyd Jones, the mysterious documents which Rosika Schwimmer carried in a black bag, the personality clashes among the delegates. Rosika Schwimmer caused conflict by her secretive and domineering ways. Henry Ford never made quite clear exactly who was going to get the money he had promised, and that led to resentment and confusion. Jane Addams did not help matters either. She told a reporter that she would not comment on the wisdom or folly of the Peace Ship. "However, the peace ship was not related to the movement of the Woman's Peace Party. The women's plan is to establish a clearing house for peace sentiment," she announced. Again, a few days later when wired for advice by Aletta Jacobs as to what stand the International Committee of Women should take toward the Peace Ship, she replied, "Keep the International Committee distinct from Ford Enterprise." Misunderstanding her meaning, the European women not only kept their organization distinct, but they held aloof entirely. This caused Rosika Schwimmer to resign from the International Committee. On Christmas Eve Henry Ford, angered and disillusioned, withdrew from the venture, having failed to get the boys home by Christmas. Despite a series of misfortunes, the neutral conference was organized in Stockholm at the end of January 1916, with representatives from Denmark, Holland, Norway, Sweden, and the United States. The conference issued reports, made studies of various international disputes, and served as a center for discussion and a source of information on peace groups in Europe, despite the failure of the Ford Peace Ship.[16]

Ironically, even though Jane Addams did not sail on the Ford Peace Ship, her name was closely associated with the venture. Many newspaper accounts at the time suggested that her sudden illness was imaginary and exceedingly convenient. Writing many years later, Walter Millis remarked that "Jane Addams suddenly discovered that she was too ill to go."[17] Her sudden illness seemed suspicious to some people, and to make matters worse Henry Ford announced in an interview on June 4, 1916, that he first got the idea for the Peace Ship from Jane Addams. She was quick to deny that it was her idea, but she also insisted that she would have gone if it had not been for her illness. Her denials did little good; in the public mind she was very much a part of the ill-fated peace venture which seemed, both hilarious and pathetic to most Americans.[18]

The Ford Peace Ship and the matter of the bayonet charge (which refused to die) provided editorial writers with plenty of material with which to denounce Jane Addams well into 1916. But she kept giving them additional opportunities as well. In January 1916, despite her ill health, she testified before the Military Affairs Committee of the House of Representatives and argued against military preparedness, suggesting that the desire for a larger Army and Navy was part of the war hysteria, and that the agitation to prepare for a hypothetical enemy, when there was no danger of actual attack, came primarily from men who were more emotional than women. She also predicted that after the war was over world disarmament would be adopted and she urged that the United States not wait until the end of the war before starting a new policy. "Your very presence was an argument," William Jennings Bryan wrote in thanking her for her testimony. "The manner in which you answered the questions put to you must have impressed the committee."[19] Not everyone agreed. "Miss Addams a Visionary," one newspaper decided. "Somebody ought to lead Miss Addams back to social service," another paper announced. "She may know how long it will take Hull House to get a job for a woman out of work, but does she know how long it takes to turn raw recruits into seasoned troops?"[20]

Some of the attack was more vicious. "About the best thing that could happen to Miss Jane Addams, President of the Woman's Peace Society of America," one writer decided, "would be a strong, forceful husband who would lift the burden of fate from her shoulders and get her intensely interested in fancy work and other things dear to the heart of women who have homes and plenty of time on their hands." Many editorial writers noted the decline of Jane Addams' reputation. "All the world has joined hands in admiring Miss Jane Addams," *The Providence Journal* pointed out, "and the regret that has been felt because of the unjustifiable and hysterical utterances which her pacifist ardor has led her to make is therefore the more extreme."

Agnes Repplier, who almost made a career during the war years of attacking the "ruthless sentimentality of Jane Addams," remarked on one occasion that she knew a Boston gentleman who told her that he was sick to death of "efficiency, reform and Jane Addams."[21]

A writer for *The Nation* using the pseudonym, "Tattler," also seemed tired of Jane Addams as he tried in his column to explain the erosion of her reputation.

> When Jane Addams was last in Washington, to preside over a world-peace gathering, the common remark was that she had lost her hold on a considerable part of her old constituency. There was a time when Miss Addams had only to open her lips and the whole country listened. . . . Jane Addams, of Hull House, loomed large in the history of her special era, and is still cherished as warmly as ever in the popular affections; but Jane Addams, of the World, seems a small figure projected against a huge background. Hull House and its work she knew from centre to circumference. As her fame spread and she was drawn into other lines of activity, however, her definiteness of vision seemed to suffer. . . . What she had lost in the intensity of her appeal appears to have been sacrificed to an endeavor to do too much in too many alien and untried fields with its incidental diffusion of her native force.[22]

It was not the diffusion of her talents that caused the decline of Jane Addams' reputation but dealing with the problems of war and peace, of armament and disarmament; by suggesting that there were ways to express the love of country other than fighting and dying in the trenches, she challenged some of the basic tenets of the American way. By taking part in controversial movements, and meddling in men's affairs, she also contradicted the stereotype of woman, as passive and gentle. No longer was she a heroine who represented the best of American democracy or the saint who symbolized the purity and purpose of American women, she was a high-minded and deluded fool, well-meaning perhaps, but impractical and well beyond her depths.[23]

Despite the Ford Peace Ship, and the ridicule heaped upon her because of her stand for peace, Jane Addams did not lose faith in the idea of mediation by representatives of the neutral powers, nor did she give up on Wilson. Even though she was in poor health, she saw Wilson again in January 1916, and was encouraged when in the course of her interview he drew out the resolutions of the Women's Congress, which she had presented to him six months before. They showed signs of having been handled and read. "You see I have studied these resolutions," he remarked. "I consider them by far the best formulation which up to the moment has been put out by anybody."[24] He did not commit himself to a time table for mediation, but the persistence and persuasiveness of Jane Addams and the other women peace advocates did influence Wilson, though similar ideas were fairly common in liberal and radical circles in Europe and America. The women presented Wilson with the most comprehensive and well-formulated plan for mediation, but in the end they helped him define the principles of his "new diplomacy," which would link mediation to the peace settlement after the war. There never was any real chance that Wilson would lead a movement of neutral nations to end the war, but through most of 1916, despite setbacks and discouragement, there remained enough hope to keep the mediation movement alive.[25]

There was enough hope that Wilson would try to end the war so that Addams, like most of the peace liberals, supported the President for re-election in 1916. The Progressive Party had collapsed, and Charles Evans Hughes, the Republican nominee, did not seem like a viable alternative. Raymond Robins, who was supporting Hughes, made a special trip to Bar Harbor to try to get her endorsement for Hughes, but Wilson had finally come around to support a national child-labor bill and other progressive measures, and he did seem like the peace candidate in 1916 so Jane Addams announced publicly for the President. Wilson responded with a warm note of thanks and after he was re-elected, he invited her to dinner at the White House.[26]

For a brief time it seemed as if Wilson was going to reward the patience and confidence that Jane Addams and the other peace liberals had shown in him. In December he asked the belligerents to state their peace terms. Then, in January 1917, in his "Peace Without Victory" speech, he suggested the need for an international organization to guarantee world peace, and argued for an end to the war before one side had achieved victory. Addams applauded his "brilliant statement of the hopes of modern internationalists," and remarked to Louis Lochner: "isn't it fine and isn't the cause moving along." But early in February the United States broke diplomatic relations with Germany over the resumption of submarine warfare, and it was obvious that Wilson had become convinced that if the United States was to have any influence in the peace settlement he must get into the war.

Jane Addams made a few last desperate appeals. She helped form an

Emergency Peace Federation, which sponsored demonstrations at the White House and a letter writing campaign. She had one last interview with the President, but he pushed aside her arguments. "How perplexing it all is," she admitted to Lillian Wald.[27] After Wilson's War message early in April, she watched her friends, even many who had been active in the peace movement, desert the cause and support the President. Paul Kellogg who, even in February and March 1917, had urged a peaceful and neutral United States as the only hope for a progressive peace after the war, capitulated in April and joined the patriots. John Dewey and the editors of the *New Republic* also accepted America's entry into the conflict, and looked forward with some misgivings to the "social possibilities of war."[28] Jane Addams could easily have joined this group of sincere and intelligent people who opposed war until war came, but then reluctantly and with fear and trembling, accepted the inevitable and began to work for social reform and world peace in the context of America's entry into the war. It was a logical and pragmatic solution, a compromise to be sure, but she had usually compromised and worked for the reasonably possible. It was an agonizing decision, the most difficult she ever made, but this time she rejected compromise. She remained a pacifist for complex reasons. In part it was because of her experience with the dedicated and aggressive women pacifists from Europe with whom she had worked for three years. These women, many of them politically and in temperament much more committed and militant than she, forced her to interpret the problems of peace and war in international terms. Then there was the controversy that had swirled about her name in the past three years. The attacks on her had almost trapped her into a position where she had to become a more ardent pacifist. Perhaps trapped is the wrong word for her hatred of war, her conviction that fighting and bloodshed solved no problems had become more adamant since her European trip. There was also her pride and honor which seemed to be at stake. All of these things combined to tip the balance and made her for peace even after the United States entered the war. But it was a hesitant decision, and she was filled with questioning and self-doubt. She did not have the advantage of a firm ideological position that made it easy for the Quakers, Eugene Debs, or Randolph Bourne to oppose the war. After the vicious attacks of the last few years she must have realized what her decision would mean in terms of isolation and personal suffering, but she had been idolized and admired for so long that she was blinded to some of the criticism. One thing was sure; she chose to oppose the war with no desire to become a martyr to the cause.

She was not entirely alone, although sometimes it seemed that way to her. There were the faithful few—Lillian Wald, Emily Balch, Alice Hamilton, and there was Mary Smith who disapproved of her stand on the war, but who remained personally loyal and supportive. There were also the socialists, and the Quakers who were pacifists, but she had little in common with either group. "I feel as if a few of us were clinging together in a surging sea," she admitted to Helena Dudley, a Boston settlement worker. Just how surging the sea and how few the faithful, she would soon discover.[29]

Confronted in the first weeks after the United States declared war with the strange situation of being completely out of step with majority opinion in America, she reacted, as she often did in time of crisis, by trying to work out her ideas in a public speech, "Patriotism and Pacifists in Wartime." It was not a revolutionary speech. "The position of the pacifist in time of war is most difficult," she began, "and necessarily he must abandon the perfectly legitimate propaganda he maintained before war was declared. When he, with his fellow countrymen, is caught up by a wave of tremendous enthusiasm and is carried out into a high sea of patriotic feeling, he realizes that the virtues which he extols are brought into unhappy contrast to those which war, with its keen sense of a separate national existence, places in the foreground." She rejected the idea that pacifists were cowards or traitors, but admitted that she was not surprised that "in the stir of the heroic moment when a nation enters war, men's minds are driven back to the earliest obligations of patriotism, and almost without volition the emotions move along the worn grooves of blind admiration for the soldier and of unspeakable contempt for him who in the hour of danger, declares that fighting is unnecessary." She argued that the pacifists, though there were many different kinds, did not want to sit passively by, but that on the contrary they believed that "this world crisis should be utilized for the creation of an international government." She spent most of the address defending the importance of international organization "To secure without war, those high ends which they now gallantly seek to obtain upon the battlefield. . . . With such a creed," she asked, "can the pacifists of today be accused of selfishness when they urge upon the United States no isolation, not indifference to moral issues and to the fate of liberty and democracy, but a strenuous endeavor to lead all nations of the earth into an organized international life worthy of civilized men."[30]

She gave the address at the Chicago City Club and the University of Chicago. Her reception at both places was cool but not especially hostile. She delivered the same speech, with minor changes, in June at the First Congregational Church in Evanston. When she finished, "There was not even a ripple of applause." Then Judge Orrin Carter of the Illinois Supreme Court, a long-time friend of Jane Addams and loyal supporter of Hull House, jumped to his feet.

> "I have always been a friend of Miss Addams, Judge Carter said when questions were called for, "but . . ."
> "The 'but,'" Jane Addams broke in lightly, "sounds as if you were going to break with me."
> "I am going to break with you. Anything which tends to cast doubt on the justice of our cause in the present war is very unfortunate. No pacifist measures should be taken until the war is over," Judge Carter said almost angrily.
> "Perhaps my subject was an unfortunate one to be discussed at this time," replied Miss Addams slowly, "but surely that should be referred to the committee which invited me to speak."[31]

The meeting came to an abrupt end. The incident was widely reported in the press and was treated as an indication of the decline of Jane Addams' reputation. Even the *Survey* which had always, as a matter of course, published anything she sent to them and clamored for more, refused to publish this address on the grounds that it was too controversial and might alienate and anger the readers as it had most of the editorial board.[32]

A few people wrote to praise her speech, to compliment her on her "great courage and devotion to truth and honor in these troublesome times." But most of the letters were critical, some vitriolic, indicating how rapidly many Americans became super-patriots, and 100 per cent loyal citizens, and how quickly they changed their minds about Jane Addams. "My dear Miss Addams, believe me, you are an awful ass, truly awful," one man wrote. "You are more than the equal of Victor Hugo in inflated self esteem and sublime egoism. You take yourself and your opinions with such solemn seriousness that only the ass is your equal. Continue to bray, my dear woman. Each time you open your mouth nowadays and each time you write one of your unpatriotic and pro-German speeches you proclaim yourself an ass."[33]

The newspapers also had a field day, calling her sentimental, impractical and a traitor. The *Fort Wayne News* denounced her in an editorial: "For three or four years past Jane Addams has gone to bizarre extremes in her advocacy of weird measures and her championship of impossible people, apparently capitalizing a reputation honestly won in a worthy work, to keep herself constantly in the headlines. She has sacrificed fame for notoriety and a place in the public heart for a place in the spotlight."

She had come full cycle, from heroine, to high-minded fool, to villain. During the early months of the war she became the symbol for everything anti-American, the betrayer of her country, the antithesis of what she had stood for for so many years. Of course, her wartime reputation as villain and fool was closely related to her earlier image as saint and feminine conscience of America. As Martin Duberman has written: "ridicule, like its opposite, adoration, is usually not the result of analysis, but the substitute for it." "When a public figure loses his heroic stature, his role often shifts to that of fool or villain," W. Lloyd Warner decided. He goes on to suggest that former heroes or heroines make the best villains, because they have been accepted as symbolizing the best of a society or culture, and by falling from grace and being transformed they express the fears and ambivalence that the people feel during a time of crisis. Just as Jane Addams was formerly praised and worshipped for her altruism by people who felt guilty about their own acquisitiveness, so now she could be denounced for her opposition to war by people who felt ambivalence and fear about the horrors of armed conflict, yet would not admit it. And she was the perfect symbol to attack because she had represented all that was good and noble about American society.[34]

Having become accustomed to being treated as a heroine, Jane Addams was not happy with her new role as villain, though she was quick to find a rational explanation for her new position. She felt isolated and alone. She found some solace in kindred spirits, and wrote to praise Randolph Bourne for his essay denouncing the *New Republic* editors and other intellectuals who saw progress and social advance coming out of the war. She attended a few meetings of the Fellowship of Reconciliation, a pacifist group dedicated to the Christian principle of love. She cherished the occasional letter of praise for her stand that she received from a stranger. But these things did not make up for the public scorn, the loss of friends, such as Louise Bowen, who broke with her over the war.

Many social workers disagreed with her position and stopped writing for advice. Mary Kingsbury Simkhovitch, president of the National Federation of Settlements, issued a public statement defending the entry of the United States into the war. "It has been very painful to many of us who hold Miss Addams in deep affection and wholly respect her," she wrote, "to find that we cannot think or act in unison with her. It is imperative for us to hesitate no longer." The Chicago Woman's Club snubbed her and informed her that the "peace committee" of the Club could no longer use the club rooms. It was very difficult after years of being treated as oracle and sage, suddenly to be ignored or denounced.

"I experienced a bald sense of social opprobrium and widespread misunderstanding which brought me very near to self pity, perhaps the lowest pit into which human nature can sink," she wrote. "Indeed the pacifist in war time, with his precious cause in the keeping of those who control the sources of publicity and consider it a patriotic duty to make all types of peace propaganda obnoxious, constantly faces two dangers. Strangely enough he finds it possible to travel from the mire of self-pity straight to the barren hills of self-righteousness and to hate himself equally in both places."[35]

She not only felt alone, but also useless and out of step. She questioned herself. "The force of the majority was so overwhelming that it seemed not only impossible to hold one's own against it, but at moments absolutely unnatural, and one secretly yearned to participate in 'the folly of all mankind.'" Only a few peace groups invited her to speak; the magazines which had clamored for her articles only the year before now had no interest in what she was writing. The realization that few were listening made it difficult to write.

She stopped talking about the effects of the war, but she learned that she was being kept under surveillance by the Department of Justice. "I am feeling far from clear about the 'path of duty' just now, although my convictions are not changing, nor wavering," she wrote to her niece in September 1917. She became more cautious and refused to sign a Civil Liberties Bureau appeal for funds. "I am obliged to walk very softly in regard to all things suspect," she admitted to Roger Baldwin.[36]

In the early months of 1918 she finally found a way to be useful during time of war. She began to speak around the country under the auspices of Herbert Hoover's Department of Food Administration. She appealed to women to help conserve and increase the production of food. She spoke at women's clubs, high school assemblies, and public meetings in California, Texas, Louisiana, and Alabama. "I am out here speaking for the Food Administration and thankful that there is something that I can do," she wrote Paul Kellogg from San Francisco.[37] Speaking about the crisis in the world's food supply brought on by the war gave her the chance to talk about the need for international organization and cooperation in order to prevent starvation. But turning her attention to food also allowed her to explore some of the basic human impulses that had always fascinated her. When the Russian Revolution broke out and the Russian soldiers refused to fight she speculated that perhaps it was the peasant's primitive impulse to work the land and produce food that was responsible. "It is quite possible that the Russian peasant soldiers are telling the East Prussian peasant soldiers in the opposing trenches what Tolstoy told them: that the great task of this generation is to 'free the land,' as a former generation had already freed the serfs and slaves; that the future of the Russian peasant depends not upon garrisons and tax gatherers but upon his willingness to perform 'bread labor' on his recovered soil and upon his ability to extend good will and just dealing to all men."[38]

The Russian peasant did not interest and excite her nearly as much, however, as the relationship between women and bread labor. Her earliest memories were connected with grain and flour and bread, and her father's mill across the street from the big house. At Rockford she had helped give her class the name "bread-givers," and in a college essay she had speculated on the proper role of women by recalling the ancient role of woman as provider. Later, inspired by the example of Tolstoy, she had even attempted to do her own bread labor at Hull House. Much of her writing that depicted a special role for women in municipal housekeeping and in international affairs was based on her understanding of the role of women in primitive societies and throughout history as provider and protector. Now she poured over James G. Frazer's *Golden Bough*, and discovered the ancient myths relating to food. She was especially fascinated with the feminine spirits representing fecundity and growth. She explored the myths of the Corn Mother, and studied the role of woman as agriculturalist in primitive societies. She became convinced that it was the desire to grow food for her children that led "to a fixed abode and to the beginning of the home, from which our domestic morality and customs are supposed to have originated." She thought perhaps that women with this conception of their historic role might "so enlarge their conception of duty that the consciousness of the world's needs for food should become the actual impulse of their daily activities."[39]

Jane Addams was much happier doing something useful, touring the country giving speeches for the Food Administration, acting again as oracle and sage, than she was sitting at home feeling isolated and out-of-step. She approved the establishment of a selective service recruiting station at Hull House and she even spoke occasionally for the Committee on Public Information and for the Liberty Bond campaign in Chicago. The crowds were not as enthusiastic as they once had been when she spoke, and there were those who continued to ridicule her efforts. "Jane Addams says that Russia quit the war because the Russian peasants love their enemies, and won't fight because they would rather work on their farms," one newspaper remarked. "Jane forgets that if the Allies did not fight the Russians would have no farms to work on. The Germans would have them all." On the other hand some of the more committed pacifists, such as Rosika Schwimmer, denounced her for supporting the government and the war effort.[40] Most of her audiences, however, were willing to listen when she talked of food and not of peace. Some even saw her as a Corn Mother or Earth Mother, feeding a protecting humanity, an interpretation her speeches and her appearance often encouraged.

The *Los Angeles Times* commented on her life and work when she appeared in the city in March 1918 to talk about food.

> Jane Addams has become a household word in the United States and there is the tender glamour of true womanhood about her. So long as she worked for the alleviation of sorrow, the betterment of humanity in the practical field of direct work and organization she was blessed indeed, and stood proud in the unalloyed appreciation of her sex and of her country.
>
> It was only when a great war raged in the world, tremendous international emotions were let loose, that this good woman essayed a task beyond her, and in an excess of zeal and shocked horror, stood forth for peace where there was no peace, and made public utterances from a full heart that were better left unsaid. . . . It will not be for her chairmanship of the Woman's Peace Party and its earnest but mistaken activities that Jane Addams will reign in the hearts of men. . . . And now she is seeing clearly again, and her service is with the country, with the administration, with the Allies, wholehearted and wholesouled. . . .

Jane Addams, as she stands upon the platform looking down upon a sea of faces seems very tired, aged beyond her years with the burden of responsibility of sorrow. Essentially the mother-woman, she looks a woman who has ever mothered humanity though herself unwed. She dresses plainly, unaffectedly, and her hair is silver gray, guiltless of the coiffeur's art. There is obviously no personal vanity in her, her face has never known the cosmetics and beautifiers dear to the modern woman. Her eyes look very earnest, very tragic and while the message she brings has been told a hundred times by voice and print, her personality gives it a deeper weight, her direct plea a greater response. . . . She obviously stands before the country now an earnest, though sad, adherent of the Allies' cause.[41]

Jane Addams seemed to have redeemed herself by lecturing for the Food Administration. In November 1918, the same month that the armistice was signed, and the war came to an end, a poem appeared in the *Atlantic Monthly* entitled "Jane Addams":

> Remember Botticelli's Fortitude
> In the Uffizi?—The worn, waiting face;
> The pale, fine-fibred hands upon the mace;
> The brow's serenity, the lips that brood,
> The vigilant, tired patience of her mood?
> There was a certain likeness I could trace
> The day I heard her in a country place,
> Talking to knitting women about Food.
>
> Through cool statistics glowed the steady gleam
> Of that still undismayed, interned desire;
> But—strength and stay, and deeper than the dream—
> The two commands that she is pledged to keep
> In the red welter of a world on fire,
> Are, 'What is that to thee?' and 'Feed my sheep!'[42]

It appeared as if she was to be forgiven for her war-time heresy, and accepted as the worn and tired American version of the Corn Mother. But once a heroine has fallen from grace, it is difficult for her to regain her former symbolic position, and the sense of united purpose, and victory achieved in the last days of the war, gave way quickly to the hate and distrust of the Red Scare. Jane Addams remained the protecting mother figure for some Americans, but to many others she became, in the decade after the armistice, "the most dangerous woman in America."

XIV

The Most Dangerous Woman in America

HE end of the war did not restore peace and rationality. In fact the armistice ushered in a period of hysteria and the Red Scare. The Russian Revolution, coming as it did simultaneously with the war, altered and confused the peace settlement and influenced American attitudes toward those who had opposed the war. Pacifists became synonymous with Communists and Bolsheviks. Fear of subversion gripped the country, and every criticism was interpreted as un-American and disloyal. Jane Addams, who had been an American heroine, representative of all the best of American democracy, was transformed into a villain by her opposition to the war. In the 1920's she became a special symbol of subversion to many of the super-patriots; she was denounced as the "most dangerous woman in America." Even those who knew that she was not disloyal, were influenced by the irrational attacks, and it was years before her pre-war reputation was restored.

It became obvious very quickly to Jane Addams that the armistice had not ended the hate and fear. A few days after the war ended, three prominent German women sent appeals to her and to Mrs. Woodrow Wilson urging them, on behalf of American women, to attempt to change the terms of the peace treaty to allow for shipment of food in order that German women and children would not starve. The government intercepted the message and she learned about it only from the newspapers. Then the State Department advised her not to answer it. The reaction in America was immediate. "Huns use Women to Try to Evade Terms of the Armistice," one newspaper headline screamed. "The world is quite justified now in suspecting that behind this row of wailing German women the Hun hides treachery and lies," another newspaper announced. "We know the Hun. He makes peace because he is beaten, not because he is starved. He remains constitutionally and determinedly a liar."[1]

"These are the women who spit at our soldiers, who carried water to our wounded, only to pour it on the ground before their suffering eyes," one man protested to Jane Addams. " 'We are mothers too,' they whine. Yes, we remember; mothers of the beasts who defiled other mothers, and tiny maids, and nuns and grandmothers," a woman complained. "Please accept sincerest sympathy at the most undeserved humiliation that has been heaped upon you by the shocking appeal made to you by the German women," another pleaded. "When it is remembered that you have given your life to save girls, to help the needy, to uplift the fallen, to have Germans, whose soldiers have made rape a system, whose bayonets have spitted innocent babes, appeal to you is too much." Some of the protests were not as polite. One newspaper referred to her as the "rather impressionable Jane Addams, who took unfortunate part in the wild and almost forgotten schemes of Henry Ford." Another newspaper asked: Can it be that it was these same German women "who told Miss Addams—and betrayed her into repeating the silly accusation in this country—that the soldiers of the allies had to be made drunk before they would fight?"[2]

The old charges soon gave way, however, to new accusations that she was a Bolshevik and a dangerous radical. In January 1919 Archibald Stevenson, a young New York lawyer, employed by the Military Intelligence Division of the War Department, testifying before a Senate sub-committee, created something of a sensation by producing a list containing the names of 62 persons whom he claimed held "dangerous, destructive and anarchistic sentiments." He also revealed that those named had long been under surveillance by the government. Included on the list were Professor Charles Beard of Columbia University, Oswald Garrison Villard, David Starr Jordan, Lillian Wald, and many other liberals and pacifists. But heading the list was Jane Addams.

The newspapers quickly dubbed those named as the "Who's Who of Pacifists and Radicals." A few of those included were amused and some who were left off were jealous. "It would be rather a disgrace not to be in that 'Who's Who,' " John Palmer Gavit, a writer who was left out, remarked, "gradually it is coming to include everybody who during the past twenty five years has tried to do anything for his fellow men. I shouldn't like to be left out of that category entirely."[3] Jane Addams and many others on the list were not so sanguine; they organized a campaign of protest letters to be sent to Secretary of War Newton Baker. They were especially shocked at the extent of military intelligence, which had kept so many outstanding and law abiding citizens under surveillance. "I am a pacifist," Jane Addams told a reporter. "I am a member of many pacifist organizations—national and international and head of several of them, but I have been loyal to my country." Paul Kellogg fired off a telegram to Secretary Baker. "In the name of common sense, fairplay and decent regard for the public service to our common country of some of the truest, most farseeing and courageous citizens of our generation has produced. Let me urge you to repudiate that indiscriminate, brutally unjust, fool-in-the-head list of Americans put under the ban by Military Intelligence. . . ." Baker responded with a public statement denouncing the list. "In the particular list accredited to Mr. Stevenson," he wrote, "there are names of people of great distinction, exalted purity of purpose, and lifelong devotion to the highest interests in America and mankind. Miss Jane Addams, for instance, lends dignity and greatness to any list in which her name appears."[4]

Baker's statement did not mitigate the effect of the publicity however. "Mr. Baker belongs to the same ecstatic class of philanthropic enthusiasts that Miss Addams belongs to, and naturally rushes to her defense when lists of antiwar workers are published," the *Boston Evening Transcript* remarked, "but it hardly adds to Mr. Baker's own reputation that he is so anxious to shield the men and women whose efforts handicapped his own department throughout the war." *The Woman Patriot*, an anti-woman-suffrage and super-patriotic journal, headlined its story: "Former Suffrage President Heads 'Who's Who in Pacifism and Radicalism,' " (mistakenly believing that Jane Addams had been president rather than vice-president of the National American Woman Suffrage Association.) Noting that Newton Baker had defended Jane Addams, they cited in rebuttal a story from a *Los Angeles Times'* reporter who stated: "I was in Berlin shortly after Miss Addams had gone there for the purpose of asking the Kaiser politely to please stop the war. All Europe was simply screaming with laughter and I was ashamed to be an American. If Miss Addams and her peace mission are a sample of women in world affairs, I want to take it all back. I am sincerely sorry I voted for suffrage."[5]

Even more disturbing than the news stories was the failure of the protest to discourage Archibald Stevenson. He convinced the New York State Legislature that they should authorize a full-scale investigation of radicalism and seditious activities. This inquiry was headed by Senator Clayton R. Lusk, but Stevenson was the driving force behind the venture which produced a four-volume study of Revolutionary Radicalism in 1920. The Lusk Report became the Bible of the super-patriots for the next decade, and provided massive documentation for the alleged connections between peace organizations, women's groups, and all those who advocated social reform, with Socialism, Communism, and Bolshevism. The technique was simple; masses of real documents and accurate information were printed with completely false and half-true statements of connections with International Communism. Jane Addams' name occurred frequently in the four volumes. Her role in various peace and reform organizations was well-documented. But the unwary or prejudiced reader could easily jump to the intended conclusion that because she was involved in the Woman's Peace Party and the campaigns for child labor reform she was therefore a Communist. The specter of the report haunted her all through the 1920's, and she never found an effective way to answer the charges which mixed fact, half-truth and outright lies.[6]

Even before the Lusk report was published, however, she was branded a Communist by some people because, in a year of hysteria, of strikes and violence and distrust of everything un-American, she dared stand up and defend the right of radicals to free speech. She was no more radical than she had ever been but the hysteria of the post-war period made her middle-of-the road position seem radical and dangerous. She even lent her name to a group that advocated recognizing the Bolshevik government in Russia. "Jane Addams in Movement to Uphold Lenine" a newspaper headline announced. "Russia should no longer be denied the presence of Jane Addams and other sympathizers with Bolshevism," the *Boston Evening Transcript* decided.[7]

Despite the growing hysteria at home, Jane Addams turned, in the first months of 1919, to the task of putting the woman's peace movement back together. The delegates at The Hague Congress in 1915 had agreed to hold their next meeting simultaneously with the peace conference, but when Paris rather than a neutral site was chosen for the official conference, the women changed their meeting to Zurich in order that delegates from the Central Powers could more easily attend. Jane Addams was president of the Woman's Peace Party, and president of the International Committee of Women for Permanent Peace. Much of the burden for arranging the meeting fell to her, but she had help from many sources, especially from Emily Balch in the United States, and from Aletta Jacobs in the Netherlands. Yet she traveled to Washington to talk to Secretary of State Lansing and Secretary of War Baker to clear the way for obtaining passports for the women delegates. She corresponded with women in the United States and in many European countries urging them to attend, and she publicized the conference as much as she dared in the face of the adverse climate of opinion in the United States.[8]

The American delegation to the Women's Conference sailed in early April 1919. Among the delegates were Emily Balch, Alice Hamilton, Lillian Wald, Lucia Ames Mead, and Jeanette Rankin, who as Congresswoman from Montana, had cast a vote against the United States entry into the war. It also included Florence Kelley, who told everyone that the only reason she was going was "to black J.A.'s boots and lug her suitcases." But Crystal Eastman, one of the most active members of the American Union Against Militarism and the Civil Liberties Union, was not a delegate because, to the rather staid and conservative leaders she seemed too radical. They also worried that her reputation as an advanced feminist and her casual sex life would give the conference a bad name.[9]

Even without Crystal Eastman, however, the women's conference received its share of ridicule, and was denounced by many as silly, irrelevant, and even subversive. "Miss Addams assures the world that she and her colleagues are law-abiding and their sole desire is to put before the world certain principles leading to permanent peace, which are cherished by women as such," the *New York Times* editorialized, but then reminded its readers that the first women's conference had started "an agitation to stop the war, regardless of who happened to be ahead at the time." The editorial recalled the bayonet-charge story, Jane Addams' part in the Ford Peace Ship, and the recent appeal to her by the German women, all of which, in the opinion of the *Times* made her unfit for leadership in determining peace terms. The editorial also suggested that the conference would do damage to the suffrage movement because those who sought the vote for women believed that women were people, sharing the same rights and duties as men, but the women's conference was being sponsored by pacifists who held the socialist theory that "women are not people; they are a class, a group, something apart, with class interests which require a congress of their own for definition; a class which apparently hates and distrusts men. . . . The millions of women who have worked and suffered to help win the war for democracy will hardly relish the revival of sex-antagonism by women who insisted that the war was wrong," the *Times* concluded.[10]

Despite the criticism and the controversy, Jane Addams approached the conference in Zurich with a sense of purpose and determination. She was once again surrounded by those who treated her with deference and respect, and she was leading a movement which she firmly believed would have a profound effect on the peace negotiations in Paris. The American women arrived in France late in April; they spent a few days in Paris, interviewing officials at the peace conference, and then Addams, Hamilton, Rankin, and Wald embarked on a five-day tour of the devastated battlegrounds under the auspices of the American Red Cross. "I can't tell you how tragic it is," Alice Hamilton reported to her family, "the villages especially. One feels that these humble little stone houses weren't the sort of thing that artillery ought to attack. It is like killing kittens with machine guns, they are so small and helpless. One was just what we had always read about, a little place of gray stone houses, pounded into a dreadful mess and in one house only in the cellar, a red-cheeked old woman living, and in a dug-out under the hill an old couple. The vitality of the old is so amazing. . . . British soldiers fill Amiens and we had to go to a queer little hotel, but the dining room was warm and we had a wonderful dinner and Miss Addams and I had a single bed in a queer little room, but clean. It was so cold we didn't mind sleeping together."

They went from Amiens to Vimy Ridge, "the place where the Canadians fell in such numbers. That was terrible. A tire blew out and we climbed out and walked a way, finally taking shelter in a bit of ruin from the cold rain that had begun to fall. All around stretched a flat plain, falling abruptly on all four sides, covered with great masses of rusty barbed wire, heaps of ammunition boxes, three great tanks looking like dead monsters and worst of all the graveyards of Canadian soldiers. Anything more desolate cannot be imagined, these little wooden crosses at the head of a pile of mud, barrenness all around, gray skies, cold rain, crazy skeletons of trees sticking up like scare crows."

Jane wanted to find the grave of her nephew, John Linn, a Y.M.C.A. volunteer who had been killed at Argonne. After a long search through the muddy, temporary graveyards they finally discovered the place where he was buried. "As we came back a bitter, cold rain began to fall with a pitiless wind," Alice Hamilton reported, "and we toiled on through the sticky mud believing that we could imagine pretty well what our men had to endure there. . . . Then there was a bitterly cold drive to Chalons where we caught a warm and fast express for Paris and last night we felt like soldiers on leave from the front. We got off our mud-caked clothes and had hot baths and slept twelve hours."[11]

Even in Zurich there were constant reminders of the devastation and human suffering caused by the war. The first day while walking along the street Addams suddenly met an Austrian woman who had been a delegate at The Hague Congress. "She was so shrunken and changed that I had much difficulty in identifying her with the beautiful woman I had seen three years before," she recalled. "She was not only emaciated as by a wasting illness, looking as if she needed immediate hospital care—she did in fact die three months after her return to Vienna—but her face and artist's hands were covered with rough red blotches due to the long use of soap substitutes, giving her a cruelly scalded appearance. My first reaction was one of over-whelming pity and alarm as I suddenly discovered my friend standing at the very gate of death. This was quickly followed by the same sort of indignation I had felt in the presence of the starving children at Lille."[12]

Despite the constant reminders of death and destruction the Congress was an exhilarating experience. It was attended by about 150 people from sixteen countries. There was a spirit of adventure, a sense of martyrdom and survival, of solidarity and comradeship about the Congress. "The will toward peace and international neighborliness, so often trampled under since the war, became alive again in that hall," an American observer reported. Even Florence Kelley, who went as a skeptic was completely captivated. "As you doubtless know my going was an act of faith, not of conviction . . . ," she wrote to Mary Smith, "but next time I would go on my knees. It was unbelievably wonderful. There were twenty-five English women sitting with the Germans in front and the Irish at one side, all alike, engrossed in the common effort. . . . The English leaders amazed everybody by emphasizing at every opportunity that they were all socialists. . . . Hitherto I have found it hard to take English women, but this time I found myself their humble admirer. . . . Never have I seen so generous a spirit in any group of human beings."[13]

The women immediately passed a resolution condemning the famine and pestilence in Europe as a "disgrace to civilization," and urged the peace conference to raise the blockade, and if necessary to transport food from one country to another. They wired the resolution to Woodrow

Wilson who replied in a telegram that Jane Addams read to the assembly. He approved the sentiment, but pleaded practical difficulties. The Congress spent much of its time reviewing an advance copy of the peace treaty. Showing remarkable foresight, they voiced criticisms that only much later became commonplace. Unanimously they condemned the harsh nature of the treaty, which called for the disarmament of only one side, that denied the self-determination of peoples, and enforced economic penalties on the Central Powers. They denounced the peace terms which, "must result in the spread of hatred and anarchy," and "create all over Europe discords and animosities which can only lead to future wars." A majority supported the League of Nations, but they regretted that the Covenant of the League, "in many respects does not accord with the fourteen points laid down as the basis for present negotiations, contains provisions that will stultify its growth, and omits others, which are essential to world-peace." The women also formed themselves into a permanent body, "The Women's International League for Peace and Freedom." They elected Addams president, and Balch secretary-treasurer.[14]

Jane Addams was in her glory at the congress, happier than she had been in five years, Alice Hamilton decided. She was an expert at presiding at a meeting, at handling resolutions, offering compromises, and soothing hurt feelings. She knew she was good and she loved it. "Needless to say J.A. presided to the satisfaction of everyone (but me! I thought she wasted one afternoon)," Florence Kelley wrote, "and I heard people saying in the English delegation, 'what an excellent chairman, so fair and not a moment wasted.' In the Austrian delegation a woman was saying, 'She is so willing to yield and say that she is wrong,' 'I'm sorry I made that blunder,'—I shall always hear her saying that, and so few blunders!" She enjoyed talking to the women from all over Europe, and she appreciated the "enthusiastic devotion," with which most of the women treated her. After the vilification and the distrust with which she had been treated at home, the admiration and the respect of the European women was doubly important.[15]

She was troubled and discouraged by the peace treaty, but she had some hope for the League of Nations despite its weaknesses. She was also encouraged by the Zurich meeting, where women from both sides sat down together "not in a pretended goodwill, not in mere outside sentimentalism . . . but in genuine friendship and understanding. . . ." "We shall have to believe in spiritual power," she told the delegates in her closing speech, "We shall have to learn to use moral energy to put a new sort of force into the world and believe that it is a vital thing—the only thing, in this moment of sorrow and death and destruction, that will heal the world and bring it back into a normal condition."[16]

She quickly discovered, however, that it was not easy to talk to diplomats and politicians, or even to ordinary citizens about a new moral force, when they were still overwhelmed by the bitterness and hate which was one legacy of the war. She went to Paris to give Wilson the resolutions passed by the Zurich conference, but had to be content to leave them with Colonel House. She did see Herbert Hoover, however, and he aided the American women in a new venture. Hamilton and Addams had been invited by a group of English and American Quakers to make a trip into Germany to investigate the needs of the German people and to make arrangements for the distribution of food and clothing collected by the Society of Friends. Hoover was able to purchase condensed milk, cocoa, sugar, and other items with $30,000 collected during the war by the Quakers. But there were long delays before the actual trip could start. The peace treaty had not been signed and the United States officials did not want American women inside Germany when there was still a possibility that Germany might refuse to sign.

Addams was frustrated by the long waits in legations; she was disturbed by the confusion and the contradictory stories, but she still had a good time. She had tea with Romain Rolland and with Alexander Kerensky in Paris, and enjoyed talking to the journalists, civilian attachés, and assorted experts who had gathered in Paris for the peace conference. Tired of waiting longer in Paris she went to London where she was entertained by Sydney and Beatrice Webb, Mrs. Henrietta Barnett, Lady Courtney, and Graham Wallas. In addition she spoke at several public meetings. "Of course you know J.A. and how she can fill up a day," Alice Hamilton remarked to Mary Smith. On the whole, Jane Addams decided, the peace movement was treated "with so much more respect and dignity here," and that disagreements and differences of opinion were much more easily accepted in England than in America.[17]

The American women were finally given special visas and arrived in Berlin on July 7, 1919. They were overwhelmed by the horror of hungry, sick, and starving children. "In Leipzig, we visited a *Landkolonie*, a large playground in which 625 children from six to twelve years of age spend the day and are given a midday dinner," Jane Addams and Alice Hamilton reported. "It consists of one pint of thin meal soup, to which had been added a little dried vegetable. Out of 190 children who were seated at one time in the dining room all except one were thin and anemic." They recorded the increase in tuberculosis, typhus, and other diseases under control before the war. They talked to doctors and nurses and social workers about the impossible task they were undertaking. "What they are facing is the shipwreck of a nation and they realize that if help does not come quickly and abundantly this generation in Germany is largely doomed to early death or a handicapped life."[18]

But when Jane Addams returned home in August she discovered that many newspapers were denouncing the treaty, not because it was too harsh, but because it was pro-German, and that few people worried about hungry German children. In the fall of 1919 and through much of 1920 she spoke frequently about the food crisis in Europe and raised money to feed German children. But even though she consciously toned down many of her remarks about the international situation and the need for a just peace, believing that "nothing is gained by pushing too hard when public opinion is so adverse," she still was called a traitor. A Red Cross worker in Cleveland denounced what she called "the most violently pro-German speech ever delivered in an American city." "Miss Addams' talk did not have a single bit of Americanism in it," she told a reporter. "It was an appeal for the mothers and babies of Germany and for their soldiers who had been wounded in fighting our own boys." In Detroit Addams was heckled for 45 minutes before she was allowed to speak. So it went around the country, and there was a new wave of abusive letters accusing her of being pro-German and un-American.[19]

The attacks became more vicious and more irrational in 1920 when she spoke out against the justice department's raids on aliens and radicals, and in opposition to the massive arrests and deportation of those whom the government considered disloyal. At a meeting in Chicago, where hundreds of aliens were rounded up, she defended the loyalty of most aliens, and criticized the government's policy.

> Hundreds of poor laboring men and women are being thrown into jails and police stations because of their political beliefs. In fact, an attempt is being made to deport an entire political party.
>
> These men and women, who in some respects are more American in ideals than the agents of the government who are tracking them down, are thrust into cells so crowded they cannot lie down.
>
> And what is it these radicals seek? It is the right of free speech and free thought; nothing more than is guaranteed to them under the Constitution of the United States, but repudiated because of the war.

It is a dangerous situation we face at the present time, with the rule of the few overcoming the voice of the many. It is doubly dangerous because we are trying to suppress something upon which our very country was founded—liberty.

The government is proceeding on the theory that because these thinking aliens demand an end of class struggle and equal rights for all they are plotting to overthrow the United States. So it was said of suffrage years ago. Anything that is radically new to the established order of things is revolution in the eyes of many.

The cure for the spirit of unrest in this country is conciliation and education—not hysteria. Free speech is the greatest safety valve of our United States. Let us give these people a chance to explain their beliefs and desires. Let us end this suppression and spirit of intolerance which is making of America another autocracy.

"Reds Upheld by Jane Addams As Good Americans," "Jane Addams Favors Reds," the headlines announced the next day. She denied, in a letter to the *Chicago Tribune*, that she had said some of the things attributed to her, but she did not retract her criticism of the government for arresting and deporting men and women because of their political opinions.[20] She was quickly denounced in the press and in a flood of letters. "Reading your letter in the *Tribune* today I notice as in all your public utterances a studied vein of cant and perversion and distortion of the facts involved," a man who signed himself Colonel Charles W. Masher wrote. "The radicals are sworn enemies of our country and should be shot to death instead of being deported." She was not a bomb thrower, he admitted, "but you are continually throwing verbal bombs and dynamite at those charged with the affairs of government and the orderly administration of law. How much better are you than those who hurled the bombs . . . ? It's high time Miss Addams that yourself and all such people were accumulating some ordinary . . . horse sense."[21]

"As you still *persist* in your pernicious, anti-American activities," another man wrote, "I will celebrate Washington's Birthday by enclosing some Healthful reading—'Who Shall be Deported,' by M. M. M., and unless, like the leopard, your spots are unchangeable, you may change your lop-sided views on what 'Freedom of Speech' etc., really means under a *Constitutional Government*. . . . I had occasion to chide you in January, 1918 for your pro-German, insidious and mischievous propaganda, but you do not appear to have profited by the sensible advice I then recommended. However, I again suggest you adopt *America First as your motto for the future*." "If your 'mouthings' were not so ludicrous, or if they emanated from an important source, they would be a stench in the nostrils of all decent people," another man wrote. "Thank God we are not afflicted with many citizens of your type."[22]

Jane Addams was troubled by the attacks, personally, but more than that, she worried about the fear and hysteria that caused someone like herself, who spoke out to defend freedom of speech, and collected money for German children, to be denounced as a communist and a disloyal citizen. Occasionally she responded to one of those who charged her with being a Bolshevik. She sent a clipping and questions to R. A. Gum who was reported to have made a speech critical of her and of Hull House. "I did not refer to Hull House specifically or its work," he replied. "I did, however, in classifying the several groups of radicals, refer to what is sometimes called the 'Hot-House, Hull House Variety of Parlor Bolshevists,' a term not original, and though somewhat facetious, is fairly descriptive. Again in the course of my remarks I was asked from the floor if in my opinion Jane Addams was regarded in Chicago as a loyal American. I answered that to my own personal knowledge she was not so regarded by many of the city's foremost citizens." He then proceeded to document instances when she was associated with pacifists or radicals. "You were known to have been a member of the Ford Peace Ship fiasco," he charged. "In May, 1918 you were denounced by the American Liberty League as cooperating with that organization which during the war opposed the operation of the Selective Service Act and encouraged conscientious objectors." On and on he went. He admitted that he could not control her actions, but argued that he should "be permitted to believe that pacifists and radicals, sometimes referred to as Bolshevists, are dangerous to the community." She replied, trying to correct his factual errors. "I am quite willing to receive any legitimate criticism," she maintained, "but charges of disloyalty such as you make with deliberate use of the word 'Bolshevist' I must repeat are not criticism, but mere innuendo."[23]

It was the use of innuendo, half-truths, and out-right lies that were the stock-in-trade of those who saw a giant Communist conspiracy at work in the United States. The election of Warren G. Harding and the end of the raids on aliens and radicals did not stop the hysteria, nor allay the fear of the super-patriots that liberals, pacifists, Bolshevists, and other subversives were conspiring to destroy the American way. In fact the 1920's saw the proliferation of organizations and the expansion of activities of the Radical Right. R. A. Gum, who denounced Jane Addams, was a member of the American Protective League. There were also the American Defense Society, the National Security League, the Sentinels of the Republic (whose motto was "Every Citizen a Sentinel. Every Home a Sentry Box"). There was the National Association for Constitutional Government, the United States Flag Association, the Women Builders of America. In addition there were older organizations that took part in the crusade to stamp out the conspiracy: the Daughters of the American Revolution, the Daughters of the War of 1812, the National Civic Federation, and of course, the American Legion.[24]

The most dangerous kind of subversive activity according to these groups was not bomb-throwing, but the more subtle take-over of the minds of men and women through the infiltration of progressive organizations, especially the colleges, settlements, and women's organizations. In 1920 the Better American Federation of Los Angeles published a booklet which pictured on the cover a college professor peeking out of a rosebud. The message was obvious: "The bomb-throwing, bullet-shooting anarchist does not worry me very much. It is the subtle, highly intellectual, pink variety that is boring into the very heart of America. Such tragedies as the explosion in Wall Street . . . are horrible—monstrous, but they will never halt our progress as a people . . . America will carry on despite . . . Tom Mooney, the MacNameras and their tribe. But when I find a slow poison being secretly injected into our body politic through the classroom, I do worry—and so should you."[25]

It was not just the colleges, however, for there was a giant communist conspiracy involving progressive, pacifist, and women's organizations. This was the major message of the spider-web charts which circulated widely during the 1920's. The first chart was apparently prepared in 1923 by Mrs. Lucia R. Maxwell, librarian of the Chemical Warfare Service of the War Department, and approved by Brigadier General Amos A. Fries. At the top of the chart was a quotation from the Lusk report: "The Socialist-Pacifist Movement in America is an Absolutely Fundamental and Integral Part of International Socialism." At the bottom of the chart was a quotation from Lenin: "If Bolshevism fails it will be because we could not get enough women interested." In one version of the chart were listed various organizations in several categories. Under "Yellow-Pacifist Internationalist and Pro-German" can be found the Women's International League for Peace and Freedom, the Fellowship of Reconciliation, etc. Under "Pink-Progressive-Collectivist," the National Child Labor Committee. Under "Red-Radical-Communist-Subversive" were listed the American Civil Liberties Union and the Third International, Moscow. Under "Red and Part Red Labor Organizations and Adjuncts," were the AFL and the National Consumers' League. Under "Rose-Colored Educational-Political-Religious" were included the Federal Council of Churches, the Federation of Women's Clubs, The National League of Women Voters, and colleges—Harvard, Yale, and over 100 others. In the other column was a list of prominent individuals: Jane Addams, Roger Baldwin, Florence Kelley, Julia Lathrop, Eugene Debs, etc. A tangle of lines connecting the individuals to the various organizations formed a giant spider web in the middle of the chart. The network of lines, of course, tried to demonstrate the interlocking directorate through which the Communists worked to take over the country. In some versions of the chart such organizations as the Needle Work Guild of America and the Girls' Friendly Society and the International Sunshine Society, by connecting various members with other organizations, were identified as "absolutely fundamental and integral parts of international socialism."[26]

Jane Addams was not mentioned prominently in the first spider-web chart, but in some of the later versions she led the list of dangerous subversives, and was denounced by General Fries as "the reddest of the red." She was singled out for attack because she was a member of so many organizations labeled "Communist," or "pink"; and also because her name always led the alphabetical lists. She was a convenient symbol to attack because she was the most famous woman in America, formerly admired and now fallen from grace. Charles Norman Fay, a retired businessman from Cambridge Massachusetts, the author of one version of the spider-web chart, denounced her in a letter to the *Boston Herald* in 1927.

> Miss Addams as all the world knows is a *Lady*, of large and winning personality; one of the most conspicuous women of our time, whose long and successful devotion of life and fortune to an unequaled Settlement-Work has earned the admiration and affection of many thousands of the very highest and lowest of her fellow men and women. All honor to her therefore! All regret for what follows! . . . She is one of those curious *Pacifists* who would disarm every nation, including her own, except the only one that plots violence against all the rest. She is one of those strange economists who would better the conditions of working-folk by thrusting them, bound hand and feet into the throttling grip of the trade-unionist and the politician, in the name of Social Justice.[27]

The Spider Web

CONSCIOUS RADICALS AND ORGANIZATIONS, AND THEIR AFFILIATIONS, IN THE U.S.

Interlocking Directorates   Memberships   and   Other   Relations   Organizations

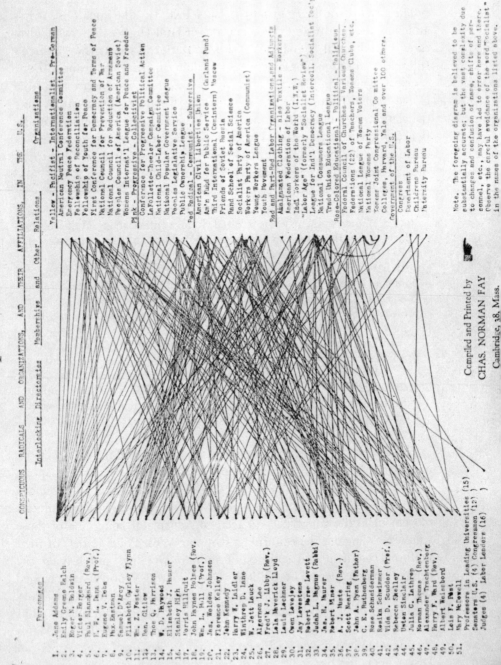

Personages

1. Jane Addams
2. Emily Greene Balch
3. Roger N. Baldwin
4. Victor Berger
5. Paul Blanshard (Rev.)
6. F. L. Dana (Prof.)
7. Eugene V. Debs
8. Max Eastman
9. Samuel D'Arcy
10. Elizabeth Gurley Flynn
11. Wm. Z. Foster
12. Ben. Gitlow
13. Thos G. Harrison
14. W. D. Haywood
15. Elizabeth J. Hauser
16. Stanley High
17. Morris Hillquit
18. John Haynes Holmes (Rev.)
19. Wm. I. Hull (Prof.)
20. Jas. Weldon Johnson
21. Florence Kelley
22. John Kennedy
23. Harry W. Laidler
24. Winthrop D. Lane
25. W. Jett Lauck
26. Algernon Lee
27. Fred'k J. Libby (Rev.)
28. Lola Maverick Lloyd
29. Laura Lachner
30. Owen Lovejoy
31. Jay Lovestone
32. Robert Morse Lovett
33. Judah L. Magnus (Rabbi)
34. Jas. H. Maurer
35. Robert Miner
36. A. J. Muste (Rev.)
37. Scott Nearing
38. John A. Ryan (Father)
39. C. E. Ruthenberg
40. Rose Schneiderman
41. Rosika Schwimmer
42. Vida D. Scudder (Prof.)
43. Rebecca Shelley
44. Upton Sinclair
45. Julia C. Lathrop
46. Norman Thomas (Rev.)
47. Alexander Trachtenberg
48. Harry F. Ward (Rev.)
49. Albert Weisbord
50. Lois F. Fast
51. Mary McDowell

Professors in Leading Universities (15)
Senators U.S. (4) Congressman (12))
Judges (4) Labor Leaders (16))

Organizations

Yellow – Pacifist – Internationalist – Pro-German
American Neutral Conference Committee
Emergency Peace Federation
Fellowship of Reconciliation
Fellowship of Youth for Peace
First Conference for Democracy and Terms of Peace
National Council for Democracy and Terms of War
National Council for Reduction of Armament
Peoples Council of America (American Soviet)
Womens Internat'l League for Peace and Freedom

Pink – Progressive – Collectivist
Conference for Progressive Political Action
LaFollette-Wheeler Campaign Committee
National Child-Labor Committee
National Popular Government League
Peoples Legislative Service
Public Ownership League

Red Radical – Communist – Subversive
American Civil Liberties Union
Am'n Fund for Public Service (Garland Fund)
Third International (Comintern) Moscow
Friends of Soviet Russia
Rand School of Social Science
Socialist Party of America
Workers Party of America (Communist)
Young Workers League
Youth Movement

Red and Part-Red Labor Organizations and Adjuncts
Amalgamated Clothing – also Textile – Workers
American Federation of Labor
Ind'l Workers of the World (I.W.W.)
"Labor Age" (formerly "Socialist Review")
League for Ind'l Democracy (Intercoll. Socialist Soc'y)
National Consumers League
Trade Union Educational League

Rose-Colored Educational – Political – Religious
Federal Council of Churches – Various Churches
Federations (22) of Teachers, Womens Clubs, etc.
National League of Women Voters
National Womens Party
Womens Joint Congressional Committee
Colleges, Harvard, Yale and over 100 others.
Government of the U.S.
Congress
Department of Labor
Childrens Bureau
Maternity Bureau

Note. The foregoing diagram is believed to be substantially accurate; but the vast complexity due to changes and confusion of name, shifts of personnel, etc., may have led to error here and there. Observe the careful avoidance of the word "Socialist" in the names of the organizations listed above.

Compiled and Printed by
CHAS. NORMAN FAY
Cambridge, 18, Mass.

The super-patriotic organizations had a field day all through the 1920's attacking the loyalty and the patriotism of Hull House, those who advocated liberal social legislation, and organizations such as the Women's International League for Peace and Freedom. In 1926 a long and vitriolic article, originally published in the *Woman Patriot*, was inserted into the *Congressional Record* by Senator Thomas Bayard of Delaware, during the campaign to defeat the extension of the Shepard-Towner Maternity Benefits Act. In this article Florence Kelley was singled out for attack because she had translated Engels' work, and according to the article, she had made Hull House into a nest of radicals.

> It is of the utmost significance that practically all the radicalism started among women in the United States centers about Hull-House, Chicago, and the Children's Bureau at Washington, with a dynasty of Hull-House graduates in charge of it since its creation.
> It has been shown that both the legislative program and the economic program—"social-welfare" legislation and "bread and peace" propaganda for internationalization of the food, farms, and raw materials of the world—find their chief expression in persons, organizations, and bureaus connected with Hull-House.
> And Hull-House itself has been able to cover its tracks quite effectively under the nationally advertised reputation of Miss Jane Addams as a social worker—who has so often been painted by magazine and newspaper writers as a sort of modern Saint of the Slums—that both she and Hull-House can campaign for the most radical movements, with hardly a breath of public suspicion. . . .[28]

The veterans organizations, retired Army officers and military societies of all kinds found Jane Addams a convenient symbol to attack. Captain Ferre Watkins, Commander of the Illinois American Legion, announced that "Hull House is the rallying point of every radical and communist movement in the country," and accused Addams of being one of those who was selling out the country by stripping West Point Cadets of their uniforms, depriving all colleges of military training, and leaving the country undefended. The Military Order of the World War charged her with trying to nullify the National Defense Act, and General Henry J. Reilly of New York remarked: "I tell you if things continue to go as they have recently in Washington we can expect to see Jane Addams President and William Z. Foster, Secretary of War." The American Legion included her in its list of black-listed speakers. "Scabbard and Blade," the publication of the R.O.T.C. Honorary Society, charged that

Jane Addams had for twenty years directed her efforts "to international and subversive channels until to-day she stands out as the most dangerous woman in America."[29]

But it was not only the military organizations which found Jane Addams a dangerous radical. She was denounced in Fred R. Marvin's column, "The Searchlight," which appeared in the *New York Commercial*. She was featured as a leading pacifist and subversive in a pamphlet published by the Industrial Defense Association, called "What's What." She was also denounced by professional medical associations, church groups, and by private citizens.[30] The Daughters of the American Revolution were among the most vindictive and persistent of the groups which attacked her, even though she had been given a membership in the organization in 1900. They denounced her for refusing to protest at a public meeting when the flag was belittled. They accused her of being disloyal, and featured her in a pamphlet, "The Common Enemy" which purported to show how a variety of liberal and pacifist organizations were conspiring to overthrow American democracy in favor of Soviet Communism. They also included her on their black list of "doubtful speakers." "Miss Addams is connected with the National Council for the Prevention of War, The Foreign Policy Association, and the Fellowship of Reconciliation, all three of them notoriously 'yellow' organizations and playing the game of the Reds," one D.A.R. attack began. "She, so far as any public records go, has never raised her voice toward the disarmament of Russia or toward the lessening of the Communist ability and willingness to carry on civil war in America and other countries outside of Russia, but she is doing everything she apparently can to lessen the ability of America and other countries to resist a Communist uprising and civil war. In other words, all her actions have tended toward the strengthening of the hands of the Communists to make for the success of a Communist civil war in our country."[31]

Carrie Chapman Catt, who had often differed with Jane Addams, over the war and over the proper role of women in politics, wrote an open letter to the D.A.R. in which she eloquently defended her. Pointing out carefully that she was not a socialist or communist she continued: "the fact is that Miss Addams is one of the greatest women this republic of ours has produced. She has given her life to serve others. She knows no selfish thought. You slap her on the right cheek; she only turns the left. Sticks, Stones, Slanders, you cast upon this highest product of American womanhood, and not a protest passes from her lips. She is the kind of Christian who might have been thrown to the lions and would have gone cheerfully." But protests, rational answers, even law suits did not stop the irrational criticism or stem the hysteria.

The attacks continued, even into the 1930's though they diminished about 1928. In 1934, Elizabeth Dilling published a book called *The Red Network* in which she leveled the same charge of radicalism and subversion against the founder of Hull House.

> Greatly beloved because of her kindly intentions toward the poor, Jane Addams has been able to do more probably than any other living woman (as she tells in her own books) to popularize pacifism and to introduce radicalism into colleges, settlements, and respectable circles. The influence of her radical protegees, who consider Hull House their home center, reaches out all over the world. One knowing of her consistent aid of the Red movement can only marvel at the smooth and charming way she at the same time disguises this aid she reigns as 'queen' on both sides of the fence.

By 1934 those attacked by the super-patriots could laugh. They gave themselves a party. "Did Mrs Dilling Denounce You?" the invitation read, "Do you wish she had? Do you want to meet the people who are undermining civilization?" But the attacks, the innuendo, the lies, were not quite as funny in the 1920's.[32]

Jane Addams was terribly hurt by the irrational attitudes toward her, though she pretended that they did not bother her. "I have never taken these attacks very seriously," she wrote to Mrs. Catt, "having learned during the war how ephemeral such matters are. . . ." But her friends knew otherwise. They answered the charges that she refused to; they tried to talk her into using lawsuits to stop the slander, and in 1927 they gave her a huge testimonial dinner in Chicago to try to counteract the adverse publicity she was receiving. Calvin Coolidge sent his greetings, Governor Alfred Smith of New York wired: "In honoring Jane Addams we honor the idealism of American womanhood." From all around the country the great and the unkown praised her patriotism. William Allen White and Mayor William Dever of Chicago spoke, and Charles Merriam of the University of Chicago called her "a statesman without portfolio, a professor without a chair, and a guiding woman in a man-made world."[33] But all the praise did not make up for the vilification. Most of the attack came from a crack-pot fringe, which did not represent majority opinion in the United States, and yet inevitably the publicity given to this propaganda affected the attitudes of many Americans. The fear of a Communist conspiracy was not just the psychological aberration of a few in the 1920's; it was close to the surface in American thought and influenced everyone, subtly if not directly. Jane Addams' reputation suffered even among those who rejected the most blatant lies told about her; and others acquiesced in the witch hunt out of fear or cowardice.

In 1920 a lecture she was scheduled to give at the University of Toronto, was cancelled because a group which called itself the Daughters of the Empire objected to her pacifism during the war, and her defense of radicals and aliens in the post-war period.[34] There were, indeed, many lectures and public appearances she was not invited to make in the 1920's because she was at best a controversial figure, and at worst a villain and traitor. Her income from lectures and royalties plummeted. "She has lost something of the shine from her halo," one newspaper commented. "In America in 1912 I learned that it was unsafe to mention Jane Addams' name in public speech unless you were prepared for an interruption, because the mere reference to her provoked such a storm of applause," Maude Royden, a British physician recalled. "And I was in America again after the war, and I realized with a shock how complete was the eclipse of her fame . . . her popularity had swiftly and completely vanished. . . . How well I remember, when I spoke in America in 1922 and 1923, the silence that greeted the name of Jane Addams! The few faithful who tried to applaud only made the silence more depressing."[35]

Another incident which indicated the decline of her reputation occurred at the annual meeting of the National Conference of Social Work in Providence in June 1922 when the social workers gathered to elect a fiftieth anniversary President of the conference. A few of her friends, Edith Abbott, Julia Lathrop, Alice Hamilton, and Graham Taylor had been organizing a campaign for some weeks. They felt it was the psychological moment for her to come back, and be recognized once again as the most important leader among the social workers after the disagreement caused by the war. They also thought it was the perfect time for her to take the reins of leadership and redirect the conference back toward the pre-war goals of social reform. She really wanted the presidency. She had never been adverse to being given honors and prizes and awards, but now after years of being attacked the recognition seemed more important. She cooperated with her campaign managers in every way she could but they quickly ran into trouble. Her principal competitors were Homer Folks, Secretary of the New York Charities Aid Association and Mary Richmond, pioneer in social case work and author of *Social Diagnosis*. It was quickly obvious that too many people opposed Addams for her stand against the war; even Robert Woods, a long-time friend, refused to support her. Rather than face the embarrassing prospect of losing, she withdrew her name, and the conference chose Homer Folks, certainly capable, but more conservative and less distinguished than Jane Addams.[36]

It was a bitter disappointment, but not nearly as painful as her failure, during the 1920's, to win the Nobel Peace Prize. Almost every year from 1920 until 1930 her name was submitted for the award, and in some years a campaign was launched in her behalf and with her knowledge. She very much wanted the prize; it would vindicate all her efforts to promote peace, and also be an answer to her critics and those who attacked the Women's International League. Emily Balch was confident in 1920 that she could get the European women to back her candidacy. Jane Addams was willing to try, but Alice Hamilton thought it was asking for trouble, that the old bayonet-charge story and other incidents would be revived and that it was much too early to attempt an all-out campaign, especially when her "claim to it rests chiefly on the founding and guiding of a League which while it is important in a lot of European countries is almost unknown over here."[37] She was nominated again and again and when the award finally came in 1931 it was not only anticlimatic, but she was also forced to share it with Nicholas Murray Butler, a conservative internationalist who had supported America's participation in the war.

Disappointed and frustrated by the turn of public opinion against her, and against social reform and pacifism in the 1920's, Jane Addams spent more and more of her time abroad, attending conferences, traveling and working for the Women's International League for Peace and Freedom. She was not quite an expatriot, but like a number of other intellectuals, she found life outside the United States more congenial than at home. While denounced in America as a traitor, it was comforting and reassuring to be viewed in Europe and Asia as a symbol of American generosity. It was also good to learn from a nun that *Twenty Years at Hull House* had replaced the *Lives of the Saints* in a German convent as inspirational reading at mealtime.[38]

Addams never contemplated living permanently abroad, but she traveled to Vienna in 1921 to attend the third conference of the Women's

International League. In 1922 she went to The Hague for a Conference for a New Peace, called by the Women's International League to deal with the international economic crisis, but attended by representatives of more than a hundred organizations from twenty countries. After the meeting was over she traveled with Mary Smith to the Far East and around the world. She stopped in Burma, India, the Philippines, Korea, Manchuria, China, and Japan. She had an emergency operation in Japan for what proved to be a benign breast tumor, and left just a few days before a disastrous earthquake leveled Tokyo. Everywhere she went she was greeted by enthusiastic crowds, entertained as if she were royalty, and treated to the reverence and awe she had once been accustomed to at home. "I have never anywhere been so fêted as a peace advocate," she wrote of her experience in Japan, "it was positively embarrassing at times, 5000 school children waving flags."[39]

In 1925, she spent a month vacationing in Mexico and the next year she went to Dublin to preside over another Women's International League conference. In 1928 she traveled to Honolulu as president of the Pan-Pacific Women's Union to chair still another meeting. The following year she was in Prague to preside for the last time as president of the Women's International League. After the meeting she resigned as president because of her declining health. She gloried in the travel even though she was almost always seasick. She loved to stay in elegant hotels, to be waited on, and to eat in good restaurants. She enjoyed being entertained by famous and important people around the world. Her work with the Women's International League was stimulating and meaningful, at a time when her reputation was at its lowest ebb at home.

In the 1920's the W.I.L.P.F. absorbed much of the energy and attention that earlier she had devoted to Hull House and to reform campaigns. The League embodied and institutionalized her conception that there was a special feminine consciousness that could be utilized to promote world peace, it stood for the proposition that women were less warlike and aggressive than men and thus had a special responsibility to emphasize the humane impulse in world affairs. She spoke of the need for a new kind of spiritual power, of a moral energy that could heal the world's wounds. She sought ways to translate this spirit into action, but that was not easy. She was fascinated by Gandhi's practice of nonviolence and passive resistance, and when she was in India she attempted unsuccessfully to talk to him. She never tried to adopt his ideas literally; like Tolstoy he was an inspiration to her because he actually applied his theories and lived his ideals.[40] She was too practical; still too much the compromiser to live like Tolstoy or Gandhi, and although she believed in the importance of symbolic action she thought that peace could be preserved through organizations and by putting pressure on governments. She had more faith in the League of Nations and the World Court, after many initial doubts, than did many of her colleagues in the peace movement. She belonged to many peace societies (she had a difficult time saying no to an organization which wanted to use her name), but her own special vehicle to promote peace was the W.I.L.P.F.

The Women's International League had its headquarters in Geneva and branches in many countries; each section was semi-autonomous. Inevitably there were conflicts and disagreements within the organization but in general the league stood for disarmament, total and universal, and subscribed to the principle of non-violence and passive resistance. It sought to remove the causes of war, rather than to alleviate the suffering resulting from war. The league demanded the revision of peace treaties, condemned the policy of reparation, and urged that conscription be abolished in all countries. Its members lobbied in Geneva to influence the policy of the League of Nations on many issues. They sent a mission to Haiti in 1926 to study the effect of the occupation of that country by United States Marines, and the next year they dispatched a team to Indo-China and China to make contact with women's organizations in that part of the world. They also launched an investigation of the opium trade. Occasionally the league, or one of its branches sponsored a more militant demonstration, such as the "peace pilgrimage" conducted by the British section in 1926, with marches, mass demonstrations, and informal classes along the way under the theme of "Law not War." But usually the Women's International League, which represented a minority within a minority, devoted a great proportion of its time and energy to filing reports, writing letters, and trying to influence the policies of governments and other peace organizations. The leaders spent a large amount of time and effort simply keeping contact with their far-flung sections and members, and in organizing their frequent conventions and summer schools.[41]

The executive committee of the W.I.L.P.F. was made up mostly of European women and several of the European sections were stronger and more active than the American branch. Still Jane Addams was the spiritual leader of the league, idolized by many of the European and American members. When she resigned as president in 1929 Lida

Gustava Heymann of Germany wrote urging her to reconsider. "We here in Europe are of [the] opinion that our W.I.L. is so deeply connected with your personality, that it is quite impossible that the League keep on without your name. Neither in America, nor in Europe exists another woman's name who would give that flavour and that atmosphere to our League and work as your name does . . . do not leave your child and our League." Not everyone shared this view. Rosika Schwimmer, who resigned from the League in protest in 1927 because the organization was not militant or aggressive enough, was a constant critic of Jane Addams and of the admirers who surrounded her. She accused her of being a "fake saint," of presenting herself as a pacifist only when abroad, and of spending much more time and effort collecting money and publicizing the work of Hull House than the work of the Women's International League. There were others who resented the way Jane Addams played the role of benevolent saint on the one hand, and of hard-nosed politician on the other. Some of them feared that her leadership was preventing more aggressive, younger women from taking command.

Jane Addams' role in the Women's International League was that of spiritual leader. She was too far away from Geneva to run the day-to-day operation, and she was too busy with other matters in any case. She did raise $500 a month to help keep the organization solvent, but it was a succession of secretaries in Geneva, Emily Balch, Vilma Gluchlich, and Madeleine Doty who kept the League alive, except during conferences and then Addams emerged as a dominant figure because she was in the chair. "I had quite a good time watching Jane," one of those who attended the Dublin Congress recalled. "She is the finest politician I have met and I have met a good few! The whole affair was well oiled and the chief aim of Jane and her group was to make it run smoothly. Of course the real people hadn't a look in. Jane is a champion streamroller. She overlooked nobody (except when they wanted to propose something she didn't want). She had everything so planned and prepared before she arrived . . . but as far as making an impression on the Irish it was nil."[42]

Jane Addams was a politician and a compromiser; that was her style. Despite the fact that she was not a militant pacifist, and that the W.I.L.P.F., especially the American branch, had little influence beyond its own circle, she still was denounced for being president of an organization which the American super-patriots thought was subversive and un-American. She was embarrassed by the way the American press and patriotic organizations treated the delegates to the Women's International League Congress held in Washington in 1924. She apologized to the delegates in her opening address. "May I assure you that Americans are not by nature and training less tolerant than the people in other countries . . ." she announced. "But a survival of war psychology is an unaccountable thing; it constitutes a new indictment, if one is needed, of the devastating effects of war upon human character." A railway coach, dubbed the "Pax Special" had been hired to take a number of delegates from Washington to Chicago for a special summer school. The plan was to stop in various cities and towns along the way, to hold sessions and public meetings to promote the cause of peace. The D.A.R., the Daughters of the War of 1812, the American Legion charged that the foreign delegates were Russian and German agents coming to undermine the government, and that the League advocated the abolition of private property and tried to extract a pledge from its members not to participate in any future war, not even to wrap bandages. "We believe its campaign to make America defenseless, and to make slackers out of American women and American youth is not only disloyal but encourages both foreign insult and oppression," a spokesman for the Daughters of the War of 1812 announced. Jane Addams, of course, was singled out for attack, because she was president of the subversive organization which was bringing spies and enemy agents into the country. She did temper her statements, and seek to minimize the publicity concerning her pacifism, because of the violent reaction of the super-patriots against her in the 1920's, but she also withdrew from other activities as well.[43]

She spent less and less time at Hull House. Even when she was in Chicago she more often stayed with Mary Smith on Walton Place than at the settlement. She still managed to influence the various programs and to raise money for all the activities. With a budget of over $100,000 and an endowment that covered only about half the expenses, raising money became more and more of a problem. Some contributors died, others declined to give because the settlement now seemed controversial. But she refused to let Hull House join the community chest or the federated fund drive as some settlements were doing, on the grounds that Hull House would lose the right to make its own decisions, and not incidentally, she would lose the power to juggle the budget. The settlement was a big operation, with many problems that ranged from keeping the furnaces and the plumbing repaired, to relationships with the changing neighborhood, and management of the music and art programs, and keeping peace among the residents. There was no formal organization, when Jane Addams was away, Mrs. Bowen or Jessie Binford or one of a number of other people made decisions, or fired off an emergency appeal to Miss Addams. Somehow they muddled through, and Addams had a genius for settling disagreements, putting the pieces back together even from afar, and the settlement survived though there were several close calls. Her management of the settlement was personal in the extreme; she was head resident and chairman of the board, and she was much more. She was "Miss Addams," treated with awe even reverence by all the residents, though secretly hated and resented by some of the younger men and women. She prepared badly, or not at all, for the day when the settlement would have to operate without her.[44]

Hull House had changed. Julia Lathrop and Grace Abbott had gone to Washington for important federal appointments. Florence Kelley had long since departed for New York, Alice Hamilton was in Boston teaching at Harvard Medical School, while Ellen Starr had entered a Catholic convent. There were able residents who remained; Jessie Binford, George Hooker, Victor and Rachel Yarros, Robert Morss Lovett and many others, but no longer was there anyone who could laugh at Jane Addams or prod her into action. The settlement movement had also changed. Most settlements had moved away from reform; many were in financial trouble, and they found it much more difficult to recruit able and energetic young residents. Social work in the 1920's was rapidly becoming professionalized, and more concerned with psychiatric case work than in social reform. One man who visited a number of settlement houses in 1922 reported to Jane Addams that he found "an uncertain vision and a bewildered attempt at comprehending the awful problems of the war and its aftermath." She went to a few settlement conferences and was treated as an elder statesman in the movement. Of course for years she had been the "grandmother" of the movement. There was a new generation of settlement workers, and they sometimes resented the pioneers. One of these young workers spoke out at a meeting of the National Federation of Settlements: "a movement needs good followers as well as good leaders," she remarked, "but after thirty or forty years it is time for new leadership to develop." Jane Addams was critical of many of the young workers and their concern for professional standards, their obsession with psychiatric counseling and individual adjustment, and their lack of interest in the community and in reform. But time brought changes, and it was difficult for the pioneers, like Jane Addams, to adjust to the new situation—it was easier to accept the applause of those who remembered the old days, and to ignore the new movements, and the new problems.[45]

She went to other conventions when she was in the United States. There was the National Conference of Social Work, the National Council of Women, the National Committee on American-Japanese Relations, the National Advisory Committee of the League for the Abolition of Capital Punishment, the Survey Associates. It seemed sometimes as if all she did was go to conventions and committee meetings. She attended the early meetings of the League of Women Voters, and there became involved in a fundamental difference with Carrie Chapman Catt over the tactics and strategy of political involvement for the newly enfranchised women. Catt and her followers argued for quick infiltration of the established parties, and the assumption of office-holding and policy-formation by the women. But as one of the observers reported: "Then there was another group lured by the beckoning finger of Jane Addams, most widely respected and influential woman in America. She felt women had important work to do to make their communities better places to live, they must follow their traditional concerns into the public arena. They must enlarge their sense of responsibility for their own families to include the whole community, because the health and welfare of their families can no longer be guarded within their own four walls. . . . Mrs. Catt was conservative in her economic and social thinking, but extremely advanced in her political thinking. Jane Addams was liberal in her social thinking, but fundamentally conservative in her conception of woman's political role as primarily a politicizing of her function. Mrs. Catt would have women remake political institutions to allow for their inclusion on equal terms with men. Jane Addams wanted to remake society over in a pattern approved by women."[46]

She had been stressing women's special responsibility and qualifications for promoting peace and municipal reform for years, but in the 1920's with younger women demanding equality, it was a position that seemed more and more old-fashioned. She opposed the Equal Rights Amendment to the Constitution, which was supported by Alice Paul and her Woman's Party. Here Addams was joined by Kelley, Hamilton, and most of the other social justice reformers who had fought hard to promote special legislation to protect working women, and did not want to sacrifice it for an amendment that would establish the idea that women were the equal of men.[47]

Like many of her social work colleagues she supported prohibition.

She was disturbed by bootlegging and the speakeasies, by the crime and violence that was a by-product of prohibition, especially in neighborhoods like those near Hull House. But she was convinced that outlawing liquor had improved conditions in most working class sections of the city. Her attitudes toward drink, however, had been formed by her Victorian upbringing. She had been taught that drinking, especially for women, was a sin, and she never outgrew that attitude. Intellectually she could appreciate the importance of the saloon as a social center and she could tolerate her friends who enjoyed a cocktail now and then, but other than an occasional glass of sweet wine, she never touched alcohol and basically disapproved its use for both the working man and for the upper class.[48] She also could not understand what she called the "astounding emphasis upon sex" in the 1920's. She appreciated the importance and the power of the sex drive before most of her generation, but her goal was to find ways to sublimate sex, not glorify it. She rejected the new freedom in sex relations and had no understanding or appreciation of the liberated woman. She was surprised, if not shocked, when her grand-niece wore shorts and used lipstick. When Judge Ben Lindsey sent her a copy of his book on companionate marriage, which advocated a kind of trial marriage she remarked: "I am afraid I do not agree with the basic principle upon which you urge the experiment, but I should like to talk it over with you very much." She remained, for all her tolerance and compassion, a Victorian lady.[49]

She seemed out-of-step with the times. Where once she had represented all that was good about America, now she seemed tired and worn and old-fashioned if not disloyal. She still appeared in most lists of "Famous American Women," but she no longer automatically finished first. In 1922 a Chilean official asked the League of Women Voters for a list of the Twelve Greatest Women in America, and her question started a national craze. Newspapers and magazines began to compile lists. Jane Addams was on most of the polls but she was sixth on the *New York Times* list, and she was not nearly as popular as Carrie Chapman Catt and Edith Wharton. The lists were clearly drawn up by middle-aged, middle-class Americans, but young actresses like Mary Pickford and singers like Geraldine Farrar began to appear.[50] The twenties produced a new kind of heroine, young, seductive, and daring. No longer was maturity a badge of honor, nor was service to society, which Jane Addams symbolized in the pre-war era, as important as personal freedom. Jane Addams was still admired and respected by many people, but she no longer served as a role model for college women. The decade that made a hero out of Charles Lindbergh for flying across the Atlantic in a single-engine plane, and admired the Fitzgerald heroine for her freedom and her casual attitude toward sex could hardly keep as its patron saint one who had founded Hull House to aid the poor. No longer was it possible to believe that women were the conscience of the nation, and that some women could do Christ's work in the world. The unity and the faith in the American dream that had allowed a pre-war generation to admire the innocence and purity of Daisey Miller, the civic virtue and social morality of Victoria Flint, and the practical spirituality of Jane Addams, was shattered in the 1920's. The pre-war unity was a mirage in any case, and most of those who treated Jane Addams as a saint did so because they thought she was solving some of the problems of poverty in the city that they feared but dared not face. The disillusionment and despair of the war and its aftermath changed all that. Even after Jane Addams ceased being a villain and a high-minded fool, she seemed out-of-step with the 1920's, and no longer a representative American, or a unifying symbol of the best of American democracy.[51]

There were still some who kept the faith, who saw her as a martyr to the cause of peace and justice. Florence Holbrook, an American peace worker, member of the Woman's Peace Party and one of these at The Hague Conference in 1915, wrote a poem honoring her in 1923, connecting her to another saint, but emphasizing the theme of martyrdom and sadness.

> One wrote of Filomena, saint of old,
>   Who bore a lamp in dark and lonesome place;
>   And with like blessed charity and grace
> Wrought England's Florence with her heart of gold.
>
> Now comes another who with courage bold
>   Dark pathways of sad souls with love both trace,
>   Light comes to all who look upon her face
> Transfigured with the faith of martyrs old.
>
> O'er sorrowing hearts her loving heart both yearn.
>   Deep grief to allay and to assuage the pain;
> Great wrongs to right her eager soul both burn,
> And always from the false the true discern.
>   Be this her joy, her work is not in vain,
>   In loyal hearts enshrined, our own Saint Jane.[52]

Despite her martyrdom and her loss of popularity in the 1920's Jane Addams was still important enough so that she was enlisted in every liberal cause, from trying to save Sacco and Vanzetti, to opposing strict immigration laws, but her involvement was more remote than it had been earlier. Her endorsement was also sought by those running for President. Both Harding and Cox tried to win her support in 1920 but she refused to come out publicly for either one. In 1924 she endorsed Robert La Follette and the Progressive Party, because they seemed to represent the progressive ideals she had fought for over many years. In 1928 she endorsed Herbert Hoover because of his work with the Food Commission during the war, and because it seemed to her that he represented the best of the progressive tradition. "It is significant" she argued, "that Herbert Hoover, the one American identified with the World War to be nominated to the Presidency, should have been distinguished not for his military prowess, but for his conservation of tender lives menaced by war's starvation." She also believed he could effectively regulate business and cooperate with labor. She opposed Al Smith, who was supported by Lillian Wald and many of her other friends, because Smith opposed prohibition, and prohibition meant that much to her. Even in 1932 after the disaster of the depression had altered politics she endorsed Hoover for re-election. Her faith and confidence in Hoover, like her continued support for Wilson in 1916 and again in 1919, went beyond the bounds of reason and was based on a liberal dream that she refused to admit had failed.[53]

Her political activity was limited in the 1920's but she did continue to write. She did not turn out the volume of books and articles that she had in the previous decade, in part because she had less to say, and in part because there was not the incessant demand for speeches, out of which she usually fashioned her books. Paul Kellogg, after a brief estrangement during the war, continued to pressure her to publish in the *Survey*, an indication that though her name was in disrepute elsewhere it still meant something to social workers. In fact the *Survey* editors were convinced that an article by Jane Addams automatically made an issue sell.[54] But the other more popular and large circulation magazines no longer clamored for her work, even the Macmillan editors, who before the war constantly badgered her to publish more, ignored her for several years before finally suggesting in 1921 that the time might be right for another book.

The two books she published in the 1920's were autobiographical. *Peace and Bread in Time of War* was an account of her wartime experiences and her philosophy of pacifism, in fact, she originally called the book "A Pacifist in Wartime." It was a straight-forward and muted account; she described the persecution and the hysteria during the war, but she understated it. She was critical of Wilson and his policies, more critical than she had been at the time. She described the formation of the Women's International League and expanded her theories, based on the myth of the corn mother, that women had always had a special role in preserving peace and feeding the community. It was generally a hopeful book, despite a note of discouragement and despair which crept in here and there. Her friends and co-workers liked it, but some of the reviewers decided that it was too idealistic, and Paul Kellogg thought she was too critical of Wilson. One of the shrewdest reviews appeared in a British journal and argued that "Jane Addams represented the best type of nineteenth century pacifist. . . . She belonged to that company of distinguished women who appeared in so many different countries who were humanists, pacifists, feminists, and who—one would have said eight years ago—stood in the van of civilization." But the war ended all of that, it created a "feeling of hopelessness and helplessness, of being either sane in a world of madmen, or mad in a world of sane. . . ." This feeling left a deep mark on Jane Addams and on her book, the review continued. "She remains a pacifist, but not a nineteenth century pacifist. Nineteenth century pacifism was founded upon a belief that ultimately man is amenable to reason. The pacifist of 1922 finds his hopes so tarnished that he carefully hides them away. . . ." But the reviewer was wrong in his conclusion, for Jane Addams in many ways remained a nineteenth-century pacifist. She was discouraged and disturbed by the irrational attacks upon her, but essentially she continued to believe in man's reason, and in woman's ability to prevent war, and that, in a decade of despair and disillusionment, made her seem out of step.[55]

The other book which she worked on through much of the decade but did not publish until 1930 was the sequel to her autobiography, which she called, rather prosaically, *The Second Twenty Years at Hull House.* She had a difficult time writing it. She was ill with heart trouble, the old kidney ailment, and finally, to complicate matters, she fell and broke her wrist. But it was more than ill health that made the writing difficult. After she finished the first chapter on the Progressive campaign she sent it off to the *Survey* for possible publication as an article. "I suspect that you will be disappointed in the chapter as I certainly am," she admitted. "I suppose that it is the experience of the war which makes it all seem so remote." Again she wrote: "The book is not going very well although I am sticking to it every day. I think that it is because I am writing about the war period. . . ."[56] There were chapters on the war and its aftermath, on the immigrants and the anti-immigration laws, education, the arts, and prohibition. She also republished the article that she liked best of all she ever did, "The Devil Baby at Hull House." But there was little unity in the book; it did not have the drama and appeal of *Twenty Years*. There were no childhood memories, no conversion experience, no search for the holy grail, no real conviction that she knew the way or had the answers. There was a large element of nostalgia for a simpler, better time, just as there was a good deal of recalling the good old days, when former residents and other dignitaries gathered at Hull House about the time the book was published to celebrate the fortieth anniversary of the settlement. Lewis Gannett, in reviewing the book for the *New York Herald Tribune*, exaggerated when he decided that Jane Addams emerged from the book as "a lovely, but a slightly anachronistic figure, quaintly and pleasantly out of place in 1930," but he only exaggerated a little. "To read Jane Addams' 'The Second Twenty Years at Hull House' . . . ," he decided, "makes one a little homesick for the days before the war when Jane Addams was a sort of national saint and we all believed in ideals."[57]

XV

The Restoration of a Saint

S the depression deepened some of the controversy associated with Jane Addams in the 1920's subsided. The economic crisis at home, and the threat of a new war abroad made her seem more relevant and less controversial. In the early years of the 1930's, the last years of her life, she was showered once more with honors, praised beyond reason, and treated, again, as a saint. There were some like Elizabeth Dilling and an occasional leader of the American Legion who continued to denounce her as a "Red," but most people approved the awards and the tributes. There was, however, something nostalgic about the honors bestowed on her in the 1930's, as if everyone were trying to recapture a more simple and idealistic age when Jane Addams was solving the problems of poverty and the slums.

In 1930 the Greek government gave her a Medal of Military Merit for her service to Greek-Americans, and specifically for allowing Greek citizens, waiting to join the Greek Army, to use Bowen Hall at Hull House for military drill. The irony of receiving a military honor did not seem to bother her. In 1931 she was awarded the C. Carey Thomas Foundation Award, given by Bryn Mawr College to a woman of eminent achievement. It was only the second time that the award had been given, and the first time it was to Miss Carey Thomas, the longtime president of Bryn Mawr. She also received the *Pictorial Review* award for 1931, made "to the woman who in her special field has made the most distinguished contribution to American life." She was named by *Good Housekeeping Magazine* as the first among "America's Twelve Greatest

Women." The twelve, which also included Grace Abbott, Mrs. Calvin Coolidge, Helen Keller, and Carrie Chapman Catt, were selected by an all male jury. "One of the committee," Jane Addams remarked, "formerly regarded me as a traitor, and I'm quite sure that two at least of the others had never heard of me before the contest."[1]

Other lists quickly followed. In fact there was something pathetic about the attention given to lists of American heroes and heroines, compiled at the very time the nation faced its worst crisis and people were going hungry in the streets. Perhaps there was a need in the face of the depression to have re-assurance that there were still heroes and heroines worth believing in. Mark A. DeWolf Howe, the Boston writer and Pulitzer Prize winner, picked "six outstanding present-day Americans" and included Jane Addams, Thomas A. Edison, Henry Ford, Alfred Smith, and Sergeant Alvin York. Another list of the "seven greatest Americans of all time" included Addams, Edison, Ford, George Washington, Abraham Lincoln, Woodrow Wilson, and John D. Rockefeller. Being bracketed once again with Edison, Ford, and Rockefeller, all self-made American industrialists and businessmen, was a sure sign that she was included again in the American pantheon of practical heroes.[2]

In 1932 the National Council of Women ran a contest for the twelve greatest American women of the century, the winners to have their portraits hung in the Hall of Science at the Century of Progress Exposition in Chicago. Mary Baker Eddy was first, Jane Addams second, Clara Barton third, and Frances Willard fourth. Susan B. Anthony, Helen Keller, Harriet Beecher Stowe, Julia Ward Howe, Carrie Chapman Catt, and Amelia Earhart followed in that order. Most of those who placed high on the list were either associated with the woman's rights movement, or as in the case of Addams, Barton, and Keller, had reputations as self-sacrificing humanitarians. But it is significant that Mary Baker Eddy and Jane Addams finished first and second in the poll, for both were treated as spiritual leaders, and both were credited, during part of their careers at least, with being the feminine conscience of the nation.[3] So Jane Addams in the early 1930's had seemingly regained her position as both practical humanitarian and saint.

Other honors came her way in the last years of her life. The colleges and universities which had failed to offer her honorary degrees during the war and in the 1920's because she was too controversial, now fell over themselves in their eagerness to honor her. Northwestern, the University of Chicago (which had refused to give her a degree much earlier),

Swarthmore, Rollins, Knox, the University of California, and Mt. Holyoke all gave her degrees. Some educators, however, still did not forgive her deviation during the war. James R. Angell, President of Yale, whose institution had been one of the first to honor her, when asked his opinion of Jane Addams by the University of Chicago replied: "I have known Jane Addams for nearly forty years and have in many ways the greatest admiration for her character and accomplishments. I am frank to say, however, that I could not understand, and I find it difficult wholly to forgive her attitude during the early part of the war. She was, from my point of view, so altogether irrationally pro-German, veiling her actual procedure under the guise of her Tolstoian pacifism. . . ."[4]

Despite the occasional dissent, there were other signs of her returning reputation. There were the favorable, even embarrassingly flattering magazine articles that had been absent for the most part during the 1920's, and a new group of accounts of her life for school children. The articles were usually sentimental, and they continued and passed on the old myth. There were the familiar stories told in her autobiography and now part of the legend—the time she told her father that she wanted to have a big house surrounded by little houses, the sights and sounds of East London and the rotting garbage; the bull fight in Spain. Most of the popular accounts de-emphasized her work for peace, and ignored the controversy that had swirled about her name. Even Edmund Wilson, one of the nation's leading literary critics, who wrote a starkly beautiful essay on Chicago and Hull House in 1932 that captured some of the hopelessness and despair of the depression, became sentimental when he wrote of Jane Addams, "A little girl with curvature of the spine. . . ."[5]

It was difficult apparently for most people to avoid being sentimental when they saw Jane Addams' tired and worn face, which seemed somehow to represent the suffering of mankind, for they sent her poems inspired by a picture, by a radio speech, by reading one of her books. The verses came from old friends, from unknown women, unemployed men, and from school children. The poems of tribute were not distinguished for their quality, but they emphasized two themes—the burdens she had born for humanity, and that she had been, like Christ, sent by God to do her work on earth. They were sentimental but they meant a lot to her for she carefully preserved each one.[6]

Grade school children wrote to tell her that they had been studying her in their history classes. Not all the school girls to whom she was held up as a model knew exactly why she was famous. Lillian Wald recalled that on one occasion a group of girls came to Henry Street Settlement and announced "Last year we did Jane Addams, . . . this year we got to do you." Not especially eager to be "done," she inquired what they had learned about Miss Addams and if they had ever seen her. "Oh sure," one of them replied, "We saw her in *Peter Pan!*" They had confused her with actress Maude Adams. Such was the penalty of being a celebrity.[7]

Her fame and reputation among adults was sometimes based on conceptions almost as ephemeral and sentimental. Even some of her friends and co-workers treated her like a good fairy, or as one who had a special spiritual presence. Sometimes they even went a step further. Alice Thatcher Post, who had worked closely with her in the peace movement, admitted: "countless times I have said to myself when confronted by a moral emergency: what would Miss Addams do?" (As Charles Sheldon asked: What would Jesus do?) The religious symbolism and comparisons and the sense of martyrdom were constant themes, but some people wrote to her in the early thirties as if they thought it would be the last letter she would ever receive.[8]

Her health was not good. She had recurring heart trouble after an attack in 1926. She had chronic bronchitis and another operation for a tumor in 1931. Despite the doctor's warnings her weight ballooned to over 200 pounds. She did not have the same energy and drive she once had, and she had to spend long periods in Arizona or Florida to escape the effects of the Chicago winter, but she remained active and involved. She finished editing the memorial addresses and funeral orations she had given over the years into a book called *The Excellent Becomes the Permanent*. The Macmillan editor was not enthusiastic about the prospects for the book in a depression year and asked her to take no royalty on the first 1,000 copies and 10 per cent thereafter. But old age and poor health had not diminished her business sense nor her ability to bargain. "May we compromise the matter," she suggested, "and say that no royalty is to be paid on the first thousand copies, but that I will begin the second thousand with 15 per cent. I suppose it took me so long to climb up to that eminence with Macmillan that I dislike the feeling of 'demotion,' as the public school teachers say." But when the book was not advertised widely and was not available in several Chicago bookstores, she protested again, and Macmillan corrected the situation, eager to demonstrate that "Miss Addams and anything that she writes are very dear to the Macmillan heart."[9]

Other publishers, magazine editors, and a variety of organizations who had ignored her for ten years now once again besieged her for articles, essays, and speeches. She no longer had the energy to go on long speaking tours or to turn out frequent articles, but she increasingly gave radio addresses, and was pleased with the results. William Hard, who interviewed her on the air, thought she was the most interesting person he had talked to on his program, and others wrote to tell her what an impressive radio voice she had.[10]

None of her activities or awards, however, received as much attention or publicity as winning the Nobel Prize. To her friends in the peace movement it was vindication at last for years of struggle and criticism. Not everyone agreed; many thought she got the prize as much for her work at Hull House as for her efforts to promote peace. And the *Outlook*, in an article called "Good Choice; Poor Choice," praised the selection of Nicholas Murray Butler, but felt that Jane Addams did not deserve to share the award. "One of the most able American charitable workers . . . and one of the most admired women alive, she nevertheless had done nothing of the first magnitude in the cause of world peace. . . . She founded and has been the guiding spirit of the Women's International League for Peace and Freedom, but with all due respect for this organization, it can scarcely be called important." But the reaction of the *Outlook* was not typical. Most of the editorial comment was favorable. The same newspapers who had attacked her during the war for being silly, or impractical or a traitor now praised her "unyielding fight for her ideals." *The New York Times*, although they gave top billing to Butler in their front page story, published a major article in their Sunday edition, entitled: "Jane Addams: Bold Crusader For Peace." Taking the theme emphasized by Halvdan Koht in his address at the awards ceremony, the article suggested once again that Jane Addams was representative of the best of American democracy. From a "childhood spent close to the fountainhead of American idealism," she went on to achieve international acclaim and an "intense sense of kinship with every member of the human race." But her success remained "an ultimate expression of an essentially American democracy of spirit."[11]

Her part of the Nobel award came to $16,480. With the Bryn Mawr and *Pictorial Review* awards each worth $5,000, her prize money represented a huge windfall in a depression year. She gave it all away. The Nobel money went to the Women's International League, and the rest she used to help the unemployed in the Hull House neighborhood. The announcement of the awards, together with the dollar amounts, caused a flurry of letters asking for help. Since the first years of Hull House she had received many letters from men, and women, and children she had never met, asking for advice, or jobs, or money. The letters had dwindled in the 1920's, but the announcement of the prizes in the midst of the depression caused a great many ordinary Americans to write. The pathos and the despair was overwhelming. "I hesitate to burden you with my problems for I realize that to one in your position every moment is precious," a woman wrote. "Although I can hardly hope for a reply, yet I must write for I am confident that I shall feel better for having bared my wretchedness to one whom I feel can understand." "I see in the paper that you are awfull rich and have $5,000 to help the poor," a fourteen-year-old girl who did not own a pair of shoes, wrote, "Moma says you will not help Texas children but I thought I would write to ask you." "Miss Addams, please if you *ever helped anyone* help us," a woman pleaded.[12]

There was little that Jane Addams or anyone else could do about the despair and the suffering. "All around the social workers of Hull-House there today stretches a sea of misery more appalling even than that which discouraged Miss Addams in the nineties," Edmund Wilson wrote. "I have watched fear grip the people in our neighborhood around Hull House," Jane Addams remarked in 1931, "men and women who have seen their small margin of savings disappear; heads of families who see and anticipate hunger for their children before it occurs. That clutch of cold fear is one of the most hideous aspects, I think of human nature, —certainly one of the most wretched things to endure. People under fear will do almost anything to rid themselves of their panic, and they are scarcely responsible for what they do." Still she was not ready to admit that it was the American system of free enterprise that was at fault, or to lose her basic optimism that one could work to promote legislation to provide old age pensions, unemployment insurance, and other forms of governmental assistance. In fact, she argued that the depression would speed the day when the federal government would take up the responsibility of caring for "our unfortunate fellow citizens." "We must not forget that a period of depression connotes vast human suffering and bewilderment," and decided that, "to avert disastrous social consequences is a primary obligation."[13]

She admitted that Hoover's actions in the face of the desperate economic situation were bélated and inadequate. Still she supported him for re-election in 1932, more out of nostalgia for the past than for any other reason. But when Roosevelt was elected she quickly went to work to support Frances Perkins as Secretary of Labor. She accepted a position on the Chicago advisory committee of the Housing Division of the Public Works Administration, under the direction of her old friend, Harold Ickes. She was also one of the vice-presidents of the American Association of Social Security. She was excited by many of the early New Deal programs. She opposed the Agriculture Adjustment Act; it seemed to her unwise and tragic to destroy food while people starved. But she defended the NRA in a radio broadcast and argued for a managed credit system, higher wages, shorter hours, and a huge public-works program. She especially approved the federal support for public housing which resulted in three large slum-clearance projects just a short distance from Hull House. "It is really a wonderful time in which to live," she wrote a friend in 1934, "in spite of much suffering due to unemployment which still exists."[14]

She remained interested in world affairs and the peace movement. After her resignation as president of the Women's International League she was given the title of Honorary President. She was unable to attend the conventions, but she raised money for the organization, an increasingly difficult task during the depression. She also maintained a wide correspondence with the women peace leaders around the world. She offered advice and encouragement, tried to settle disagreements and calm the resentments that developed. She had long advocated the recognition of the Soviet Union by the United States and rejoiced when it was finally accomplished during the first year of the Roosevelt administration. She deplored the international competition and trade in the weapons of war, which she saw developing in the thirties. She urged the use of moral energy, not physical force in settling international disputes and she favored the withdrawal of American marines from all countries where they were stationed to protect American citizens and property. She criticized the self-righteous failure of the United States to disarm, which she decided was "doubtless due to the fact that we are so sure that our intentions are beneficial, that our army is small, and that no one would suspect us of unworthy ambitions." She was horrified by the invasion of Manchuria by Japan and by the rise of Nazism in Germany, but she had faith that peace could be preserved through moral sanctions, international trade agreements, and the gradual end of the war psychology. "A great Kingdom of Peace lies close at hand ready to come into being," she announced, "if we would but turn toward it."[15]

She could not attend all the conferences of the organizations she belonged to, but she remained concerned and involved. In 1932 when a young social worker in New York announced that men made better head residents of settlements than women, she fired off a note to Lea Taylor, president of the National Federation of Settlements: "I think that the Federation of Settlements might consider disciplining this young man. It's a voice of forty years ago." She no longer was an aggressive leader of the settlement movement, but her opinions still counted. She lived with Mary Smith on Walton Place and did not get to Hull House as frequently, but she still managed the finances and when she was at the settlement there still was a magic about her presence, at least to some people. A young woman just out of college, living at Hull House, reported her reaction to Jane Addams' return after a long absence:

"The first thing I heard—I had just come home—was her voice. I heard it all the way from the third floor the minute she walked into the house. There isn't any other voice like it is there? Suddenly it seemed as if everything clicked, as if the tonic note had been struck and the chord was complete. I can't explain just how I felt, but when I walked downstairs . . . and saw her sitting there in a black velvet dress and her heavy amber beads, talking to Mrs. Lovett whose face looked as if she had just watched a sunrise, I felt as if she had been sitting there always, as if there must have been something unfinished about the room all the time she wasn't there. Her hair is whiter—that's all, and it's beautiful. Otherwise she looks so exactly the way she always did and always will. I think she has the most familiar face in the world."[16]

Sometimes it seemed like a face from the past. She was getting older, and the small circle of settlement pioneers was getting smaller. Florence Kelley and Julia Lathrop both died in 1932. Mary Smith died in 1934 and that was a great blow. Ellen Starr, herself an invalid and paralyzed from the waist down wrote in condolence: "I could never think of a flaw in her character, or suggest any way in which she could have been improved." Without Mary she was more impatient and less serene. Yet she worked hard on a biography of Julia Lathrop she was writing with Grace Abbott, and she was well enough in the spring of 1935 to attend the twentieth anniversary celebration of the Women's International League in Washington.[17]

The celebration turned out to be in her honor. Sidney Hillman, Gerard Swope, Alice Hamilton, Oswald Garrison Villard, and many others were there. Harold Ickes called her the "truest American" he had ever known. Eleanor Roosevelt, soon to replace her as the most loved and the most hated woman in America, thanked her for her example and praised her as "a pioneer who was still pioneering." It was a festive occasion filled with nostalgia and hope for the future. Jane Addams enjoyed every minute of it. Ten days after the celebration, however, she was taken ill, and on May 21, 1935, she died of cancer.[18]

There was a genuine outpouring of grief from all around the country, and the world. A heroine during her lifetime, she was deified in death. She lay in state at Bowen Hall at Hull House. The Hull House Woman's Club, the Hull House Dramatic Association, and graduates of the Boys Club formed a guard of honor, while the boys and girls from the various clubs acted as ushers. Thousands of men, women, and children from all walks of life stood in line to file past her casket. The funeral was held in the Hull House courtyard with thousands crowding in every available spot; they overflowed the fire escapes, and perched on the roof tops. Old friends were there, working men and curious strangers, even some of the famous bootleggers and gang leaders in the city were observed paying their respects. The next day her body was taken by train to Freeport, then by hearse through roads lined with mourners, to Cedarville where she was buried in the Addams lot, in the cemetery begun by her father.[19]

Telegrams and letters of sympathy poured in. Obituaries and memorial tributes appeared in magazines and newspapers. Her death gave editorial writers and essayists, as well as her friends and co-workers, one last chance to evaluate her. It also gave them an opportunity to explain her prominence in relation to American society, and to evaluate that society at a particular juncture of history. "Jane Addams was usually on the minority side, and not seldom with the most unpopular remnant in the field," one writer pointed out. "Yet this persistent nonconformity did not affect her essential standing. Most truly and fully was she a representative American. She could have come to maturity in no other land than her own." To most writers that special quality that made her an American came from her rural mid-western upbringing. "Miss Addams was the essential American. She took from the soil of Illinois and from her Quaker ancestry all that was finest and best in the pioneer tradition of the old Northwest," The *New York Herald Tribune* decided. "Miss Addams was typical of American womanhood in her training, her aspirations, her opportunities, her democratic sympathies and her neighborliness, inherited or acquired in the frontier, rural community which she knew as a child and carried into the congested city," the *New York Times* remarked.[20]

Walter Lippmann saw her special American qualities in broader perspective:

> She had compassion without condescension. She had pity without retreat into vulgarity. She had infinite sympathy for common things without forgetfulness of those that are uncommon.
>
> That, I think, is why those who have known her say that she was not only good, but great. For this blend of sympathy with distinction, of common humanity with a noble style is recognizable by those who have eyes to see it as the occasional but authentic issue of the mystic promise of the American democracy. It is the quality which reached its highest expression in Lincoln, when, out of the rudeness of his background and amidst the turmoil of his times, he spoke in accents so pure that his words ring true enduringly. This is the ultimate vindication of the democratic faith, not that men can be brought to a common level, but that without pomp or pride or power or privilege, every man might and some men will achieve again and again the highest possibilities of the human spirit.[21]

Others saw a close affinity to the American tradition of the self-made man and the successful business executive. "She may have championed unpopular causes and rebelled against conservative thought, but there was in her makeup those very elements which when directed into other channels, result in big business executives and successful politicians." She was a woman of action, a tireless worker, an executive with common sense. She was a true pioneer and inventor. The "'social service' which she in a sense invented, was quite as definitely an invention as Edison's electric light." "She crystallized and vitalized the idea of social service, which has become part of the American creed and what she accomplished by the application of intelligence and perseverance to practical projects; she never tried to whistle in the millennium."

There were a few writers who questioned or almost questioned her Americanism. "A hater of war, she became an extremist in her advocacy of peace. It was commonly said she believed in 'peace at any price,' a view not in conformity with the spirit of American nationalism," one writer decided. "Despite her views on peace, she was an outstanding patriot who spurned to be identified with the so-called 'pink' movements which made insidious attacks on the stability of our form of government," another suggested.

Most agreed that she represented the best of American democracy. Her life spanned a crucial period in American history, and marked the development of social service and opportunities for women, immigrants, and all who called themselves American. "She stands as the very symbol of an era of advancement." But many of the tributes betrayed a worry that perhaps the three-quarters of a century that her life spanned was a golden age in American history, and that the future would not be as bright. "Look back over her record and one finds that she was American in the sense of the term that has almost been lost sight of these past few years. She believed deeply in service to her city, her state and like a real democrat all peoples of the world." She represented the best kind of American womanhood, an "exemplification of the spirit of unselfish service." But "it was doubtful whether the young woman of today will hold Jane Addams up as their ideal; Amelia Earhart is probably nearer being the 1935 model than Jane Addams." To some, the New Deal, with the Social Security Bill being considered by Congress when she died, was a culmination of the progressive social legislation that she had fought so hard to promote over the years, but to others the ominous rise of fascism in Europe, the invasion of Manchuria by Japan, boded ill for Jane Addams' dream of peace. In addition, social work, to which she had devoted herself over more than 40 years, seemed at a crossroads, "it must decide whether it is to remain behind in the area of caring for the victimized or whether it is to press ahead into the dangerous areas of conflict where the struggle must be pressed to bring to pass an order of society with few victims."

To many then, the passing of Jane Addams was a sad event not only because it was a personal loss, but also because it marked the end of an era. There was a fear that the next decades would be worse than those just past. Not everyone expressed this fear for it was easier just to praise, and to repeat all the old stories and myths and to believe that the example of Jane Addams vindicated American democracy in a time of crisis and uncertainty. A writer in the *Christian Century* said:

> Much nonsense has been written about Miss Addams as "the angel of Hull House," and an unfortunate amount of it has been repeated in the days immediately following her death. The mistaken purpose has been to establish a traditional figure of the St. Francis sort—the figure of a woman who surrendered comfort, ease, all the amenities of life to lose herself in the poverty of Chicago's needy, and to share her crusts as she passed from tenement door to tenement door. The very idea requires a

complete misconception of Miss Addams' outlook on life. She had no interest in descending to the poverty level. Her interest was in lifting the level all about her to new heights. For that reason, Hull House under her hand was always a place in which beauty was served, and the emphasis was on the maximum of enjoyment to be extracted from the widest possible spread of human interests and activities.

If Miss Addams visited the tenements of Chicago's slum areas—as she did—it was not as a romantic sharer of crusts. She went there as the duly commissioned inspector of streets and alleys, determined to make the agencies of government operate in such a way as to protect the dwellers in underprivileged areas. Her "theory" of social work, if she had a theory, was always to insist that the fullest possible good be required from the working of existing public and social agencies, to demand new agencies when the old had been proved inadequate, and to deal with people on the level of their highest potentialities.[22]

The article did not end the nonsense. The legend of Jane Addams, already well developed during her lifetime, and based in part on her own autobiographical writings, was exaggerated and extended by the tributes and biographies and appeared shortly after her death. The legend which pictured her as superhuman and saintly distorted her real importance, but it was destined to live on in school books, children's biographies, and even in scholarly accounts. The legend also had its affect at Hull House, where one head resident after another discovered that they were compared unfavorably to Miss Addams.

The legend of Jane Addams lived on but in many ways she seemed like an historical figure, long dead even a year after her passing. A memorial fund drive brought in only a modest amount. A plan to erect a shrine in her honor, with marble statues and ionic columns, was abandoned for lack of money. A script for a motion picture, called "The Lady of Hull House," was prepared, and Irene Dunne engaged to play the lead, but the movie was never produced. A few schools were named after her, and an occasional park honored her name. One of the federal housing projects near Hull House, became officially The Jane Addams Homes, and in 1940 a stamp bearing her likeness was issued by the United States in a series honoring famous American scientists. But few articles or books were written about her in the two decades after her death. World War II and the cold war made her pacifist ideas unfashionable and the post-war reaction against reform, together with the professionalization of social work, made her work at Hull House seem less important. A few social workers even dismissed her as sentimental and unprofessional, while Richard Hofstadter cited her as an example of those progressives who became reformers out of a sense of guilt in order to satisfy an internal need. In the 1960's, however, with urban reform and the peace movement again in fashion, Jane Addams was rediscovered, and her achievements praised once again. Yet the legend which made her a self-sacrificing saint survived and colored even the most sophisticated interpretations.

Despite the distortion of the legend, or perhaps because of it, Jane Addams remains endlessly intriguing. She no longer provides a role model for young women; her insistence on the special intuitive nature of women, and her Victorian attitudes toward sex have partially cut her off from the present generation. Her reform schemes and her attempts to promote peace often seem naïve from the vantage point of the 1970's. Yet her struggle to overcome the "family claim" and her attempt to do something worthwhile and important on her own still have meaning for both men and women today. In addition, those seeking to improve life in the cities and to promote peace in the world have to build on what Jane Addams and her co-workers constructed even as they reject that generation's optimistic faith in human nature. But more than that, anyone wishing to understand the course of American history from the Civil War to the New Deal must come to grips with Jane Addams—the books she wrote, the battles she fought, the compromises she made. And one cannot avoid the legend that made her first a saintly heroine and then a traitorous villain, for her shifting reputation reveals a great deal about the hopes and dreams and fears of the American people.

Bibliographical Notes

Location of Manuscript Collections and Abbreviations Used

Edith and Grace Abbott Papers, University of Chicago.

Jane Addams Papers:

Swarthmore College Peace Collection (SCPC): correspondence, clippings, and published material. Most of the Jane Addams' correspondence has been microfilmed and is available at several centers. Unless otherwise noted all references are to this collection. Also at Swarthmore is the Ellen Starr Brinton Collection (Brinton), a film of Jane Addams' correspondence. Some of the originals are now at the Jane Addams Memorial Collection, University of Illinois-Chicago, and at the Lilly Library, University of Indiana, Bloomington, Indiana.

Jane Addams Memorial Collection (JAM): University of Illinois-Chicago: correspondence, including copies of letters from many other collections, clippings and other material.

University of Kansas (KU): film of copies of Jane Addams' letters written during her two European trips. Some of the originals are now at the Jane Addams Memorial Collection or at the Lilly Library.

Stephenson County Historical Museum (SCHM), Freeport, Illinois: early Jane Addams correspondence.

Emily Greene Balch Papers, Swarthmore College Peace Collection.

Anita McCormick Blaine Papers, McCormick Collection, Wisconsin Historical Society, Madison, Wisconsin.

Sophonisba P. Breckinridge Papers, Library of Congress.

Dorothy Kirchway Brown Papers, Arthur and Elizabeth Schlesinger Library, Radcliffe College, Cambridge, Massachusetts.

Mary Dewson Papers, Arthur and Elizabeth Schlesinger Library.

Richard T. Ely Papers, Wisconsin State Historical Society.

Ford Peace Ship Papers, Library of Congress.

Margaret Haley, MS autobiography, Chicago Historical Society.

Alice Hamilton Papers, Arthur and Elizabeth Schlesinger Library.

William R. Harper Papers, University of Chicago.

Jenkin Lloyd Jones Papers, University of Chicago.

David Starr Jordan Papers, Hoover Institute of War, Revolution and Peace, Stanford University.

Florence Kelley Papers, Special Collections, Columbia University.

Paul Kellogg Papers, Social Welfare History Archives, University of Minnesota.

Mary Kenny MS autobiography, Arthur and Elizabeth Schlesinger Library.

Esther Kohn Papers, Jane Addams Memorial Collection, University of Illinois-Chicago.

Julia Lathrop Papers, Rockford College Archives, Rockford, Illinois.

Ben Lindsey Papers, Library of Congress.

Salmon Levinson Papers, University of Chicago.

Henry Demarest Lloyd Papers, Wisconsin State Historical Society.

Robert Morss Lovett Papers, University of Chicago.

Louis Lochner Papers, Library of Congress.

National Federation of Settlements Papers (NFS), Social Welfare History Archives, University of Minnesota.

Louis Post Papers, Library of Congress.

Rockford College Archives (RCA), Rockford, Illinois.

Raymond Robins Papers, Wisconsin State Historical Society.

Julius Rosenwald Papers, University of Chicago.

Rebecca Shelley Papers, University of Michigan.

Ellen Starr Papers, Sophia Smith Collection, Smith College, Northampton, Massachusetts.

Survey Associates Files, Social Welfare History Archives, University of Minnesota.

Graham Taylor Papers, Newberry Library, Chicago.

Lillian Wald Papers, New York Public Library. (Wald MSS)

Lillian Wald Papers, Special Collections, Columbia University. (Wald MSS Columbia)

Women's International League for Peace and Freedom Papers. Swarthmore College Peace Collection (WILPF).

Woman's Peace Party Papers (WPP), Swarthmore College Peace Collection.

A Note on Newspaper Sources

Many of the newspaper articles cited come from the massive clipping collection maintained by Jane Addams during most of her life and now located in the Swarthmore College Peace Collection. I have also checked many other newspapers during crucial periods, for Jane Addams had the habit of sending clippings to friends.

Notes

Notes to Chapter I

1. Biographical and genealogical information on the Addams family may be found in James Weber Linn, *Jane Addams: A Biography* (New York, 1935) and Edwin B. Yeich, "Jane Addams," *Historical Review of Berks County* XVII (Oct.-Dec. 1951), 10-13. Report of the administrator of the estate of John Addams, filed Jan. 5, 1885, Stephenson Co. Courthouse, Freeport, Ill.; also notebook, JAM.

2. Linn, *Addams*, 1-21; John Addams to Mrs. Addams, Feb. 20, 1869; Weber Addams to John Addams, Jan. 16, 1869, Box 45, SCPC.

3. Marcet Haldeman-Julius, "The Two Mothers of Jane Addams," typescript SCPC.

4. JA to Alice Haldeman, Aug. 20, 1890, Brinton, SCPC.

5. Anna Addams to John Addams, Jan. 11, 1869, Box 45, SCPC.

6. Marcet Haldeman-Julius, *Jane Addams as I Knew Her* (Girard, Kansas, 1939), and "Two Mothers of Jane Addams," MS, SCPC.

7. Sarah C. T. Uhl to Jane Addams, Nov. 16, 1896; JA to Alice, March 5, 1871, SCHM. See also other childhood letters in this collection and in SCPC.

8. JA to Vallie Beck, March 21, 30, 1877.

9. Jane Addams, *Twenty Years at Hull House* (New York, 1910), 86; JA to Vallie Beck, March 30, 1876.

10. *Memorials of Anna P. Sill: First Principles of Rockford Seminary, 1849-1889* (Rockford, Ill., 1889); *Annual Catalogue of the Officers and Students of Rockford Seminary*, 1877-78, Rockford College Archives; Jane Addams Report Book, SCHM.

11. Anna P. Sill, *A Letter of Our Old Girls and to Them Only*, 1882, Miss Sill's Scrapbook; Carrie L. Jones to Mrs. Dederburg, Feb. 16, 1925, RCA.

12. Quotation is from Frederick Rudolph, *The American College and Uni-*

versity (New York, 1962), 326. The argument over the affect of higher education on women went on for years. For extensions of Clarke's argument see G. Stanley Hall, "From Generation to Generation," *American Magazine* LXVIII (July 1908), 250-54 and A. Lapthorn Smith, "Higher Education of Women and Race Suicide," *Popular Science Monthly*, LXVI (March 1905), 466-73.

13. Florence Kelley, "When Co-Education Was Young," *Survey* XVII (Feb. 1921), 559; also see Vida Scudder, *On Journey* (New York, 1937), 66.
14. Sarah Anderson to JA, Sept. 11, 1878; *Jubilee Book of Alumnae Association of Rockford College, 1854-1904*, 82; *Annual Catalogue*, 1877-78.
15. Helen Harrington to JA, July 23, 1881; Clara Lutts to JA, Aug. 26, 1878; Sarah Anderson to JA, Oct. 26, 1881. A friend wrote to JA from another female seminary: "The girls here are afflicted with the same sentimental 'spooning Malady' which you say infests Rockford. I heartily agree with you old fellow that it is both disgusting and horrible and demoralizing to us women. . . ." Unidentified to JA, Dec. 5, 1877.
16. Addams, *My Friend Julia Lathrop* (New York, 1935), 38.
17. Mary Downs to JA, Nov. 14, 1880; JA to Starr, Aug. 11, 1879; Jan. 29, 1880, Starr MSS.
18. Quotations are from Jane Addams notebooks. Box 42, SCPC. A similar dilemma confronted many others; see Walter Houghton, *The Victorian Frame of Mind* (New Haven, 1957), 93-109.
19. JA to Starr, Aug. 11, 1879, Starr MSS.
20. JA to Starr, Aug. 11, 1879, Starr MSS.
21. JA to Starr, Jan. 29, 1880, Starr MSS.
22. JA to Starr, Nov. 22, 1879, Starr MSS.
23. Houghton, *Victorian Frame of Mind*, 101-22; JA to Starr, Nov. 22, 1879, Jan. 29, 1880, Starr MSS.
24. JA to Starr, Jan. 29, 1880, Starr MSS.
25. JA report book, SCHM; also Jane Addams Records, RCA.
26. JA to Mrs. Addams, Jan. 14, 1880, SCHM; JA to Alice, Jan. 22, 1880, Brinton; JA to Mrs. Addams, March 7, 1880, in possession of Mrs. John Woodhouse, Freeport, Ill.
27. JA to Starr, Aug. 11, 1879; *Rockford Seminary Magazine* VI (April 1878), 81-82; JA to George, April 26, 1881; John Farrell, *Beloved Lady: A History of Jane Addams' Ideas on Reform and Peace* (Baltimore, 1967), 37.
28. *Rockford Seminary Magazine* VII (June 1879), 163-64; James Weber Linn, *Jane Addams*, 54; Mary Downs to JA, May 23, 1880.
29. College themes and essays, gift of Mrs. Karl Detzer, JAM. On one manuscript in JA's handwriting: "written for Harpers Magazine but not yet published."
30. JA to Alice, Jan. 23, 1880, Brinton.

31. Debate: "Resolved that French Women have exerted a greater influence through literature than through politics." JAM.
32. *Rockford Register*, April 2, 1880. Also *Rockford Seminary Magazine* VIII (April 1880), 110.
33. She stressed the role of women as breadgiver in her later writings, especially *Peace and Bread in Time of War* (New York, 1922).
34. JA to John Addams, May 8, 1881; JA to Alice, May 8, 1881, JAM; JA to George, May 8, 1881; *Rockford Seminary Magazine* IX (June, 1881) 173-74. To her brother she also said she sometimes doubted the wisdom of the undertaking. She makes the trip to Jacksonville a major incident in her autobiography, but there she tells the story quite differently. See Chapter 9.
35. JA to George, May 8, 1881, SCHM; Helen Harrington to JA, March 9, 1882. She did return the next year with two others to receive a BA.
36. *Essays of the Class of 1881*, 36-39, RCA.
37. Quoted in Farrell, *Beloved Lady*, 34, note.
38. Sarah Anderson to JA, July 14, 1881.

Notes to Chapter II

1. Helen Harrington to JA, July 23, 1881. Most accounts assume she planned to go to medical school after college, and they blame the illness and depression on her father's death. See Linn, *Addams*, 65-66; Farrell, *Beloved Lady*, 39; Christopher Lasch, *New Radicalism in America* (New York, 1965), 15. This letter makes clear that she had decided not to go to Smith at least a month before her father's death and that her despair and illness, although increased by her father's death, was not caused entirely by it.
2. Quotations are from William Dean Howells, *Suburban Sketches* (Boston, 1872), 96; Elaine and English Showalter, "Victorian Women and Menstruation," *Victorian Studies* XIV (Sept. 1970), 83-89; see also Carroll Smith Rosenberg and Charles Rosenberg, The New Woman and the Troubled Man, forthcoming in *Journal of American History*.
3. "A New Woman's College," *Scribner's Monthly* VI (Oct. 1873), 749; see also Donald Meyer, "The Troubled Souls of Females," *The Positive Thinkers* (New York, 1965), 28-41.
4. Starr to JA, n.d. (1881), Starr MSS.
5. Linn, *Addams*, 65-67; *Freeport Budget*, Aug. 20, 1881.
6. JA notebooks and note fragments, JAM.
7. JA to Starr, Sept. 3, 1881, Starr MSS; Starr to JA, Sept. 10, 1881, JA MSS, Box 45, SCPC; Sarah Anderson to JA, Sept. 21, 1881; George to Mrs. Addams, Sept. 21, 1881, JAM.
8. Emma Briggs to JA, Nov. 13, 1881, Brinton; George to Mrs. Addams, Sept. 21, 1881, JAM.

9. See Ernest Ernest, S. *Weir Mitchell: Novelist and Physician* (Philadelphia, 1950); Nathan G. Hale, Jr., *Freud and the Americans: The Beginnings of Psychoanalysis in the United States, 1876-1917* (New York, 1971), 57-62.
10. JA to Alice, Oct. 23, 1885, JAM.
11. JA notebooks, entries for 1883, SCPC; Helen Harrington to JA, March 9, 1882.
12. JA notebooks; Mary Ellwood to JA, June 8, July 30, 1882.
13. Quotations from Houghton, *The Victorian Frame of Mind,* 64-76.
14. O'Neill, *Everyone Was Brave: The Rise and Fall of Feminism in America* (Chicago, 1969), 79; only those classmates who got married seem to have been happy in the first years after college, those who sought further education or a career seem to have been troubled by the same illness and self-doubt that beset Jane Addams. Helen Harrington to JA, July 23, 1881; March 9, 1882; Nora Frothingham to JA, Sept. 25, 1881.
15. O'Neill, *Everyone Was Brave,* 79.
16. Alice to JA, Sept. 10, 1882, Brinton; Farrell, *Beloved Lady,* 40. A great many other young women seem also to have had back problems. See Scudder, *On Journey,* 73-74; Donald Meyer, *The Positive Thinkers,* 28-41.
17. JA to Starr, Jan. 7, 1883, Starr MSS.
18. Report of the Administrator of the Estate of John Addams, filed Jan. 5, 1885, Stephenson Co. Courthouse, Freeport, Ill.; also notebook, JAM.
19. JA to Alice, May 1, 7, 22, 29, 1883, JAM; Anna Sill to JA, May 3, 1883; Frank Woodbury to JA, May 1, 1883.
20. JA to Alice, May 22, 1883, JAM.
21. JA to Starr, July 11, 1883; Farrell, *Beloved Lady,* 40; Lasch, *New Radicalism,* 18-19.
22. JA to Starr, Aug. 12, 1883, Starr MSS.
23. Alice carefully copied her sister's letters into notebooks (leaving out only a few references to family affairs). Microfilm copies of these notebooks are now at the University of Kansas Library. Most of the originals are either at The Lilly Library, University of Indiana, or at the Jane Addams Memorial Collection, Chicago.
24. JA to Alice, April 26, 1884, KU.
25. JA to Mary, Aug. 31, 1883, KU.
26. JA to Weber, Oct. 29, 1883, KU.
27. JA to Mary, Nov. 4, 1883, KU.
28. JA to Weber, Jan. 27, 1884, KU.
29. JA to Starr, July 11, 1883, Starr MSS.
30. JA to Starr, March 30, 1885, Starr MSS.
31. JA to Mary, April 15; JA to Alice Nov. 5, 1884.
32. Ida Tarbell, *The Business of Being A Woman* (New York, 1912), 179; JA to Alice, Nov. 30, 1884, KU.
33. JA to Mary, Dec. 6, 1883; JA to Weber, Jan. 27, 1884, KU.
34. JA to George, Jan. 4, 1884. Mistakenly dated 1883, KU.

35. JA to Weber, March 20, 1884, KU; JA to George, Jan. 4, 20, 1884, both mistakenly dated 1883, KU.
36. JA to Alice, Dec. 22, 1883; JA to George, March 8, 1884, KU.
37. JA to Alice, Oct. 24, 1884, KU.
38. JA to Starr, June 8, 1884, Starr MSS.

Notes to Chapter III

1. Quoted in Cushing Strout, "The Pluralistic Identity of William James, A Psycho-historical Reading of the *Varieties of Religious Experience*," *American Quarterly* XXIII (May 1971), 135-52.
2. Lasch, *New Radicalism*, 6.
3. Addams, "The Subjective Necessity for Social Settlements," "The Objective Value of a Social Settlement," Henry C. Adams, ed., *Philanthropy and Social Progress* (New York, 1893), 1-56.
4. Abraham H. Maslow, *Toward a Psychology of Being*, 2nd ed. (New York, 1968), 34-35. For a perceptive article which suggests that the humanistic school of psychology provides an alternative to an emphasis on deficiencies in personality and style in understanding the motivation of reformers see: Gerald W. McFarland, "Inside Reform: Status and Other Evil Motives," *Soundings* LIV (Summer 1971), 164-76.
5. "Three Days on the Mediterranean Subjectively Related," *Rockford Seminary Magazine* XV (Jan. 1886), 11-17. See *Twenty Years at Hull House* (New York, 1910), 69-71, where she uses De Quincey again to illuminate her own failure to react to the misery of East London.
6. MS essay, JAM.
7. JA to Alice, Oct. 23, 1885, JAM.
8. JA to Mrs. Addams, Oct. 16, 1885, JAM.
9. Jane Addams, "The College Woman and the Family Claim," *The Commons*, IV (Sept. 1898), 3-4.
10. JA to Alice, Feb. 17, 28; March 7, 1886, JAM. JA to Starr, Feb. 7, 1886, Starr MSS.
11. JA to Alice, Sept. 23, 1886, JAM. Lasch, in his essay on Jane Addams in *New Radicalism in America* has made much too much of the conflict between Jane and her stepmother. It is true that later there was real conflict, but at this point Jane got along with Mrs. Addams probably better than any other member of the family. Her role as compromiser was more important than the conflict.
12. JA to Alice, Nov. 12, 14; Dec. 8, 15, 1886, JAM. JA to Alice, Jan. 27, 1887.
13. JA to Alice, March 2, Dec. 10, 1887; Brinton.
14. JA to Alice, Jan. 10, 1887, Brinton; JA to George, July 5, 1887, Brinton; George to Mrs. Moyer, June 24, 1887, JAM; JA to Alice, Sept. 30, Oct. 9, Nov. 28, 1887, Brinton.

15. JA to Flora Guiteau, Jan. 7, 1888, KU; JA to Alice, Jan. 6, Jan. 26, 1886, KU; cf. Addams, *Twenty Years*, 82-83.
16. JA to Alice, Feb. 27, 1888, KU; Mary to JA, Jan. 31, 1888, JA to Mary, Feb. 5, 1888. Daniel Levine, *Jane Addams and the Liberal Tradition* (Madison, 1971), argues that the illness was psychological.
17. Sarah Anderson to Mrs. Addams, Feb. 26, 1888.
18. JA to Starr, April 23, 1883, Starr to JA, n.d.; JA to Starr, Jan. 24, 1889, n.d., Starr MSS; Starr to JA, Jan. 1, 1882, April 25, 1883.
19. Starr to Alice, March 4, 1888, JA to Alice, March 22, 1888, KU.
20. Quotation is from Gordon Haight, introduction, K.A. McKenzie, *Edith Simcox and George Eliot* (Oxford, 1961), xv. For other discussions of feminine friendships, see William R. Taylor and Christopher Lasch, "Two 'Kindred Spirits' " Sorority and Family in New England, 1839-1846," *New England Quarterly* XXXVI (March 1963), 23-41; Philip Rahv, Introduction, Henry James, *The Bostonians* (New York, 1945).
21. JA to Alice, March 15, 22, April 6, 1888, KU; JA to Alice, April 14, 1888, KU.
22. Addams, *Twenty Years*, 85-86.
23. JA to Laura, April 25, 1888, KU.
24. JA to Mrs. Addams, April 27, 1888, JAM. For the bull fight as recorded in her autobiography, see Chapter 9. Most accounts simply accept her version of the experience. Lasch notes the discrepancy between the autobiographical account and the letters but essentially accepts the bull fight as a conversion experience, *New Radicalism*, 26-27.
25. JA to George, June 9, 1888; JA to Alice, June 14, 1888, JAM; Mrs. Samuel A. Barnett, *Canon Barnett: His Life, Work and Friends*, 2 vols. (London, 1918), I, 22-28; Addams, *Twenty Years*, 87. Most accounts assume that she knew about Toynbee Hall before arriving in London; Robert A. Woods, and Albert J. Kennedy, *The Settlement Horizon* (New York, 1922), 46 suggest that she happened on an account of the settlement before going to Europe and clipped the address.
26. JA to Alice, June 14, 1888, JAM. In an essay that she wrote soon after founding Hull House, "The Outgrowths of Toynbee Hall," she emphasized the importance of culture and art, and the fact that the residents could live as they were accustomed to live. MS, SCPC. "Congress of Protestant Missions," *London Times*, June 14, 1888.
27. JA to Alice, June 14, 1888, JAM.
28. Walter Besant, *The Children of Gibeon*, New ed. (London, 1894), 134.
29. Walter Besant, *All Sorts and Conditions of Men* (New York, 1882), 154-55.
30. JA to Alice, June 14, 1888; JA to Alice, n.d. (June 1888), JAM.
31. See Allen F. Davis, *Spearheads for Reform: The Social Settlements and the Progressive Movement, 1890-1914* (New York, 1967), 3-11.
32. Baptismal and membership record, Presbyterian Church, Cedarville, Hulburt MSS, JAM.

Notes to Chapter IV

1. JA to Mrs. Addams, July 9, 1888; George to Harry Haldeman, Sept. 14, JAM. The most serious of the family problems was the complete mental collapse of George Haldeman in the fall of 1888.
2. JA to Starr, Jan. 24, 1889, Starr MS.
3. JA to Mary Blaisdell, Feb. 13, 1889.
4. Starr to Mary Blaisdell, Feb. 23, 1889, Starr MSS.
5. JA to Mary, Feb. 13, April 1, 1889; James F. Findlay, Jr., *Dwight L. Moody: American Evangelist, 1837-1899* (Chicago, 1969), 321-35.
6. JA to Starr, June 4, 1889, Starr MSS.
7. JA to Mary, Feb. 19, 26, 1889.
8. JA to Mary, March 13, 1889, SCHM.
9. JA to Mary, Feb. 19, 1889.
10. JA to Mary, Feb. 13, 1889.
11. JA to Mary, Feb. 26, 1889.
12. Starr to Mary Blaisdell, Feb. 23, 1889, Starr MSS.
13. Helen Harrington to JA, July 25, 1886.
14. JA to Mary, March 13, 1889, SCHM; Starr to Mary Blaisdell, Feb. 23, 1889, Starr MSS.
15. *Ibid.*; JA to Starr, Jan. 24, 1889, Starr MSS.
16. JA to Mary, April 1, 1889.
17. JA to Mary, March 13, 1889, SCHM.
18. Ellen Starr to Mary Blaisdell, Feb. 23, 1889, Starr MSS.
19. Linn, *Jane Addams*, 94-95; Helen Culver to JA, n.d. (1889); JA to Mrs. Addams, May 9, 1889, JAM.
20. JA to Alice, Aug. 6, Sept. 13, 1889, Brinton; Addams, *Twenty Years*, 94. See John P. Rousmaniere, "Cultural Hybrid in the Slums: The College Woman and the Settlement House, 1889-1894," *American Quarterly* XXII (Spring 1970), 45-66.
21. JA to Alice, Sept. 13, 1889, Brinton.
22. JA to Mrs. Addams, May 9, 1889, JAM.
23. "To Meet On Common Ground: A Project to Bring the Rich and Poor Together," *Chicago Tribune*, March 8, 1889.
24. Leila G. Bedell, "A Chicago Toynbee Hall," *Woman's Journal*, XX (May 25, 1889); JA to Starr, May 31, 1889, Starr MSS.
25. Starr to Mary Allen, Sept. 15, 1889, Starr MSS.
26. See Barbara Welter, "The Cult of True Womanhood, 1820-1860," *American Quarterly* XVIII (Summer 1966), 151-74; Clifton J. Furness, ed., *The Genteel Female* (New York, 1931), 88-119.
27. Bedell, "A Chicago Toynbee Hall"; articles, *Chicago Times*, March 3, 23, 1890; *Chicago Journal*, May 17, 1890 and n.d. all from Scrapbook, JAM.
28. Starr to Mary Blaisdell, Feb. 23, 1889, Starr MSS.

29. A note written by Starr attached to letters given by Starr to the Jane Addams Papers in the Swarthmore College Peace Collection maintains that she carried the organizational ball through most of the summer of 1889 while Jane was taking care of family matters, but the letters do not substantiate this. Both Jane and Ellen were away from Chicago during part of the summer and Jane, who did go home, seems to have spent most of her time taking care of her duties as a member of the Board at Rockford College. In any case there is no evidence of major disagreement or resentment between them.

30. Bedell, "A Chicago Toynbee Hall"; David Swing, "A New Social Movement"; Mary H. Porter, "A Home on Halsted Street," *Advance*, April 11, 1889; XXIII (July 11, 1889), 500. "A Chicago Belle's Scheme to Help the Poor," *New York World*, June 16, 1889, scrapbook, JAM.

31. Bedell, "A Chicago Toynbee Hall."

32. Anne Forsyth, "What Jane Addams Has Done For Chicago: A Fight for The Betterment of a Great City," *Delineator* LXX (Oct. 1907), 493.

33. Quotations are from "Outgrowths of Toynbee Hall," MS, *Ca.* 1890, SCPC; the same idea is expressed in "A New Impulse to an Old Gospel," *Forum* XIV (Nov. 1892), 345-58 which was republished as "The Subjective Necessity for Social Settlements" in Henry C. Adams, ed., *Philanthropy and Social Progress* (New York, 1893), 1-26, and republished again in part in *Twenty Years at Hull House*, 115-27. The same idea in somewhat different form is in "The College Woman and the Family Claim," *The Commons* III (Sept. 1898), 3-7.

34. *New York World*, June 16, 1889; *New York Times*, March 3, 1890; *Chicago Journal*, May 17, 1890 clippings, scrapbook, JAM.

35. Quoted in David Kennedy, *Birth Control in America* (New Haven, 1970), 53.

Notes to Chapter V

1. Addams, *Twenty Years*, viii.

2. *Ibid.*, 109.

3. JA to Alice, Oct. 8, 1889, Brinton; Florence Kelley, "I Go to Work" *Survey* LVIII (June 1, 1927), 271-74; Starr to Mary Blaisdell, Dec. 19 [1889?], Starr MSS.

4. JA to Alice, Nov. 23, 1889, Brinton.

5. Jane Addams, "The Art Work Done at Hull House, Chicago," *Forum* XIX (July 1895), 614-17; Ellen Starr, "Art and Labor," *Hull-House Maps and Papers* (New York, 1895), 165-82.

6. Starr to her father and mother, Nov. 3, 1889, Starr MSS; JA to Alice, Nov. 23, 1889, Brinton.

7. JA to Alice, Oct. 8, 1889, Brinton.

8. For an assessment of Mrs. Bowen, see Linn, *Jane Addams*, 140-44.

9. JA to Jones, May 20, Oct. 27, 1890; Aug. 20, Dec. 6, 1891, Jenkin Lloyd Jones MSS, University of Chicago.

10. Starr to Mary Blaisdell, May 18, 1890, Starr MSS.

11. *Ibid.* See also, newspaper account of party, Nora Marks, *Two Women's Work*, *Chicago Tribune*, May 19, 1890. Both letter and article are reprinted in Allen F. Davis and Mary Lynn McCree, eds., *Eighty Years at Hull House* (Chicago, 1969), 28-33.

12. JA to George, Nov. 24, 1889, JAM.

13. "Outgrowths of Toynbee Hall," SCPC; JA to Alice, Jan. 22, 1890, Brinton.

14. Addams, *Twenty Years*, 102-3.

15. Addams, "Hull House: An Effort Toward Social Democracy," *Forum* XIV (Oct. 1892), 231.

16. JA to George, Nov. 24, 1889, JAM; JA to George, Dec. 21, 1890, SCHM.

17. JA to Alice, March 13, 1889, Brinton; JA to Jenkin Lloyd Jones, Nov. 3, 1890, Jones MSS; the Rev. J. Frothingham, "The Toynbee Idea," *Interior*, Aug. 7, 1890; Janes Addams, "The Objects of Social Settlement, *Union Signal* XXII (March 5, 1896), 49.

18. Residents Meeting Book, Nov. 25, 1893, JAM; Edward Burchard to Starr, Jan. 16, 1938, Starr MSS.

19. See Davis, *Spearheads for Reform*, and Davis and McCree, eds., *Eighty Years at Hull House*.

20. Quotation from Francis Hackett, "Hull-House: A Souvenir," *Survey* LIV (June 1, 1925), 275-79. See also Jane Addams, *My Friend Julia Lathrop* (New York, 1935); Linn, *Jane Addams*, 133-36.

21. Florence Kelley, "I Go to Work," *Survey* LVIII (June 1, 1927), 271.

22. Josephine Goldmark, *Impatient Crusader* (Urbana, 1953); Frances Perkins, "My Recollections of Florence Kelley," *Social Service Review* XXVIII (May 1954), 13-19; Mary Dewsen, to Ramona Mattson, April 1954, Dewson MSS.

23. Graham Taylor to JA, Feb. 15, 1913, quoting Mary Kenny; Mary Kenny MS autobiography; *Notable American Women* (Cambridge, 1971), II, 655-56.

24. Quotation from Alice Hamilton, *Exploring the Dangerous Trades* (Boston, 1943), 62; see also *Notable American Women* III, 368-69.

25. On this point see Jill Kathryn Conway, "The First Generation of American Women Graduates," (unpublished Ph.D. thesis, Harvard, 1969).

26. JA to Mary Smith, Feb. 3, 4, 1895, n.d (1894); Francis Hackett, *American Rainbow* (New York, 1971), 196.

27. Addams, *My Friend Julia Lathrop*, 52-53.

28. Gertrude Barnum to JA, Aug. 16, 1899.

29. JA to Alice, July 5, 1890, Aug. 12, 1891, Brinton.

30. An interesting, perceptive, though not always accurate or unbiased, account of the family conflicts is Marcet Haldeman-Julius, *Jane Addams*

As I Knew Her (Girard, Kansas, 1936). The author was the daughter of Jane's sister Alice. JA to Alice, May 11, 1894; Brinton; JA to Alice, Dec. 11, 1896, JAM.

31. JA to Alice, n.d. (1894), April 16, 1894, Feb. 4, 1904, Brinton; JA to Mary Smith, Sept. 4, 1899, quotations from JA to Alice, Nov. 15, 1896; Dec. 6, 1891, Nov. 9, 1891, Brinton.

32. Quotations from JA to Alice, Feb. 16, 17, 1896, Brinton; JA to Alice, Sept. 23, 1900, JAM; JA to Mary Smith, Aug. 14, 1899; Jane Addams, "The College Woman and the Family Claim," *Commons* III (Sept. 1898), 3-7.

33. Starr to JA, April 12, 1935.

34. JA to Mary Smith, June 14, 1890.

35. JA to Mary Smith, Feb. 3, 1891; July 4, 1892; JA to Alice, Feb. 23, 1893, Brinton.

36. JA to Mary Smith, Aug. 26, 1893; May 15, 1901, n.d. (1902), April 6, 1902.

37. FK to Mary Smith, Feb. 14, 1899; JA to Mary Smith, n.d. (1894).

38. JA to Mary Smith, Aug. 15, 1895; Jan. 18, 1896; Mary Smith to JA, March 16, 1896.

39. JA to Alice, March 16, 1896, Brinton; Mary Smith to JA n.d. (March 1896); Aylmer Maude, "A Talk with Miss Jane Addams and Leo Tolstoy," *Humane Review* III (Oct. 1902), 203-5.

40. JA to Mary Smith, Jan. 20, Feb. 21, 1897, Feb. 23, n.d. (1897); Aug. 24, Dec. 27, 1899; July 15, 1900.

41. JA to Mary Smith, May 26, 1902; March 22 (1904); n.d. (1904).

42. Written sometime in the 1890's reprinted in Linn, *Jane Addams*, 289-90.

43. Edith Finch, *Carey Thomas of Bryn Mawr* (New York, 1947); Vida Scudder, *On Journey*, 217-28; *Notable American Women* I, 309-13; III, 137-39.

44. Frances E. Willard, *Glimpses of Fifty Years: The Autobiography of An American Woman* (Chicago, 1889), 641-42.

45. William O'Neill, *Everyone was Brave*, 141-42. In August 1963 I had a discussion with Dr. Alice Hamilton, then in her nineties, about the relation of women to other women at Hull House. She denied that there was any open lesbian activity involving Hull House residents, but agreed that the close relationship of the women involved an unconscious sexuality. Because it was unconscious it was unimportant she argued. Then she added with a smile that the very fact that I would bring the subject up was an indication of the separation between my generation and hers.

Notes to Chapter VI

1. See Davis, *Spearheads For Reform*, 3-25.

2. Edward Burchard, to JA, Dec. 10, 1910; Addams, "Hull House, Chi-

cago: An Effort Toward Social Democracy," *Forum* XIV (Oct. 1892), 226-41.

3. Addams, *My Friend Julia Lathrop*, 54-55.
4. *Forum* XIV (Oct. 1892), 226-41; (Nov. 1892), 345-58.
5. Woods to Mark De Wolf Howe, quoted in Eleanor Woods, *Robert A. Woods: Champion of Democracy* (Boston, 1921), 130; Graham Taylor to JA, Dec. 25, 1895.
6. JA to Alice, Feb. 23, 1893, Brinton.
7. For example see Jane Robbins to JA, June 28, 1897; John Gavit to JA, July 11, 1897; Woods to JA, June 5, 1898, July 11, 1898.
8. Jane Addams' remark recalled by Albert Kennedy "The Settlement Heritage," June 4, 1953; MS, NFS; Mary E. Richmond to Florence (Converse?) June 3, 1899, republished in Ralph E. and Muriel W. Pumphrey, *The Heritage of American Social Work* (New York, 1961), 259-68.
9. Quoted in Frederick Whyte, *The Life of W. T. Stead* (New York, 1925) II, 42; Stead to JA, Dec. 29, 1894.
10. William Hard, "Chicago's Five Maiden Aunts," *American Magazine* LXII (Sept. 1906), 489; David Shannon, ed., *Beatrice Webb's American Diary, 1898* (Madison, Wis., 1963), 107-9.
11. Dewey to JA, Jan. 27, 1892, RCA; Jane Dewey, "Biography of John Dewey," Paul Schillip, ed. *Philosophy of John Dewey* (New York, 1939), 29-30; Dewey, "The School as Social Center," *NEA Journal of Proceedings*, 1902, 374-83.
12. On Zueblin, see *National Cyclopedia of American Biography* XIV, 454-55.
13. See Chester McArthur Destler, *Henry Demarest Lloyd and the Empire of Reform* (Philadelphia, 1963), 241ff. Also Starr to Lloyd, Oct. 21, 1891; JA to Lloyd, Dec. 15, 1891, Jan. 2, Dec. 15, 1892, Lloyd MSS.
14. Dorothy Rose Blumberg, *Florence Kelley: The Makings of a Social Pioneer* (New York, 1966), 112-16; Kelley to Ely, Dec. 11, 1890, Ely MSS. On Ely, see Benjamin G. Rader, *The Academic Mind and Reform: the Influence of Richard T. Ely in American Life* (Lexington, 1966).
15. Quoted in Blumberg, *Florence Kelley*, 128.
16. Kelley, "I Go to Work," 273; JA to MS, Aug. 26, 1893.
17. *Hull-House Maps and Papers* (New York, 1895).
18. Kelley to Ely, Nov. 14, 1894, Ely MSS.
19. JA to Ely, Nov. 27, 1894, Ely MSS.
20. JA to Ely, Dec. 4, 1894, Aug. 22, 1895; "Settlers in the City Wilderness," *Atlantic Monthly* LXXCII (Jan. 1896), 119-23.
21. JA to Ely, March 12, 1895, Ely MSS; Albion Small, "Scholarship and Social Agitation," *American Journal of Sociology* I (March, 1896), 567; Addams, "A Belated Industry," *Ibid.* I (March 1896), 536-50. An example of an article done at Hull House is Ernest C. Moore, "The Social Value of the Saloon," *Ibid.* II (July 1897), 1-12.

22. JA to Mary Smith, June 27, 1896; JA to Starr, May 29, 1896, Starr MSS; Addams, *Twenty Years*, 262-64.
23. Henry May, *The End of American Innocence: A Study of The First Years of Our Time, 1912-1917* (New York, 1959), 29; on the influence of Geddes, see Jill Conway, "Stereotypes of Femininity in a Theory of Sexual Evolution," *Victorian Studies* XIV (Sept. 1970), 46-62.
24. JA to Alice, Jan. 7, 1908; Brinton; JA to Ely, Dec. 24, 1904, Ely MSS; *Chicago Record*, May 6, 1895.
25. *Springfield Republican*, July 31, 1892, scrapbook, JAM; Addams, *My Friend Julia Lathrop*, 56.
26. *Religious and Philosophical Journal*, March 29, 1893; *Philadelphia American*, n.d.; *Indianapolis Journal*, Feb. 28, 1896, *Memphis Appeal*, Jan. 10, 1899, May 19, 1895, and Dec. 1895 clippings not identified SCPC.
27. *Harrisburg Independent*, Feb. 27, 1899. On the changing image of women in the 1890's see John Higham, "American Culture in the 1890's *Writing American History: Essays on Modern Scholarship* (Bloomington, Ind., 1970), 82-83, also William Wasserstrom, *Heiress of all the Ages: Sex and Sentiment in the Genteel Tradition* (Minneapolis, 1959), 3-19; Leslie A. Fiedler, *Love and Death in the American Novel* (Cleveland, 1962), 49-50.
28. *Woman and Home*, Philadelphia, n.d. (1895), clipping not identified 1895, scrapbook, JAM. The first reference to her as "Saint Jane" which I have been able to discover is in Julian Ralph, *Our Great West* (New York, 1893) as quoted in Bessie Louise Pierce, *As Others See Chicago: Impressions of Visitors, 1673-1933*, 319. Emily Herdon, "Hull House: A Swept-Out Corner of Chicago," *The Christian Union* XL V (Feb. 20, 1892), 351; F. Herbert Stead, "The Civic Life of Chicago," *Review of Reviews* VIII (Aug. 1893), 182.
29. Agnes L. Hill to JA, Oct. 14, 1897; Emma Graves to JA, March 22, 1896.
30. See Leonard Covello, *The Social Background of the Italo-American School Child* (Leiden, 1967), 103-45. Quotation from Rudolph J. Vecoli, "Prelates and Peasants: Italian Immigrants and the Catholic Church," *Journal of Social History* III (Spring 1969), 226.
31. Linn, *Jane Addams*, 139.
32. Addams, *Twenty Years*, 152; Addams, *The Excellent Becomes the Permanent* (New York, 1932), 152; See John M. Mecklin, *The Passing of the Saint: A Study of a Cultural Type* (Chicago, 1941), for a discussion of replacement of saints in America by people not connected with institutionalized Christianity.
33. JA to Helen Culver, March 7, 1890; Culver to JA n.d., JAM.
34. Starr to Mary Blaisdell, May 18, 1890, Starr MSS.
35. JA to William Harper, Dec. 1895, Harper MSS, JA to MS March 3, 1894.
36. JA notebook, JAM.

37. JA to Anita Blaine, Nov. 3, 1904, Blaine MSS; JA to MS, Jan. 15, 1895. Paul Kellogg, "Twice Twenty Years at Hull House," *Survey* LXI (June 15, 1930), 265-67; Hull House Association Minutes, 1895-1936, JAM.

Notes to Chapter VII

1. Floyd Dell, *Women As World Builders* (Chicago, 1913), 32-33, 35.
2. JA to Lloyd, Dec. 22, 1895, Lloyd MSS.
3. Addams, "Domestic Service and The Family Claim," *World Congress of Representative Women* (Chicago, 1894), 630.
4. Addams, "Trade Unions and Public Duty," *American Journal of Sociology* IV (Jan. 1899), 444-62.
5. This and the following paragraphs are drawn from Stanley Buder, *Pullman: An Experiment in Industrial Order and Community Planning, 1880-1930* (New York, 1967) and Almont Lindsey, *The Pullman Strike* (Chicago, 1942).
6. Kelley to Lloyd, July 18, Aug. 1, 1894, Lloyd MSS.
7. Her essay was finally published as "A Modern Lear," *Survey* XXIX (Nov. 2, 1912), 131-37. Dewey to JA, Jan. 19, 1896; Lloyd to JA, Feb. 23, 1896; H. E. Scudder to Mrs. Wilmarth, April 18, 1896.
8. "Defense of Unions: Miss Addams Speaks in Behalf of Walking Delegate," *Chicago Post*, Dec. 1, 1900; Davis, *Spearheads*, 119.
9. Jesse Binford told me this story in the summer of 1963. Winifred Wise, *Jane Addams of Hull House* (New York, 1935), 171, tells a similar story. It may be apocryphal but it is in character.
10. Sara Hart, *The Pleasure is Mine: An Autobiography* (Chicago, 1947), 88, 146-47; Matthew Josephson, *Sidney Hillman, Statesman of American Labor* (New York, 1952), 47-58; JA to MS, Nov. 8, 28; Dec. 1, 1910.
11. Starr to Lloyd, April 8, 21, 1896; JA to Lloyd, March 25, 1896, Lloyd MSS.
12. Eleanor Grace Clark, "Ellen Gates Starr, O.S.B.," *Commonweal* XXXI (March 15, 1940) 446-47, quoting a contemporary newspaper account.
13. A. C. Bartlett, to JA, Dec. 5, 1900; *Chicago Chronicle*, April 12, 1904; Oct. 7, 1903; Wallace L. DeWolf to JA, July 17, 1916.
14. Robins to Medill McCormick, Sept. 5, 1914; Louise Wade, *Graham Taylor, Pioneer for Social Justice, 1851-1938* (Chicago, 1964), 134; Allen F. Davis, "Raymond Robins: The Settlement Worker as Municipal Reformer," *Social Service Review* XXXIII (June 1959), 131-41.
15. *Central Christian Advocate*, Sept. 18, 1901; *Burlington* (Iowa) *Gazette*, Sept. 10, 1901.
16. *Chicago Inter-Ocean*, March 4, 1908; *Chicago Evening Post*, March 5, 1906; Graham Taylor, *Pioneering on Social Frontiers*, 325-26; Addams, "The Chicago Settlements and Social Unrest, *Charities and the Commons* XX (May 2, 1908), 155-66.

17. *Chicago Chronicle*, Sept. 16, 1903; A. D. Traveller to Dr. William F. King, Jan. 25, 1904, copy JAM.
18. *New York Call*, April 25, 1912.
19. Margaret Robins to JA, Feb. 10, 1907; Rauschenbush to JA, Feb. 24, 1910, JAM.
20. *National Single Taxer*, Oct. 1898.
21. JA to Mary Smith, n.d. (1904).
22. See Davis, *Spearheads for Reform*, 103-47; 208-13.
23. *Chicago Evening Post*, July 23, 1895; *Chicago Times-Herald*, July 31, 1895; *Topeka Journal*, May 28, 1895; Addams, *Twenty Years*, 281-87.
24. Ray Standard Baker, "Hull House and the Ward Boss," *Outlook* LVIII (March 28, 1898), 769-70. I have written about Powers in another connection and much of the following is drawn from that account. Davis, *Spearheads*, 151-62.
25. JA to Lloyd, Dec. 22, 1895, Lloyd MSS.
26. Addams, "Ethical Survivals in Municipal Corruption," *International Journal of Ethics* VIII (April 1898), 372-91.
27. Woods to JA, April 28, 1898; Ely to JA, Feb. 3, 1898; Richmond to JA, May 11, 1898.
28. *Chicago Tribune*, Jan. 24, March 7, 1898; *Hartford Times*, March 8, 1898.
29. A Voter to JA, Jan. 17, 1898.
30. JA to MS, March 26, 28, 1898; Baker, "Hull House and the Ward Boss," *Outlook* LVIII (March 28, 1898), 769-71. *Chicago Tribune*, April 6, 1898.
31. Kelley, "Hull House," *New England Magazine* XVIII (June 1898), 566. A recent article suggests that the reformers could have defeated Powers if they had cooperated effectively with the Italian community, Humbert S. Nelli, "John Powers and the Italians: Politics in A Chicago Ward, 1896-1921," *Journal of American History* LVII (June 1970), 67-84.
32. JA to Mary Smith, May 19, 1902; JA Itinerary, Feb. 1899; JA to Alice, March 1, 1899, Brinton; Louise de Koven Bowen, *Open Windows: Stories of People and Places* (Chicago 1936), 206-7.
33. JA to Mary Smith, June 27, 1900; April 6, 1902.
34. Ely to JA, Jan. 1, 1901; Ely to Harper and Brothers, Sept. 25, 1899, Ely MSS. He later moved his series to Macmillan.
35. Quotations from *Democracy and Social Ethics* (New York, 1902), 270, 276. There is a new edition edited with introduction by Anne Frior Scott, published by Harvard University Press, 1964.
36. *International Socialist Review* II (June 1902), 885-87; *Charities* VIII (May 24, 1902), 517-20; William James to JA, Sept. 17, 1902; Edwin Seligman to JA, April 26, 1902. O. W. Holmes to Ely, June 18, 1906; Ely MSS; Elizabeth Stebbins to JA, July 18, 1909.
37. Addams, "Social Education of the Industrial Democracy," *Commons* V (June 30, 1900), 17-20.

38. *Utica Dispatch*, Aug. 21, 1899; *Los Angeles Express*, May 5, 1902; Mrs. William English Walling to JA, June 8, 1909; Addams, "Respect for the Law," *Independent* LIII (Jan. 1901), 20.
39. Edith Abbott, "Grace Abbott and Hull House, 1908-1921," *Social Service Review* XXIV (Sept. 1950), 374-94.
40. Addams, *Democracy and Social Ethics*, 199; "Social Education of the Industrial Democracy," *Commons* V (June 30, 1900), 20.
41. *Chronicle*, quoted in Levine, *Jane Addams*, 82; *Tribune*, Oct. 19, 1906.
42. Margaret Haley MS autobiography. The controversy can be followed in the *Board of Education Proceedings*, 1905-08. Two different perspectives are provided by Louis Post, "Living a Long Life Over Again," MS Autobiography, Post MSS, and Mary Dreier, *Margaret Dreier Robins: Her Life, Letters and Work* (New York, 1950), 28, 33. A brief and generally accurate account can be found in Levine, *Jane Addams*, 80-86. Also see Robert L. Reed, "The Professionalization of Public School Teachers, *The Chicago Experience 1895-1920*" (Ph.D. thesis, Northwestern, 1968).
43. Quoted in Dreier, *Margaret Dreier Robins*, 31.
44. *Chicago Record-Herald*, May 23, 1907.
45. Mary Dreier to Raymond Robins, May 27, 1907, Robins MSS; Florence Kelley to Lillian Wald, Sept. 11, 1907, Wald MSS, Columbia.
46. Haley, MS autobiography; Harry Clay comment quoted by Margaret Carol Dunn, "Jane Addams as a Political Leader" (Unpublished MA thesis, University of Chicago, 1926), 79.

Notes to Chapter VIII

1. Quoted in Staughton Lynd, editor, *Nonviolence in America: A Documentary History* (Indianapolis, 1966), Introduction, xxxii.
2. JA to Mary Smith, Sept. 4, 1895.
3. Addams, *Twenty Years*, 267-68.
4. JA to Gertrude Barnum, July 25, 1896, Starr MSS; Aylmer Maude, "A Talk With Miss Jane Addams and Leo Tolstoy," *Humane Review* III (Oct. 1902), 203-18.
5. JA to Mrs. Barnett, July 31, 1896, JAM; "Jane Addams at Home," *Chicago Record Herald*, Sept. 23, 1896.
6. Quoted in Maude, "A Talk With Miss Jane Addams and Leo Tolstoy," 216-17, also Maude, *The Life of Tolstoy*, II (N.Y. 1910), 521-25; JA to Graham Taylor, Dec. 24, 1910, *Twenty Years*, 268.
7. George Herron to JA, Nov. 21, 1897.
8. *New York Evening Post*, Dec. 21, 1898; the published version of her speech, "A Function of the Social Settlement," *Annals* XII (May 1899), 33-55, is slightly different.
9. James' notes for Philosophy 4, 1888-89, quoted in Ralph Barton Perry,

The Thought and Character of William James (Cambridge, 1935), II, 265.

10. JA to Mary Smith, Oct. 6, 1898.
11. On anti-imperialists, see Robert L. Beisner, *Twelve Against Empire: The Anti-Imperialists, 1898-1900* (N.Y. 1968).
12. Fragment of letter, JA to Mary Smith, Oct. 18, 1899; Frederick Bancroft, ed., *The Papers of Carl Schurz*, VI, 88, 119-20.
13. "What Peace Means," *Unity* XLIII (May 4, 1899), 178.
14. "Commercialism Disguised as Patriotism and Duty," *St. Louis Post Dispatch*, Feb. 18, 1900; this is the first version of the incident with the spade which she tells in a slightly different way in *Twenty Years at Hull House*, 444-45.
15. *Chicago Times Herald*, Jan. 28, 1900; *Inter-Ocean*, May 3, 1903.
16. JA to Mary Smith, Oct. 5, n.d. (1904); Addams "The Interest of Labor in International Peace," *Universal Peace Congress, Official Report* XIII (New York, 1905), 145-47; James, untitled address, *Ibid.*, 266-69.
17. James' essay is republished in Lynd, ed. *Nonviolence in America*, 135-50. I have profited from reading Sandra R. Herman, *Eleven Against War: Studies in American Internationlist Thought*, 1898-1921 (Stanford, 1969), which contains a perceptive essay on Jane Addams.
18. JA to Ely, Nov. 27, 1902; May 2, 1903; Nov. 9, Dec. 24, 1904; Aug. 6, Nov. 20, 1905; Sept. 5, Oct. 12, 13, 17, 1906; Ely to JA, April 19, Nov. 11, 1905, Richard T. Ely MSS.
19. Quotations are from *Newer Ideals of Peace* (New York, 1907).
20. James to JA, Feb. 12, 1907.
21. A. H. Nelson to JA, Jan. 11, 1907; fragment of review, Kelley to JA, Jan. 20, 1907; *Chicago Inter-Ocean*, Feb. 9, 1907.
22. Theodore Roosevelt to Florence Lockwood La Farge, Feb. 13, 1908, in Elting Morrison, ed., *Letters of Theodore Roosevelt* (Cambridge, 1952), VI, 942-43; Roosevelt, "Tolstoy," *Outlook* (May 15, 1909), 103-5; *Chicago Evening Post*, May 21, 1909.
23. Clipping, n.d., *North American Review; Chicago Post*, Feb. 22, 1907; Elia W. Peattie, "Miss Jane Addams' *Newer Ideals of Peace*, A Remarkable Book," *Chicago Tribune*, March 9, 1907.
24. For the Psychopathic Institute and the Juvenile Court, see Joseph M. Hawes, *Children in Urban Society: Juvenile Delinquency in Nineteenth Century America* (New York, 1971).
25. On Hall's ideas, see Lawrence A. Cremin, *The Transformation of the School: Progressivism in American Education, 1876-1957* (New York, 1961), 101-4; and Nathan G. Hale, Jr., *Freud and the Americans*, 100-109.
26. Edward Marsh to JA, Feb. 23, 1909.
27. Marsh to JA, Feb. 15, 23, 1909; JA to Marsh, Feb. 25, 1909.
28. JA to Julia Lathrop, n.d. 1909.
29. Vida Scudder to JA, Nov. 13, 1909.
30. *American Journal of Sociology* XV (Jan. 1910), 553. He said about the

same thing in a letter to Jane Addams, but added that it was "hard not to cry at certain pages." William James to JA, Dec. 13, 1909; Walter Rauschenbush to JA, Feb. 22, 1915.

Notes to Chapter IX

1. Addams, *Twenty Years at Hull House* (New York, 1910), viii.
2. Erik H. Erikson, *Gandhi's Truth: On the Origins of Militant Non-Violence* (New York, 1969), 57.
3. William C. Spengemann and L. R. Lundquist, "Autobiography and the American Myth," *American Quarterly* XVII (Fall 1965), 501-19. Other useful studies of autobiographies are: Roy Pascal, *Design and Truth in Autobiography* (London, 1960); Anna R. Burr, *The Autobiography*, A *Critical and Comparative Study* (Boston, 1909); Robert F. Sayre, *The Examined Self: Benjamin Franklin, Henry Adams, Henry James* (Princeton, 1964).
4. "Jane Addams' Own Story of Her Work; Fifteen Years at Hull House," *Ladies Home Journal* XXIII (March 1906), 13-14; "Jane Addams' Own Story of Her Work: the First Five Years at Hull House," *Ibid.* (April 1906), 11-12; "Jane Addams' Own Story of Her Work: How the Work at Hull House has Grown," *Ibid.* (May 1906), 11-12.
5. Elia M. Peattie, "Women of the Hour: No. 1. Jane Addams," *Harpers Bazar* XXXVIII (Oct. 1904), 1003-08.
6. On the problem of why people write their autobiographies, in addition to the items in footnote 3, see Bruce Mazlish, "Clio on the Couch: Prolegomena to Psycho-History," *Encounter* XXXI (Sept. 1968), 46-54.
7. Commager "Foreword," *Twenty Years at Hull House*, Signet Classic edition (New York, 1961), vii-xvi.
8. Marcet Haldeman-Julius, *Jane Addams As I Knew Her* (Girard, Kan., 1936) 10-11.
9. William Wasserstrom, *Heiress of All the Ages*, 70-74. Some of the emphasis on her father may have been stylistic for there is not the same emphasis in the early version published in the *Ladies Home Journal*.
10. Orrin E. Klapp, *Heroes, Villains and Fools: The Changing American Character* (Englewood Cliffs, N.J., 1962), 31; Joseph Campbell, *The Hero with a Thousand Faces* (N.Y., 1949, 325-26), writes: "The folk tales commonly support or supplant this theme of exile with that of the despised one, or the handicapped, the abused youngest son or daughter, the orphan, stepchild, ugly duckling, or squire of low degree." Many popular accounts of Jane Addams' life make her an orphan and, of course, a stepchild.
11. *Twenty Years*, 4-5.
12. Letter from A. C. Berry to *Kansas City Star*, 1935, clipping SCPC, tells of being a guest in the Addams home in the '70s and of hearing Jane's

father tell a version of the story. Clara Doty Bates, "Our Lady of the House," *Chicago Inter-Ocean*, March 20, 1892, scrapbook JAM. For a discussion of the impact of the story on writing about Jane Addams, see Christopher Lasch, *New Radicalism in America*, 29-31.

13. Gerda Lerner, *The Grimké Sisters of South Carolina* (Boston, 1967), 19.

14. Campbell, *Hero*, 319-29, William J. Browne, M.D. (a psychiatrist) makes a great deal of these early dreams in "Jane Addams and the Rescue Fantasy," *Psychiatric Communications* (Jan. 1971), 13-18.

15. Charles Shinn to JA, Feb. 15, 1911; Ellen Frost to JA, Dec. 31, 1910.

16. *Twenty Years*, 23-27; of Jane Addams, "A Village Decoration Day," JAM; "Most American Autobiography from Taylor through Franklin to Henry Adams has aimed at some form of edification. At least it has formed an argument, a recommendation, a special plea of some sort. Indeed ours has been a notably sermon-ridden literature from the beginning." Daniel B. Shea, Jr., *Spiritual Autobiography in Early America* (Princeton, 1968), 95.

17. *Twenty Years*, 23-42. On the Importance of the Lincoln ideal or myth see Ray Ginger, *Altgeld's America: The Lincoln Ideal versus Changing Realities* (New York, 1958); Dixon Wector, *The Hero in America* (New York, 1941), 222-72.

18. *Boston American*, Feb. 15, 1911.

19. *Twenty Years*, 54-57.

20. JA to John Addams, May 8, 1881, JAM.

21. Report of the contest in *Rockford Seminary Magazine* IX (June, 1881), 173-74; and George R. Page, "College Career of William Jennings Bryan," *Mississippi Valley Historical Review* XV (Sept. 1928), 177-82, confirms the account in the 1881 letter and indicates that Bryan did not take part. Years later a man who claimed to have been at the contest wrote to Jane Addams and even recalled how she and Bryan looked. Henry Read to JA, April 9, 1917.

22. *Twenty Years*, 85-86.

23. Spengemann and Lundquist, "Autobiography and the American Myth," 507. "This experience creates the intensified self-consciousness which prompts them to write autobiography in the first place, and it usually appears in the narrative itself as a 'calling.'" Not all autobiographies, of course, contain conversion experiences; Henry Adams, because he assumed that it was his right by birth to be a symbolic figure has no need for conversion to a special calling. The experience is not obvious in Benjamin Franklin though he made his break with the past, and took up his secular calling when he moved from Boston to Philadelphia.

24. Campbell, *Hero*, 30.

25. Emma Goldman, *Living My Life* (New York, 1931), 10.

26. Mrs. H. C. Mowry to JA, Feb. 24, 1906; Emma Engle to JA, Feb. 24, 1906; Jesse Gordon to JA, Feb. 28, 1906; Cora Patterson to JA, March 23, 1906, Mrs. M. to JA, March 20, 1906.

27. W. H. Page to JA, Nov. 8, 1905, April 6, 1906; JA to Page, April 10, 1906; *Current Literature*, XL (April 1906), 377-79.

28. *Twenty Years*, 162, 246-47.

29. *Nation* XCI (Dec. 29, 1910), 634-35; John Haynes Holmes, "Routine and Ideals," *Survey* XXV (Feb. 25, 1911), 883.

30. Ralph Gabriel, *The Course of American Democratic Thought* (New York, 1940); Charles Sanford, *Quest for Paradise: Europe and the American Moral Imagination* (Urbana, 1961).

31. *Twenty Years*, 42, 38-39, 79, 257-58.

32. The sales figures are from royalty statements, JA MSS, SCPC.

33. *Baltimore Sun*, Jan. 21, 1911; *Portland Evening Telegram*, Dec. 10, 1910; *Review* IV (April 1911), 153-54; Anna Lindermann to JA, April 24, 1914.

34. Julia Lathrop to JA, Jan. 11, 1911; R. T. Ely to JA, Dec. 16, 1910; Eleanor Woods to JA, March 7, 1911; JA to Mary Smith, n.d.; Taylor, "Twenty Years of Industrial Democracy," *Survey* XXV (Dec. 3, 1910), 377-79. Ella Flagg Young to JA, Dec. 10, 1910.

Notes to Chapter X

1. Robert E. Riegel, "Changing American Attiudes Toward Prostitution," *Journal of the History of Ideas* XXIX (July-Sept. 1968), 437-52; Roy Lubove, "The Progressive and the Prostitute," *The Historian* XXIV (May 1962), 308-30. Egel Feldman, "Prostitution, the Alien Woman and the Progressive Imagination, 1910-1915," *American Quarterly* XIX (Summer 1967), 192-206.

2. Alice Hamilton to JA, Aug. 14, 1911; Norah Hamilton to JA, Aug. 14, 1911.

3. S. S. McClure to JA, Aug. 15, Sept. 1, 1911; JA to McClure, Aug. 21, 1911; Edward Marsh to JA, Aug. 17, 1911.

4. Riegel, "Changing American Attitudes."

5. Mrs. Joseph H. Willets to JA, July 11, 17, 1912.

6. Charles Sheldon to JA, Dec. 8, 1911; Mary Goldman to JA, July 14, 1912; Dr. J. A. Corn to JA, Dec. 19, 1911; John Doe to JA, Nov. 2, 1911.

7. Frederic T. Bowers to JA, Aug. 6, 1912; H. H. Herbst, to JA, Jan. 20, 1912.

8. Alice Hamilton, *Exploring the Dangerous Trades*, 91-93.

9. Walter Lippmann, *A Preface to Politics* (New York, 1914), 78-79, 135.

10. Rhoda Brooks to JA, Dec. 22, 1911; Robert Hewitt to JA, Nov. 15, 1911; Mary Jones to JA, Nov. 10, 1911.

11. *Knoxville Sentinel*, May 11, 1912; Charlotte Rowett Lansey to JA, Jan. 27, 1912.

12. Allen F. Davis, "The Social Workers and the Progressive Party, 1912-1916," *American Historical Review* LXIX (April 1964), 671-88.

13. Paul Kellogg, "The Industrial Platform of the New Party *Survey* XXVIII (Aug. 24, 1912), 668-70; Owen Lovejoy, "Standards of Living and Labor," *Proceedings of the National Conference of Charities and Correction* (Fort Wayne, Ind., 1912), 376.

14. Kellogg to Robins, July 10, 1912, Robins MSS; Elizabeth Cady Stanton, et al., editors, *History of Woman Suffrage* (New York, 1881-1922), V, 705.

15. Kellogg to Addams, Feb. 9, 1929, Survey Files, also quoted in Jane Addams, *The Second Twenty Years at Hull House,* (New York, 1930), 27.

16. Mary Dreier to Lillian Wald, n.d. Wald MSS; "Jane Addams Tells Why," *New York Evening Post,* Aug. 8, 1912.

17. Addams, "My Experiences as a Progressive Delegate," *McClure's* XL (Nov., 1912), 13; JA to Lillian Wald, Aug. 15, 1912, Wald MSS.

18. Addams, "The Working Woman's Need of the Ballot," *Western Womanhood,* Nov. 1898, also *Woman's Journal,* Nov. 20, 1897.

19. Addams, "Why Women Should Vote," *Ladies Home Journal* XXVII (Jan. 1910), republished in Jane Addams, *A Centennial Reader* (New York, 1960), 104-07. She made similar statements in many other articles and in her books, especially *Newer Ideals of Peace.* This emphasis on the special feminine intuition was present even in her college themes, but for the influence of Patrick Geddes see Jill Conway, "Stereotypes of Femininity in A Theory of Sexual Evolution," *Victorian Studies* XIV (Sept. 1970), 47-62.

20. *Chicago Record-Herald,* April 1, 1906; *Survey,* Oct. 23, 1915, 85; Aileen S. Kraditor, *The Ideas of the Woman Suffrage Movement, 1890-1920* (New York, 1965), 142-43.

21. Daniel Levine, *Jane Addams and the Liberal Tradition,* 183-85.

22. Telegram, TR to JA, Aug. 9, 1912; There is a story that Jane Addams convinced Roosevelt to support votes for women on the way to his speech in Chicago. Edith Abbott, "Grace Abbott and Hull House, 1908-1921," *Social Service Review* XXIV (Dec. 1950), 502.

23. *New York Times,* Aug. 8, 1912.

24. New York Globe, Aug. 26, 1912; *Boston Journal,* Aug. 20, 1912; *Philadelphia North American,* Aug. 14, 1912.

25. Roosevelt to JA (telegram), Aug. 8, 1912; Mary McDowell to JA, Aug. 16, 1912; Katharine Coman to JA, Aug. 8, 1912; Ellen Gay to JA, Aug. 18, 1912; Lydia Shaneck to JA, Aug. 10, 1912.

26. JA to Sophonisba P. Breckinridge, July 19, Sept. 5, 1912; Breckinridge MSS; "The Progressive Party and the Negro," *Crisis* V (Nov. 1912), 12-14; "My Experiences As a Progressive Delegate," *McClure's Magazine* LXXV (Nov. 1912), 12-14; "The Progressive Dilemma: The New Party," *American Magazine* LXXV (Nov. 1912), 12-14; "Pragmatism in Politics," *Survey* XXIX (Oct. 5, 1912), 12.

27. Chairman of the Speakers Bureau to JA, Oct. 2, 1912; S. P. Breckinridge to Mrs. Aleck Twedie, Oct. 8, 1912, Breckinridge MSS; Anna Howard Shaw, "Campaigning for Suffrage in the West," *The Ameri-*

can (Trenton, N.J.), clipping, n.d. "Jane Addams Chorus Organized," *Los Angeles Tribune*, Aug. 29, 1912; Mary Moore Flint, to JA, Aug. 23, 1913.

28. Paul Kellogg to JA, Oct. 10, 1912; Henry Morgenthau to Lillian Wald, Aug. 8, 1912; Wald to Morgenthau, Aug. 12, 1912; Wald MSS. *Chicago Tribune*, Aug. 15, 1912; *N.Y. Sun*, Aug. 18, 1912; *Chicago Evening Post*, Aug. 15, 1912.

29. Devine, "Politics and Social Work" *Survey* XXIX (Oct. 5, 1912), 9; Devine to Emily G. Balch, enclosed in Devine to Addams, Sept. 2, 1912; Taylor to John P. Gavit, Oct. 16, 1916; Taylor MSS; "The Lamb Tags on to the Lion," *New York Call*, Aug. 11, 1912.

30. Unidentified to JA, Aug. 10, 1912; Herman Green to JA, Aug. 10, 1912; Rachel Steer to JA, Aug. 18, 1912; Emma Gates, Aug. 27, 1912.

31. Charles Beals to JA, Oct. 2, 1912; Erving Winslow to JA, Aug. 7, 1912. Jenkin L. Jones to JA, Oct. 10, 1912; "Jane Addams is Criticized by Baroness," *Illinois Journal*, Aug. 14, 1912.

32. Dr. N. F. Mossell to JA, Aug. 8, 1912; George Cook to JA, Aug. 17, 1912; "One of them," to JA, Aug. 9, 1912.

33. John Kingsbury to JA, Jan. 17, 1913; Davis, "Social Workers and the Progressive Party," 685-86.

34. Kingsbury to JA, Dec. 23, 1912, Jan. 17, 1913; William Draper Lewis to JA, Feb. 17, 1914; JA to Robins, n.d., Robins MSS; TR to JA, Feb. 4, 1913.

Notes to Chapter XI

1. Levine, *Jane Addams*, 186.

2. The best bibliography of her work, though not definitive, is in Farrell, *Beloved Lady*, 221-41.

3. For a discussion of the importance of the magazine revolution see Theodore P. Greene, *American Heroes: The Changing Models of Success in American Magazines* (New York, 1970); Ernest May uses the concept of the "opinion leader" in *American Imperialism: A Speculative Essay* (New York, 1968).

4. *Los Angeles Tribune*, Jan. 21, 1912; *Jersey City Journal*, Aug. 14, 1908, *Atlanta Constitution*, May 23, 1908.

5. Unidentified clipping, 1906; *Ladies Home Journal* XXV (March 1908), *New York World*, Feb. 28, 1912; *New York Times*, Jan. 10, 1913; "The Most Useful Americans," *Independent* LXXIV (May 1913) 956-63.

6. See for example, "Portrait of a Woman," *Colliers Weekly*, April 1909.

7. White quote is from *Unity* CXV (July 15, 1935), 203. On the American traits of disinterested virtue and American heroes see Fred Somkin, *Unquiet Eagle: Memory and Desire in the Idea of American Freedom, 1815-1860* (Ithaca, 1967), 200ff; Greene, *American Heroes*, 3-15.

8. *St. Louis Republic*, May 21, 1910; *Jersey City Journal*, Aug. 22, 1908; *New York Star*, April 6, 1912.

9. Elia W. Peattie, "Woman of the Hour," *Harper's Bazar* XXXVIII (Oct. 1904), 1004; *San Francisco Chronicle*, Aug. 14, 1909; *Chicago Evening Post*, Aug. 14, 1909; "Jane Addams at Fifty," unidentified clipping; *Omaha Gazette*, Aug. 14, 1909; *Holyoke Nautilus*, Aug. 11, 1910; *St. Louis Post Dispatch*, May 22, 1910; *St. Louis Globe Democrat*, May 22, 1910. *Chicago Evening Post*, Aug. 14, 1909. "President Jane Addams," unidentified clipping. I have not done a formal content analysis on the huge mass of newspaper clippings in the Jane Addams' collection at Swarthmore to determine "public" attitudes toward Jane Addams, but I have studied thousands of individual clippings, and arranged them according to the attributes credited to her. Those I have quoted are representative.

10. "People Who Interest Us: Jane Addams, the First Woman to Receive an Honorary Degree from Yale," *Craftsman* XVIII (Aug. 1910), 574: William Hard, "Chicago's Five Maiden Aunts," *American Magazine* LXII (Sept. 1906), 489. On the development of community symbols and their importance see, Murray Edelman, *The Symbolic Uses of Politics* (Urbana, Ill., 1964), 73-113.

11. Philip Davis, *And Crown Thy Good* (New York, 1952), 86-88; Francis Hackett, "As an Alien Feels," *New Republic* III (July 24, 1915), 303-6.

12. *Leslie's Weekly*, Dec. 9, 1909; Leslie A. Fiedler, *Love and Death in the American Novel*, 79-80, 330; William Wasserstrom, *Heiress of All the Ages*, 3; Alfred Kazin, "Heroines," *New York Review*, Feb. 11, 1971, 28-34.

13. *Kansas City Gazette*, May 2, 1912; *N.Y. Journal*, March 12, 1912; *Pearsons*, Oct. 1911; Mrs. Ethelbert Stewart to JA, Dec. 9, 1909.

14. *Springfield Caxton*, Aug. 1910; *Philadelphia Record*, March 4, 1912; unidentified clipping, 1910. On self-sacrifice of heroes see Orrin E. Klapp, *Heroes, Villains and Fools: The Changing American Character* (Englewood Cliffs, N.J., 1962).

15. *Pittsburgh Gazette Times*, June 16, 1909; unidentified newspaper from Memphis, Feb. 28, 1911; *Milwaukee Leader*, Jan. 17, 1912.

16. Margaret Deland, "The Change in the Feminine Ideal," *Atlantic Monthly* CV (March 1910), 291-302; Caroline Ticknor, "The Steel-Engraving Lady and the Gibson Girl," *Atlantic Monthly* LXXXVIII (July 1901), 105-8; Wasserstrom, *Heiress of All the Ages*, 3-19. Beatrice K. Hofstadter, "Popular Culture and the Romantic Heroine," *American Scholar* XXX (Winter 1960-61), 98-116.

17. Simone de Beauvoir, *The Second Sex* (New York, 1953), 41; Harvey Cox, *The Secular City* (New York, 1965), 192-216; Jill Conway, "Jane Addams: An American Heroine"; Robert Jay Lifton, *The Woman in America* (Boston, 1965), 247-66. My analysis owes much to this essay and to Conway's dissertation (Harvard, 1969), though I often differ from her interpretation.

18. Rebecca Shelley to Franciska Schwimmer, Oct. 27, 1956, Shelley MSS, University of Michigan (Barbara Kraft kindly loaned me a copy of this letter).
19. Paul Kellogg to JA, July 23, 1929; Edward Bok to JA, Jan. 22, 1913. See Jill Conway, "Women Reformers and American Culture, 1870-1930," *Journal of Social History* V (Winter 1971-72), 164-82.
20. Addams, *The Excellent Becomes the Permanent*, 17, 29.
21. "Unexpected Reactions of a Traveler in Egypt," *Atlantic Monthly* CXIII (Feb. 1914), 178-86, reprinted in revised form in *The Long Road of Women's Memory* (New York, 1916), and *The Excellent Becomes the Permanent*.
22. Addams, "The Devil Baby at Hull House," *Atlantic Monthly* CXVIII (Oct. 1916), 441-50. An earlier, shorter version appeared in *American Journal of Sociology*, XX (July 1914), 117-18, and it was republished in the *Long Road of Women's Memory* and *The Second Twenty Years at Hull House*.
23. Arnold quotation from John Holloway, *The Victorian Sage: Studies in Argument* (London, 1953), 15. Jane Addams would certainly fit his definition of a sage "all of them sought (among other things) to express notions about the world, man's situation in it and how he should live. Their work reflects an outlook on life, an outlook which for most or perhaps all of them was partly philosophical and partly moral." The last quotation is from Andrew Kopkind review of Ralph de Toledano, "R. F. K.: The Man Who Would be President," *New York Review* VIII (June 1, 1967), 3.

Notes to Chapter XII

1. Wald statement quoted in Robert L. Duffus, *Lillian Wald: Neighbor and Crusader* (New York, 1938), 148; Addams interview *New York Evening Post*, Sept. 30, 1914.
2. Kellogg to JA, Sept. 11, 15, 1914; John Gavit to Kellogg, Oct. 23, 1914; minutes of meeting Sept. 29, 1914, Balch MSS; Jane Addams foreword to "War and Social Reconstruction," *Survey* XXXIII (March 6, 1915), 603; Jane Addams *et al.*, "Toward the Peace that Shall Last," *Survey* XXXIII (March 6, 1915), unpaged.
3. Donald Johnson, *The Challenge to American Freedoms: World War I and the Rise of American Civil Liberties* (Lexington, 1963), 1-9ff. Blanche Wiesen Cook, "Woodrow Wilson and the Anti-Militarists" (unpublished Ph.D. thesis, Johns Hopkins, 1970); David S. Patterson, "Woodrow Wilson and the Mediation Movement, 1914-17" *Historian* XXXIII (Aug. 1971), 535-56.
4. On Rosika Schwimmer, see the sketch in *Notable American Women* III, 246-49. Also see Marie Louise Degen, *The History of the Woman's Peace Party* (Baltimore, 1939). Edith Wynner, who is preparing a biog-

raphy of Rosika Schwimmer, kindly allowed me to consult her notes on the Schwimmer-Lloyd Collection in the New York Public Library relating especially to the relationship between Schwimmer and Addams.

5. On Pethick-Lawrence, see Degen, *The History of the Woman's Peace Party*, 33ff, and her autobiography, *My Part in Changing the World* (London, 1938).

6. JA to Catt, Dec. 21, 1914, WPP, Box 1; JA draft of form letter, Dec. 28, 1914.

7. Degen, *History of Woman's Peace Party*, 52-54; Addams to Mead, Dec. 28, 1914; Jan. 3, 1915; WPP, Box 1. Blanche Wiesen Cook "The Woman's Peace Party: Collaboration and Non-Cooperation in World War I," *Peace And Change*, I (Fall, 1972), 36-42.

8. Quoted in Degen, *History*, 40-41.

9. JA to Lillian Wald, March 6, April 6, 1915; Mary Smith to Wald, March 31, 1915; Wald MSS, JA to Emily Balch, March 26, 1915 Balch MSS; JA to David Starr Jordan, Apqril 9, 1915; Jordan MSS.

10. Quoted in Linn, *Jane Addams*, 301.

11. Balch Journal, Balch MSS; Alice Post's remark quoted in Mercedes Randall, *Improper Bostonian: Emily Greene Balch* (New York, 1964), 145-46.

12. Mary Chamberlain, "The Women at The Hague," *Survey* XXIX (June, 1915), 219.

13. Quoted in Randall, *Improper Bostonian*, 156.

14. *International Congress of Women at The Hague, 28th April, 1st May, 1915, Report* (Amsterdam, 1915).

15. Quoted in Randall, *Improper Bostonian*, 156-57.

16. Alice Hamilton to Mary Smith, May 5, 1915.

17. Alice Hamilton to Louise Bowen, May 16, 1915; JA to Mary Smith, May 9, 1915.

18. Quotation from Edward Marshall interview with Jane Addams, 1915, Kellogg MSS. There are many sources for the story of the trip to the capitals of Europe. See especially Jane Addams, Emily Balch, and Alice Hamilton, *Women at The Hague* (New York, 1915); Degen, *Woman's Peace Party*, 92-126; Alice Hamilton, "At the War Capitals," *Survey* XXXIV (Aug. 7, 1915), 417-22; Alice Hamilton to her family, May 15, May 30, 1915; Hamilton MSS.

19. JA to Starr, June 19, 1915; *New York Times*, June 24, 1915. Addams, Balch, Hamilton, *Women at The Hague*, 30.

20. Report of Emily Balch to JA, July 3, 1915; memorandum by R. Schwimmer and Chrystal Macmillan, Aug. 2, 1915.

21. *Philadelphia Press*, April 10, 1915; *Charlotte (N.C.) Observer*, April 29, 1915; *New York Evening Mail*, June 19, 1915.

22. *Chicago Evening Journal*, April 16, 1915; *Portsmouth (Ohio) Star*, July 21, 1915; Eric Goldman, *Rendezvous With Destiny* (New York, 1952), 245.

23. *New York Evening Mail*, July 2, 1915; *New York Evening Post*, July 6,

1915; *New York Times,* July 6, 1915; *Indianapolis Star,* May 20, 1915; *Detroit Free Press,* July 12, 1915; *Rochester Democratic Chronicle,* July 12, 1915.

24. Jane Addams, "The Revolt Against War," *Survey* XXXIV (July 17, 1915), 355-59. This is the only complete version of the speech which was transcribed by a stenographer.

25. *New York Times,* July 13, 1915.

26. *Cedar Rapids Republican,* July 17, 1915; *New York Call,* July 15, 1915.

27. *New York Times,* July 13, 1915.

28. Addams, *Second Twenty Years at Hull House* (New York, 1930), 133.

29. *New York Topics,* July 15, 1915; *Pittsfield Journal,* July 3, 1915; *Louisville Courier-Journal,* July 21, 1915; *Rochester Herald,* July 15, 19, 1915.

30. *Meadville Messenger,* Aug. 17, 1915; *New York Evening Telegram,* July 16, 1915.

31. Elizabeth G. Evans to JA, July 22, 1915; Laura Hughes to JA, Nov. 21, 1915; Ellen Henrotin to JA, July 23, 1915; *Wichita Eagle,* July 30, 1915.

Notes to Chapter XIII

1. Quotation from *Presidential Address, Report of International Congress of Women at The Hague,* 1915, 18-22. For similar ideas see Addams, "Women and Internationalism," *Women at The Hague* (New York, 1915). For her thinking in 1915 see, "The Food for War," *Independent* LXXXIV (Dec. 13, 1915), 430-31; "Peace and the Press," *Independent* LXXXIV (Oct. 11, 1915), 55-56.

2. JA to Wald, July 24, 1915; Wald to JA, July 14, 23, 1915; Wald MSS. A shrewd and generally perceptive analysis of Jane Addams' ideas on peace can be found in Sandra R. Herman, *Eleven Against War* (Stanford, 1969), 114-49.

3. Paul Kellogg to Louise Lochner, July 20, 1915, Lochner MSS; Wald to O. G. Willard, July 23, 1915, Wald MSS Columbia.

4. For the complicated but important story of the relationship between Wilson and the mediation movement see David Patterson, "Woodrow Wilson and the Mediation Movement," *Historian* XXXIII (Aug. 1971), 535-56; Blanche Wicsen Cook, "Woodrow Wilson and the Anti-Militarists (unpublished Ph.D. thesis, Johns Hopkins, 1970).

5. Woodrow Wilson to Lillian Wald, July 3, 1915, Wald MSS.

6. The Addams, Kellogg, Lochner, Balch, Wald, and Jordan papers are all filled with a great many letters documenting the attempts to influence Wilson.

7. Charles Seymour, *The Intimate Papers of Colonel House,* 4 vols. (Boston, 1926-28), II, 22.

8. Ray Standard Baker, *Woodrow Wilson: Life and Letters*, 8 vols. (Garden City, N.Y., 1927-39), VI, 122-24.

9. Degen, *Woman's Peace Party*, 121; Schwimmer to JA, Aug. 4, 1915; Lochner to Jordan, Nov. 2, 1915, Jordan MSS.

10. Seymour, *Intimate Papers*, II, 96.

11. Lochner to Jordan, Oct. 23, 1915, Lochner MSS; Paul Kellogg to Graham Taylor, Dec. 8, 1915, Taylor MSS; Witter Bynner, "Jane Addams," *Harper's Weekly* LXI (Aug. 21, 1915), 174.

12. Degen, *Woman's Peace Party*, 125; JA to Wald, Nov. 24, 1915; *New York Times*, Nov. 27, 1915.

13. Kellogg to Lochner, July 20, 1915; Lochner to Jordan, Oct. 23, 1915; Lochner MSS; *New York Times*, Nov. 25, 27, 1915; The story of the Ford Peace Ship can be followed in Degen, *Woman's Peace Party*, 127-50; Louis P. Lochner, *Henry Ford: America's Don Quixote* (New York, 1925).

14. Burnet Hershey, *The Odyssey of Henry Ford and His Peace Ship* (New York, 1967), 81.

15. Addams, *Peace and Bread in Time of War* (New York, 1922), 37-40. Telegram Vachel Lindsay to Henry Ford, Nov. 28, 1915; Ford Peace Papers (courtesy of Barbara Kraft who is doing a full-length study of the Ford Peace Ship).

16. Events surrounding the Ford Peace Ship and the organization of the neutral conference are very complicated and contradictory. They can be followed in Degen, *Woman's Peace Party*, Lochner, *Henry Ford*, and in the Lochner, Addams, Woman's Peace Party, and Ford Peace Papers. Barbara Kraft's book on the Peace Ship and Edith Wynner's biography of Rosika Schwimmer should clear up some of the difficulties.

17. Walter Millis, *The Road to War: America 1914-1917* (Boston, 1935), 244. There seems to be no doubt from the contemporary evidence that JA was genuinely ill.

18. *New York Times*, Jan. 4, 6, 1916.

19. *Hearings before the Committee on Foreign Affairs, 64th Cong., 1st sess., on H. R. 6921 and H.J.R. 32*, pp. 4-5; Bryan to JA, Jan. 22, 1916.

20. *Champaign News*, Jan. 16, 1916; *Minneapolis Journal*, Jan. 17, 1916.

21. *Ogden* (Utah) *Examiner*, Jan. 15, 1916; *Providence Journal*, Jan. 1916; *Hartford Courant*, March 27, 1916, with Repplier quote. For other attacks on Jane Addams see: Agnes Repplier, *Counter Currents* (Boston, 1916), 125-26.

22. *The Nation* CII (Feb. 3, 1916), 134.

23. Quoted by Jane Addams, *Report of the International Congress of Women* (Zurich 1919), 196.

24. David S. Patterson, "Woodrow Wilson and the Mediation Movement," *Historian* XXXIII (Aug. 1971), 549.

25. JA to Kellogg, Aug. 10, 1916; Survey Files; "Jane Addams States Why," *Quincy* (Ill.) *Herald*, Nov. 6, 1916; Wilson to JA, Oct. 17, 1917; invitation Dec. 12, 1916.

26. JA and S. Breckinridge to Wilson, Jan. 23, 1917; JA to Lochner, Jan. 23, 1917, Lochner MSS.
27. JA to Wald, Feb. 13, 1917, Wald MSS; Addams, *Peace and Bread*, 63-65.
28. Clarke A. Chambers, *Paul Kellogg and the Survey* (Minneapolis, (1971), 62-63; Allen F. Davis, "Welfare, Reform and World War I," *American Quarterly* XIX (Fall 1967), 615-18.
29. JA to Helena Dudley, April 19, 1917.
30. Addams, "Patriotism and Pacifist in War Time," *City Club Bulletin* X (June 16, 1917), 184-90.
31. *Chicago Examiner*, June 11, 1917.
32. Kellogg to JA, May 5, 1917; Kellogg to Graham Taylor, May 5, 1917; Memos from editorial board, Survey Files.
33. John Henry Hopkins to JA, June 11, 1917; James Atkinson to JA, May 11, 1917; William Webb to JA, June 11, 1917.
34. Martin Duberman, "The Northern Response to Slavery," Martin Duberman, ed. *The Anti-Slavery Vanguard* (Princeton, 1965), 403; W. Lloyd Warner, *The Living and the Dead: A Study of the Symbolic Life of Americans* (New Haven, 1959), 85-86. See also Orrin E. Klapp, *Heroes, Villains and Fools: The Changing American Character*.
35. Linn, *Jane Addams*, 330-31; Addams, *Peace and Bread*, 139. Addams' pacifism is put in context in Charles Chatfield, *For Peace and Justice: Pacifism in America, 1914-1941* (Knoxville, 1971).
36. Addams, *Peace and Bread*, 140; *Philadelphia Public Ledger*, Dec. 9, 1917; letter to Baldwin quoted in William Preston, Jr., *Aliens and Dissenters; Federal Suppression of Radicals, 1903-1933* (Cambridge, Mass., 1963), 143-44; JA to Marcet Haldeman-Julius, Sept. 29, 1917, JAM.
37. Herbert Hoover to JA, March 2, 1918; JA to Kellogg, March 28, 1918, Survey Files.
38. Addams, "The World's Food and the World's Politics," *Proceedings of the National Conference of Social Work*, 1918, 650-56; "Tolstoy and the Russian Soldiers," *New Republic* XII (Sept. 29, 1917), 240-42.
39. Addams, *Peace and Bread*, 73-80; "The Corn Mother," *World Tomorrow* I (Nov. 1918), 277-80.
40. Linn, *Jane Addams*, 338.
41. *Los Angeles Times*, March 20, 1918.
42. Ruth Comfort Mitchell, "Jane Addams," *Atlantic Monthly* CXXII (Nov. 1918), 634.

Notes to Chapter XIV

1. *Buffalo Enquirer*, Nov. 15, 1918; *Boston Evening Record*, Nov. 18, 1918.
2. Alfred Clark to JA, Nov. 15, 1918; Sarah Coreant to JA, Nov. 18, 1918;

Frances Johnson to *New York Tribune*, Nov. 17, 1918, *Boston Record*, Nov. 18, 1918; *Cleveland News*, Nov. 18, 1918.

3. John P. Gavit to Kellogg, Jan. 26, 1919, Survey Files.

4. JA to Wald, Jan. 25, 1919, Wald MSS; *Brooklyn Times*, Jan. 26, 1919; Kellogg to Baker, Survey Files; *New York Times*, Jan. 28, 1919.

5. *Boston Evening Transcript*, Jan. 31, 1919; *Woman Patriot* II (Feb. 1, 1919).

6. *Revolutionary Radicalism: Its History Purpose and Tactics*, 4 vols. (Albany, 1920); Robert K. Murray, *Red Scare: A Study in National Hysteria 1919-1920* (Minneapolis, 1955), 98-102.

7. *Cincinnati Times Star*, Jan. 28, 1919; *Boston Evening Transcript*, Jan. 28, 1919.

8. Degen, *Woman's Peace Party*, 218-22; Randall, *Improper Bostonian*, 258ff.

9. Florence Kelley to Mary Smith, May 22, 1919; Lucia Ames Mead to Balch, Dec. 13, 1918, Balch MSS.

10. *New York Times*, Nov. 30, 1918.

11. Alice Hamilton to Family, May 1, 1919, Hamilton MSS.

12. Addams, *Peace and Bread*, 158-59.

13. Quoted in Addams, *Second Twenty Years*, 149; Kelley to Mary Smith, May 22, 1919.

14. *Report of the International Congress of Women, Zurich, May 12-17, 1919*, 162, 241-44.

15. Degen, *Woman's Peace Party*, 226-34.

16. Alice Hamilton to Mary Smith, May 12, 19, 1919; Florence Kelley to Mary Smith, May 22, 1919.

16. *Report of Zurich Conference*, 237-38.

17. JA to Mary Smith, May 28, June 4, 14, 24, July 5, 1919; Alice Hamilton to Mary Smith, May 30, June 8, July 5, 1919.

18. Jane Addams and Alice Hamilton, "After the Lean Years: Impressions of Food Conditions in Germany when Peace was Signed," *Survey* XLII (Sept. 6, 1919), 793-97.

19. JA to Miss Prenter, Feb. 25, 1920; "Declares Jane Addams' Talk Un-American," *Cleveland Press*, Dec. 15, 1919; "Quizzers Buzz and Miss Addams Talks League," *Chicago American*, Nov. 29, 1919. JA apparently destroyed the abusive letters, but she mentions them in JA to Kellogg, Aug. 28, 1919, Survey Files.

20. *Chicago Tribune*, Feb. 23, 1920.

21. *Ibid*; Jane Addams to Editor, *Chicago Tribune*, Feb. 24, 1920; *Philadelphia Public Ledger*, Feb. 23, 1920; Col. Charles W. Masher to JA, Feb. 24, 1920.

22. Robert Lanyon to JA, Feb. 23, 1920; H. Rowland Curtis to JA, Feb. 23, 1920.

23. R. A. Gum to JA, Feb. 18, 1920; JA to RA Gum, n.d.

24. The best guide to these organizations, though it must be used with care is: Norman Hapgood, editor, *Professional Patriots* (New York,

1927). Also see J. Stanley Lemons, *The Woman Citizen: Social Feminism in the 1920's* (Urbana, 1973).

25. Hapgood, ed., *Professional Patriots*, 16.
26. Several versions of the spider-web chart can be found in SCPC, the W.I.L.P.F. MSS. Another version is in *The Dearborn Independent* XXIV (March 22, 1924), 11.
27. C. N. Fay to Editor, *Boston Herald*, May 17, 1927; Fay to Sherman Stetson, Jan. 24, 1927; Louise Bowen to Fay, Jan. 24, 1927.
28. *Congressional Record*, 69th Congress, 1st session (1926), 12946-47.
29. *New York Times*, Nov. 11, 1926; "Attacking Jane Addams," *New York Evening World*, Nov. 13, 1926; *New York Sun*, Sept. 21, 1922; George L. Dart to A. E. Palmquist, July 30, 1924, W.I.L.P.F. MSS, box 5. These papers are an important source for the attacks in the 1920s on JA and other liberals. *The Scabbard and Blade* charge is quoted in Oswald Garrison Villard, "What the Blue Menace Means," *Harpers Magazine* CLVII (Oct. 1928), 529-40.
30. Emily Balch to Edward Hunter, March 16, 1926, W.I.L.P.F. MSS box 6; *New York Commercial*, May 20, 1926; "A Study of Patriotic Propaganda," *Information Service* VII (May 5, 1928) published by Federal Council of Churches of America.
31. Carrie Chapman Catt to JA, May 26, 1927; *Boston Herald*, March 10, 1925; Elaine Eastman to JA, March 25, 1925; Carrie Chapman Catt, "An Open Letter to the D.A.R.," *Woman Citizen* XII (July 1927), 10-12.
32. Elizabeth Dilling, *The Red Network* (Chicago, 1934), 51; invitation, JAM, reprinted Davis and McGree, *Eighty Years at Hull House*, 149.
33. JA to Mrs. Catt, Jan. 3, 1925; Graham Taylor, "Chicago's Civic Dinner to Jane Addams," *Survey* LVII (Feb. 15, 1927), 618-20.
34. "Jane Addams Scorned," *Toronto World*, Feb. 26, 1920; R. M. MacIver to JA, March 2, 1920.
35. *Indianapolis Star*, Feb. 27, 1921; "Address given by Dr. Maude Royden," *Pax International* X (May-June, 1935), unpaged.
36. The story of the unsuccessful campaign to get Jane Addams elected can be followed in the Julia Lathrop MSS. See, especially, Alice Hamilton to JA, June 12, 1922; Lathrop to Allen T. Burns, May 29, 1922; Lathrop to Alice Hamilton, June 16, 1922; Lathrop to JA, n.d.; Sec. of Conference to JA, June 25, 1922, Lathrop MSS.
37. Alice Hamilton to Emily Balch, Oct. 15, 1920; Balch to Hamilton, Nov. 2, 1920, Balch MSS; Balch to JA, Nov. 2, 1920.
38. Sister Maria to JA, July 2, 1920.
39. JA to Emily Balch, Aug. 6, 1923, Balch MSS.
40. JA to Ida Lovett, Feb. 7, 1923, Lovett MSS; JA to Bruno Lasker, Feb. 20, 1923; Survey Files; Addams, "Tolstoy and Gandhi," *Christian Century* XLVIII (Nov. 25, 1931), 1485-88.
41. Gertrude Bussey and Margaret Tims, *Women's International League for Peace and Freedom* (London, 1965), 34-80.

42. Heymann to JA, March 1, 1929; Bussey and Tims, *Women's International League*, 78-80. Kathleen O'Brien and Rosika Schwimmer quotations, courtesy of Edith Wynner.

43. William Scarlett to JA, May 10, 1924; Louise Atkinson to JA, May 22, 1924, W.I.L.P.F. box 5; *Washington Times*, April 24, 1924; "Opening Address by Jane Addams," Fourth Biennial Congress, Washington, May 1-8, 1924.

44. JA to Mrs. Lovett, May 25, 1923; JA to Julia Lathrop, May 13, 1923, Lathrop MSS; JA to H. S. Kissel, Nov. 19, 1923, JAM; Davis and McCree, *Eighty Years at Hull House*, 141-74.

45. Charles Cooper to JA, Aug. 31, 1922; Isabel Taylor, "New Settlement Leadership," *Neighborhood* I (July 1928), 19-24; Addams, "How Much Social Work Can the Community Afford," *Survey* LVII (Nov. 15, 1926), 199-201; Davis, *Spearheads*, 228-42; Clarke Chambers, *Seedtime of Reform, passim.*

46. Louise Young quoted in "The Excursion," Dorothy Kirchway Brown MSS.

47. For a discussion of the controversy over the equal rights amendment see: O'Neill, *Everyone Was Brave*, 127-29.

48. Addams, *Second Twenty Years*, 221-62.

49. *Ibid.*, 192-99; JA to Ben Lindsey, Oct. 19, 1927, Lindsey MSS. For her rejection of the liberated woman and any kind of sex outside of marriage see her review of Rachelle S. Yarros, "Modern Woman and Sex," *Survey* LXX (Feb. 1934), 59. Jane Linn, "At Arizona with Aunt Jane," MS, JAM.

50. The various lists are discussed in "The Twelve Greatest Women in America," *Literary Digest* LXXIV (July 8, 1920).

51. On the changing nature of American heroines in the 1920's, see Wasserstrom, *Heiress of all the Ages*, 99-122; Beatrice K. Hofstadter "Popular Culture and the Romantic Heroine," *American Scholar* XXX (Winter 1960-61), 98-116; Leslie A. Fiedler, *Love and Death in the American Novel*, 215ff. Fiedler sees a transition from James' Daisy, "The heiress of all the ages," to Fitzgerald's Daisy, "The real bitch."

52. Poem printed on card, dated Oct. 8, 1923, SCPC.

53. James Cox to JA, July 21, 1920; "Why I Shall Vote for LaFollette," *New Republic* XL (Sept. 10, 1924); Addams MS essay on Hoover, n.d. (1928), Salmon Levinson MSS; Herbert Hoover to JA, Aug. 24, 1932.

54. Memorandum, Arthur Kellogg to Paul Kellogg, May 4, 1920, Survey Files.

55. Kellogg to JA, Dec. 13, 1921; Jan. 26, 1922; Kellogg comments Dec. 1922, Survey Files; Review of *Peace and Bread, Nation and Atheneum* Sept. 16, 1922.

56. JA to Kellogg, May 10, 1929, Survey Files; JA to Mrs. Lovett, Feb. 24, 1930.

57. *New York Tribune*, Dec. 18, 1930.

Notes to Chapter XV

1. Quoted in Linn, *Jane Addams*, 380; *New York Times*, March 18, 1930, Feb. 24, April 17, Oct. 14, 1931.
2. Linn, *Jane Addams*, 381.
3. *Ibid.*, 404; Gail Parker, "Mary Baker Eddy and Sentimental Womanhood," *New England Quarterly* XLIII (March 1910), 3-18.
4. Tufts University, was the only exception. It awarded her an honorary degree in 1923 at the height of the reaction against her. James R. Angel to Edwin Embree, n.d. 1930, Rosenwald MSS.
5. Jeanette Eaton, "Jane Addams: The First Citizen of America, *Pictorial Review* (Jan. 1932), 8-9, 54; Alice Booth, "America's Twelve Greatest Women: No. 1 Jane Addams," *Good Housekeeping* XLII (Jan. 1931), 18, 163-64; Laura Antionette Large, "A Woman Who Lived in a Rich Home But Shared it with Poor Children," *Little Stories of Well-Known Americans* (Boston, 1928), 64-79; *Daughters Known to Fame* (New York, 1932), 11-14; Devere Allen, ed., *Adventurous Americans* (New York, 1932), 141-53; Edmund Wilson, "Hull-House in 1932," *New Republic* LXXIII (Jan. 18, 1933), 261.
6. See, for example, Isabel Eaton to JA, Jan. 1, 1932; Dorothy Hughes to JA, March 21, 1932; "To Miss Addams," June 1932.
7. Grade 6A Montgomery Street School, Newburgh, N.Y. to JA, Dec. 21, 1931; 7th grade class, Mansfield, La. to JA, Dec. 11, 1931; Nancy Naumberg to JA, n.d.; Lillian Wald, "Afterward," Jane Addams, *Forty Years at Hull House* (New York, 1935), 457.
8. Alice Thatcher Post to JA, April 27, 1932; Mary E. Callson to JA, June 2, 1932.
9. JA to H. S. Latham, Oct. 28, April 22, 1932; Latham to JA, April 26, 1932.
10. Mrs. E. A. Maisland to JA, Sept. 6, 1934; Kellogg to JA, Sept. 26, 1932, Survey Files.
11. Villard to JA, Feb. 4, 1932; *Outlook*, Dec. 23, 1931; Eunice Fuller Barnard, "Jane Addams: Bold Crusader for Peace," *New York Times Magazine*, Dec. 20, 1931.
12. Gladys Smith to JA, April 6, 1931; Josie Lee Lewis to JA, Oct. 17, 1931; Mrs. A. G. McAndrew to JA, Dec. 16, 1931.
13. Edmund Wilson, "Hull House in 1932," *New Republic* LXXIII (Jan. 18, 1933); "Casting Out Fear," *Pax International* VI (Feb. 1931), unpaged: *Social Consequences of Business Depressions*, (Chicago, 1931), 1-10.
14. JA to Mrs. Barnett, Feb. 9, 1934; Jan. 10, 1935, JAM; Radio address, Nov. 2, 1933 Esther Kohn MSS; Wald, "Afterward," Addams, *Forty Years*, 443-46.
15. Addams, "How to Build a Peace Program," *Survey* LXVIII (Nov. 1,

1932), 550-53; "Exaggerated Nationalism and International Comity," *Survey Graphic* XXIII (April 1934), 168-70. Farrell, *Beloved Lady,* 211-13; Wald, "Afterward"; Addams, *Forty Years,* 443-40.

16. Lea Taylor to A. J. Kennedy, Sept. 12, 1932, NFS MSS: Katherine Everts Ewing to her father and mother, March 30, 1932, in possession of Katherine Ewing Hocking and used with her permission.

17. Starr to JA, Feb. 23, 1934. Jane Linn, "At Arizona with Aunt Jane," an essay by her grandniece that has some interesting insights into her character and personality as an old woman. The book on Julia Lathrop was published after her death as *My Friend Julia Lathrop.* The part Grace Abbott was preparing was never published.

18. *New York Times,* May 3, May 23, 1935.

19. Linn, *Jane Addams,* 410-28; Louise Bowen letter to friends, May 27, 1935. Esther Kohn MSS, reprinted in Davis and McCree, *Eighty Years at Hull House,* 182-83.

20. S. K. Ratcliffe, "Jane Addams of Chicago," *Contemporary Review* CIII (July, 1935), 38; *New York Times,* May 23, 1935; *New York Herald Tribune,* May 23, 1935. See Sigmund Diamond, *The Reputation of the American Businessman* (Cambridge, 1955), for an analysis of obituaries as a way of studying and evaluating the values of a society. Ford and Rockefeller, like Jane Addams were treated as uniquely American.

21. Lippmann's article was syndicated in many newspapers, May 23, 1935.

22. These generalizations are based on a study of more than 500 obituaries collected in the Jane Addams MSS, SCPC. Quotations are used from the following: *Marquette* (Mich.) *Journal,* May 23, 1935; *Liberty* (Miss.) *Southern-Herald,* June 7, 1935; *Mobile* (Ala.) *Press,* May 24, 1935; *Literary Digest,* June 1, 1935; *Rock Island Argus,* May 24, 1935; *Philadelphia Labor Record,* May 24, 1935; *Winona* (Minn.) *Republican-Herald,* May 24, 1935; *Richmond* (Ind.) *Item,* May 23, 1935; *Winnipeg Tribune,* May 25, 1935; *Muncie* (Ind.) *Press,* May 24, 1935; *Christian Century* LII (June 5, 1935), 751-53.

Index

Abbott, Edith, 78.
Abbott, Grace, 78, 178, 209.
Adams, Henry, 29, 165.
Addams, Alice (Haldeman), 61, 31-32, 43, 83, 105.
Addams, Anna Haldeman, 6-7, 28, 31, 43, 45, 83, 160.
Addams, James Weber, 6, 31, 43, 83.
Addams, Jane: appearance, 8, 33, 103, 205, 249-50, 284, 289; attacks on, 111, 116-18, 132, 148, 192, 195, 223-24, 226-30, 240-41, 245-47, 251-56, 260-70, 282; birth, 3; and bayonet-charge story, 226-30, 236, 252, 255; and blacks, 129-30, 186, 195; and bull fight, 47-48, 168-69; compared to businessmen, 202-3, 283, 291; as businesswoman, 31, 34, 106-9, 178, 285; on Chicago School Board, 131-34, 158, 175; joins church, 51, 168; attitude toward city, 72-73; as college woman, 10-23; as compromiser, 18, 31, 43, 95, 107, 110, 130, 133-34, 219; death, 290; and depression, 287-98; need for loving disciples, 85, 94, 104-5; influence of John Dewey, 96-97, 131; attitude toward drinking, 36, 72, 276-77; influence of Richard T. Ely, 97-98, 100-101, 144; first European trip, 32-37; second European trip, 43-52; family problems, 31, 41-43, 82-85, 113; relationship with father, 3, 9, 21, 25, 26, 160-61; works for Department of Food Administration, 247-50; and Ford Peace Ship, 237-40, 252, 255, 262; as garbage inspector, 121; influence of Gandhi, 271-72; health, 6, 24, 27-28, 30, 32-33, 38, 45, 235-36; honorary degrees, 158, 202, 283-84; early years at Hull House, 67-91; motivation behind Hull House, 38-39, 48-53, 65; organizing Hull House, 53-59; role at Hull House, 81-82, 95-96, 105-9, 274-75, 289; inheritance from father, 31; at International Congress of Women at The Hague, 217-25, 237, 254, 257; influence of William James, 140-45, 155; relationship with Florence Kelley, 77-78, 125, 134; and organized labor, 79, 110-19; connected with Lincoln, 162-64; influence of Henry Demarest Lloyd, 97-98; speaks against lynching, 129-30; relationship with men, 13-14, 29, 88-89, 93-94; movie about, 293; Nobel Peace Prize, 270, 286; New Deal, 287-88; President of National Conference of Charities and Correction, 185, 198, 206; and peace move-